Katrina Kittel holds undergraduate degrees majoring in history and geography, as well as a Master degree. She has been writing about POWs since 2012 including articles for *Sabretache*, the journal of Military Historical Society of Australia, and for Department of Veterans' Affairs Our Mob Serving Country website. She was invited in 2016 to write preface for an Italian translation of *Australian Partisan: a true story of love and war* by Ian Sproule and Lynette Oates. Katrina was selected for ACT Writers Centre's Hardcopy 2017 program for emerging non-fiction writers.

This is her first book.

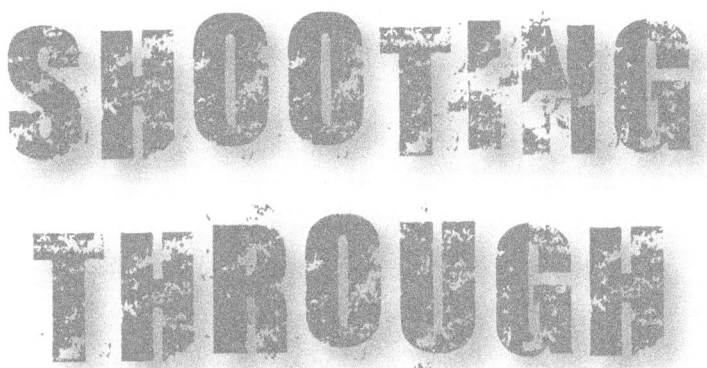

SHOOTING THROUGH

Campo 106 escaped POWs after the Italian armistice

Katrina Kittel

First published in 2019 by Barrallier Books Pty Ltd,
trading as Echo Books

Registered Office: 35—37 Gordon Avenue, West Geelong, Victoria 3220, Australia.

www.echobooks.com.au

Copyright ©Katrina Kittel

Creator: Kittel, Katrina: Author.

Title: Shooting Through: Campo 106 escaped POWs after the Italian armistice

ISBN: 9780648554042 Paperback

A catalogue record for this book is available from the National Library of Australia

All reasonable efforts were taken to obtain permission to use copyright material reproduced in this book, but in some cases copyright could not be traced. The author welcomes feedback to the text and nominal roll and is contactable on katrinakittel9@gmail.com

Cover images: Mattmark Hotel - photographer Peter Bates, copy in author's collection. POW group – with permission Bob Kerr, Bruce Wilson, Mat Sincock

Aboriginal and Torres Strait people are respectfully advised that this publication contains names and images of deceased persons.

Book layout and design by Peter Gamble, Canberra.
Set in Garamond Premier Pro Display, 12/17 and Smudgers Regular.

www.echobooks.com.au

for Col and Peter

*This is no story of heroes,
but of plain common ordinary men,
Who came from the farms, cities and towns,
To fight for the so-called freedom of men,*
—Harold Sanderson,
New Zealand 18 Battalion

Contents

Foreword	x
Prologue: 'There's more that I can tell you'	xiii
1 'The war is over for you': Capture and captivity	1
2 'Smoko': Sabotage and subversion at Campo 106	10
3 'Go grey thinking about it': POWs' privations	19
4 'Keep calm and stay put': Italy's capitulation 1943	26
5 'That's when our war started': Walking into German-occupied Italy	33
6 'The familiar rice mill': Shelter at Campo 106 farms post-Armistice	44
7 'South to the River Po': Towards Allied Lines	53
8 'Our train ride began': Officers jump-start to the Swiss-Italian border	61
9 'Coffee plonk': Italian hospitality	71
10 'Charlie did the talking': Teodulo Pass, late September 1943	82
11 'The Italian man with an American accent': Monte Barone's Hotel Alpe Noveis	91
12 'A bloody German frontier guard': Coal-shuttle helmets at the border	99
13 'North was the grim line of the Alps': Climbing towards the frontier	108
14 'None of us were prepared to argue with two rifles': Re-capture at the frontier	116
15 'First time I had been on a bike for nearly three years': Late departures	122
16 'Monte Moro was testing our resolve': From Turlo to Moro	130
17 'Whilst we were eating the last of our grub': Monte Moro and Mondelli Pass	142

18 'Quiet resort equally suitable for rest-seekers and mountaineers': Saas Valley	150
19 'I'm sorry mate, we've bungled it': Leadership and loss of bearings	159
20 'The mountain gave the impression of being alive': Mountaineering, late October 1943	167
21 'Along the way we lost Snowy': POW mates separate	178
22 'The last station in Italy': Hidden help by escape organisations	186
23 'The easy way to Switzerland': Border lake crossings	199
24 'Through German Lines': South to Allied Lines	209
25 'Marking time': A year in Switzerland and coming home	219
26 'Contribution towards the final collapse of German armies in Italy': POW-partisans and SOE	234
27 'Don't shoot, we're English': Ambush in the hills	243
28 'Never, ever heard us speak about it': Repatriation, resilience	253
Epilogue: 'I am now ready to meet my father'	263
Acknowledgments	272
Notes	275
Bibliography	306
Appendix 1: Nominal roll of Australian POWs at Campo 106	312
Appendix 2: New Zealander POWs reaching Switzerland	324
Index	326

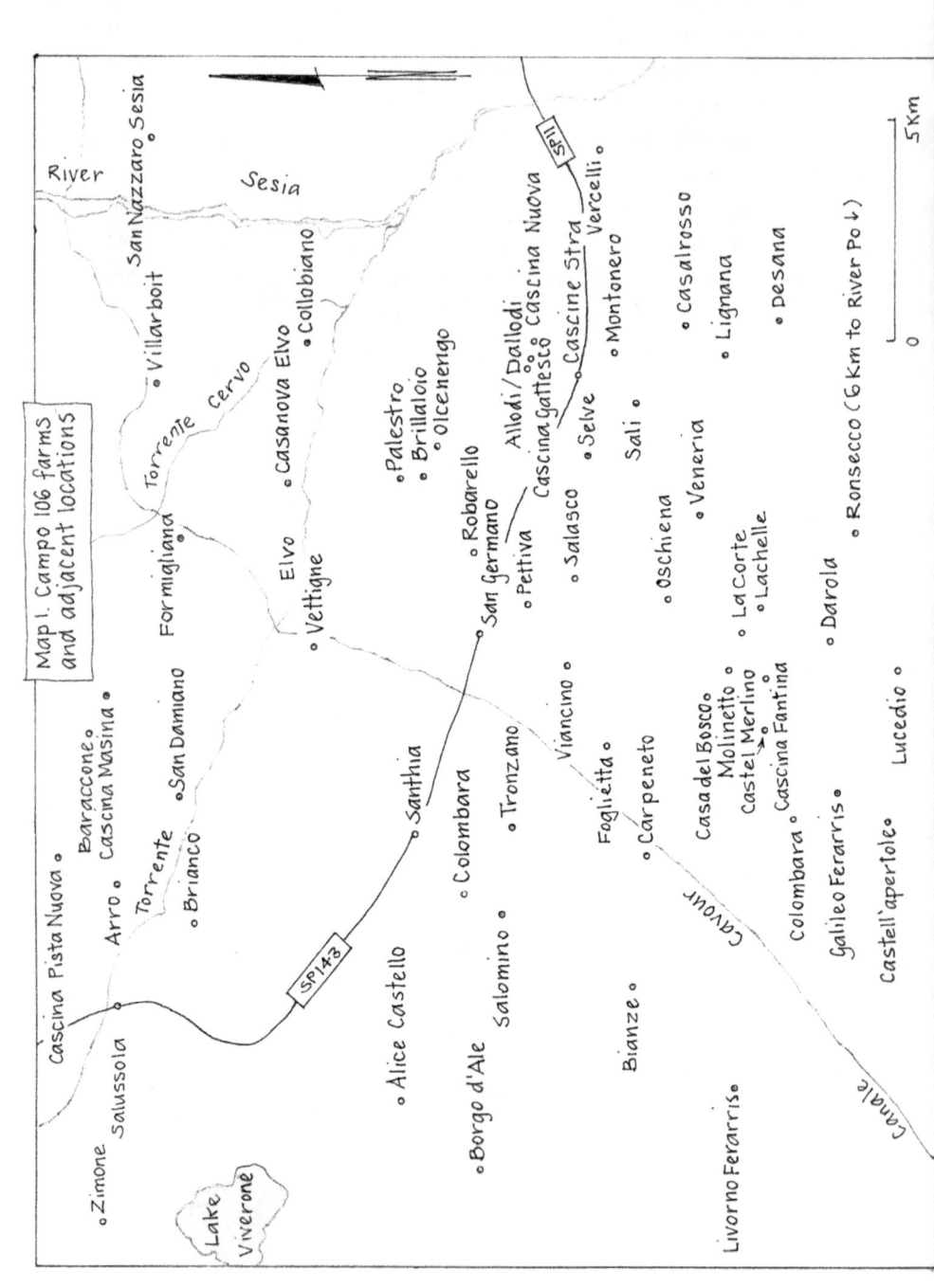

Map 1. Campo 106 farms and adjacent locations

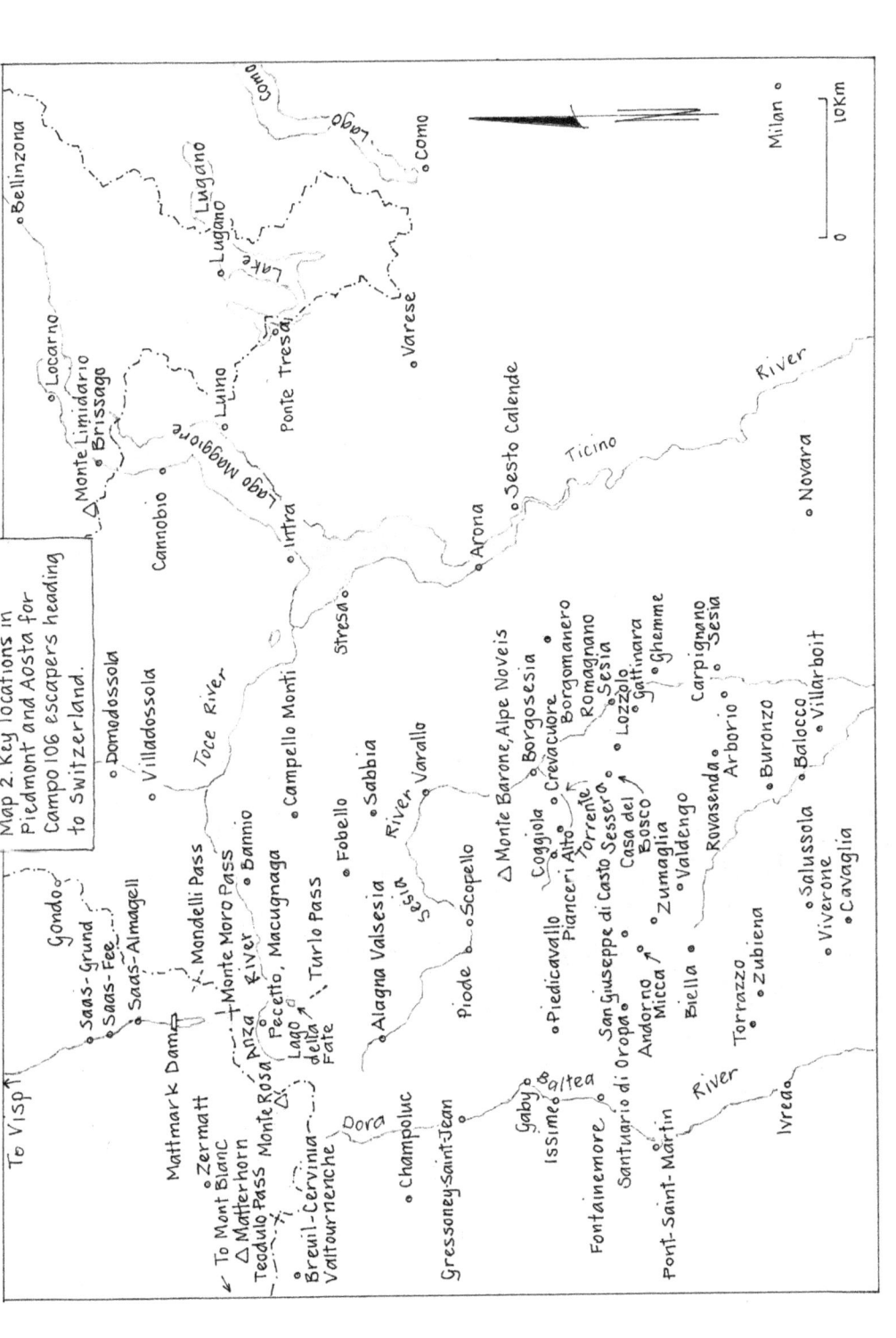

Map 2. Key locations in Piedmont and Aosta for Campo 106 escapers heading to Switzerland.

Foreword

There is much about war that defies the imagination. When Australians enlisted in their thousands after the outbreak of war in September 1939, they had little sense of what awaited them. At that time Italy had not even entered the war, so who could have imagined spending months or years in a country about which most knew very little? And who could have imagined working, living and even fighting alongside the enemy?

Truth is indeed sometimes stranger than fiction, and the history recounted here belongs firmly in the world of truth. The very first enemy to be confronted by the Australians sent to the Middle East was Benito Mussolini's Italy. In pursuit of the *Duce*'s own fantasies of a modern Roman Empire, Italians forces clashed with Australian and other British Empire forces in the Western Desert. In 1941 and in 1942, whether nabbed by Mussolini's men or by Erwin Rommel's *Afrika Korps*—who duly handed them to their Axis partners—the fate of some two thousand Australians was to be shipped to Italy and confined to one of many Italian POW camps.

Not only were their capture and detention in Italy unimagined, there were challenges for which most were woefully prepared. While soldiers feared death or maiming in advance of battle, few contemplated capture, and even fewer were given any advice on how to cope with it. To be suddenly 'in the bag' provoked responses ranging from shame and despair through to defiance and a steely determination to carry on the fight through whatever means available. To be a POW, as Winston Churchill once put it, was to find oneself in 'a melancholy state'. No matter when or where they were captured, POWs had to call on their resources and initiative to deal with the travails of a life behind barbed wire.

It is a huge credit to these men that they adapted to these unforeseen circumstances as well as they did. For so many of them, the moment of capture was not the end of their war but rather the start of a new phase. They adapted the legendary Anzac resourcefulness to the bleak world of the POW camps and then, finally and most impressively of all, to the extraordinary challenges of post-Armistice Italy. The reader of the stories in this book will be astounded at how many solutions Australians found to deal with their plight. There were those who were lured by the prospect of refuge in Switzerland, and followed multiple paths toward that destination. Then there were those who aimed for France or, further south, for Allied lines. Others experienced the good fortune of prolonged stays with generous Italian families or even with partisan groups, eager to take trained soldiers into their ranks in fighting a brutal civil war. A small and remarkable group renewed their war by working in collaboration with the clandestine British organisation the Special Operations Executive. Fortune did not smile on all of these Australians, as the possibility of recapture or death followed them wherever they went.

This might be a very Australian story, built around the adventures of Australians in wartime Italy, but at the same time it is an Italian story as well. It foreshadows a multicultural Australia yet to be created in the Antipodes. Countless unlikely yet enduring friendships were formed in the crucible of war. That so many Italians were willing and able to offer life-saving assistance to so many is in itself difficult to fathom. To harbour an escaped or evading POW exposed Italians to the threat of severe punishment, whether by fascists or by the Germans who had set themselves up as the brutal overlords of northern Italy. Yet despite those acute risks, Italians in their thousands, and from all walks of life, opened their homes and their hearts to these desperate men on the run. Their exemplary courage and hospitality were all the more remarkable because the men they protected had been the very same men who had comprised the enemy until just a short time earlier, and who over years had been depicted in fascist propaganda as wild, uncouth colonials. Few words can express the gratitude Australians should feel to this day toward those men and women who preserved their decency and humanity during such dark times.

This book has its origins in a loving family relationship. In part it is an attempt by a child to understand a parent, an element of whose past remained well concealed for so long. To that extent it is a labour of love. Much more than, that, however, it is a passionate and determined quest for the truth about a piece of the past too long hidden in the footnotes of history. Katrina Kittel has quite literally followed in the footsteps of those men like Col Booth who, when confronted with one of the most vexing questions of their lives, opted to 'shoot through' and find their way to freedom. In search of the stories of countless others she has tracked down the descendants of others to piece together a great web of escape and survival stories. And on top of all that, she has trawled archives and libraries to ensure that this book is not just a remarkable tale, it is a true one. It defies the imagination, and it satisfies it too.

—Peter Monteath

Prologue: 'There's more that I can tell you'

Monte Rosa's snow-covered face blinks at us through scant mist. In 2013, my husband, Brett, and I zigzag uphill on a medieval trail through larch forests, towards the summit of Rosa's neighbour, Monte Moro. We trek to the cable-car station at Alpe Bill and admire Rosa's gleaming face, the longest face in these Alps.

We decide to abort our uphill attempt and retreat to Staffa village, then travel by bus down the valley to Domodossola, a medieval frontier town and railway junction between Italy and Switzerland.

The following day, Brett and I arrive at Monte Moro's Swiss mid-slopes that descend into the Swiss Saas Valley. We trudge up from the valley towards Moro with our guide, Bernhard; a Swiss archivist, Jurg; and Jurg's wife, Barbara. Above the tree-line and scree slopes we rest at Saastal's damp meadow, a junction of time-worn trails squiggling down from Moro and nearby Mondelli passes. Jurg snaps chocolate and cuts chunks of bread with his Swiss army knife. Marmots fleetingly perch atop huge rocks to screech their territorial warnings.

Amongst the scraggy line of peaks, Bernhard identifies and points to Moro's summit. The sky is clear, broken only by fleck of moon. There is no mountain mist to obscure our panorama, or us from other observers.

Four decades ago my father Colin 'Col' Booth, former anti-tank gunner and a prisoner of war, spoke about escaping an Italian prison camp and reaching this place. He called it the frontier.

My planning for this trip started in 2011 when Col's grandchildren wore his medals on Anzac Day. When they asked me about his war, I could not fully answer their questions.

To fill in more about the grandfather my children never met, I yearned to understand Col as a fresh-faced soldier. In 2011, we removed Col's papers, photos and paraphernalia from a brown Globite case. In a family photo-album full of tiny black-and-white photos, unfamiliar faces and places had remained silent, stuck in their time. On the reverse of some photos and postcards of Swiss mountains and pretty villages, Col's handwriting hinted at people, localities and events from his war. In beautiful handwriting on postcards sent from Switzerland in 1946, a woman named Eva reminded Col of delightful times sitting amongst alpine flowers. On other cards, she expressed disappointment and sadness that Col had not written to her after his repatriation to Australia. She was unaware whether he'd made it home.

He had. Col met his Bundanoon guesthouse sweetheart Evelyn not long after returning home. Dressed in his army uniform, in July 1945 Col married his beautiful Kamilaroi-heritage teenage bride who wore flowing white. In 1946, they named their first child—dark-haired and brown-eyed Peter—in honour of Col's army mate, Peter Erickson. Another son, blue-eyed, fair-haired Brian, nicknamed 'Snow,' arrived in 1949. I was the daughter who cost Col two pounds, he'd later tease me, for a Sydney parking fine when he and Evelyn collected me, their adopted 'Doll', in 1959.

As the Booth photo-album shows, the family enjoyed camping and fishing on the New South Wales south coast in the 1950s, sometimes with Peter Erickson and his wife and daughters. Contact between the two families dwindled by the sixties, and I did not meet Peter Erickson's family.

All I can recall is Dad's comment that, 'Peter killed the person who was about to kill me'. Or had he said '... about to shoot me'?

Col, or Collie as he liked to be called in later years, died in 1989, aged seventy-one. With nothing else to go on, I presumed that Peter and Col's critical incident took place during their breakout from a prison camp in Italy.

Blue-eyed Col left hints about wartime events and people in a small hymn-and-calendar notebook. The notebook was issued to POWs by Pope Pius XII and, as a gift from the Pope, were presumably immune from confiscation by prison-camp authorities. Col scribbled names, places and events in this notebook, his words squeezed into small blank sections amongst hymn notation and Papal quotations. At the top of Col's list of places is 'Grupignano'.

More than twenty years after Col's death, I learned that he and most of the Australian and New Zealand POW cohort captured in North Africa spent Christmas 1942 at Grupignano, known as Campo 57, or PG57, located near Udine in north-east Italy. It was a purpose-built camp for prisoners of non-commissioned rank. Only a small number of officers were kept there.

In my early scrounges for information in 2011, I stumbled upon a website created by a former POW. Several of Col's photos glared back at me from its pages. I phoned the web author, Bill Rudd, to ask whether he knew my father. He did not. As we spoke, I clicked that he was taken prisoner at Alamein's Ruin Ridge on the same day as Col and Peter Erickson. Bill's POW experience parallels Col's and, better still, Bill is an authority on POW history in Europe.

In 2014, I sit in his South Yarra home. I ask, 'What did it feel like to be a prisoner of war?'

'Shame,' he blurts without hesitation.

I do not get his drift. 'Bill,' I ask, 'why feel shame when we are proud of our veterans?'

'We felt shame and humiliation being taken prisoner of war,' he declares. 'One does not take liberty for granted after that.' It now made sense: capture meant disgrace.

Ninety-six-year-old Bill is not only sharp, he's busy. For decades, he has gathered accounts by fellow POWs for his web publication; he analyses prisoner lists sourced from British and Swiss archives.

Bill explains my father's contexts of captivity through several camps. Col and his mate Peter, and Bill, were crammed with hundreds of other Australian POWs into cattle-train compartments and carted from Campo 57 in April 1943 to work Campo 106 farms scattered on the plain between Turin and Milan. I learn that it was from Campo 106 that they effected their escapes five months later.

Bill has built a researcher network in Australia and Europe which includes Swiss archivist, Jurg. He introduces me to Jurg by email and I fire off several of Dad's wartime photos in case these are of interest. One photo, of a dishevelled Swiss building nestled amongst boulders near Monte Moro, is annotated by Col as 'Mattmark Hotel'. Jurg is surprised; he's never heard of this hotel.

I am not alone in searching for information about POW experience. If fathers and grandfathers were quiet on their war stories, their descendants grab at whatever they find. I search *White Pages* listings, draft search letters and fire out dozens across Australia. One letter quickly finds Nick Emery and his wife Enid. I speak with Enid on the phone several times but Nick's hearing-aid makes it difficult for him. Enid implores me to visit. 'He may talk to you about his war, if you come.'

As I step across the threshold of their home, Nick, at ninety years old, reaches out to greet me. He's straight into it: 'Let's start with Alamein.'

Nick settles into his favourite armchair, locking me into his gaze. We pause to munch Enid's tall sponge layers sandwiched with fresh fruit. I admire a faded green tattoo on Nick's forearm that reads 'Liberty Forever, 1941'. Seventeen-year-old soldier Nick and mate Charlie Mills had taken leave in the old city of Jerusalem to search for grog and a tattoo parlour. Charlie changed his mind about getting a tattoo but tipsy Nick invested in one. He was at liberty in 1941. Within a year of the tattoo ink drying, Nick was captured at Alamein on the same day as my father Col and Bill Rudd.

On the Emery's living-room wall, a young uniformed Nick is artistically positioned within a photo collage. Crafted by his grand-daughter for a senior school project, it shows a teenage Nick before he became the father of her father. Watching over our morning feast are other wartime images held captive by the plastic of Enid's laminating machine; a backdrop of small black-and-white portals into the 1940s. I recognise these photos of young smiling soldiers sturdy on skis, soaring mountains and gun-slinging sentries as the same cluster of photos on Bill's website—and the same as those in my father's Globite case.

A morning with story-teller Nick drifts to lunchtime. We nibble our bread. Nick and I trek onward, fleeing into the hills beyond the POW camp, practising our pronunciation of village names, looking over our shoulders for German troops. Enid's tap on the shoulder jolts me back. It's dinner time. 'Will you stay for tea?' she asks. Nick gestures for me to stay.

Leftovers from lunch are mostly left over as we listen to Nick's anecdotes, to those stories heard before and others never heard. Nick's tales take us to little huts in the misty foothills of northern Italy in which cauldrons of warm stew bubble and then fill his belly. He speaks of his gratitude for Italian women, priests and shepherds. Nick takes me with him on mountain-goat tracks in autumn of 1943 where we hear the splosh of freezing feet in icy streams. '*Sempre sul*', Nick says. I nod, knowing from my Italian lessons that it means 'always onward'.

I worry that Nick will tire but young Nick needs to keep going. We're at a critical stage in this journey of evasion, this life on the run, heading higher into the foothills leading towards the Anzasca Valley, the site of Macugnaga's mountaineer churchyard. Its old grey stone bell-tower signals the summit-searching trails weaving up to high Alps.

A young blond soldier barely out of his teens is right next to me. Guides desert us; they've gone as far as they dare. We giggle about the women's shoes tied by scrappy filthy bandages to his blistered feet.

With nightfall, our time-travel to the dangerous days of 1943 is over. We rest. A stooped but steady Nick grips the rim of my car door to say his farewell. 'There is more I could tell you,' he declares, 'but I cannot, I'm too embarrassed.' Unspoken memories almost spill from his blue eyes.

In 2013, as my husband and I rest and snack at the Saastal meadow with our Swiss guides, I wonder whether alpine conditions were this mild in late September 1943 for Nick Emery, Peter Erickson, Bill Rudd and Col Booth. Three of them—as their notebooks and archival records inform—reached this frontier on the same day. In darkness or daylight, under drizzle or dry skies, Col's shoddy boots crunched this same stony trail downhill towards the old Mattmark Hotel. The hotel, as Jurg discovered, is now gone.

Post-war, Col declared to a newspaper journalist that in the strain to reach this frontier, he was cold, hungry and often desperate. My soldier father was frightened. I prickle with this sense of menace. I imagine it right on my heels, and just over the hills. Safety in Switzerland, the 1943 fugitives hoped, was just a few stumbling steps downhill. Other POWs were right on their tails, or heading in the opposite direction; others were stuck in the hills.

1
'THE WAR IS OVER FOR YOU': CAPTURE AND CAPTIVITY

'Australians entered every campaign with some expectations of their enemy. Whether or not these impressions were confirmed depended on which enemy unit the Australians faced, and where and when the action took place ... the Australians found distinctive traits in each of their enemies ...'

'The first enemy soldiers who fought Australians in World War II were Italians. The average Italian soldier was poorly trained, poorly led, poorly fed and poorly armed ... Australians went into action carrying not only weapons to defeat the Italians, but a set of attitudes that reflected a sense of superiority. Even before face-to-face hostilities began, the Italians were considered somewhat ludicrous.'

—Mark Johnston, 2000[1]

When Herbert 'Nick' Emery accompanied his older brother to Sydney Showground's AIF recruitment centre on 4 July 1940, a recruitment officer also handed Nick a form. Noting his youthful exuberance, he implored Nick to get his mother to sign the attestation form.[2] Nick trotted around the corner, forged the signature of his mother Bridget and trotted back to the officer. Nick declared his birth year as 1920, although he'd just turned sixteen.³ Bridget's blond fresh-faced boy was swiftly snapped up by the Australian Imperial Force (AIF).

Overseas service sounded like an adventure for naive young Australian men who lined up at army recruitment centres in 1940. Yet 2000 Australian enlistees, most during the North African campaign, were taken prisoner of war—'in the bag'– to enter Italian captivity during 1941 and 1942.⁴ 'I was like a lot of us,' Paul Lavallee, also from Sydney, said. 'I couldn't imagine being a POW. I could imagine being wounded, killed, shot up, but I never saw that I would become a POW.'⁵

West Australian Ron Maitland's World War One veteran father planted the seed about volunteering to go to war. Ron expected army life to inflict restrictions on freedom, so with mates he let his hair down before leaving for overseas service. In his published memoir, he quips: 'A number of us from the rough old mining town of Kalgoorlie enlisted. I remembered how we loaded ourselves with enough booze to last us to Perth and as a final gesture to our guileless youth, some of the lads blew up the remainder of our issue of French letters and hung them from the carriages!'⁶ With the 2/32nd Battalion, Ron Maitland was nabbed into captivity with buddies at the second battle of Alamein, late October 1942.

The October Alamein battle would bring in the tailender Australian POWs of 1942 to end up in Italian hands.

Australian troops destined to populate a string of Italian prison camps began to be captured at various locations in North Africa from as early as the beginning of 1941.

The site of the first Australian–Italian contact was the Italian fortress of Bardia, a coastal town in Libya. By 5 January 1941, Bardia had fallen. The 6th Division advanced westwards through Libya, and by 7 February were in Benghazi, ahead of being withdrawn for operations in Greece. German troops landed at Tripoli, on the North African scene, in March 1941. The 9th Division fought Italians, as well as Germans, until November 1942 when it was relieved after victory during the

October battle at El Alamein. The Italians, unlike the Germans, had a reputation as poor fighters.[7]

The 2/13th Battalion's troubled turn came in the early days of April at El Regima. 'My section was attached to D Coy [Company] on patrol at the minefield when we were surrounded and isolated by an enemy column,' recalled Sydney-based George Clarke. 'We could receive no orders or assistance.'[8]

Of the soldiers of Queensland's 2/15th Battalion, many were picked up on 7 April 1941. 'During the withdrawal from Barce,' Jim Wilson jotted in his 1944 report, 'the column stopped just outside Derna. A convoy approaching from the south rounded us up with tanks.'[9] Also on that day, Colin Gardner, in a signaller's unit, was 'ambushed by Germans, stunned and taken prisoner while unconscious'.[10]

All up, approximately seventy 2/15th soldiers would later become POWs of Italy's Campo 106.[11]

Speaking about the suddenness of being removed from active service at 2am on 7 April 1941,[12] 2/17th Battalion's Lance Corporal Paul Lavallee said, 'I didn't fire a shot.'[13] Paul and some of his unit were rushing back to Tobruk from Benghazi on a signaller's truck. About 2am, the convoy was halted in its tracks by Germans. 'The only war that I saw was from our planes. That's all I saw. It was overwhelming, I was in a daze for days, no food. Rommel got sick of us and he said I'll hand you over to the Italians.'

The active service of Major Raymond Binns, an Adelaide medical practitioner posted to the 2/8 Field Ambulance, with others from his unit, also came to an abrupt end on 7 April 1941 when they mistakenly turned down a road towards the Derna airfield, to be duped by a man wearing Australian uniform, a deceptively easy ploy to whisk them into a German trap.[14] [15] Major Binns had stepped off the boat in the Middle East only two months earlier.[16]

The next batch to go into the bag were 2/3rd Anti-Tank Regiment gunners and bombardiers. Regarding 8 April 1941, Moree's Carl Carrigan reported that his section was 'in a defensive position at Fort Mechili. After two days' fighting, we were left to fight the rearguards. The Fort surrendered.'[17] Lance Bombardier Lloyd Moule was caught in the same web as Carl and his brother Paul Carrigan. Lloyd listed a string of North Africa's transit camps that he trawled through: Mechili, Derna, Benghazi and Sabratha in April. Then, in Italy he was held five weeks at Sulmona, five months at Prato Isarco,[18] before a 16-month stint at Campo 57, commencing the end of October 1941.[19] For POWs captured later in 1942, most went directly to Campo 57 from southern Italy transit camps including Capua.

Less than four weeks after the Mechili mauling, Victorians of the 2/24th Battalion took a hammering. Cornered with most of his battalion's company and his two brothers at Tobruk at the start of May 1941, Eddie Sincock described the downfall: 'Surrounded by tanks and infantry, and strong bombing by German planes. Forced to surrender.'[20] For about 145 2/24th men, Campo 106 captivity eventuated.[21]

Forced into captivity, some prisoners 'jacked up', snatching short-lived freedom outside the barbed wire. 2/24th's Tom Anderson, Fred Tabram and Rupe Sheridan shot through from a poorly guarded camp, 120 kilometres outside Derna. With 'no map, no plan and only a few tins of food', the trio slid down an electrical cable rope from a washroom and strolled east into the Libyan desert. As narrated by Tom in his wartime notes, nomadic Arabs shared beans and goats' milk, and directed them to fresh springs.[22]

On the coast the truants snuck into a rowboat, rowing out for about forty metres until water seeped in. Despondent, they returned to shore, apprehended four days later. To Tom's relief, 'We were fed well when recaptured by German frontline troops. They seemed pretty decent, not like hard-core Nazis.' Interrogation concluded with a feed of dark stew and coffee, and within the Italian theatre of war, they were offloaded to Italian troops.

Similarly, Australians facing the Afrika Corps won a positive reputation among the Germans.[23] Brunswick Junction's Charles Warburton,

2/28th Battalion, sustained wounds in action outside Tobruk in 1941, copping machine-gun bullets to his arm and neck. Grenade splinters penetrated the side of his head. Charles concurred with Tom's summation that German troops in North Africa acted professionally. Detailed within his war memoir, Charles reflected on his six-week convalescence in a German field hospital in North Africa. 'In the hospital there were a lot of Jerries [German troops], with all sorts of wounds, German doctors and orderlies were very busy and doing a fine job,' Charles noticed. 'They attended to me the same as the rest. There was quite a bit of excitement due to the impending visit of some German brass. A German officer came over and spoke to me. He was wearing a few medals including an Iron Cross and he looked every inch the soldier. He congratulated me for the rest of us on the way we had fought and he hoped I would soon recover.'[24]

Charles was later appraised that the visiting officer was General Erwin Rommel, the Desert Fox. General Rommel's memoirs reveal his awareness that the struggles of units under his own command had spanned limits of human endurance. 'I had made tremendous demands on my forces ... I knew that the fall of Tobruk and collapse of the Eighth Army was the one moment in the African war when the road to Alexandria lay open and virtually undefended, and my staff and I would have been fools not to have gone all out to seize this unique opportunity.' As Commander-in-Chief of the Italian formations, Rommel applauded many Italian generals and officers who'd won his admiration.[25]

'The Italian was willing, unselfish and a good comrade, and considering the conditions under which he served, he had always given far better than the average.' Rommel attributed Italian defeats to an interplay of factors: lower standards of command and training, inferior quality of the Italian armament, poor supply of anti-tank weapons, insufficient food rations. 'All in all,' Rommel surmised, 'it was small wonder that the Italian soldier, who incidentally was extraordinarily modest in his needs, developed a feeling of inferiority which accounted for his occasional failure in moments of crisis.'

A minority of Australian POWs who came into Italian hands were captured in locations other than North Africa. On 29 May 1941, Bill Waller of 2/3 Light Anti-Aircraft Attack Regiment (3LAA) was aboard HMS *Hereward* whilst evacuating Crete when targeted by German stukas. 'Lifeboats destroyed, every man for himself,' feared Bill and regimental comrades, 'paddling a half-submerged float by hands'. Mercifully, a small boat approached and hauled Bill aboard. The passengers handed Bill and others over, depositing them within a Rhodes staging camp ahead of relocation to Capua camp's tents and barbed-wire.[26] About 88 3LAA soldiers became POWs.[27]

At Italian camps, the 'old hands', POWs who fell into captivity in 1941, greeted newly captured POWs in 1942.

1942's large round-up of Australian prisoners occurred at El Alamein.

West Australian Jack Wauhop, like Nick Emery, was one of the younger Australian soldiers. Born in North Fremantle in March 1920, Jack celebrated his twenty-first birthday while undergoing army training with 2/32 Battalion at Northam in early 1941. Jack spoke candidly about his war memories in 1989 when interviewed for the Keith Murdoch Sound Archive of Australia. Initiation began light-heartedly: 'I had my first imbibing of alcohol and my first pipe full of strong Havelock tobacco, that black stuff chopped up with a pocket-knife—it took a box of matches to keep it going.'[28]

Grim initiation came like a shot at Alamein on Friday 17 July 1942. 'It wasn't nice to see one of my mates running past me without a head; it was cut clean off by a shell that didn't explode. I will never remember anything in my life with such nightmarish feelings as seeing that.' Of the 2/32nd POWs, 104 worked the Campo 106 fields.[29]

Within their respective military units, Bill Rudd, Colin Weekes and Nick Emery were snatched into captivity on the morning of 27 July 1942 following a disastrous night battle at Ruin Ridge, Alamein.[30] Bill, born in December 1917, served as sapper in his unit whereas Colin served as anti-tank gunner, within their respective units, both of which supported the large West Australian 2/28th Battalion, into which Nick was posted before the Ruin Ridge offensive.[31] The 2/28th Battalion suffered huge losses, as 2/3 anti-tank gunner Colin Weekes observed during a full night battling alongside their ranks, 'a single battalion advanced through a hail of machine-gun cross-fire from nests, which the promised arty [artillery] barrage had failed to effect.'[32] The ill-fated 2/28th, as it panned out, contributed more soldiers to the POW cohort in Italy than any other Australian unit, of which about 163 men ended up at Campo 106.[33]

Colin voiced the humiliation for all Ruin Ridge warriors: 'We became prisoners of war, very upset and wild because we had been left out in such a hopeless position, without the support attacks of the infantry and tanks. The Jerry said "the war is over for you" but really it had just begun. We had a long fight ahead of us, against hunger, illness and wire complex.' About 41 of Colin's regimental colleagues captured at Alamein or Mechili were tapped on the shoulder to work at Campo 106 farms in 1943.[34]

After battle-dead and POWs were hauled away, an Allied soldier searching the pebble-strewn battlefield scooped up Nick's dog-tags. The find triggered official dispatch to Bridget Emery's door to inform that Nick was missing, presumably killed in action. Another telegram followed. Bridget tearfully read that Nick was alive, albeit a prisoner of war.[35]

On 17 August 1942, her teenage son Nick was worn down with dysentery on deck of the POW transport ship *Nino Bixio*,[36] crossing the Mediterranean to Italy from North Africa when, off Crete, it copped torpedo fire from British submarine HMS *Turbulent*. Young Nick absorbed the horror of seeing men killed instantly, dying slowly, afloat in the sea. Ship authorities forced survivor Bill Rudd to clean up human carnage sickeningly strewn in rigging and on deck.[37]

'I stumbled into Campo 57, Gruppignano,[38] Udine after a long train trip up the boot of Italy from Bari,' Bill Rudd wrote of a night he'd never forgot. 'It was dark and I was among a small rag-tag group of POWs, ex-El Alamein, who were among the survivors from the *Nino Bixio* torpedoed off Crete en route to Italy from the Benghazi POW camps. Cpl Gordon Dare of the 2/24 Bn was one of the curious onlookers watching our small party trudge into 57. Gordon took pity on a fellow Melburnian and nursed me through successive attacks of amoebic dysentery, influenza and jaundice after my arrival.'[39]

To document the impoverished condition of POWs arriving at Grupignano from the Alamein battles of July 1942, Major Raymond Binns typed his report. 'After capture these men were in concentration camps in Libya which were not properly organised. They suffered from lack of food and bad camp conditions and dysentery was rife. Survivors arrived at Grupignano camp in feeble condition, many being wasted and exhausted.'[40] These battered POWs bolstered Grupignano's capacity to its highest occupation numbers.

Veteran accounts concur on the harsh conditions of Campo 57, an expression of deeply felt negative impressions of Italian authorities and guards. 'Unfair severe punishment for petty offences', Col Booth summarised about Grupignano.[41]

In two waves during April 1943, POWs were marched four kilometres under armed guard from compounds at the large Australian and New Zealander Grupignano camp to the small medieval town of Cividale del Friuli.[42] At Cividale del Friuli station, near the Yugoslavia border, POWs were jammed into overloaded cattle-train 'truck' compartments, to head west to the rice-cultivation plains of the Piedmont plain between Turin and Milan, and north of the Po River. Because young Italian men were away fighting the war, POWs provided a ready labour source.

Travelling mostly at night, the train rattled the packed prisoners for fifteen hours. Sleep was not a priority. 'Changing camp is bad enough,' thought Colin Weekes, 'but at night it is no picnic at all.' POWs yearned to snatch bearings of main roads, rail-lines, rivers and mountains but darkness dampened opportunity. To the guess of Geelong-born Ian Knight, the train passed through Verona, Brescia and branched south from Milan.[43]

At a small railway siding near Vercelli, the Italian capital of rice, POWs disembarked, were divided into billet groups, and marched to assigned camps. Under the umbrella of Campo 106, its administration spanned as many as thirty farm camps where POWs slept or worked as the season required.[44] Rice, maize and corn grew on farms scattered within an area bordered by the River Po in the south, River Sesia in the east, River Dora Baltea in the west and Salussola village in the north.

Fred Tabram was downhearted when Tom Anderson was rounded up within the first group of about four hundred POWs in mid-April 1943 to be sent to work.[45] 'He was only sixteen when he left school to join up,' Tom jotted about Fred in his wartime notes. Before he enlisted, Fred was touted as a young footballer with talent, a rising player with the style of Haydn Bunton, a fellow Albury talent, and a Brownlow Medal recipient.[46]

Two weeks after Tom and the first batch of POW farm recruits departed Grupignano, Fred's name was called out to register for work. On Easter Sunday, 25 April 1943, Fred's cluster of POWs dragged their feet in the heat for a few kilometres, shouldering blankets and private gear. Several marchers fainted. Doug Le-Fevre, also in this second wave of POW farm recruits, estimated it comprised five hundred Australian and New Zealand POWs.[47]

At some stops, Fred was stupefied that local people proffered morsels of food.

He was relieved to be carted away from 'twenty months of starvation and misery'. His 'growing hate for Italians and all things directly and indirectly connected with them' niggled at his Catholic faith as 'these people were the heart of it'. In his notes of this period, Fred is adamant he'd never be in circumstances to befriend an Italian.

2
'Smoko': Sabotage and Subversion at Campo 106

'A working POW had the option of sabotage in the workplace. The frustrations of the prisoners were taken out on guards where possible; any changes in the balance of power were exploited to the full.'

—Adrian Gilbert, 2006[1]

Private Fred Tabram stepped off a train at Tronzano, west of Vercelli.[2] Lorry wagons carried the despondent and sore-footed while stronger men dawdled behind. Tronzano locals stared in curiosity. Some smiled. To good-looking girls, Fred smiled in reply.

As the POWs scrambled for bread and cigarettes thrown at their feet, Fred felt overwhelmed by a sense of empathy: 'the first kindness anyone had shown for nearly two years'. Sixty-five POW farm recruits marched into their prison courtyard, measuring '18 yards square'.

Each man clutched three blankets, a pillow slip, two sheets and a paillasse for their wooden two-tier beds. They eagerly scoffed the meagre but wholesome dinner. Recognising that they'd need a ration commensurate to the required labour, Fred's gang elected stockily built Corporal Wally Hampson as camp leader and emissary to argue the case. 'We had a book on the Geneva Conventions,' Fred stated, 'we knew where we stood.'

On Wednesday morning, the *padrone* divvied the POWs between nearby La Corte, Lachelle, Molinetto and Cascina Fantina's farms.

Gunner Colin Weekes recalled his arrival to the western part of the Piedmont plain on or about 26 April 1943.³ He was twenty-two at the time. During the transfer from Campo 57 to the farms, Colin's mind may have harked back to his first prod into POW transport trucks, 'three-tonners, packed in like cattle' at Alamein nine months earlier, and to when he was shuffled from Tarhuna on the Libyan coast to another transit camp at Tripoli in November 1942.⁴ 'Changing camp is bad enough, but at night it is no picnic at all.' From the African desert to the Italian plain, Colin kept record of each stage of captivity.

Colin and fellow farm recruits walked from the train station near Vercelli through a hamlet called Arro. Local field-workers waved to them. Old horse-carts trundled behind POWs on their way to nearby Salussola, a small town built on the western side of the narrow river Torrente Elvo, eight kilometres north-west of Vercelli. Eighty Australian and New Zealand prisoners, forty of each, were allocated to Salussola's adjacent farms, Baraccone and Tenuta Masina.⁵

Peering through a blanket of mist, Colin's first impressions of Baraccone were akin to being dropped into a previous century. 'Here and there a large block of farm buildings could be seen with groups of haylofts and store sheds scattered about them.' The buildings, Colin guessed, were more than one hundred years old. Within a compound secured by huge gates, the main building stood four storeys high. Colin estimated its brick wall to measure 180 metres by 90 metres.

'In the old days,' Colin learned, 'roving bands came down from the mountains so that each farm had to be protected and was therefore built like a small fort.' Heavy bars on all ground-floor windows deterred breaking and entering, and dampened prisoner thoughts about night-time escapes. Nearby, the more modern mixed farm, Tenuta Masina, was owned by a wealthy nobleman who, they were relieved to discover, was pro-British.

POWs were also relieved that, on the whole, Campo 106 farms offered superior conditions compared to the stench and squalor of transits at Tripoli, Benghazi and the harsh conditions at Grupignano. Improved food rations boosted POWs' fitness for eight-hour days, six days of the week. Physical labour buffed POWs' muscles; summer sun warmed their skin. Being outside the wire lifted morale. POWs slept more comfortably in farm buildings than in crowded Grupignano barracks. POWs harvested titbits about the wider war, albeit peppered with propaganda and rumour, through engaging in, and overhearing, conversations with farmers. Intelligence was gathered from chats with villagers and itinerant workers.

Wielding farmer's forks, POW recruits flicked cow and horse manure on the fields of the Italian rice-cultivation zone, feeling chuffed about their first days of farm work.

As weather warmed, POWs donned shorts, their skin gleaming with holiday tan. Once they discerned how much they could get away with, Fred Tabram, like Doug Le-Fevre, relished testing the boundaries of hours worked. 'We argued with the *padrone* about five times a day,' rejoiced Fred.[6] Locals were incredulous that prisoners opposed authority and enacted strikes. Evening singalongs solicited applause from villagers who listened in.

By June, summer heat seethed while they prepared for the flooding of the fields. Legs sloshed and sunk into the water and slime. Insects swarmed up legs and pestered faces. More than once, as Fred's gang went on strike, Italian guards gestured them to barracks and locked them in. Red Cross parcels were withheld, rations tightened and cigarettes confiscated. Clamped into handcuffs, POWs savvily negotiated their release. They fossicked barracks for nooks and crannies to stow Red Cross rations.

The Antipodean POW crew based at Salussola camp, to the north of Fred and Doug's fields, included Bill Rudd. Colin Weekes respected Bill's command of the Italian language and skills in gathering intelligence. 'Bill was working with a couple of bricklayers on the farm house so he could be close to camp,' noted Colin. 'These chaps gave him the [news] papers and from them Bill gave us a nightly newsletter session. He was very clever at reading between the lines and tipped the invasion of Sicily, and Italy, and almost predicted the capitulation of that nation to the very day.'

Ten kilometres south of Salussola, other Australians adjusted to their new billet at Tronzano and surrounding farms. Getting his bearings, Victorian Don Radnell made mental note of Tronzano's location west of Vercelli city and about thirty kilometres north-east from Turin.[7] Don would have been relieved that his mate and fellow Victorian Norm King was with him. Don and Norm were captured together at Tobruk on 1 May 1941. By the time they'd settled into working for the Italians, the duo had cooled their heels in captivity for two years.

At Tronzano farm, rice harvest was in full swing by the end of summer. Laboriously, farm workers cut rice and bound sheaves by hand. 'Modern machinery hadn't got to them,' bemoaned Don. 'Although the ear of the rice is dry and ripe, the stalk is still green which makes it very heavy, not like wheat or oats. They thrashed the rice hay like we thrashed wheat or oats years ago in Aussie.'

At twenty-three years of age, the former furnace-worker from Footscray[8] didn't take long to devise ways to shirk farm work and to subvert authority. 'Not long after we got to this camp,' Don recounted, 'we were asked to unload a load of bricks on a Sunday. We refused, saying that this is our Sabbath as well as theirs. They asked us what religion we were so we said we are all Catholics. They gave in. The next Sunday they sent a Catholic priest from the village to us for a church service in our yard. Out of forty of us only three were Catholics but most of us went along just to keep the peace.'

Sabotage was a subtle form of resistance: a means for prisoners to bait captors, to resist orders and to regain some control. Stones slipped from prisoner's hands into threshing machines used for wheat and oats; split pins were mysteriously dislodged from cartwheels. Nuts and bolts were plucked from farm equipment and POWs placed these into their pockets; when in the fields, they dropped the metal components one by one, and trod these into the ubiquitous mud. Unionists amongst prisoner ranks invented non-existent clauses in the Geneva Convention, citing an inability to work in stinking stagnant water or to work without boots. Guards wondered as to the forgetfulness of the prisoners as many boots became lost. POWs feigned ignorance about how to operate a shovel. With wry smiles and wide eyes, they watched the guards demonstrate shovel technique. Chores were completed by guards who taught duties that the POWs knew how to do. Merry hell was played with the crop. When guards turned their heads, the foreign farmhands ripped up rice stalks, leaving weeds to flourish.

Australian Private Doug Le-Fevre grew up resenting authority.[9] As a four-year-old orphan in 1921, he lived in a Barnados home on London's outskirts before he was fostered by a 'dear old lady'. She died when Doug was ten years old. He came under the auspices of the Fairbridge Society's scheme which deported orphaned children to farm schools throughout the British Empire. As a teenager at the Fairbridge Farm School at Pinjarra in West Australia, he detested work at farms where he was mistreated and underpaid.

As a POW allocated to a working farm of an enemy nation, Doug rebuffed rules, busily devising sabotage and subversion strategies to undermine the Italian and German war effort. At twenty-six years of age, Doug was still 'a stirrer'. As Doug put it, the 'little things we got up to' were also a boost to the prisoners' self-efficacy. Doug cottoned on that 'some of the Italians belonged to partisans. They had a clandestine radio so through them we knew probably more of what was happening than the average Italian.'

German occupying authorities demanded Italian farmers provide bags of produce for Germany; Doug, a veteran of Tobruk and Alamein, was determined to reduce the export quantity. Self-proclaimed 'staunch unionists' within Doug's prisoner gang of thirty-five men claimed that four-bushel capacity bags of rice were far too heavy for one prisoner to carry, and that two men must be allocated to lift one bag. Four busy hands tampered with the rice bags 'when nobody was looking'.

'We would put excreta in them or bricks or any dirt we could think of—anything to sabotage this food that was sent to Germany.' In another tactic, while one prisoner distracted guards by offering a cigarette, another fiddled with the water flow to the fields by altering the sluice gates.

Sergeant 'Popeye' Hanson, the senior Australian officer at Doug's prison camp, was charged with keeping an eye on Doug and 'Blossom' Anderson who were ploughing the fields with a Fiat tractor.[10] Hatching a mischievous idea, Popeye called to the tractor drivers: 'Your turn to sabotage today; that tractor has to stop.'

Doug promptly obeyed instructions from his senior officer. 'In those days,' Doug recollected, 'the Fiat tractor had an oil gauge above the driving seat with a little winding handle, and before you started the motor you had to wind this handle a dozen times to bring the oil up. However, this time I conveniently "forgot" and I went up once and she ran all right and coming back the second time I could hear a distinct knock. By the time I was on the third leg the motor had blown up.'

In the ensuing kerfuffle, a guard rushed to Doug, demanding something be done about the tractor, and for someone to inform the boss. Tractors were new technology in these areas, few and far between. 'I went up to the *padrone*, the farm boss, and I said that the tractor had gone bung. He said, "Explain it, what do you mean by going bung?" I said, "It is like me, it doesn't work." He said, "Well, that's fair enough." And so they had to take the tractor away.'

From March to October, the labour-intensive stages of rice cultivation—land preparation, planting, flooding, weeding, harvest—dictated POWs' tasks, and opportunities to tip the power balance.

Colin Weekes also relished the satisfaction of small victories over the guards. 'Taking a smoko' was insidiously incorporated into the farm's daily repertoire. 'One day we were on the thresher, and we overfed a drum and blocked the hay shoot, putting a great strain on a drive belt. Bang! It broke. Twenty minutes smoko. Bang! Snaps again. A further twenty minutes smoko.'[11]

'While we innocently conducted our Sunday hymn session in the boot room,' Colin recounted of another occasion of subversive serendipity, 'two chaps cut two bars in the window near my bed (no glass in the windows). Later that night while we made plenty of noise, they bent the bars and slipped away. Next morning, we went to work as usual and that night we replaced the missing boots with two spares.' Guards counted the POWs' boots each night. 'For four days we concealed their absence,' Colin rejoiced.

'Between Bill Rudd's cunning and [camp leader] Lou Moir's Scottish blood,' Colin added, 'we had the Italians licked on the diplomatic side. No sooner would one chap get into trouble would these two lads talk his way out.'

Not all relations between prisoners and guards were amicable, or as easy to manipulate. Colin's regimental mate Col Booth, who pre-war 'earned a quid' as a farmhand at Bundanoon[12] was at a farm near San Germano, a few kilometres east of Tronzano. San Germano and its closest farms, Pettiva and Robarello, were administratively clumped by authorities as Campo 106/1.[13] POWs marched from barracks to adjacent farms and were relocated as farmers needed during the summer season.[14]

Col's first escape was short-lived. At a river guarded by Germans, presumably the Po River, he was forced back to the rice farm area.[15] Some POWs were punished for escape attempts.[16]

A few kilometres from Col's camp, at the hamlet of Carpeneto, Maleny's Jim Wilson[17] was encamped. The farm was managed by the Pino brothers and Garlanda family. Forty prisoners, Jim tallied, were living in a two-storey farmhouse surrounded by fields.[18] Canale Cavour, a large irrigation canal, flowed 200 metres to the east.

While other POWs worked the fields, including several from his 2/15th Battalion, Jim worked within the blacksmith's workshop alongside local carpenter Giovanni Bonello. On Sundays, anti-fascist Giovanni made his own subversive statement by putting his black work shirts in the wash and donning a white shirt, in contrast to the black shirts of fascist patriots.[19]

One hot summer day in mid-June 1943, Jim caught sight of 2/17th Batallion's John 'Paddles' Laws speaking to Giovanni's fifteen-year old daughter, Carla, through the barbed-wire fence. Like many local girls, Carla became fond of chatting with the Australian men: 'They were just like our own.'[20]

John had intimated to Jim that he was planning an escape. Jim advised John that 'it would be far better to make a break in broad daylight rather than in the night'. As a water-carrier who cycled between the fields on the large Pino brothers' property, Carla wondered whether John might flee during daylight hours. John fantasised about going to France to locate relatives.

About midnight on 15 June 1943, Jim was jolted awake by a sharp rifle shot, followed by a fusillade fired from the courtyard below. Bullets penetrated the upstairs dormitory windows where POWs slept. Military police, *carabinieri*, barged into the dormitory, rapidly speaking in Italian to thirty-year-old Sergeant Brinley Jones, one of the few senior-ranked POWs at Carpeneto.[21] Brinley was escorted downstairs. Within minutes he was back to barracks, telling the others that John had been shot dead. John had just turned twenty-six years of age.[22]

Jim helped move John's body, dressing him for burial. Carla came to pay her respects.

Throughout her post-war life, she retained fond memories of the POW who tried to teach her English. 'It seemed a monstrosity to kill him for so little,' Carla said in 2017. 'They could have shot a bullet in the air; he would have come back. They had to send away the guard who killed John. No one wanted to see him again.'

A POW at an adjacent camp heard that the scheduled night guard had been given Red Cross chocolate to turn a blind eye to a POW leaving the compound, but a late replacement guard was unaware of the arrangement.[23] In his post-war affidavit for a war crime investigation, Jim Wilson attested that he hadn't previously seen a guard stationed in the courtyard at night. His verdict was that John was shot while climbing the kitchen wall, and that the guard had somehow got wind that John would try to escape. Jim was blunt about the close-range shooting: 'John had been shot in the head, the bullet entering under one jaw and coming out the opposite temple.'

Unsettling gossip fanned out to neighbouring camps that an Australian with the nickname of 'Paddles' had been unnecessarily murdered. As the war and the summer hotted up, many POWs grew edgy.

3
'GO GREY THINKING ABOUT IT': POWS' PRIVATIONS

> *'POWs who worked at a farm or in a factory often came across women who were curious about them ... Females who came into the camp to work frequently became the focus of sexual fantasies and some bestowed favours in return for Red Cross bounty.'*
>
> —Midge Gillies, 2012[1]

Privations permeated POW existence. They eagerly anticipated letters from home, from wives, girlfriends and mothers. They delighted in issues of Red Cross boxes containing familiar, enjoyable foodstuffs to augment prison-camp 'grub'.

A by-product of POWs' chronic hunger was a marked diminution in sexual appetite.[2] Prisoners expected their camps to be a male domain and became accustomed to long periods without setting eyes on women. Only men sent to working camps had any possibility of heterosexual relations. Campo 106 farms provided an unexpected and unique captivity opportunity to interact with women.

POWs' thoughts also turned to the issue of cigarettes. Many servicemen smoked, as the armed forces supplied nicotine as standard ration issue. To tolerate irregular receipt of Red Cross cigarettes, POWs conjured coping strategies. Heavy smokers swapped Red Cross items for cigarettes with non-smokers. Paul Lavallee and Norm Freeberg adopted this arrangement.

At ninety-seven years of age, Paul sparkled as he retold the story: 'As well as our English cigarettes (fifty Capstan in a tin), we received a cigarette quota from the Italians called Populare—they were the strongest cigarette ever and, as the saying goes, would blow the top of your head off. I didn't like them so Norm smoked my issue as well as his—he loved them. Cigarettes became our means of currency. The Italians liked our cigarettes so we could trade one or two English cigarettes to ten Italian cigarettes.

'Another way of accumulating smokes was in player poker—the Italian tobacco in the cigarettes was very loose and when betting with them we had to twist both ends to prevent the tobacco from falling out. They would pass through many hands before they were actually smoked.'

As camp currency, 'two English cigs would buy one egg from the Italians, likewise five English cigs could buy a kilo of sugar.'[3]

Paul and Norm ran quiz shows in a 1941 transit camp at Prato Isarco, north of Bolzano, 40 kilometres south of the Swiss-Italian border, and later at Grupignano. Smokes were integral to quiz routine. 'The entry fee was two English cigarettes and of course the prizes were in cigarettes,' Paul quipped.

Don Radnell told a similar yarn. 'We played a lot of cards: poker, bridge and pontoon. I mostly played poker and the lurk was to play on your bunk as most of our cigarettes were Italian and the tobacco would fall out when they got dry so one would finish up with quite a few smokes in loose tobacco. At this stage, I still hadn't taken up smoking.'[4]

Elsewhere in Italy, POWs played out frustrations against their guards. At Fontanellato, approximately 100 kilometres south-east of the Campo 106 farm complex, a Canadian prisoner baited guards with quality Canadian cigarettes from Red Cross parcels. 'A favourite trick was to light up in front of a guard, take a couple of puffs, then throw the cigarette at his feet. You could see his eyes widen, waiting for you to move on so that he could retrieve the butt. Instead you would grin at him, step forward and grind it under your heel.'[5]

According to Charles Warburton, a former farmhand in West Australia, cigarettes were valuable for bribing guards and civilian overseers to turn a blind eye to minor infractions, or to barter. 'Cigarettes were very scarce in Italy,' Charles remembered, 'and most of us had brought as many as possible from Grupignano to exchange for food. Guards would give a large loaf of bread for a packet of ten and everyone took advantage of this as we needed the bread very much. Soap was also very much sought, and used to bring in three loaves of bread.'[6]

Bill Rudd was not fond of Italian tobacco; he described it as 'ratshit'.[7] Doug Le-Fevre concurred, saying that not even the Italians liked the ironically named Populare brand. Doug lamented the paucity of cigarette papers to roll his preferred loose tobacco.

Doug empathised with civilians, recognising them as prisoners within their own war. As he observed, wartime privations afflicted everyone: 'especially when we got the Red Cross parcel and the Italians saw such things as chocolate that they hadn't seen for a number of years because Mussolini forbade it, powdered milk and all these different foods.'[8]

Carpeneto's Carla Bonello watched POWs making chocolate pudding, a rare treat for Italians living at subsistence level. Carla was grateful that Jim Wilson shared cocoa from Red Cross parcels but she didn't have the heart to tell him she didn't enjoy all the foodstuffs. 'One day he showed up with a nice box of rice cooked with milk and another box of stewed plums. I feared the idea of having to eat the rice and milk, which I hate, and then he mixed it with the cooked plums that I didn't like. Poor man! He was depriving himself of food to give it to me.'[9]

Don Radnell's work crew exploited amiable relations with guards: 'Each Saturday evening, after we finished work, we had one of our guards go into the village [Tronzano] and get wine. We traded woollen clothing for money. A pair of socks would keep one in plonk for over a week. I flogged a pullover and had enough money to keep me going for over a month. When we got into full swing, bartering and stealing, we would be pissed from Saturday night until Sunday evening. We would try to taper off until about Thursday, swear to God that we would never drink again, but by Friday, we would be so dry that Saturday evening couldn't come quick enough. Between forty of us we would get a demijohn of about 80 litres. This demijohn was a glass bottle built into a wicker frame. It took two men to pick it up! Each Saturday night the guards would come in with their vino and drink with us.'

From Maleny to Melbourne, Bundanoon to Bullfinch, Wagin to Winton, Australian townspeople missed their young men absent from mines, factories and farms. Their mothers had lived through the First World War; they remembered friends and relatives who never came back. Exchange of letters lifted both POWs and relatives' wellbeing, a tangible link and expression of hope for a future beyond wartime. Campo 106 prisoners made good use of small standard-issue postcards, *poste Italiane cartolina postale per prigionieri de Guerra,* to write to loved ones.

On 6 June 1943, six weeks into his stint on farms around San Germano, Col Booth penned one to his mother Ruby, hospitalised in Sydney. Chosen carefully, Col's words aimed to appease censors, to reassure Ruby, and dig with a tinge of sarcasm about his plight:

> Dear Mum,
> Well, everything's going fine. I'm still working on the rice farm and as fat as mud. Today being Sunday, we've just received our weekly parcel and a huge straw hat each. I can speak Italian fairly well now. Cheerio Mum till next week, and I hope you are well. Love, Col.[10]

While Col and POW comrades toiled rice and maize fields during long hot days, they chatted with itinerant *mondine* labourers who'd been drafted from nearby towns and cities. But unlike seasonal workers in Australia and New Zealand, the assiduous Italian *mondine* were mostly female.

Many of the internees, in their twenties and unmarried, could not be blind to the women working with heads down and bottoms up. With many young Italian men away fighting their own war, the arrival of unexpected itinerants of the opposite sex was a pleasant surprise. Prisoners suddenly developed interest in learning Italian.

In typical boldness, Don Radnell described the unexpected POW perks: 'We all got the shock of our life when we had to work alongside these sheilas, most of them bloody beautiful, all about eighteen to nineteen years old. Our first embarrassment was when we wanted a piss, we would ask the guard, and walk over behind a tree, but to our surprise the sheilas just dropped their daks and let go where they worked. You can imagine the eyes on twenty or so blokes that were girl-starved for about two years, so after that all we did was turn our back to have a leak.'

Tom Anderson concurred with Don about the female *mondine* at work: 'It was very pleasant to watch them lined up across the paddy, heads down, bottoms up and skirts hitched high ... They would each take a bundle of seedlings, line up across the paddy, then all move forward in unison. It was hot, strenuous toil, knee-deep in mud all day long, but they used to sing as they worked.'[11]

At a large 12th-century estate, Cascina Veneria, a government's experimental rice farm[12], where Paul Lavallee was appointed official interpreter and put in charge of about eighteen prisoners including Norm, female *mondine* received a 'pittance of pay, meals and a bag of rice when labour was finished'.

Charles Warburton mentioned the mutual ogling between POWs and the 'generous and wonderful' girls at Montonero, six kilometres east of Don's camp at Tronzano. With typical politeness, Charles expressed that 'there is no doubt about the vivacity of the average Italian girl. They have the best carriage I have seen.' Montonero prisoners relaxed by chatting with the girls through windows of their quarters. After work, Charles was enchanted when girls 'changed into trim costumes, and with lipstick added, it was hard to realise they were the same girls'.

Mondine, like the POWs, were drafted to work the fields, removed from their city jobs as factory workers, typists and dressmakers. At Montonero village's mill, prisoners worked the wheat in a large room underneath the girls' quarters. Charles was cheered in 'their company and singing. We used to have some fun.' He reiterated that 'there were many strikingly beautiful girls, and with their brightly coloured hats and scarves they certainly made our dull existence a lot brighter'.

Under *padrone* chaperonage, exchanges between female *mondine* and prisoners were mostly platonic. As anti-tank gunner Dick Gill said, 'It was hilarious as an armed guard stood between us. We would go grey thinking about it.'[12]

Despite POWs' proximity to young women at the Italian farms, POWs also had eyes for escape opportunities. West Australian Ron Maitland does not disclose the date of a fortuitous evening when he was afforded chance to walk out of camp.[13] Standing close to the camp's barbed-wire, he was handed 'a mud map' by a guard called Aldo. Then, as Aldo held up the wire, Ron slid underneath. 'All the while I wondered if Aldo would shoot me in the back for the glory of thwarting an escape attempt. Miraculously, nothing terrible happened. I felt safe in this field of velvety husks, cradled and comforted by the anonymity of the night.'

'As an escapee, on the run in Italy, I still thought and behaved like a soldier in battle. I lived by my wits and survived because of it.' The romance of rough sleeping under the stars quickly wore thin in coming days. A 'wretched loneliness' gnawed at Ron's so-called freedom, and he yearned for 'a full belly and a warm bed'.

After desperately wandering in search of shelter in the Piedmont hills, his body frozen and his gut aching with hunger, Ron stepped up to a rustic wooden door to tug the cord of a large bronze bell. The door opened to reveal a small man with piercing 'intelligent black eyes' wearing a rough woollen jumper over baggy grey pants and black boots splattered with mud. Huddled behind the man were three women snatching glimpses of the shivering stranger. In a moment of intuition, Ron put trust in them.

Ron was summoned inside. The women served polenta, cheese and wine. The warmth of the fire eased his frozen, aching bones and he looked forward to a safe, comfortable night of uninterrupted sleep.

'As if reading my mind,' Ron recalled, 'the old man offered some frayed old coats to use as blankets and directed me to a fine straw bed in the barn. As I lay there gazing out the small aperture above my cot, it struck me that here on the other side of the world even the sky was foreign to me. I knew I would have no trouble sleeping; I was numbed by my host's Italian homemade wine.'

In the morning, a small hand timidly shook Ron's shoulder. He thought it to be a dream. 'An ethereal, young beauty hovered before my sleepy eyes.' One of the farmer's daughters had come to wake him. 'I had a sudden and overwhelming urge to make this moment last as long as I could; maybe there would never be another chance. As I mulled over this depressing prospect, my hand gently reached for hers. She made no attempt to move away so I drew her a little closer and felt the warmth of her body next to mine. Never before had a woman looked or felt more inviting.

'The next day the other daughter came to my hiding place. I do not really know who seduced whom but I soon found that I was romantically entangled with both sisters.'

For men and women in wartime, often there was a sense of living for today. Ron simply seized the moment. 'Death could come on any day,' he declared, 'I really was so terribly alone.' Before leaving the house of the old Italian with piercing eyes, Ron became 'involved with an amazing woman': the two girls' mother.

4
'KEEP CALM AND STAY PUT': ITALY'S CAPITULATION 1943

'Much more than in Germany, the treatment of Allied prisoners in Italy was determined by the character of the individuals guarding them. Moreover, Italy was unique, in so far as it was the only Axis power to sign an armistice mid-war and then become partially an Ally, helping rather than holding British, Commonwealth and American prisoners.'

—Charles Rollings, 2008[1]

At Montonero, Charles Warburton could not shake the feeling that 'always the war was looming in the background'. In conversation with local people, Charles became aware of their deep-seated grievances and frustrations. A bullock driver who regularly cycled to Montonero from nearby Salasco frequently bleated that although Australians had been prisoners for two years, he'd been a prisoner of fascism and its fallout for twenty-five years. One Montonero guard exclaimed to Charles 'that it was alright fighting a war where just men got hurt, but it was no good when the bullet, which misses you, might strike your mother or sister'.[2]

Charles Warburton watched, and wished for unfolding events to bring about POWs' liberation. He'd learned that 'Allied troops had completely vanquished the Axis out of Africa and had taken Pantellero [Pantelleria] and Sardinia and had now gained a foothold on Sicily.' As he recalled, 'Mussolini had said that if Italy was invaded, the Italians were to defend it tree by tree. The air was filled with the droning of our bombers ... Montonero locals rushed about cheering and spitting at posters of Mussolini. An Italian neighbour sat on his doorstep, head in his hands, crying with joy.'

During the summer of 1943, Allied bombardment pounded the large cities of Milan, Turin and Genoa. Propaganda permeated conversations; it agitated the locals who worried that every city would be bombed if Italy didn't surrender. Nearby, Vercelli's valuable rice mills and large quantities of stored rice were sitting ducks. Charles reasoned that 'chaos would be caused if our bombers launched attacks against the numerous mills just as harvest was due'.

Montonero, approximately equidistant from Milan to its north-east and Turin to its south-west, was smack in the middle of the aerial action. As Montonero prisoners watched waves of bombers fly over, the reverberations of exploding bombs, explosions and lights from ack-ack and the drones of engines 'was like music to our ears,' diarised Charles. 'We realised the powerful blows being dealt to Axis powers must soon bring about our release.'

News vendors reported that on 12 and 13 July, Turin was hammered by British Lancaster, Stirling, Wellington and Halifax aircraft dropping 760 tons of bombs. Fire-fighters struggled to minimise damage thrust on Turin's infrastructure, buildings and industrial facilities by cluster bombs and incendiary devices. 790 people were killed.[3]

Montonero *mondine* expressed their distress. 'Girls would be escorted upstairs in a pitiable state, crying and broken-hearted,' remembered Charles. 'We'd be told by her friends that her home had been bombed or her parents killed.' One girl spoke candidly: 'Mussolini, it's him we have to thank. I hope you bomb more, then we will be out of this war'.

British bombing of Rome also aimed to cripple military targets but old churches copped the blasts. 'This,' Charles understood, 'struck home at the Italian people as nothing else could. It was obvious that the Vatican would suffer if the threat of bombing were to continue.'

An Italian article, reprinted in a POW newspaper in 1944, highlighted war's cultural collateral. The journalist's plea targeted the British: 'Have you ever thought of the future? War is a terrible tragedy but only temporary. What will happen tomorrow if a bomb was to reduce, to a heap of ashes, the Scala Opera House? Or is the Last Supper of da Vinci, honoured by the world, to be crumpled to pieces?'[4]

From a farmhouse at Casa Foglietta, a marching distance of four kilometres west from Montonero, Private Bert Lockie of 2/15th Battalion also watched RAF aircraft heading towards Turin. Bert penned that 'well-primed POWs would cheer them on but the guards weren't happy as many had relatives in Turin.'[5]

At nearby San Germano, Private Ernie Sparnon, 3LAA, diarised that 'we were often kept awake at night by the raids of our air force,' and 'when Mussolini went, we were kept inside for three days.'[6]

At Carpeneto, Italian teenager Carla Bonello was fearful after sundown because a machine-gunned plane roamed around. 'It was dangerous in particular for those who were working as herdsmen in the stables and woke up at night to milk the cows. The curfew started when it was dark. Even a small light from a window could trigger an attack.'[7]

In July, Charles Warburton was wheelbarrowing rice at Montonero when he heard that 'old Mussolini has gone, he cleared out this morning'. Prisoners grasped the Italians' rising hatred toward Mussolini. 'Even we in our prison camp,' Charles jotted, 'had inkling of the tremendous undercurrents beneath the still-united fascist regime, working for the Royalists; and now, with Mussolini's prestige and power falling every day, the Royalists were making their organisation ready.' Doug Le-Fevre concluded that most locals he encountered were communists 'as red as beetroots' and opposed to fascism.[8] POWs tried to discern loyalists, Royalists and the Roman Catholics amongst those they met.

Italians and POWs rejoiced together when British and American troops landed at Sicily on 10 July. Marshal Pietro Badoglio formed government following the overthrow of Mussolini and began secret peace talks with the Allies. British and US governments and their respective escape organisations MI9 and MIS-X had begun to consider the fate of their prisoners within Italy.[9] Allied authorities feared that a mass POW breakout would lead to German reprisals.

Mussolini was placed under arrest and Marshal Pietro Badoglio became head of government on 25 July. 'Practically every man of us believed we would be on our way home in a few days,' Charles said. 'However, on the next day news came that the fascists had regained control under German authority.'

Whether the prisoners could fully comprehend the historical significance of the events to Italians, a world war churned its wheels while they toiled the fields.

During his interview to Keith Murdoch Sound Archive, Jack Wauhop remarked that despite bouts of beriberi, he tolerated farm work. Jack, like many Campo 106 POWs, was reasonably content to bide his time, with ears to the ground for developments in the wider war. As did many others, Jack worked for a *padrone* who was 'a decent fellow'.[10]

With this in mind, and anticipating the Allied troop advance, Jack 'didn't make a decision to escape'. In August 1943, Jack's stay-put plans were dashed by a frightening exchange with a fascist guard, a veteran of the Russian front. The Italian targeted Jack for gloating about the roar of aerial bombardment. In broken English and Italian, the guard ranted: 'You *Australiano*, you say "*Viva il Duce*".' Jack, also 'a little hot under the collar', replied with an enigmatic, 'Ned Kelly forever!' and a defiant thumbs-up. Infuriated, the guard prodded Jack to a shed where he drew a bayonet from his scabbard, fixed it on his rifle and gestured towards the northern mountains. Jack cottoned on that he wanted him to run but Jack stood his ground to avoid a bayonet in the back.

Incensed, the guard 'blubbered', eyes rolling in his head. Jack eyed a three-pronged pitchfork and flashed back to bayonet training at Northam's army camp. 'I left him with a pitchfork in him and took off.'

Jack sprinted to a clump of trees, took breath, and headed for the hills. Three weeks later, Jack was 25 kilometres north of the farm, hiding out near Biella, wondering why the countryside was 'lousy with soldiers, night and day'. He got wind that Italy had 'chucked in the towel. German numbers in the vicinity of Biella had increased. There were at least 10,000 German troops watching everybody and always on the move, and you had to get through them.'

While early escapers like Ron Maitland and Jack Wauhop were on the run, having decamped before the armistice, Allies landed at Salerno during Operation Avalanche on 9 September 1943. Nick Emery, Bill Rudd and most of their Australian POW cohort were still in camps, contemplating what to do.

The communique about an Italian armistice with the Allies on 3 September 1943, coincident with British and Canadian assault on the toe of Italy, rippled to the rice bowl within days. Italy's capitulation was a watershed event. Three main choices were now before the prisoners: to head south to aim for advancing Allied forces; to head north to neutral Swiss territory; or to stay put in camp until Allied forces liberated them. Outside prisoner barracks there was growing pro-British sentiment amongst the Italian populace: a shifting of alliances as a shared understanding emerged between former foes. The option to stay put within camp barracks was the least attractive to most prisoners unless injury held them back.

At 8pm on Wednesday 8 September, just one week after a strike concluded, Ted Peachey crept into Fred Tabram's night barracks to blurt news of the armistice.[11] Bob Ward diarised that he interpreted Ted's wide grin as signalling delivery of 160 kilograms of 'precious spuds' to supplement food rations of the forty Tronzano-based POWs.[12] The flip of playing cards ceased. All looked up to digest Ted's announcement.

'I've just heard the news over the wireless and confirmed by both bosses that Italy has signed the armistice, but for God's sake don't make too much noise, we're not supposed to know about it!'

Ted was fortunate to be one of few Australian soldiers to have a head start in Italian before the war.[13] At the time of his enlistment, he frequented a fish-and-chip shop owned by an Italian who engaged him in conversation.

Confused from hearing unconfirmed rumours over the previous weeks, the Tronzano POWs were hesitant to get excited until an Italian corporal trotted in to confirm the news. Prisoners and guards hugged. After a potato feast, Bob Ward's gang bunked down to restless sleep.

The next morning, an officer came to Tronzano advising that plans for their repatriation were under way. 'Within fifteen days, you'll be on your way home,' the officer optimistically announced, shaking their hands. Although he was not staying put, he asked the POWs to keep up the good behaviour and stay in camp. Allied forces had landed near Genoa on the coast and would soon, he expected, reach the Piedmont plain. Fred remembered this scoop came at 8am. He heard that men from different camps 'got out of control and were wandering everywhere'.

On 11 September, the gates of Tronzano barracks were flung open. Mindful of hearsay about German round-ups of newly escaped POWs, prison-breakers juggled food and clothing and scattered into the fields. Men drifted into small groups or mateship pairs. Ted Peachey took off with Gordon Dare, Ralph Abercrombie, George Weedon, Stan Booth and Jimmy Dean.[14] Bob Ward and fellow 2/28th Battalion private Max Wills went fishing at the canal with mosquito nets and frames doubling as nets.

'Our first drive wasn't very successful, only two fish,' diarised Bob. 'Later we tried again and boy, did we get a haul! Twenty-eight fish in the second drive. Max and I cleaned them, and then set to work boiling them.'

Tom Anderson begged Fred Tabram to go south with him to flee across the Po River towards Genoa on the coast. Tom was won over by the rumour that Allied forces had landed and were moving northward. But Fred and others were unconvinced, opting instead to tackle the high mountains visible on the northern horizon. In his notes, Tom refers to Palestro as his base, eight kilometres north-east of Tronzano. Many farms were close to others; POWs knew where some of their mates were working.

On 9 September, Fred sought permission from his camp officer to buy wine at the *dopo lavoro* (after-work tavern). 'Les Clare and I had quite a few mixed drinks. One of our mates told us two girls waited outside for us, girls we'd worked with, who wanted to take us home.' But when they were nearly there, guards nudged the duo back to camp.

Fred was going stir-crazy, waiting for orders the next day. His Lachelle work gang opened gates and walked out. The sergeant watched, smiled, and walked away. Fred and Les, with Jack Bristow, Mickey Peel and Frank 'Bluey' Blewett went to town to drink, probably at nearby Ronsecco. Fred and Bluey formed an escaper party and left Lachelle but stayed nearby, hedging bets that Allied forces would soon arrive. On 19 September, Fred followed advice by an unknown source to assemble at nearby La Corte. A 'Dr Rossi',[15] Fred heard, was preparing to help them but 'plans did not come off'.

On the canal banks, fishing or sitting tight, clusters of POWs marked time, awaiting bulletins. They briefly joined up with fellow Lachelle workers Doug Le-Fevre and 'Bloss' Anderson. Fred and Bluey swam in the canal at night. Locals 'claimed' them. They were 'booked every night', Fred delighted. One day Fred had invitations from six girls, including Josephine, to go home with them or to the pictures. 'One day the four of us visited eight different homes, hospitality was rich. My dislike of Italians died of fright.'

5
'THAT'S WHEN OUR WAR STARTED': WALKING INTO GERMAN-OCCUPIED ITALY

> *'The life of a soldier on active duty is unpredictable at best, but army organisation, standing orders and unit discipline carry him along, even in a prison camp. Not so the AIF POW 'Free Man' who has to exist in a very harsh environment indeed. He has to live off the land. Harassed and hunted by the enemy, he enjoys neither the protective benefits of the Geneva or Hague conventions. And for many, the knowledge that his own risks may be even greater for the local population who help him to survive.'*
>
> —Bill Rudd, 2012[1]

As elucidated by historian Roger Absalom, 'Italy had become a field of desperate and complex struggle between armies, classes and ideologies. On the battlefield itself the contending forces were, on one side, the forces of the German Reich; an 'alliance' between Germans, Austrians, and a motley collection of Czechoslovaks, Russians, Ukrainians and Cossacks were joined, within a few weeks of the Italian surrender to the Allies, by the armed formations of Mussolini's born-again Fascist Italian Social Republic, an equally uneasy mixture of reluctant conscripts and elite units. Fighting its way northward against these defending forces was an even more heterogeneous army, officially known as the United Nations.'[2]

Regardless of their place of impoundment in Italy in early September 1943, few Allied POWs were in a mood to keep calm or stay put. Most POWs fled, worried that Germans would soon learn the locations of their prison farms. For Australian, New Zealand, British and South African POWs scattered across Italy, the armistice promulgation came like a celebratory bell-toll from an Italian church tower, calling them back into action.

At Tronzano farm or barracks nearby, sapper Frank 'Arthur' Jobson was not in the best position to pull on his boots when the armistice newsflash hit town.[3] Arthur was laid up with malaria, stricken with it on 19 July, his twenty-ninth birthday. For most of August 1943, he lay prostrate on his bunk.

On the evening of the armistice promulgation, when POWs tramped in from the fields, he was puzzled about a guard's exultant proclamation: '*La guerra finite! La guerra finite! Armistissio! Armistissio!*' in premature optimism that war had finished. Another guard raised his rifle, emptying the magazine skywards. Camp gates were flung open and guards vigorously shook hands. Arthur may have wondered if he was delirious. He barely had strength to stay on his feet and crawled back into his bunk to be 'kept awake until after 2am by my mates and the guards celebrating, mistakenly, the end of the war'.

Arthur and younger brother, sapper Ian 'Tim' Jobson, belonged to one of four work gangs of sixty men billeted in the communal hall of a small village. Tim reported their transfer from San Germano to Tronzano camp on 17 June as farmers' needs changed. One work gang's relocation swelled their farm workers to eighty-six men.

According to Arthur's account, this cohort was divided into six gangs working separate farms. In June, female *mondine* arrived, immediately transplanting rice plants on fields from which the early maturing wheat had been harvested. This technique enabled a crop of wheat and a crop of rice to be obtained every year between the winters. The Po valley plain yielded good maize crops and may have reminded the Jobsons of familiar home territory at Gooburrum Shire and of the warm climate of Rosedale, north of Bundaberg. By day the Jobsons' work gang was patrolled by two men on pushbikes while at dusk resident mosquito hordes patrolled for blood.

The day after the armistice announcement, Arthur dragged himself back to work. Italian farmhands chimed their chorus: *'Mussolini finito! Italia libra'*—Mussolini is finished, Italy is free. The senior officer-in-charge instructed prisoners to stay put. Two days later, a guard named Carlo drove the farm's truck to Vercelli to collect rations and petrol, later returning hours overdue, on foot. Germans had taken over Vercelli and had confiscated their truck, but Carlo was nonplussed. 'If we have no truck, we have no petrol, and we have no food. But we will win!'

Arthur and Tim, with corporal Thomas 'Joe' Newbey of the 2/28th Battalion, and a prisoner they knew only as 'Five-Miler', strolled to an adjacent farm to touch base with trusted farmhands. They were invited to bunk in farm buildings and to work there until the Allies reached the scene. Five-Miler's prediction that Allied liberators would soon arrive seemed very feasible. Tim reported that nine POWs stayed put for a week after the armistice.[4]

Arthur benefitted from a week of convalescence before an incident put wind up their sails: German bullets sprayed into an Italian lieutenant's car; a subtle warning to Italians who sympathised with POWs. Strategies mooted by German local command included 'a death penalty on any Italians found aiding Allied POWs'. Next morning, while POWs and *mondine* were knee-deep in the paddock, a pamphlet was handed around, communicating German proclamation that Italians harbouring or aiding prisoners of war would incur the death penalty.

The Jobsons' quartet agreed to leave after dark, aiming to cross the busy Milan–Turin road and journey towards Switzerland. None of them felt certain if this was the best strategy—to become interned in another foreign country for war's duration. First priority was to assemble with Italian friends for the evening meal.

The Italians concurred that they make haste for the Alps and perhaps consider joining partisans. Back in camp, Italian farmhands kissed the POWs on the cheek, an Italian custom that Australian and New Zealand POWs had become reasonably comfortable with. The Italian colonel gave a 50 *lire* note to each POW, and retrieved two folded maps from his coat pocket. He tore off the covers to remove his name and handed the maps to Joe Newbey as senior officer. The maps detailed roads and trails west of Genoa to France, to the central north of Italy, and into Switzerland. Joe, the Jobsons and Five-Miler were equipped with full bellies and a sense of direction.

They listened diligently to the colonel's spin on the situation: 'Under the Geneva Convention, if food or water could not be supplied to prisoners within 24 hours, they must be released.' The Italian colonel added that, 'If you decide to stay, we will not hand you over to the Germans, we will resist them. If you wish to be released, I will open the gate.'

The subtext sang clear: Italian guards preferred not to resist the Germans, and neither did the Jobson quartet. A vote was taken amongst camp-wide POWs: stay put or leave? Eighty-six prisoners voted to open the gate; no prisoners voted to stay put. Guards packed up and took off, fearing German round-ups for involuntary deployment to the Russian front.

The wider work gang split into three small groups and rendez-voused at a copse of trees near the farm buildings. Maps were laid out; intelligence was discussed: were the Allies now at Genoa on the coast, about 200 kilometres to the south? Had anyone heard whether German soldiers were marching up and down the highways?

Joe Newbey tucked the tattered funeral pall ribbons from the coffin of Ted, his older brother, under his shirt.[5] Ted had died at Grupignano camp nine months earlier. The official cause of death as annotated on his army file was 'bronchial pneumonia, severe organic decay'.[6]

Like Joe Newbey, Ian Knight grieved for a brother who died before they left Campo 57. Ewen Knight died on 31 January 1943[7] in the midst of a severe winter. When Ewen took ill, he was taken from Campo 57 to a 'hospital in nearby Udine [convent hospital] where, in spite of the most careful attention from doctors, sisters and staff, he died within a few days from meningitis'. Ian wrote in his notes that the death of his younger brother 'had a profound effect on myself in particular; and the whole Australian area of the camp'.[8]

As autumn cooled the steamy summer in early September 1943, Ian Knight and a New Zealand mate were encamped at Castellone, located five kilometres east of Tronzano farms. Like the Jobson gang harboured at a nearby camp, Ian's duo stalled, in a quandary about escape routes. 'Where best to go,' Ian quavered. 'We were aware of massive movement via the *autostrada*, of southbound heavy war transport such as tanks, guns and troop-carriers laden with troops, indicating that the Germans were really mounting a full-scale occupation of Italy. All guards and officers of the Italian army in charge of our camp disappeared during the night.

'Our first thought was to travel south to join the advancing Allied army. Of course, this would entail passing through the already strengthening German lines of defence ... but after travelling south, avoiding the main roads, we encountered the River Po, and considering that all bridges would be under military guard, we returned north ... by avoiding the valley roads, we would have a reasonable chance of getting through to neutral Switzerland.'

Like the Jobson brothers and the sole Knight and Newbey brothers, Col Booth felt the war sticking to his tail.

During post-armistice exuberance at a farm, Col worried about a dalliance in an abandoned guard house between a prisoner and one of the female *mondine*. Col ramped up his plans to decamp, anxious that this tryst could enflame any guard looking for an excuse to fire a gun.[9]

Col, probably with Peter Erickson, shot through, seizing their first or second breakaway on 9 September according to Col's POW report,[10] and headed south with another POW, name unknown.[11]

Col's trio reached Balzola, about ten kilometres south of Vercelli. The River Po flowed across their path. On the southern banks, Col noted Casale Monferatto, but their hopes to cross the Po were crushed as German patrols held guard. There seemed no other option but to turn around and head north, regardless of the anticipated support of advancing Allied forces coming their way, if indeed they trusted this rumour. Col missed his smokes. Would they be let down again as happened at Ruin Ridge a year previous, when Allied support did not arrive? With German forces and fascist spies everywhere, was there high probability of succumbing to another ambush, a humiliating recapture, or worse?

During training in the unforgiving desert of North Africa, troops in Col's regimental battery had been trained for battle and close combat with the enemy. On the loose in Italy, the best tactics were to avoid the enemy at all costs. Enemy lines in Italy's countryside were often indistinct to the unknowing escaper in unfamiliar territory. Enemy could attack at any time of day, on any mountain, or in any village. Friend or foe had to be discerned amongst the Italian men, women and children they approached for assistance.

A POW mate to Col, Havaland Park, reported in 1945 that he walked out of an open-gated camp with forty-three other POWs.[12] Havaland carried war-wounds to his leg and was presumably unable to travel with fast-footed friends. At Cascina Gattesco, near to Allodi, he fell into the care of Armando Ardizzone until 1945 and also Silvana Salvarini. Havaland reported that Armando 'also clothed nine other ex-POWs after their escape'. All dispersed, except Havaland, in coming weeks, due to 'fascist attention'. Havaland listed Col and Peter as well as Rossett Wycherley, Edwin 'Ted' Price, John 'Chocka' Johnson, George Woodyard, Gorden Rickard, William 'Bill' Blair, and Charles Stouse.

Round-ups soon after the armistice rattled POWs and Italians. 'There were difficult times even after 8 September,' reiterated Carla Bonello, recalling the day that a senior-ranked fascist and his militia came from

Vercelli to the Pino brothers' Carpeneto farm to see whether partisans were there. 'In the Pino's warehouse, partisans were already there ready with rifles to shoot him in the back. Domenica Pino said, "No boys, for god's sake. You kill those there and their comrades will kill us all."'[13]

Unlike the Jobson brothers in company with their sergeant Joe Newbey, Col's trio were typical of most Australian escapers in Italy: men of non-commissioned rank without commanding officers. In this new battlefield, as it had been in the dust of Ruin Ridge, soldiers dug into physical toughness and psychological resilience, survived on low rations, lack of sleep, and a great deal of looking over shoulders. Like towns blackened-out to reduce chance of bombings, escapers were hell-bent on being inconspicuous to reduce the chance of recapture.

Rules of war changed once they stepped out of prison camps. Italians proffered tips about being Italian. To look like peasants, walkers must not walk abreast nor talk to each other. Better still, one should adopt a slouch and walk slowly with hands down or in pockets. No military bearing was to be conveyed by the walker.[14] Men with red hair must source hats. If a POW's unusual Italian accent was queried, a POW could pretend to be mute, or to hail from south of Rome. Northern Italians were mostly unfamiliar with southern Italy, akin to another country. Italians swiftly spotted a non-Italian. One British escaper, a medical officer, was aghast that Italian peasants recognised him as British despite best efforts to pass himself off as a local. Locals told him that his hair was parted the wrong way, that he walked and sat the wrong way, and that anyone as scruffy-looking as him would not have possessed glasses.[15]

Doug Le-Fevre's escaper garb of 'quite a dapper blue outfit' may have drawn more attention than he desired.[16] He'd slipped the collar of captivity with former Bayswater gardener Norm Terrell, Ron Bryant and 'Bloss' Anderson. Their farm guards included veterans of the Russian front and, unlike Jack Wauhop's guard, most were sympathetic to their walkout.

Initially, the four escapers hoped to stick together, but as Doug found out, 'the Italians in those areas of course were as poor as church mice and though they were generous, we knew we were stretching the bonds of friendship. We split up and Norm and I went on our own ... Some members of the camp went north, some south, some east, some west; a few remained. Those who remained were picked up a few days later and taken to Germany.' At that time, Doug thought there were not many Germans about. As Norm was young, fair, tall, and knew little Italian, he and Doug concocted that he'd pretend to be mute.

Doug and Norm moved from village to village. While drinking water at a village pump, the tinkle of a bicycle bell announced a young German toddling towards them on an army bike. In Italian, he asked for help to paste a poster on the pump. As if thrown into an acting audition, Doug and Norm dug deep in search of the safest persona. As the Australians stepped back to check whether the poster was on straight, they noticed the image of a desperate villain and the message that large rewards were on offer for information leading to the apprehension of POWs. The German pulled out bologna sausage and wine from his haversack to thank his 'Italian' helpers. He told them that the poster was nearly redundant because the German SS believed that they'd have all escapers rounded up within a month. The young German said he was aware of subversion activities happening under the Germans' noses. He told Doug and Norm that he had 'called into a village a couple of nights ago and had put up a poster, and in the morning, it was gone'. The German confided he heard that 'four "Australianos" had come by in the night and had taken the poster with them'. He added: 'I believe those buggers would too.' Norm and Doug watched the young German wobble unsteadily on his bicycle, and when out of sight, they breathed relief and hurried northward.

At the Baraccone and Salussola camps, ten kilometres to the north of Montonero, Bill Rudd recalled the euphoric attention to the *vino* stocks and the female *mondine*.¹⁷ Bill chose to be a sober sentry to 'the biggest celebration. They rolled out gallons, huge drums of vino, everybody had a big party, and it was reminiscent of a Roman orgy at one stage, but that didn't interest me.' With eighty Australian and New Zealand POWs and about one hundred *mondine* in residence, Bill saw 'quite a party going on in the midst of the general confusion'. Compound gates stood welcomingly open.

Geraldton brothers Bert and Bill Wilson participated in Salussola's post-armistice party. 'We were able to walk out at ease. In the evening, four of us and a guard had a meat-roll party with biscuits and butter, washed down with litres of vino.'¹⁸ Bill Rudd listened to the BBC on Friday 10 September to learn that Germans were in nearby Novara, Turin, Milan, Vercelli and Biella. As his Salussola colleague Colin Weekes elaborated: 'In fact, Jerries were all around us. Four days was spent in wild celebrating, and instead of rising, the balloon began to settle down on us again. From then we saw that we were not on top of the world.'¹⁹

Generic terms of derision referring to the Italian enemy as *Itie* and *Wop*, and the German enemy as *Jerry* and *Hun*, permeated POWs' lingo. 'We had to post a man every night with the Wop guard,' Colin put it, 'so we'd get fair warning if the Hun did come.' Conscript guards at the camp were the first to leave, 'gone in civilian clothes in two shakes of a lamb's tail'. Disarmed Italian soldiers aimed to avoid being rounded up for labour or fighting.

On 11 September, several Baraccone POWs reconnoitred to surrounding farms. Bill Rudd plucked a map of northern Italy from a local school's wall. Being a graduate geologist, he was skilled in map interpretation. Situational awareness of roads, rivers and railways was a distinct advantage for successful evasion. To Bill's reckoning, the distance to Switzerland was about 140 kilometres. He tried persuading his mate and fellow sapper John 'Jock' Smith to head to the north with him. Scottish-born Jock, a former scaffolder and rigger from Queensland, had however resolved to head south.

Each man chose his strategy; each man sought camouflage. Bill's clobber inspired him to adopt an alias of a navy deserter. 'My civilian clothing included a canvas-type naval shirt, I had a reasonably good watch which in conjunction with the sun was a rough compass, some Italian money, a good swag, some condensed milk, Ovaltine, jam etcetera from Red Cross parcels and a battered but efficient vacuum flask which was to prove invaluable.' Bill did not wish to stick around for too long. 'I foresaw the Germans digging in against the advancing Allies, and I was much nearer Switzerland than them. Moreover, I had skied there before the war when my sister was at school at Lausanne.'

Bill struck a deal with Nello Cugnasco, an overseer in charge of camp discipline and a sergeant of the *carabinieri*, the Italian military police. Nello had fought alongside British forces in the First World War. Bill deduced that Nello was 'no German lover'. Although the official line was that *carabinieri* cooperated with the Germans, many *carabinieri* acted informally to assist escaped prisoners or to turn a blind eye. Bill had his eye on Nello's alpine quality boots and negotiated with Nello that Bill hand over his battle dress, army equipment, army boots and some Red Cross items in return for Nello's boots. Bill obliged Nello's request to carry a package for personal delivery to the British military attache in Switzerland. From what Bill gleaned, the cheesecloth-wrapped package included a letter and a sketch map of the farms where POWs had been interned.[20] He did not open it, a decision that prayed on his mind into his 102nd year of life.

Nello accompanied Bill for a ten-kilometre train trip from Salussola to the textile town of Biella, the limit of Nello's jurisdiction. There, Bill was introduced to Nello's contact, but something niggled at Bill's gut. This was the beginning of a new phase of his war, and he needed to trust his instinct.

Bill declined the stranger's assistance and set off alone on foot. He covered ground during daylight hours, opting to walk parallel to roads on their high side to maximise reconnaissance. Night was for rest. Bill found it easy to 'bandicoot' crops. 'Chestnuts, grapes and tomatoes were easily gathered, and poor though the mountain people undoubtedly were, it was easy to ask for a flask of hot water in exchange for a cigarette, and sometimes cold boiled potatoes or polenta could be obtained. In retrospect and hindsight, those mountain peasants were extremely helpful to Allied POWs on the loose, but I was taking no chances. I was free, on my own and so less likely to attract attention, and could doss down for the night with a good warm drink of Bovril or Ovaltine.'

Bill considered it best not to trust anybody, so he employed his Italian to make inquiries only to children and the very old. On the whole, the weather was fine as he headed north during the middle of September. In his adopted guise of a Yugoslav naval deserter with imperfect Italian, Bill Rudd felt pretty confident he was on the right track.

6
'The familiar rice mill': Shelter at Campo 106 farms post-armistice

> *'The Australians and other POWs in the region faced quite a quandary. They might remain with the people who offered them shelter and succour, albeit at great risk. Or they could hope to avoid the Germans and their Italian minions by seeking refuge in more isolated areas, moving when necessary from one hiding place to another, but always relying on the almost unfathomable kindness of strangers ... An alternative was to try to leave Italy altogether.'*
>
> —Peter Monteath, 2017 [1]

In September 1943, individual escapers could not know the bigger picture of 79,000 men from Allied nations in Italian captivity, nor that nearly 50,000 of them had moved out of camps dotted across Italy.[2] Perhaps as many as 800 Australian escapers from Campo 106 were a microcosm of this mass escape, and a fewer number of New Zealanders.[3] As Roger Absalom concludes, the records in the public domain are insufficient in detail to make it clear what proportion of POWs transferred to Germany were scooped up at or near farm camps soon after the armistice or were captured at some point after escape.[4]

Some prisoners embraced days of sitting tight to evaluate the best course of action, or to await further direction from locals. Many escapers discovered that initial euphoria of escape waned with the realisation that they'd need helping hands to survive. Although many farmers were sympathetic to their plight and shared what they could, the *contadini* peasants were mostly poor.

For escapers who forged strong connections to villagers, it was commonplace to stay close to working farms for days or weeks during the tumultuous post-armistice period. Farm routine was constant, and provided a shelter from the storm. Many tried to repay their farm hosts, content to work for food and somewhere to sleep. The rice mill was vital to the localised economy, regardless of the changing war. Mutually dependent on each other, farmers relied on young strong POWs during the 1943 summer while local men served in the war. Peasant farmers empathised with the escaper's plight and vulnerability.

On Wednesday 8 September 1943, Charles Warburton was halfway through a shave when the silence was broken by cheering and the thud of feet running down the main street of Montonero.[5] His hand shook while he held his razor. Other POWs quit washing their utensils. 'It came like the bolt out of the blue,' Charles exulted, 'the great moment when Italy would throw down her arms and surrender. Before the day was finished, I would no longer be a prisoner of war, but a free man waiting to return to my country.'

Italian villagers surged the compound gate, 'half hysterical men and women shouting *finito la guerra*.' An officer requested everyone to go to bed, to be patient for 'arrangements'. Villagers cheered prisoners as they scaled stairs to their quarters. For the first time, guards declared that they'd not lock the door.

Around the farms, topography was as flat as a tack. To the north, rising above the horizon, Alps with white tips rubbed the white clouds and blue sky, about 70 kilometres away to Charles's calculation. 'Even at so great a distance, the mountains looked high and rugged.' Many Montonero POWs thought it timely to sell surplus utensils, bedding and clothes for Italian *lire*. In a flash, villagers heard about the sale. 'There are few people in the world who like buying and selling as do the Italians, and soon the Italians were drifting into the compound. At first, they waited below and when any of the lads had anything to sell, they bid for it and the guards changed the article for *lira*. As the crowd grew bigger and the bidding brisker, the people were soon in our rooms.'

Charles was enthralled by the frenzy but hesitant to sell because others were selling gear without strategic weighing up of respective merits of blankets, boots and a 'few bob' for escape kits. 'The Italian people saw themselves able to buy first-class woollen stuff for a song,' Charles observed. 'The noise and arguments rose to a crescendo. Men and women were surging about our beds as a chap showed an article for sale'. Quality fabric had become scarce in Italy.

Nearby at Carpeneto, Carla Bonello put her seamstress skills to good use to refashion a POW's shirt for her own use, decorating the chest pocket with the four suits of a deck of playing cards.[6] With the virtual collapse of the usual official purchasing and distribution system for agricultural produce, informal arrangements and black-market economies grew. 'The peasant with a surplus of food or other home-produced goods (either his own or what he could conceal from the landowner) was able to generate a larger cash income than before.'[7]

Mid-morning on 10 September, Montonero's senior camp officer passed on orders from Campo 106's command in Vercelli. POWs were to be turned loose in order to contravene German orders from German HQ in Vercelli to turn POWs in. The officer suspected that records of farms holding POWs had deliberately been destroyed to prevent German knowledge of prisoner numbers and locations. The officer and guards donned civilian clothes in the hope that advancing British troops would soon free them from duties, advising POWs to head south towards the British, carrying as much *lire* as available.

It was time for another sale. Charles now joined in. 'Everything was being sold including food from parcels, and the Italians were even grabbing our sheets and rugs. Against emergency, I had kept three tins of meat and biscuits, and these I put in my haversack; the rest of the stuff I gave away. As for clothes, I had very little and, after keeping my overcoat, a jersey and a singlet, I gave the rest away.' In the ruckus, a farm worker known to Charles as Johannah, clambered over beds to grab a tin trunk that Charles had fashioned from food tins at Grupignano, and nestled it under his arm. 'Our rooms were now being thoroughly stripped of everything, and I had to watch my overcoat and pack very sharply, else they would have vanished.'

Shedding of military uniforms rendered escapers unrecognisable as military personnel. Out of uniform, the protection of the Geneva Convention was no longer applicable and POWs could be shot as spies. Charles contemplated his understanding of the rules. 'If we were caught, we were only prisoners doing our duty trying to regain our lines; whereas in civilian clothes I imagined we could be taken for spies, and our treatment would then be in the hands, or the feelings, of whoever captured us.'

Charles opted to wear the POW uniform of woollen British battledress plastered with a conspicuous red patch. Military boots were good compared to the Italian boots, but were more conspicuous. All in all, a no-win situation. Cold weather would soon snap at the heels of all boots regardless of colour or make. Charles worried that some of the Montonero gang were unfit. 'Three of the seven of us were still recovering from the effects of the wine of yesterday, and this morning, the rest of us had to help them get some gear together. One of them had his boots stolen but luckily, had a pair of white sandshoes ... he looked rather odd striding along with khaki uniform topped off with white shoes.' Charles squirrelled a packet of Red Cross parcel coffee to give to an old lady who lived next door. Coffee was a luxury that she would welcome and Charles silently hoped for a few tomatoes from her garden.

While Charles juggled packing his gear with Italian handshakes, the *padrone* whom the POW nicknamed 'Bull' offered to give them clothes and work for a month. 'By then the English would be up,' Bull predicted. Many Montonero men were less certain. Over the course of the last five months,

Charles's attitude transformed to 'think a bit more kind of the people'. Despite some fights and strikes for improved conditions, the farms were respite from previous appalling captivity conditions.

Except for a few who opted to stay in camp, most of Charles's group left at 3pm on 10 September, stopping at a shady spot less than a kilometre from Montonero. 'Some lads were still not the best in the head owing to the wine of yesterday; it was a good idea to make a fire and some tea.'

Not all POWs had lay of the land, an awareness where roads, rivers and railways ran; and only the sketchiest of notions of the overall geography of Italy. Charles learned their location sat within a geographical triangle, noting Vercelli as practically half way between Turin and Milan. The main artery of communication between the two cities formed the top of the triangle. One side comprised the road through Turin heading south; the other was the road from Milan. These roads converged at the Po River. All roads heading south carried enemy traffic. The Po River, they understood, flowed the full length of the Piedmont Plain. 'The river is 20 kilometres south of Vercelli, and we'd been told Germans were patrolling the banks, had the bridges guarded, and were feverishly erecting defences along its whole length.'

The prospect of swimming an unfamiliar river in enemy territory while protecting their small but precious stash of notebooks, army paybooks and personal items made Charles uneasy. A man they met fishing on the canal bank eyed their uniforms, recognising POWs, and told them it was hopeless to try crossing the Po. He said they'd be shot. Locals alighted their bicycles, hurried the men across a road and offered similar advice to return to Montonero and await the British. Women toiling the rice stopped, as usual, to gaze curiously at them. It was impossible to be inconspicuous wearing uniforms.

As the sun dipped to the plain, the POWs spotted a clump of trees but the camping spot was occupied. They froze, thinking 'Jerries' there, but it was Australians. Their *padrone* sent out food to them. All decided to sleep out to prevent trouble for the farmers if 'Jerry' raided. Charles lay flat, looking up at the stars, the first time he'd slept on the earth since being captured at Tobruk, almost two years earlier. Countless frogs and marauding mosquitoes soon spoiled Charles's mood. Fed up, POWs crept back to the farm.

Early on 11 September, Charles woke with a busy head: it could take months for British troops to arrive, he could drown in the River Po, travel by night would be tricky because Germans had set a ten o'clock curfew, travel in daylight was risky. 'Unless we were in civvies, we may as well be preceded by a brass band.' To confuse him more, two POWs were sick and winter was approaching. Charles felt he was 'in pretty good nick' but knew reserves would drop if food was light.

The group argued about the best short-term strategy but conceded to return to Montonero. 'Only the next day, I was seeking to come back.' As if to solidify this decision, another escaper told them that an armoured car had approached a POW, ordering him to halt but when the absconder kept going, he was shot.

Three men went ahead to check if Montonero looked clear. Riding his bicycle, Pedro, one of the familiar locals, spotted them and, with friendly chiding, was agreeable to their return to work. 'Turning into the square, we were surrounded by people greeting us cheerily, patting our backs.' Charles was moved. 'Women were wiping their eyes.'

The *padrone* Bull looked surprised, and pleased. After a few comments in jest, he said he'd pay 12 *lire* for each eight-hour day, and insisted on civilian clothing. The 'crook' men could rest and work when ready. 'Yacko' arranged for blankets, straw palliasse mattresses and clothes. Charles had missed the 'old familiar mill'.

Next morning, the fittest men were given shovels to dig irrigation drains and to level ground in preparation for pasture. Working alongside the main road, it was a nervous four days. German vehicles rumbled by at any time of day. 'As Germany had refused to withdraw her troops from Italy, she was now at war with her former allies, and was busy gathering up all the young Italian men she could lay hands on and sending them to work.'

One evening, Charles was approached by a man on a bicycle. He was a former guard, a Dutchman, who'd gone to work in an aeroplane factory. The Dutchman said that he easily spotted Charles amongst the Italian workers. He asked Charles whether he wanted to go to Switzerland or 'join the *alpini* in the mountains'. Charles hesitated to disclose his intentions. The Dutchman handed over a letter. It attested to the trustworthiness of its bearer, and was signed by an Australian officer based in Vercelli. It claimed that men joining Italian *alpini* troops would be given rifles to fight their way through to Switzerland.

Charles didn't know what to make of it. How could an Australian officer operate without detection within Vercelli, now overrun by Germans, he wondered. 'I had an idea we would, if captured, be treated not as British soldiers but as traitors, and probably shot down. Even if we did reach the *alpini*, we knew nothing about mountain warfare, and not being fluent in Italian, would be unable to follow directions quickly.'

Unsure as to its integrity, Charles's gang shook their heads at the Dutchman's proposal and opted to work on a bridge. By the middle of September, rice-cutting was in full swing and the bridge was repaired to withstand drays.

Within hours, Bull startled the men with a sudden request to leave. A German officer was coming to inspect the farm's capacity to billet 140 soldiers. Bull advised the Australians to hide in the maize crops but the men chose a vantage point, a thick belt of trees some distance from the village from where the main road could be monitored. In the middle of the day, they heard their corporal's name called out by frustrated villagers who'd searched in vain for their hideout. They wanted to transfer food across a 12-foot-wide canal to them. Charles enjoyed the unfolding comedy. 'They had loaves of bread besides some cooked rice in bowls. We were at a loss how to get it. Audranna's father started to strip the clothes off his son so that he could bring it over, but eventually one of our chaps rolled his trousers up and managed to wade halfway across the canal. He had strict instructions not to let any vessel turn the wrong way up.'

At nightfall, heavy rain spurred the men into the village and they took refuge in a disused room outside the square. Several other escapers returned, bringing fugitive numbers to fifteen. POWs dispersed to haylofts, a room above the workman's kitchen, and to haystacks. Loose straw helped keep blankets dry as POWs feared catching pneumonia. Each night, they had packs ready to grab should Germans approach their lair. A manifesto had been issued stating that northern Italy was now a German province. When local labourers drifted to the mill, POWs worried that any person could be a fascist sympathiser.

At night, Charles's throng savoured a quick drink at the local bar, *osteria*. 'Each day, whilst out scything, we would see either Jerry trucks or, quite often, whole convoys going along the road, huge lorries loaded with tanks or artillery. Often, a reconnaissance plane would buzz overhead from its aerodrome near Vercelli.'

Living on one's nerves became wearing for Montonero's mob. On the morning of 18 September 1943, Germans issued a 'final warning' to all Italians that anyone helping Allied fugitives faced the death penalty.[8] The German proclamation, to Charles's interpretation, stated that each POW was worth 4000 *lire*.

Further north, dark-haired Colin Weekes and red-headed Alan 'Blue' Neave were similarly unnerved watching armoured German traffic pass by. After their breakout, they'd also taken work near to their farm, two hundred yards from a main road.[9] Concern niggled Colin when 'Jerry staff' called into the farm to arrange water supplies. Relocating to nearby San Damiano, several Italian guards fled with them. Colin diarised that they 'worked over tourists maps all morning and with the help of civilians, managed to form a route to follow ... so after receiving our 40 *lire* pay and about two-pound fresh bread we said "so long" and at intervals of half an hour each group of two moved quietly from the rear of the village... Prison life had come to an end, and we began our trek as free men, escaping from behind the enemy lines.'

Like Charles's gang, the German proclamation heightened their situational awareness of the precarious security of the farms. Receiving 40 *lire* pay as farm workers while attracting a bounty of 4000 *lire* was a poor bet. Hanging around sympathetic villagers on the Piedmont plain was a risky strategy presenting strong moral dilemmas. Stay-put options were scrapped.

When POWs decided to make tracks, 'that's when our war started' discovered Lloyd Moule, a lance bombardier in the 2/3 Anti-Tank Regiment.[10] 'It became a cat and mouse sort of war, and you were motivated towards your complete freedom. It became an entirely different warfare then to them and us. You didn't know who they were.'[11]

From 12 September to 13 October, Lloyd was taken under the wing of Margherita 'Rita' Perazzo.[12] Despite the passing of seven decades since his war, Lloyd was moved when he spoke of this 'brave' woman who provided food, shelter and guides.[13]

Rita lived at the farmhouse Economia di Salasco, where arose spontaneously an organisation for assistance, concealment and transfer of ex-prisoners to Switzerland, with links to a Dr Roberto Saviolo.[14] Within this mix of Italian populace were the subversion activities of various partisan groups on an ideological spectrum of goals and grievances. Joining with a partisan 'red scarf' band near Biella, Lloyd Moule was frustrated by the absence of anticipated food drops. With winter drawing closer, Lloyd was convinced to move on.

Lloyd, in his nineties, recalls these days with a chuckle: 'like Rambo with a gun and bread hanging on my belt.'

7
'SOUTH TO THE RIVER PO': TOWARDS ALLIED LINES

'Evading POWs travelled over much of the Piedmont after the Italian Armistice. Not just Australians and New Zealanders, but also large numbers of British and South African evaders who also sought immediate refuge in the region, and passage to the alpine passes, or tried to reach Allied frontlines far away in the south of Italy.'

—Ken Fenton, 2011[1]

Escaper choices to head north for the hills or south to the River Po were a proverbial flip of a coin. If a POW did not like the look of the soaring Alps in the north, he hedged his bets on rumours that Allied forces were advancing from the south. Whether it was German lines in the south, or Germans patrolling northern roads and snooping in villages, the chance of ambush and recapture was at the back of POWs' minds.

In the lead-up to the Italian armistice, authorities plucked 28-year-old Dick Gill and 34-year-old Jack Duggan[2] from rice fields in the large Cascina Veneria holdings and plonked them behind high walls of a warehouse used as a prison in Vercelli city.[3] Anti-tank gunners Dick and Jack had been prisoners since being nabbed at Mechili on 8 April 1941.[4]

The transfer of POWs to the Vercelli warehouse came after an incident at Veneria,[5] about eight kilometres west of Vercelli, when a horse and old dray driven by a prisoner clumsily collided with the new car of the farm owner, according to Dick's account. Whether it was an act of insubordination or accidental is not clarified in his post-war memoir. The right-hand man to the *padrone* tearfully farewelled the POWs. Dick recorded that 'sixty of us' crammed in with existing internees. One of the farm girls came to visit, waving at the men through the armed gate.

At the Vercelli prison, the warehouse-cloistered throng, fed up with 'walking around like caged animals' discovered loose bricks in the toilet block. When whisper came about the armistice, accompanied by a roar of heavy vehicles on roads outside, it was like a nudge to the ribs to Dick and companions. 'Four of us who banded together decided to start on the wall with the only tools we had: spoons and pieces of tin with which to scrape the mortar out of the brick joints. All that was needed when the opportunity arose was a sudden push on the weakened wall.'

As the four escapers scrambled through the rubble and ran for cover into a neighbouring yard, a rifle shot rang out over their heads. 'Tony [Giddins] was dressed in Italian uniform and [Bill] Garrigan in overalls. I had overalls on. Duggan had his army tunic with our regimental colours on his shoulders.' A voice called out to them, offering to help. The men had landed in the caller's backyard.

They returned to Veneria 'like drowned rats'. One of the Italian workers gave them a note from Bryce Jones saying that 'Baker, Wilson, Armitage and Berg[6] were with him at Viancino, south of San Germano, and were aiming for Switzerland'. The *padrone*, they discovered, conceded to food demands by Germans based in nearby Vercelli, hoping this would preclude demands on his *cascina* and cattle. Italian go-betweens passed on notes on behalf of escapers harboured at neighbouring houses and farms.

Dick's gang chose new refuge on a half-acre island in the rice fields, isolated by a canal on either side. Jim Wood of Dick's regiment sheltered nearby. Nightly, Veneria friends carried food to their campground.

Three days of drizzle dampened their groundsheets and straw bedding. Feeling increasingly wary, they packed up. A haystack on a river bank was chosen as next hideout. 'Maria', one of the peasant women, 'was more concerned for my safety than I was for myself,' Dick acknowledged.

One day, in a rush of panic, Maria noticed Germans near her home and shimmied the downpipe to warn the men. Abruptly abandoning their haystack, the POWs farewelled their helpers.

A day and a half passed without food. The men wrung the necks of two fowl, sharing the birds with another POW group preparing a fire and simmering their cooking pot in an adjacent glade. 'We plucked the feathers off,' Dick exulted, 'and not having a knife, threw them in the pot without cleaning out the insides and with the legs still on. After two hours we tore them apart with our hands, a wonderful meal washed down with three bottles of wine. Being without blankets we slept huddled together on the damp ground like animals seeking warmth from each other.'

Next morning, Dick's gang continued south towards the Po, edging around Trino on the northern banks. Trino was over-run by Germans and Po had guarded bridges. Fuelled by the warnings of locals about German visits to the farms, Dick's anxiety swelled. Five weeks had elapsed since their dramatic warehouse escape.

In October, Dick's quartet crossed the Po River with the generosity of a rowboat owner. They reached Brusaschetto, falling into the friendly arms of the Bianco family. Tony Giddins and Bill Garrigan sheltered in another part of the village. The Bianco family told Dick that another Australian, Nicol Lawrie, was nearby, visiting the home of a local priest.

Describing his camp breakout, Nicol recalled, 'Four of us noticed that the big wire compound gate hadn't clipped shut properly as the trucks went through. We crawled underneath the trucks, squeezed open the gate, and kept crawling through the scrub until we came to a neighbouring rice paddock which was privately owned. We entered a shed where we found old clothes, put them on, then rolled our prisoner uniforms in a bundle and threw them in the creek.' They aimed southward. 'We were used to being without food but after three days we were exhausted,' Nicol recollected.[7]

Displaying similar flair to the toilet block escape by Dick's quartet at the warehouse, Don Radnell and his mate Norm King had staged their exit from a farm camp several weeks earlier.[8] As Don boasted: 'Norm and I kicked the boards off the back of our shit house and we shot through into a maize crop for cover. We stopped at the *casa* that night.

'The next morning the boss told us that Italy had capitulated so the whole camp and guards shot through. After a few days walking south, Norm wanted to head north towards Switzerland so we split up. I met up with two other Victorian mates, John 'Brian' Green and Jimmy Hughes. We crossed the Po River by boat; an old Italian fisherman gave us a lift across. We couldn't use any bridges as they were being patrolled by Germans and fascists. We used to camp in any hayloft we could get into without being seen but most times the farmers saw us and gave us a feed. Our ambition each day was to get one meal. Somehow, we were lucky, there were still plenty of grapes and other fruit on the vines and trees but most women would give us food.'

Don's trio crossed the River Po on a Sunday. As the men stood on the southern banks, townspeople strolled to church. A cyclist looked hard at them. Picking them as escapers, he alighted and introduced himself. Don was astounded that this man's brothers had lived in Queensland, and when the war loomed and Mussolini called all Italians back to Italy, the brothers stayed put in Australia. This fellow chose to return to troubled Italy. 'He was a mug bastard,' Don judged, 'working his guts out for nothing while his brothers, being interned in Australia, were living on the fat of the land.'

Don's trio chucked their stand-out uniforms for civvies and tucked away their army paybooks and dog-tags. They helped the man with his wine harvest. 'The first night he got the girls from the next farm to tramp grapes, they do this singing. Then a chap had an accordion and played music, so we, being half pissed, joined in dancing in a vat of grapes. We drank wine and it took this family three days to get us sober. They started to get frightened that Germans would find us and get them into trouble, probably shot, so we left.'

Foot-soldiering southward, Don's field army were floored to see reward notices for information posted on trees and public walls about escaped POWs. 'We ripped them down.' As a German convoy rumbled through a village, Don was aghast that locals stood outside and waved at them. Don presumed it was safest to appear nonplussed, and do the same. Don pitied the passing enemy troops. 'The poor dickheads were only going up to get killed.'

After a couple of weeks hiding in wheat fields and with local families near Foglietta and Tronzano, Queenslander Bert Lockie took stock and ambled south with POW friends, 2/28th's Fred Vardy and 2/23rd's Jack Fullarton.[9] Their Campo 106 *padrone* had plumped their contextual awareness by sharing snippets of BBC news. Bert felt doleful that prisoners were generally bereft of war news, as were many camp guards. 'Rumours and counter rumours were heard. The Germans had occupied Italy in force—our troops were still 1000 miles to the south.'

Lockie's lads swapped their good-quality English boots for Italian footwear. 'We were to regret that later,' he lamented. Clutching road maps and wearing 'rather nondescript civilian outfits', Bert and his friends aimed for the Apennine mountains. Former clerks, carpenters, miners and farmers roamed the Italian countryside looking like their status: homeless and vulnerable hobos.

South of the Po, the lads were hailed frequently with offers to stay and help with the grape harvest. Matt Knight of the 2/24th joined up with the Lockie group. Matt was younger than the others, having enlisted at only eighteen in 1940.[10] He had put his age up to twenty-one. Matt's blonde hair, surprisingly, did not raise local eyebrows. People were generally fairer of hair and complexion in the south.

At night, the lads were divvied up between different families for meals and reunited to sleep in a communal hayloft. Next day, they followed the family to gather grapes, filling a wooden cart pulled by snow-white oxen. The farmer emptied grapes into casks in a wine cellar. 'We three would strip to shorts and then into the cart and stamp the grapes,' Bert Lockie enthused. The grape-stomping and good food gave the men stamina to forge on.

Hearing that Corsica had fallen into Allied hands, Bert tossed around an idea of heading to the coast to nab a boat. Hearing from Italian sailors that German presence was thick on the Genoa coast, controlling shipping and fishing fleets, the lads disapproved of Bert's suggestion. Two British officers 'trying to look like Italians' told the lads that the River Arno near Florence was guarded.

As with the Po, Germans on the Arno's banks awaited prisoner prey like hawks.

Across Italy, large numbers of escapers from other Allied nations were at large, dispersing in various directions. Wearing Italian cast-off clothing or the prisoner garb with a red cross emblazoned on the back, all escapers were marked men. Victorians Fred Tabram and Tom Anderson shared this undesirable status. Two years after their first prison escape into the Libyan desert, Fred and Tom were on the run, but this time they were separate. Tom disappeared into the countryside on 10 September, guards having idly watched him toddle out of camp. 'These people weren't fascists,' Tom concluded. 'They were farmers who'd share their lunch: cooked frogs.'[11]

Towards the end of September, Fred Tabram penned a letter to his family in Albury, with Tom's family in Geelong in his mind. During the war years, informal Australian family networks acted as bush telegraphs passing on news. Fred wrote that he was the closest to finding freedom for nearly three years but was in dangerous territory: 'Escaped prisoners had to be watchful, day and night. All prisoners rely on the poor people of Italy for food. The family we are living with are marvellous, also the neighbours.

We have been given clothes, food, a bed to sleep in and also money for our pocket. I am in the same area where I worked as a prisoner. We are no longer in military clothes. I have destroyed my military equipment and letters from home. Betty's rosary has been stolen. Tell Tom's people he's OK. Some of the boys have been captured by Jerry. Well, my people, cheer up. The long-awaited armistice has been signed. I intend to remain free. Fred.'[12]

Fred's parents and sister may have felt more disquiet than reassurance about his predicament. Like Fred, Tom was gathered up by generous abettors, some of whom tuned to the BBC. Through its broadcasts in Italian, the BBC's reporting of the war was backed up by talks and features more or less subtly exhorting Italians to help the Allied cause.[13]

'About a month into our trek,' Tom narrated, 'the Italians started telling us that Churchill was promising to reimburse them. Churchill was encouraging them to help the thousands of Allied POWs who were on the loose. They had to get us to fill in a chit. We'd fill in our name, number, date and a line to the effect that "the bearer of this chit has helped T H Anderson with food and shelter". We never did learn if they were reimbursed.'[14]

Mail delivery in wartime Italy was erratic and delayed, to Tom's frustration. 'Letters from home would catch up with me months after being sent. One I received from Ma in March '43 had been sent in November '42.' In that parcel, Tom's Ma had stuffed in a pair of boots. Its timely arrival to Campo 57 came a couple of weeks before Tom was relocated to the Campo 106 farms. For Ma Anderson's 29-year-old son's fugitive feet in September 1943, the boots were spot on.

In addition to his mate Fred, Tom thought highly of two Queenslanders, Garvan 'Snowy' Drew and ex-jockey Joseph 'Joe' Andrews. Snowy volunteered to be cook at Palestro camp. By that stage, men were fed up with rice, macaroni and watery stew. Tom said that Snowy 'didn't receive any complaints and no one called the cook a bastard'. Snowy knew a thing or two about food. When he enlisted during Brisbane's 1940 winter, he declared in black pen on the pink attestation form that his occupation was 'fruit hawker'.[15] In camp, Snowy monitored food stock to plan camp meals as well as escape rations. At Palestro farm, Snowy stockpiled Red Cross coffee and other foodstuffs in the kitchen. Red Cross coffee commanded good prices from civilians. It was better quality than the local variety: 'a substitute made of roasted wheat or barley'.[16]

Snowy served in the Queensland-raised 2/15th Battalion with Jim Wilson. Jim shared Tom's respect for Snowy.[17] In 1941, in a POW holding camp west of Tripoli, Jim witnessed an incident when Snowy was in strife. A guard looked like pulling the trigger but instead put Snowy in a small room and bashed him. He was there for a week. Jim sneaked in food and cigarettes.

At Carpeneto, ahead of the armistice, Jim rejoiced that he was 'suntanned and had learned sufficient Italian to pass for one of them'. In August 1943, two months after John 'Paddles' Laws's murder, Jim swapped clothes with civilians while working in the blacksmith's shop. 'In early September, I was told not to work. I was taken by a guard, along the canal, to another camp nearby. I found POWs who'd been locked in a building for a couple of weeks. I'd worked alone in the blacksmith's shop and they in the fields. Then came the day when guards downed weapons, unlocked doors and cleared off. The CO advised me to go south.'

Meanwhile, Tom Anderson, Joe Andrews and Snowy Drew lugged their stash of non-Italian coffee, setting off in a northerly direction. Just one day later, they changed their minds and went south, conquering the Po River crossing. 'The Po was very wide and deep, some 50 metres wide. Bridges were guarded,' Tom worried. 'After a few inquiries we were told of a man who would row us across ... we overcame our first obstacle. Now all that lay between us and freedom were 600 miles of German-occupied Italy.'

8
'OUR TRAIN RIDE BEGAN': OFFICERS JUMP-START TO THE SWISS-ITALIAN BORDER

'Those who stayed put in their camps ... were easily gathered together as German forces descended from the north, collected the men and deported them to the overflowing camps of the Reich, to places like Moosburg, Gorlitz, Spittal or Lamsdorf.'

—Peter Monteath, 2011[1]

The Italian armistice ended captivity in Italian camps for approximately 2000 Australian prisoners of war.[2] They moved out of Italian camps by choice or by control. While Campo 106 escapers took off into northern Piedmont or south to the Po, most Australian POWs interned on the other side of Italy at places like Grupignano and Bologna had little choice but to head north out of Italy—on trains bound for German-controlled camps.

Frank Sharp and his son Keith were in the thick of September 1943 prison camp round-ups by Germans.[3] The Sharp men were cramped in a cattle-truck compartment on 11 September, the same day that some of their 2/3 Anti-Tank Regiment comrades escaped from Campo 106 farms.

Frank Sharp was a decorated veteran of World War One. His twenty-year-old son Keith, a projectionist pre-war, had fronted up to enlist in Toowoomba in 1940.[4] Frank followed suit in Sydney three weeks later. Despite war injuries to Frank's leg that left an indentation 'big enough to put a fist in'[5] he sailed through enlistment checks on 21 July 1940. He filled in his attestation papers, including contact details for his wife, Elsie. He attested that his age was thirty-nine and three months, that he was born in Newcastle on 6 April 1901.[6]

Both father and son served in North Africa until nabbed at Mechili on 8 April 1941.[7] When secure in his net, a German officer apologised to Frank. 'I am sorry to be taking a prisoner of your age.'[8]

Father and son Sharp intended to stick together, and throughout a string of camps, they did. With the Italian armistice, Keith was promoted in rank to be Frank's batman[9] to remain with his father at the officers' camp at Bologna, Campo 19. Ordinarily, Keith would have been detained with his fellow gunners and other non-commissioned ranks at Grupignano.

Keith wrote in his wartime summary that Bologna POWs wasted no time putting into practice what they'd rehearsed if escape windows went ajar.[10] Bologna prisoners packed their meagre belongings. They cut the wire entanglements at the camp's rear and devised an agreed signal to communicate timing of mass escape. Australian officers assumed camp control but Italians maintained guard. No one was allowed to leave. The Italian commander advised that prisoners would be protected until Allied troops took over, and also if Germans showed a strong hand. POWs strongly doubted that protection would be enforced against the latter; Germans would jump to control a camp full of officers. That night, the Sharps went to bed fully clad and within reach of a small pack of emergency rations.

Bologna POW Tom Elliott had other ideas and although Germans surrounded the camp, he broke through a troop cordon to be recaptured 'after seven hours liberty'.[11] During this break, one officer was killed and two wounded. 'There were 30,000 Germans in the Bologna district and our position was not rosy,' noted Australian airman Fred 'Eggie' Eggleston.[12] From behind the barbed-wire fences, Eggie heard bursts of machine-gun and tommy-gun fire as Germans rounded up the escapers. An English escaper Captain 'Podge' Johnson was wounded in the hand and thigh, and later died of shock and loss of blood. Fred believed he was the only fatality. He considered this to be 'amazing in the circumstances and indicates the excellent discipline of the German outfit that took the camp. Its commander was an army lieutenant aged twenty-two.'

Keith and Eggie documented that on the morning of 11 September, orders were given for their transfer to Modena, a New Zealand camp, about 30 kilometres away. Desirable Red Cross items were divvied up, surplus food and clothing was destroyed. Again, the men obeyed instructions to sleep in full kit, ready for evacuation. Keith, Frank and Eggie watched as 'hide-up artists' tried to conceal themselves in ceilings, cupboards and drains.

The prisoners left Bologna packed in motor trucks like sardines, covered in canvas to keep them hidden from view. At Modena, they were permitted to clamber out of oppressive box-cars to stretch their legs. At the station yard, Eggie keenly watched as Ted Paul 'grabbed a case of fruit from an Italian vendor and quietly walked to the fence, vaulted it and disappeared. Jack Kroger borrowed a pair of blue airforce pants.' Unlucky in his attempt, Jack Kroger was ushered by a German with a tommy-gun back to the POW crowd.

Keith Sharp and Tom Elliott tallied the captive cargo as comprising about one thousand officers. Destined for Austria via the Brenner Pass, they were crammed into cattle trucks, thirty men per compartment. There was room for only some to lay down and sleep at any time. As well as the officers, 250 other men were loaded on, Keith estimated. He noted the set-up of the trains and guard. After every third cattle-truck, a flat platform bristled with machine-guns. German guards travelled in a compartment at the end of each wagon. The irony of their situation didn't bypass the men: German captors had handed them to Italians in North Africa, and now the Italians were letting them slip back into German grip.

The train stopped frequently and both Keith and his father watched as other prisoners effected their escapes. 'A railway guard walked past our open door carrying a red flag. A prisoner grabbed the flag and walked calmly down the line out of view,' Keith lauded. 'Another, seeing

Italians unloading cases of apples from a goods train that had pulled up beside us, coolly joined them and was still unloading apples when our train went on.'

Inspecting the box-car floor, they eyed rotten floorboards under the cattle dung. It took a while to lever up a plank to make an opening large enough for a man to slither through. They drew lots to jump, agreeing that father and son Sharp could go together. 'Dad and I were ninth on the list,' according to Frank's narrative. 'Eventually, while moving slowly up a hill Dad and I jumped, after dropping a pack of food. It was about four o'clock in the morning and we found ourselves just outside Trento.'

'It proved a lucky area for us,' Keith realised, 'as the Germans had shot up the Trento division and numbers of civilians in the area, so the Italians were definitely pro-Allied. Dad and I decided to hide in a cornfield and get the lie of the land. Later in the morning we noticed three men and a boy creeping along the riverbank and were surprised to find that two of them were British officers who had also escaped from the train.' The Italian boy proved particularly helpful, risking his life to help them. The little Italian that Frank had learnt in prison camp was very useful.

Bright moonlight helped to facilitate Eggie's safe leap from one of the box-cars. To monitor the train's approach to the northern border and to time his jump, he'd read signposts through the box-car window while referring to a Red Cross silk map. Fred and others hit the ground about 4am near Lavis, eight kilometres north of Trento.

At dusk, Eggie delighted in seeing fellow train-jumpers Bob Jones and John 'Sandy' Mair crawling towards him. Peasants offered clothes and bottles of Chianti. The POWs disguised their boots with mud and manure to look like peasants' footwear. According to Eggie, fellow airman Sandy Mair 'looked the part with his neat, pointed moustache and freckled face set off by a smart blue-and-yellow chequered shirt, and dark-grey striped trousers. I had a cream shirt and a light-grey golf jacket and "plus fours" with long socks.'

At a level crossing, a woman in black asked Eggie if he was English. She added, 'There is a German guard on the bridge. Take my hand and he will think you are my son.' Besotted by her bravery, Eggie gripped her hand, glancing behind to see Sandy and Bob holding the hands of her children. Safely escorted over the bridge, Eggie's trio climbed to the village of Fai della Paganella, in central Trentino Province, and in pitch darkness reached Andalo's plateau. On the morning of 15 September, they thanked an overnight host and climbed to Malga Spora to rest before trudging onto Brenta Pass. Its beautiful mountains and pine forests form part of the Dolomites.

By dusk on their first day out of the train, the Sharps were led by their Italian boy to a steep pass, possibly Brenta, although Keith does not specify. As the boy turned on his heels, he told them to climb to the top and he'd bring food in the morning. Frank ditched his battle-dress for a scraggy Italian suit but 'the trousers reached no more than halfway down my shins; I must have looked a peculiar sight.'

Frank and Keith ascended the rugged path. Through the darkness, in the direction of the valley of the Brenner Pass, southward-bound German convoys' lights glimmered like warning flares. Moving on, a sudden rustling in the bushes sharpened their attention. Hearing English voices, they called to them and got a very Australian reply, realising that their path converged with other train-jumpers. Out of hiding came 'Don' McDonald, Bob Donnan and a Canadian pilot, later identified by Eggie as Gordon Reneau.[13] Bob Donnan told Keith and Frank he'd similarly 'disembarked', making his jump near Lavis in the province of Trento, south of Bolzano.

Father and son Sharp craved sleep. 'We lay beneath bushes by the track and tried to rest, but drizzling rain began to fall and cramps developed as we stopped.' The hills seemed steeper, and it was bitterly cold. The help of Italian boys proved reliable in sourcing directions and leads to Andalo, about ten kilometres north-west of Trento.

The locals, 'very decent people', wanted them to stay and join the Italian Resistance, but the Sharps opted to go along mountain tracks marked every few hundred metres by a splash of red paint, en route to Malge Spora, a refuge in the hills several kilometres north-west of Andalo. They frequently halted, exhausted, taking shifts to watch while the other snoozed by a fire. On 14 September 1943, they despaired when Malge Spora was found to be deserted by people, with no food.

Keith and his father were 'right on top of the world, 10,000 feet' on 15 September. Mountain streams surged with water, but drinking too much made them sick and giddy, which was hazardous on the narrow and slippery trail with a sheer drop on one side.

In the early afternoon they began a descent towards burnt-out barracks where the track branched three ways: they chose to keep straight on. Frank was worried. 'It was late and none of us was fit enough to spend another night in the open.' Late afternoon they approached Rifugio Tuckett, an alpine refuge built in honour of an English alpine explorer. The building was deserted. The Sharps feared they'd taken the wrong track. 'We came face to face with a glacier—the first one I'd seen.' There, they were startled to be hailed by three Australian officers who'd jumped the same train. Sandy Mair, Bob Jones and Eggie Eggleston had been put on the Sharp duo's trail by the Italian who'd helped them the day before.

On they went, with the Sharp duo in the lead. At dusk they reached the home of an Italian woman. She was frightened, but on learning they were British POWs seeking aid, she felt more at ease for the men to wait until her husband returned. Sure enough, accommodation was rustled up, but they could not share food. 'The Germans had commandeered it,' Frank explained. 'These people and their two children were in dire straits. At the beginning of winter, it was customary to have full storerooms to tide them over the long winter. They hoped for Allies to arrive quickly.'

While the Italian family boiled potatoes, the fugitives nibbled their biscuit supply and raked together tea-leaves from remaining Red Cross provisions to provide tea for all. The Italians had not sipped tea for years.

In peacetime, guides would've been readily available but due to German warnings about assisting POWs, none were forthcoming. Early on 16 September, the host led them to the foot of the range, advising which direction to take.

The Sharps occasionally resorted to begging. 'At one such place we met an American,' Frank recalled, 'who gave us an excellent lunch, and told us where to contact another American. We lost Mair, Jones and Eggleston during the afternoon, and by dusk they came upon the house of the other Italo-American. He proved quite a character, claimed to be an ex-bootlegger and looked every inch the part. He fed us, gave us each a bed, and wanted us to stay with him in the mountains until the war ended.'

At 3am on the 17th, they were guided to the foot of another mountain. According to Keith: 'Here we ran into some villagers who, for no apparent reason, burst into tears on seeing us. They dug potatoes and gave them to us. Mair, Jones and Eggleston caught up with us. Dad and I were now bringing up the rear, as he wasn't feeling well. The next stage was steep and dangerous, and proved the worst of the journey.'

A cup of tea from an old woman at Madron peak was welcomed. She was a carrier of '100-pound packs of barbed-wire' lugged on her back down the mountainside. She was accustomed to the terrain but the Sharps battled exhaustion, breathing difficulties and mountain sickness. Eggie Eggleston, who'd experienced glacier environments before the war, led them slowly towards a man on the glacier. He was digging up old shell cases from the First World War and salvaging the driving bands for the Axis war effort. Sympathetic to their plight, he led the way for an hour, sometimes on hands and knees, gingerly moving forward, averting feet from deep deadly crevices.

On reaching solid earth, and a steep path, the seemingly remote frontier yielded more helpers despite German patrols. A boy showed them a shed and the men dossed down in a bed of hay.

Eggie remembered 'Pop' Sharp as worldly, having 'learned all the tricks and all the answers. We got to admire his guts and determination in the face of difficult conditions. He and Keith worked as a team and it was a relief to us, when the mountains made the going tough, that Keith was standing by his father.'

At daybreak on 18 September the POWs spearheaded in a north-west direction, slipped around Ponte de Legno, an operational centre for German patrols, and lumbered through thickly wooded country. They met three English officers—probably Guy Greville, Richard Dennis and Peter McDowall—who had been in the same train compartment.[14] Keith and Frank dropped behind the others. Keith estimated he and his father had come about 55 kilometres, as the crow flies, north-west from Trento. They kept to a steep road and proceeded in pouring rain.

Late in the day they faced a building marked *Bruno Mussolini Refuge for Alpinists*. Frank joked that they'd become 'fair mountaineers by now'. Breaking in, they saw a 'pleasant club-room adjoining the kitchen with cupboards bare'. While his father rested in an upstairs bedroom, Keith was spotter.

The posse woke with fresh legs. To Eggie Eggleston's memory, Sandy Mair limped from 'a blood blister on his heel the size of a bantam's egg'. Sandy drained the blister to make it bearable. Despite rain, their goal was to soon reach Switzerland.

By dusk they touched down at Santa Caterino di Valfurva in the province of Sondrio. A lad guided them to an inn where the owner, an *alpini* major, had bluntly been told by Germans that anyone harbouring escapers would be shot. Nonetheless, the major snubbed the message and offered food and a resting place until 3am. The inn was a family hotel called Albergo Compagnoni and the owner, Signor Compagnoni, was a lieutenant colonel from a famous marksman division, Bersaglieri. Bormio, a known German headquarters on the route to Austria via the Stelvio Pass, was six kilometres north-west from their location.

The POWs went through outlying parts of Bormio by the light of the moon on Sunday 19 September. About this time, the Sharp duo decided to take a divergent route from the others as they had differed on which direction to follow to Switzerland.

At a log-cabin in the valley near Livigno, Eggie's three met *contrabandieri* who smuggled saccharine and condoms across the border and were heading north-west via Fuorcla Trupchun Pass. In thin clothing, the POWs were cold enough with a bitter wind blowing sleet into their faces but the sight of uniformed soldiers sent more shivers. Worrying about Swiss internment, Eggie asserted to the soldiers that his party were Italians seeking refuge. In response to the strongly worded reply that Italians would be turned back, Eggie confessed their POW status. 'We were ushered into a hotel where an army of Swiss girls rubbed our backs with hot towels and gave us brandy. We were the first British they had seen since the start of the war.'

Meanwhile the Sharps walked through a small congregation gathered outside a church. With the Swiss frontier less than six kilometres away, they were lucky to source an Italian smuggler willing to guide them for payment. The smuggler led them several kilometres, gave advice about the border crossing, then disappeared. According to Eggie, the Sharps had travelled via a pass, Passo Val Viola, located well south of Eggie's preferred entry point.

At 3pm on 19 September, the Sharps spotted flags flying over a small brick building. They observed the scene from a rocky lookout. When they heard movement close by at 5pm, they gingerly skimmed the outside of the building and proceeded through nearby gullies. Without warning, two soldiers in greenish-grey uniforms and a shuttlebox-type helmet jumped up, covering them with rifles. The soldiers told the Sharps they'd been watching their movements all afternoon. They were Swiss.

The Sharps would have been unaware that their train jump gave them a starting line much closer to the Swiss border than that of most Australian counterparts heading north from Campo 106 farms. Frank Sharp had attested on enlistment that he was born in 1901 because his actual birth year of 1895.

To enlist, he put his age down by six years. Like the German officer who apologised to Frank in 1941, Swiss border officers in 1943 may have been awed to greet an old soldier, 48-year-old 'Pop' Sharp, and his son as two of the first twenty Australians to knock on Switzerland's door.[15]

9
'COFFEE PLONK': ITALIAN HOSPITALITY

'Women had negative precedence in Italian peasant culture—they did not rest, eat, nor sleep until men had been served ... Not a single case of rape or sexual assault by escapers on female helpers was ever reported to the Allied Screening Commission. As a contribution to 'liberation' the fact deserves attention as much as joining the partisans and blowing up bridges.'

—Roger Absalom, 2005[1]

Hundreds of Australian escapers ventured to the extents of the Piedmont and beyond, far from the routine of familiar farms on the plain. The territory in front of them comprised the Elvo, Oropa, Cervo, Strona and Sessera valleys, rivers, streams and torrents, leading to the Pennine Alps of the Swiss–Italian border that extend into the Valais canton of Switzerland and Italy's Aosta and Piedmont regions. The Italian side is drained by the rivers Toce, Sesia and Dora Baltea, tributaries of the Po River.

When escapers tentatively tapped on rustic doors, the greeting by Italian occupants often contravened the wartime rules dictated by the German regime and fascists. Women and girls proved themselves again and again to be as effective as men as resistance fighters, couriers and safe-house keepers.[2] As POWs snuggled into haylofts, washed at old troughs and dined on Italian staples, they became subsumed within everyday lives of peasants, farmers and shepherds, many of whom willingly exhibited subversion to the occupying regime and compassion to escaped POWs. *Contadini* drew on a long tradition of hospitality to strangers and travellers. In wartime, this attribute intermixed with hopes that someone may extend compassion to their soldier sons fighting with Italian military divisions in Russia, or working as forced factory labour.[3]

Drawn into Italian lives, escapers absorbed new sights, sounds and tastes. Some POW accounts focus on these times as akin to culinary and cultural tour experiences. As Colin Weekes reasoned, when editing his wartime memoir, 'Mostly I shall relate the little humorous items we mostly remember to try to blacken out the bad side of POW life.'[4]

While Bill Rudd travelled alone in his guise of Yugoslav deserter, his former Baraccone colleague Colin Weekes joined forces with Fremantle-born 'Blue'.[5] Alan 'Blue' Neave reported that food and lodging were provided by a woman Ida Donne at Tenuta Masina, near Baraccone farm in the early days after the armistice.[6]

On Saturday 18 September, Colin and Blue headed off from San Damiano village into the Italian countryside. It was raining lightly and they were dressed in dirty old clothes. Approaching a bridge, they found a detour by crossing a ditch. Hearing vehicular rumbling on either the Turin–Milan or Vercelli–Biella roads, they crouched low behind hazelnut trees, watching 'a very large and very real German troop-carrier with a fair complement of field-grey soldiers complete with black-uniformed officers'. A New Zealand prisoner passed them, sharing information from Bill Rudd that a troop-carrier was heading straight for Baraccone. Within ten seconds, Colin reckoned, he and Blue were waist-deep in cold water, possibly Torrente Cervo, 'making upstream as fast and as quietly as was humanly possible'.

Once in the false security of the foothills, Colin relaxed to take in views overlooking Biella, north-west of Milan. Blue recalled a one-night stopover at Valdengo, on Biella's outskirts. 'We were on the edge of the Alps, and green pastures gave way to vineyards to bright leafy green trees. The area was one mass of rolling hills and little valley flats. The houses were built on the hillsides and were clean and bright, a complete change from the rice farmlands.'

From a ridge they discerned the main road from Biella to Novara, carrying patrolling motorcycles. Biella was 'one mass of high factory chimneys and red roofs', Colin summarised, 'a very large weaving town and in peacetime made cloth for English woollen mills'. Colin's brown hair and brown eyes may have blended in with locals, but Blue's red hair was a stare-catcher.

As they contemplated crossing a high concrete bridge near Vigliano, an old farmer gave unsolicited advice about English-speaking locals and 'an old Spar wagon loaded with Jerries rumbled across the bridge'. They crossed rail-lines at Vigliano, east of Biella on the banks of Torrente Cervo, and noticed tomatoes growing. 'We naturally borrowed a couple each and continued on our way', weaving through side streets.

On the morning of 19 September, they woke, exhausted, only a few kilometres on from Vigliano. Colin had slept little, despite securing comfortable digs with a wealthy *padrone* at Valdengo. His hayloft was decorated with a large red bedspread and a few dozen chicks that chirped all night.

Colin asked the *padrone* for a map. A large tourist map was duly unfurled. After stilted conversation, one of the children in the family ran to ring for a friend of the family to ask for an interpreter, with definite instructions not to mention the prisoners in the house. Colin got the gist that 'Nazis might have a phone-listening post'.

At dinner, Colin and Blue feasted on a 'magnificent spread of soup, cutlets and creamed potatoes with bread and butter, and of course, wine was served with the meal'. It was surreal, Colin mused, to stumble upon such a well-appointed residence with English-style oak and silverware. Hitherto, poorer families, Colin reminded himself, had been equally as attentive to their needs.

An interpreter arrived who 'spoke just enough English to be useful, with A's E's and I's added to many words'. The *padrone* flattened out maps and discussions flowed. 'A knock on the door made the Italians jump and freeze.' A softly spoken warning from the *padrone* prompted the women and children to rush from the room. When the door-knocker was assessed as safe, the door opened for three Italian women. All house guests craned over the map, collaborating to mark a recommended route, one frequented by contraband runners. When the map was flipped over, the name of the *padrone* was boldly printed on the backing. 'All seemed lost,' wrote Colin, dejected, 'until we suggested a strip be cut out which covered our route. In two shakes of a lamb's tail the map was cut, the remaining sections committed to a fire, thus destroying all evidence of help to us.'

The interpreter still hovered next morning. He gave Colin and Blue sacks to prepare for their travel into the valley. POWs and *padrone* exchanged good wishes and Colin and Blue were directed to follow a river, bypassing kilometres of winding roadway. About six kilometres north of Biella, they navigated north-west, losing sight of Valdengo, and bypassed tiny Ternengo, their first route-marker. 'On the way up, we passed an old cow-herder who was leading in his cows, one by one, talking to them, allowing them to lick his hand.'

They were halted in their tracks by a woman in Zumaglia who recognised them as escapers and beckoned them to follow her. She shared wine, milk and eggs. Her brother directed them via a shortcut to the next place on their itinerary, Callabiana. Climbing a ridge, they took a moment to peer down the green valley towards Valdengo, their respite the night before. Valdengo's red-roofed white and cream buildings stood out, overseen by 'the ever-present church-tower' with its clock and bells. As bells struck each hour and beautiful chimes heralded each quarter, Colin concluded that a 'watch was an unnecessary weight to carry up here'.

They passed Callabiana quickly but Colin memorised its features: 'This village consisted of one shop, some half-dozen old houses and a bakery' as well as the village hub: a grey stone water-trough and drinking fountain. As the clock struck one, they stepped into Camandona, immediately north of Callabiana and about ten kilometres north of Biella. Colin was famished. 'We ate our ration of meat and bread which the Valdengo family had given. In our lunchbag we discovered two fried eggs which the cook at Valdengo tried to coax us to eat the previous night. They went down well, but unfortunately Blue put his twelve-odd stone on the fresh eggs, with the natural outcome.'

Climbing to higher terrain, they stopped to ask for water but were given lemonade. On an almost bare mountainside, they studied the long valley to Biella's maze of chimneys and smoke haze. From Camandona, the POW tourists navigated north-west towards their objective of Bocchetto Sessera. 'A rather striking young lass' spoke to them in extremely good English. She was American and had been studying in Italy when war broke out. She informed them about a clutch of farmhouses, and there Colin and Blue met four Italians who were going their way so they tacked on the end. 'They led us along the side of the ridge and we halted for the night.' Colin was chuffed. They'd gone eight miles beyond the planned distance.

Into the afternoon of 19 September, Colin and Blue kept walking. 'We found three little stone buildings clinging to the steep mountainside with a little spud patch just below the track.' This small dairy farm was run by an elderly woman and her son. Two parties of Australians had already been accommodated there. As evidence, she proudly showed Canadian Red Cross soap and box. A little waterfall provided Colin and Blue—and their dirty socks—with a refreshing icy wash. Colin hung the socks in front of the fire and enjoyed a meal. 'As the last drop slipped over my tongue, a party of nine alpine troops marched up, a sergeant major and eight youngsters of about eighteen years, all loaded with fifty-pound packs.' They'd been disarmed in France and were now heading home.

The elderly woman rustled up lodgings for everyone. After sunset, Colin and Blue retreated to the rear of the cow-bail; a door led to a small loft.

Only branches and a thin layer of grass separated them from cows and pigs below. 'We crept across a pile of goat skins and soon were bedded down in comparative comfort. Cold was our least worry as the cows kept us warm as well as supplying us with an excellent sleeping draft (*sic*).' With these alpine comforts, and proximity to alpine troops, Colin and Blue slept solidly.

From Bocchetto Sessera Colin and Blue trudged north to Scopello. The duo woke at 4 o'clock on 20 September to the sound of milking in the barn below. They and the Italians decided to move on. Cold blue moonlight provided them dim torchlight and in drizzling rain, the track disappeared. While the Italians argued about which route to take, Colin suggested they descend the slope to Bocchetta della Boscarola. Downhill, the River Sesia, a tributary of the Po, flowed from the Alps in sunrise light. 'A silver tumbling river ran away from the high mountains to the west and down to the right it was lost in pine-clad gorges,' Colin noted. 'The trees were pine and fir so the colours were dark and deep. Almost at our feet, some 4000 ft below, the little logging village of Scopello nestled amongst pines on a little flat by a bend in the river.'

About 8 o'clock, after three kilometres treading downhill, the trekkers sought local reassurance that Germans were not known to be around Scopello. While the Italians sipped wine in a small café, the Australians ate bread and bully from Red Cross supplies. An hour later, they were directed to board a blue bus. The Australians heaved themselves onto the roof, sitting on the luggage. The passenger behind them was 'a fully dressed *carabiniere*, rifle and all'. He seemed to ignore them, so Colin and Blue settled for the ride.

'At each village a church almost invariably shone out as the largest, most prominent building. Their style was different to foothill churches and was very simple. The whole front of the church would be painted in vivid colours of some holy scenes. Quite often a pious scene of Heaven on one side and Hades with its flames and tortured souls on the opposite made one almost horrified. This was Italy, we took it all in.' Colin and Blue, former city clerks, relaxed to absorb the sights of Italy's rural and remote high country. The route Colin described likely passed the parish church of Rivo Valdobbia, Chiesa di San Michele. Its pointed stone arch sits above a large fresco that covers much of the church facade.

Weaving along the valley floor, Colin was aware the bus was taking them closer to the frontier: the Pennine Alps of the Swiss–Italian border. Blue estimated the bus had travelled 25 kilometres.[7] At Alagna, alongside the river Sesia, buildings exemplified regional Walser heritage. With awe and trepidation, they noted early snowfall on the mountains, and the coldness of rain squalls. 'On the green and brown peaks, a sudden dusting of white made them look like huge cakes with icing sugar shakings,' poeticised Colin.

On the edge of Alagna, the Italians led them to a chalet. The lunch menu featured macaroni and lard. Pulling off socks for washing, Colin noticed that a toe was blistering. He did not cut it, 'afraid it would poison'.

Their next move was '3000 feet' uphill to a dairy farm. The rising range looked almost perpendicular with masses of fine gravel strewn down the slopes. Along the edge of a gorge, Colin kept up with the accompanying Italians' energetic pace. Colin admired an unusual bridge with a sharp roof, necessitated by winter snowfalls. On its span, a small shrine and an opposing seat awaited passing pilgrims.

On 20 September, the men took lodging at farm holdings comprising six low stone buildings along a track. One small family lived there. Placing their sacks in a hayshed, the family summoned them for polenta and 'a funny soft type of cheese, quite palatable and not sour like cream cheese' made in little porous pots. While the men ate supper, the girl of the family kept watch with a spy-glass.

Colin and Blue warmed with a breakfast cup of fresh milk, wetting their last scraps of bread. 'The officer, pilot and one soldier decided to carry on while two decided to return south,' leaving five men to climb the steep track snaking its way above the grass and timber line. Very large rocks were strewn about the rough mountainside. A stone table and a seat with a marble plate that read *Passo di Turlo, constructed by the Alpine Regiment* marked the pass. Colin's description indicates he had reached a high point of the Turlo Pass trail, Colle di Turlo, at 2730 metres, where stone seats oppose a small rock grotto containing a Madonna shrine, dated 1929.[8] Contemporary signage points to Alagna, from where Colin had come. It was three hours away.

To check his throbbing toe, Colin sat on the stone seat. It was so cold he quickly jumped to his feet, peeling off his sock to inspect his engorged toe. Deciding against putting the boot back on, he fetched his handmade slippers from his sack. 'Slippers I made from parcel cord and cardboard covered with white cloth allowed the toe to rest.' At an altitude of more than 2900 metres, Alagna was visible and to the north, Colin looked across a wide valley. 'Beyond it a larger valley [probably Anzasca] passed at right angles, and like a little toy village set in tiny pine trees.'

The craggy unkempt peaks of Monte Rosa massif stared sharply in reply. 'Monte Rosa shone in pale pink like a huge lump of fairy-floss,' Colin gushed. With fairy-floss on his mind, Colin nibbled crumbs of very stale bread, then followed the others snaking down on the well-made path, tottering through dirty white patches of last winter's snow and ice. Colin groaned: 'This did not do the old slippers any good at all; I prayed that the cardboard held OK.' They stepped onto the valley, reaching little rock haysheds, *baite*, about midday. A dry rock offered seating for a snack of sardines and stale bread. The POWs' walking tour passed a gold mine experimental station near pretty Lago della Fate, Fairies Lake.

On 21 September, as soon as they stepped into a valley village, an old woman rushed to tell them that Germans were about. 'This knocked the wind completely out of me. I felt utterly tired for the first time,' Colin despaired. 'I took one look at the sheer cliffs and stated, "If Jerry comes now, he can have me."'

The Italian lieutenant whipped out a smart coat from his sack and reconnoitred into town. In less than an hour, he returned with news that a German officer was stationed only a few kilometres away at Macugnaga at the end of the road along the Anzasca valley. The lieutenant secured a local agent to guide them up the soaring slopes.

Colin's party were tickled pink by 'this romantic figure [who] arrived on the scene dressed in brown velvet corduroy plus-fours, jacket and mountaineering cap, long thick socks and huge boots'. Colin couldn't decipher the hand signals of this character, who sported 'a pointed black beard and dark skin, a strong face with flashing dark eyes'. With preparations afoot, Colin whipped out a dirty used razor blade from his shaving kit and slashed skin on his aching toe, releasing fluid under the nail and flushing it in icy cold water. He razor-sliced a slot into his boot to reduce pressure.

Waving a small piece of paper, the Italian lieutenant drew their attention to diagrams depicting the terrain, bringing Monte Moro and the pass at over 2870 metres to life. Moro's bluff was dark brown against the green pines, he explained, and above the tree-line the grass gave way to bare rock with sections of slippery sloping slabs. While the Italians flitted and the lieutenant sorted out guides, the Australians rested within underbrush.

At this juncture, Colin and Blue met New Zealand privates, Eddie Scanlan and Jerry Neame. They, too, had escaped from Salussola camp near Arro and Baraccone. Eddie reported that after Italians fled the camp on 10 September, he hid in fields and an unoccupied house until about 19 September.[9] Jerry Neame picked up the ensuing events: 'I had a map showing the route to Switzerland, made for us by a *carabiniere* at the camp. I and Private Scanlan set out, mostly by foot, and rode ten kilometres by bus.'[10] Jerry added that they routed north from Arro to Cossato, then north-west to Alagna, as Colin and Blue had done, before descending into Macugnaga.

Colin and POW companions watched a group of 'Tommies' slowly winding their way up the mountainside, their progress marked by bobbing Italian lamps at both ends of the column. At 9pm a whistle by the lieutenant came through the night mist and Colin quietly whistled his acknowledgement. It was time to move.

The lieutenant led the four POWs to a small miner's cottage and its hayloft. Colin made a note of the typical Walser architecture of the two-storey house, solidly built of deep brown weather-stained timber with a steep-pitched stone roof allowing snow to slide off easily. Three small pairs of homemade skis hung, hopeful for action, over the door.

'There we met the miner,' Colin narrated, 'a little old fat man with white hair and bushy moustache, dark sunken eyes and smoke-stained teeth.' He'd resided in British Columbia and hadn't used spoken English for twenty years, but anxious about the hay in the cow, goat and sheep stable below their quarters, he found words to insist guests refrain from smoking.

In the early hours of 22 September, the men awoke to the snip-snip of clippers. An old woman shearing a black sheep peered up at them. A breakfast of potatoes and two litres of hot milk awaited them. Like a magician delighted with his trick, Eddie gingerly retrieved two fresh eggs from his rucksack. Colin produced a cache of sugar. 'Egg flip was the order of the day,' delighted Colin, although it was rich for their 'strained tummies'.

The POWs exchanged chat and hand gestures with the miner, poring over a huge map. With a top-up snack of rice and milk soup, they packed ready to accompany the miner's son to the track's base. Rustling up their remaining cash, the POWs gave the miner 140 *lire*. The escapers wrote a chit to evidence the miner's assistance.

The miner's worried face contemplated the wet black night. He shook his head at the conditions. Colin layered up: 'I had all my clothes on, a pair of underpants (long woollen), a woollen singlet, two shirts, a pair of worn-out trousers, waistcoat and coat plus my skiing cap.'

With generous expressions of good fortune, the miner provided a bottle of warm coffee and wine mixed together, *grappa*. By torchlight, the miner's son led a fast scramble around the still-darkened village and crossed a river. At the base of a white-rock track, the boy reiterated his father's instructions that the POWs follow it 'for 200 yards' then a black track until reaching stone huts. In the hush of night, footsteps reverberated unnervingly loud as they kicked loose stones. Rain softly splashed the pines. On their right they saw the black track and climbed it for an hour.

Suddenly the black night became a dark rock bluff blocking the path. Realising they'd turned off too early, they doubled back. Soaked to the skin, the return trip was tedious, two hours in single file, and on all fours using feet as feelers. With their torchlight off, the terrain beyond their toes was eerily indiscernible. Frequently stopping, they took turns being leader. They lit a 'precious' wax match to skirt a '20-odd foot drop'. They staggered into the outskirts of a village, and into a dry hayshed, with no hay. Colin didn't relish sleeping on hard flooring the night before tackling the infamous Monte Moro. It was time to drink the *grappa*, 'coffee plonk'.

Saturated but charged by the plonk, Colin decided to explore the village. He eyed a house with electric light. An old woman greeted him and gestured to the huge open fire. Her family crept out of bed to look at Colin. 'They almost cried over me. I asked if we could sleep in their hayloft. Within a quarter hour we were walking quietly down the stone path and sitting by the fire.'

As he dried clothes on 22 September, Colin could not know that camp colleague Bill Rudd was also close to the border, and that his regimental buddy Col Booth was bunkered down only eight kilometres away at Monte Barone. A fortnight had elapsed since the armistice announcement. Like athletes in a mountain marathon maze, mates made in the army and inside prison camps were scattered throughout the hills and valleys, all seeking safe finishes.

10
'CHARLIE DID THE TALKING': TEODULO PASS, LATE SEPTEMBER 1943

'Indeed, during the months after the armistice, Italy was full of large, fair-headed "Italians" with speech difficulties.'

—Gilbert, 2006[1]

While many Campo 106 escapers hoofed from Scopello to Alagna and the Turlo Pass to reach the foothills of the Monte Moro pass at Macugnaga, others headed north-west from Biella, moving out of Piedmont and into the Aosta, towards the Teodulo Pass.

Bert and Bill Wilson's younger brother Harry would have been on their minds in September 1943.[2] Harry had been killed in September 1942 in New Guinea but the news of his death reached the brothers when at the rice farms. The brothers, from Geraldton, left Campo 106/20 at or near Salussola on 11 September[3] with two New Zealand prisoners, Norm Allen of Auckland and Stan Avery of Christchurch, setting off after lunch 'in the direction of the hills, our destination unknown.'[4]

Within three hours they called into a farmhouse to find that the owner, Giovanni, had been one of their farm bosses.[5] They stayed with Giovanni, and with another farmer Bruno, for several days, contemplating whether to make a dash for Switzerland. The helpers loaded them up with cash, wine, bread, rice and tomato puree.

The Wilson brothers used maps as they headed north of Biella. They crossed the rock-strewn Torrente Cervo, a ribbon stream at the western edge of the Piedmont province. The torrent flowed from the Alps, with seasonal changes in volume, through tiny villages south to skirt Biella and flow to join the Sesia River just north of the Campo 106 rice farms. The Wilsons reached Vigliano immediately east of Biella, where Colin and Blue also passed through; but the Wilson group slanted their route north-west towards Andorno.

In Andorno, a crowd of adults and children surrounded the uniform-clad POWs, offering money, fruit and advice to catch a train to Balma. Two *carabinieri* officers were watching and pulled pistols on them. 'It looked as though the game was up,' Bert recounted in his notes for 16 September. 'The crowd put on a show in favour of us, so did we, Bill doing the most talking. They finally decided to let us go, scaring us into moving, by saying that *Gerry* was close handy.'

As they charged over a hill, children ran after them. Adults waved. 'It was just as well *Gerry* wasn't about, as we certainly wouldn't have got away, with people acting as they did.' Locals yelled that the train pulled up so the POWs raced down the hill and piled on board. 'We weren't by any means feeling comfortable as we sort of expected *Gerry* to put his head into the door any minute.'

Their train followed the Cervo Valley, carved by the Torrente Cervo. Disembarking at Balma village, about 12 kilometres upstream, the POWs then boarded a bus: another nervous leg of public travel. Along the valley, the bus weaved for about seven kilometres through tiny places higher into the valley, dotting the edge of Torrente Cervo. Locals eyed them off at every stop. Nearing the green-sloped, grey rock-roofed village of Piedicavallo where the road ends, a female passenger spoke to them in English, inviting them to her home. The brothers snapped up the chance to bathe, shave and rinse their socks, and to study maps while their hostess prepared soup, steak, eggs, cheese, bread and wine. Bert was chuffed about the hospitality, and the 'jolly nice' table set for lunch.

During the afternoon, other escapers rendezvoused, rousing them from their nap. 'The woman, who we later called Aunt Ellis, just didn't seem to be able to do enough for us.' She put out generous food for supper topped off by baked pears and coffee. A former Italian soldier joined the throng. He was seconded to lead the POWs across nearby ranges.

At 3am on 17 September, Aunt Ellis farewelled them with coffee and bread. 'It was climbing from the word go,' recalled Bert, 'and it got harder as we went on,' but he felt relief to cross Col Ranzola, in the lower Val d'Ayas, part of an ancient pass between Brusson and Gressoney-Saint-Jean, to the top of Grande Mologna at 2346 metres elevation. From then on, the trekking eased as they descended on a gradual slope. Their guide gave them further directions before he turned back. To check that they were on the route, the Australians asked directions at every opportunity. They knew they were now in the Aosta region.

At Gressoney-Saint-Jean, amongst Walser heritage buildings, they sped across the main road to the Torrente Lys for a rest and snack. They foot-slogged westwards towards Brusson. The steep country and rain made it precarious underfoot but despite many falls, no one was injured.

Tired, wet and miserable, the Wilson brothers' group set down in a small room at a Brusson hotel. With wine and meal on offer, they freely spilled the beans about their aspirations to reach Switzerland. 'A chap came in who spoke English. He frightened the devil out of the folks by telling them just what would happen to them if *Gerry* found out they were helping us. We felt like slitting his throat but we couldn't. He had us taken away before our meal was ready.' As they were taken to a shed to sleep, the female owner gave them bread. They changed their uniforms for civilian clothing, 'old and ragged'.

Well fed, the Wilson group tracked due north to Champoluc, avoiding main roads as much as possible. Within eight kilometres of the frontier naturally well-guarded by the Matterhorn and Monte Rosa, locals besieged the POWs with bread, jam, cheese, sausage, biscuits, coffee, macaroni stew and cigarettes. On 18 September, on Champoluc's outskirts,

Bert mentions that red-haired 2/24th Battalion sergeant Charlie Fraser—who could 'speak Italian like nobody's business'[6]—went on ahead to contact a new guide.[7]

Having procured a guide, the Wilson party trimmed their gear to bread and greatcoats. A doctor readied accommodation with mattresses and wine at his house. Bert Wilson enjoyed his first taste of polenta and savoured the impressive scenery.

On 20 September, the travellers snaffled lodging, steak, salad and polenta at the Hotel Breithorn. An English colonel and a captain gave them 200 *lire* and paid for their food. They crept across the road to hotel sleeping quarters. The doctor found a guide on 21 September; the fee was 800 *lire*. At 10pm, the Wilsons packed trip rations and bread loaves, but omelette and wine were 'put away right there and then'. Bert Wilson welcomed an old pullover.

Early on 22 September, the Australians left the hotel and commenced with an easy walk, following their guide on the road for four kilometres to Saint Jacques. Heading into deeper 'bush', constantly climbing and crossing water courses, they took a breather at a small *baita* rock hut. Mid-afternoon they set out again, the temperature cooling as they neared the snow-line. They pulled on overcoats. Bert Wilson put socks on his hands. He tripped three times when crossing two sloping glaciers under an aerial railway. When an air-carrier rumbled overhead, they heaped together to reduce visibility, Bill gripping tight to brother Bert's coat.

Their guide farewelled them at dusk, telling them to continue over the ridge-top and down into Switzerland, warning them that a pass was patrolled by Italian sentries. With no guide, the men poked their sticks into surfaces, discerning secure footholds. By 8pm, light dropped low. With the Swiss border clearly within reach, they wanted to arrive safely. They reposed, huddled, on a rocky platform sprinkled by light rain and heavy mist. With little prospect of sleep, each man stood up every ten minutes, stamping frigid feet and clapping chilled hands to warm up.

At 6am on 23 September, the men opted to continue in low light to reduce their visibility to patrols. As if the mountain suddenly woke up and thrust off its misty blanket, the clearing haze unveiled a guard's hut directly above their path. The men stopped dead in their tracks and began tentatively retracing their steps and tracing the footprints of unknown others. In steep terrain they sludged through 'eighteen inches of snow'. Atop a ridge, they believed that downhill was Switzerland.

A shout came from behind. 'Up blew three Italian guards, one with a pistol.' Although they were on Swiss terrain, the Wilsons dismayed that 'all was up', that their near-success had unravelled. The sentries led them under guard to a hut. 'Charlie did most of the talking as he could speak Italian well,' Bert recalled. The Italian sergeant listened attentively, shook their hands and directed them on. Charlie eased his companions' shaken nerves, saying that the Italian was Royalist and not a fascist.

The hut was alpine refuge Rifugio Teodul at 3320 metres, located adjacent to the Theodul Pass, an important communication and trade route used since Roman times linking Zermatt in the Swiss canton of Valais and Breuil-Cervinia in the Italian Aosta region. The pass lies between the Matterhorn known to Italians as Monte Cervino, on the west and the Breithorn, passing between the valleys of Zermatt and Valtournenche. The east side of the pass is covered by large glaciers.[8]

Relying on their sturdy sticks, the escapers descended on uneven ground. Three Swiss guards caught up with them, taking the lead with ice-picks and ropes. 'It looked rather funny,' Bert thought, 'to see them so equipped and us with just old sticks and boots with nails in them.' The tired POW hikers negotiated glacial crevices that seemed bottomless and braced themselves to jump over the gaps. At midday, they stepped off the glacier onto solid ground, with Swiss guards in front and one behind. Inner panic rattled the POWs when one Swiss guard unexpectedly suggested they consider going back into Italy, but to their relief the other guards welcomed them, understanding their predicament. The Swiss distributed tea, bread and tinned meat to replenish energies for the walk to Zermatt, two-and-a-half hours downhill. There, Swiss officers welcomed them with cigarettes, wine and an opportunity to wash.

Thirty-six-year-old Charlie Fraser had left Tronzano camp with Henry 'Harry' Sibraa and Roy Jenks about a week before the armistice promulgation, according to Harry's account.[9] Their route into the Aosta was similar to that of the Wilsons. Like Nicol Lawrie, Harry was one of the last Australian POWs captured at Alamein at the end of October 1942.[10]

On the night of 1 September, the POWs' wine ration issue was due. Harry's gang roared bush songs, urging the guards to drink with them. When the gate guard left his post to join in, Harry, Charlie and Roy slid out, carting Red Cross chocolate, greatcoats and *lire*. They dashed for nearby wheat fields.

At daybreak, local girl Maria who'd worked near them in the fields, approached their hiding place. Harry jumped out, blurting that he'd escaped and needed clothes. Maria's husband was a POW of the British in North Africa. In spite of her wariness about aiding escaped prisoners, she fetched one suit, which Harry donned.

Wandering westward, they crouched motionless in long grass on a roadside when a German convoy trundled past; they could hear a German officer shouting orders from his armoured car. At nightfall they called into the hamlet of Borgo d'Ale, six kilometres west of Tronzano. Harry, the only one in civvies, went ahead to inquire whether Germans were stationed there. The bottleshop owner instantly recognised him as a POW. He'd worked as a cook in London for thirty years before the war. Harry left the shop cradling two ragged suits and a bottle of wine, and obeyed his directive to get out of town.

For four days, Harry's trio lived on chocolate and green grapes stolen from vineyards. The latter made them sick. Taking a lie down in a hayloft at a deserted farm, they abruptly awoke at midnight to the headlight blaze of an approaching truck. Wary of Germans, the weakened men toddled into the night, aiming for Biella, twenty or so kilometres to their north. They had limited knowledge of places and geography along their planned route but heard about Swiss entry points near Domodossola in the province of Verbano-Cusio-Ossola, about 140 kilometres from Borgo d'Ale.[11]

Travelling past the western reaches of Lake Maggiore, Harry's trio ran into partisans. With limited language exchanges, the POW gleaned the partisans intended to blow a railway line. 'Being a Pioneer (2/3 Battalion), I had visions of slabs of gun cotton, FID and detonators,' Harry recalled, 'but the method was to undo fish plates, pull out dog spikes and spread the rails, done in several places over viaducts.'[12]

Along the way, an English-speaking woman gave several warnings to the POWs: partisans' allegiances did not always align with the Allied cause; Germans had a rest camp at Domodossola and Italian Blackshirts were active there. Harry's trio scooted back down foothills to Biella Province west of Salussola, traversing Viverone, Zimone and Massaza.[13] On Biella's outskirts, they lost bearing amongst the side streets to emerge in the railway square and almost collided with a German soldier.[14] The POWs retreated, unfollowed, into a side street. Charlie's watch gave navigational aid to get out of the town and proceed north-west to Piedicavallo.

Harry, Roy and Charlie halted to hear an Italian's unsolicited directions—'Go to the white house on the right'—where they met an American woman married to an Italian. In English, she reminded them that Germans knew of POWs in the vicinity and of a 40,000 *lire* reward for each prisoner. Carrying provisions of bread and milk, she led them to a goat track leading higher to Grande Mologna. The POWs swam the chilly Lys River and slogged to Brusson and Col Ranzola. Saturated by rain and 'freezing to the bone', the trio crawled under a chalet's foundations. Rainwater ran down their backs while they tried to sleep. Within an hour, music roared and jackboots thumped above their dodgy shelter. They skedaddled, realising that hiding under a dancefloor crawling with Blackshirts was ill-advised.

The trio approached Champoluc on 18 September, the same day as the Wilson brothers. A schoolmistress located a guide, who came to the schoolhouse at 4.30 am on 23 September to meet the escapers. Abiding to the guide's request to stay '300 yards behind', they stepped above the snow-line. By 9am drizzling mist increased. The guide went on ahead to verify the track, and he decided not to proceed with them. That night the trio crouched on the slopes like drowned rats, in dread of the thundering crash of avalanche falls.

Dawn mist hung heavy as the erstwhile mountaineers put trust in their makeshift fence-post poles with nailed tips. As the three wrecked Australians clung close together within wraps of mist, they feared their journey would end in a deep crevasse. Nearby, they understood, was the border, and a heavily armed Italian frontier post.

Mercifully, the mist began to lift like a curtain revealing a beautiful stage. Harry, Charlie and Roy gasped in delight. A survey pole reared out of the snow. Slowly and painfully the men limped across the border.

But with the dissipating mist, their curtain of invisibility disappeared and they felt completely exposed. A harsh Italian voice bawled, 'Halt!' The Australians whirled to see the menace of pointed rifles. Speaking in Italian, Charlie Fraser calmly elucidated that they were now in Switzerland and Italians had no jurisdiction over them. The click of cocked rifles was the only reply. The trio were shunted into a blockhouse. Charlie kept talking. He pleaded for their release, offering money. The guards guffawed, pointing out that the trio were worth 120,000 *lire*.

When one of the guards went into the kitchen and a second guard went outside, five guards stayed behind. After a few minutes, a third guard went for a coffee in the kitchen. The POWs pounced. Two of them tussled the remaining guards; the third dived for a rifle against the wall, jammed a shell into its breech and aimed it at the nearest guard. As each guard returned to the room, a POW grabbed him. Wasting no time, the armed escapers sent the Italian soldiers into the snow to lead them across the Gornergrat Glacier.

Within an hour, they met Swiss soldiers. In safe hands, the POWs walked downhill to Zermatt. Charlie celebrated by devouring five Swiss apples. Swiss documentation confirms that the Fraser and Sibraa group and the Wilson party reached the border on 23 September.[15] As Bert Wilson diarised that he allowed Charlie to do most of the talking at the border post, the two groups presumably made safe landing about the same time of day.[16]

Red Cross staff obtained their names and particulars before putting the men on an electric train for Visp in the late afternoon. Other Australians were already there, arriving by various border areas, enjoying soup and potatoes at the gardens of the Hotel Cervin. 'We were taken to our barracks, and after some talking with other chaps retired to our bed of straw and one rug,' wrote Bert. 'We were that tired that I think we could have slept anywhere and we had certainly earned our rest.'

11
'THE ITALIAN MAN WITH AN AMERICAN ACCENT': MONTE BARONE'S HOTEL ALPE NOVEIS

'Not the least of the disincentives to pressing on was the problem of communicating with local populations ... In such circumstances the temptation to shrink from continuation of the stresses of travelling blind and to settle down, or at least pause for reflection, at some spot where a welcome, and perhaps some language bridge, had been found, was very often overwhelming, particularly during September and October 1943.'

—Roger Absalom, 1991[1]

Outside the towns a limited number of Italians could speak standard Italian with confidence, and some not at all; the use of local dialect was commonplace. Illiteracy was prevalent, especially among women. For the escapers, an important, if unexpected, ingredient in this socio-cultural cocktail was the sprinkling of middle-aged and elderly former emigrants who had returned from many 'promised lands' in the Old and New Worlds, often with divided loyalties.[2]

Returned emigrants from America were commonly referred to as *l'americani*. They had experienced different socio-political contexts and glimpsed more just and equitable societies. Not being captive to fascist propaganda that portrayed Australian and New Zealander escapers as savages seeking to rape and murder Italian women and children, *l'americani* and other pro-British civilians reached out to foreign soldiers. The assistance they offered was a soft but significant subversive gesture to snub fascist rule and German occupation.

Paul Lavallee and Norm Freeberg clocked in at Campo 106's Veneria farm on 26 April 1943 with sixty others.[3] On 30 August 1943, Paul and Norm adjusted to transfer from Veneria to a new prison abode inside factory buildings within industrial Cervetto on northern Vercelli's outskirts.[4] With news of the 'somewhat shaky armistice' between the invading Allies and the Italian government, Paul, Norm, Alfred Collins and 'tall blonde' Ray Crook were tipped off by Vercelli civilians that the River Sesia was close by. Ditching early debate on heading to Lake Maggiore because 'the whole lake was infested with German troops', the quartet decided on the Sesia as a 'guiding light' to the Alps.[5]

In the same way the Po River put up barriers to southward-bound POWs, Paul and Norm realised after launching themselves from riverbanks near the railway bridge that the Sesia's 'swirling waters' and 'uneven riverbed' was dangerous, particularly without moonlight. The saturated soldiers bedded uncomfortably amongst thick nettle bushes.

Next morning, 'an economical breakfast was the order of the day. A swig from the water bottle and a cigarette.' With word that Germans swarmed Vercelli, they revisited their route plans, re-entering the 'rapid milk-green waters' trudging northward. In daylight, the Sesia gave less of a fright. Italians gave them tin mugs, and the POWs took brief respite in nearby woods and in cornfields.

On 15 September they encountered fellow Cervetto-held POW Arthur Caffrey and companions whose hideout was three kilometres south of the main Milan–Turin *autostrada*. Two days later Paul and Norm's quartet 'acquired' Neil Corke and A. Campbell, probably Andrew Campbell,[6] and they skirted San Nazzaro Sesia, further upstream, and just north of there they approached the Cavour Canal which crosses the Sesia. Finding a nearby bridge unguarded, they crossed the canal. Along this stretch, north of the canal, they were welcomed at a large farmstead, *cascina*. 'Across a heavy wooden table lighted by the glow from an old-fashioned oil lamp, a map was spread.' *Contadini* risked their lives to help them, Norm knew. 'The crippled son who was twenty years old proceeded to plot a course for us to the border,' leaving the 'grape country' for the foothills.

Next morning the six POWs refreshed on the riverbank. After they passed the village of Carpignano Sesia, an Italian working in a vineyard warned them that two kilometres upstream the hospital at Ghemme had many Germans who frequented the riverbank. They crossed the river again and headed northwest. Neil Corke lists Rovasenda on the trip list, about five kilometres further north of the canal and Sesia junction.[7] Aiming to keep going to Alagna as a route to the Alps, via Lozzolo about six kilometres to their north, a six-lane *autostrada* carrying heavy traffic blocked safe passage south of Lozzolo.[8] Utilising a culvert, they had to 'crawl on hands and knees through foul water about a foot deep', then trudged a winding stony road to Lozzolo.

On dusk, they met *l'americano*, a man who spoke good English and had lived in America for twenty years. The 'stout bald fellow with a ruddy complexion and ragged moustache' made them welcome. With a straw bed, fowls roosting above and a pig in a pen in the corner, the POWs fought restless sleep.

Next morning, 19 September, Paul and Norm's party passed many roadside shrines on a five-kilometre walk northward to find a warm village embrace at Sostegno, located four kilometres south of the small river Torrente Sessera junction with the Sesia. At Sostegno, Paul entered a general store with his shopping list of peroxide, cottonwool, bandages, talcum powder and chocolate. The shop attendant refused to take payment.

The POWs steered around Coggiola, due to warnings about Germans. An Italian told them that former Cervetto internees Don Steele and Colin Gardner were hidden in a shack, planning to get to Switzerland via Lake Maggiore.

Paul and Norm rendezvoused with Steele and Gardner at Monte Gemevola, several kilometres north-west, and climbed three hours. Villagers handed them biscuits, jam, cheese, fruit and an alpine pack. Whether their route was with referral by the recent host or by their new POW companions, the POWs spearheaded directly towards a hotel on Monte Barone—the Hotel Alpe Noveis.

Norm was struck by the superb view from a 2000-metre vantage point at Monte Barone, and its hotel at 1200 metres. On clear days when the mountain repelled blankets of dense fog, Norm took in a vista of Monte Rosa to the north and Po Valley cities to the south. On the slopes below Monte Barone, 'the hotel was rather small, sitting beside an ornamental pond, and among many beautiful trees. In between the trees sat a number of small stained timber holiday cabins, sparsely furnished, and for sleeping only, guests eating at the hotel.' Norm souvenired a small strip of pink ribbon from one of the cabins where guests slept, to take home to his girlfriend Phyllis.

The hoteliers offered new guests a long glass of a strong white wine, grappa, to ward off chills after the ascent from the valley. 'The proprietor was Angelo Zaninetti, about sixty, with stout build and a shock of thick white hair.' With socialist sentiments, he welcomed Italian antifascisti, partisans and Allied escapers. His sister was 'some ten years younger'. Both spoke good English. Norm discovered that pre-war the hotel was involved with contraband. Prisoners in the vicinity were directed to the hotel.

Around this time, Italians had suggested to Nick Emery and Charlie Mills to go to a hotel in the hills north of Coggiola.[9] The description fits Hotel Alpe Noveis. The duo passed through Pianceri Alto[10] a few kilometres south of the hotel, but feeling uneasy about partisans, they avoided the hotel and kept going north-west.

Col Booth and another POW, probably Peter Erickson, met l'americano Francesco 'Frank' Secchia[11] at Rovasenda, 15 kilometres east of Biella.

Frank, who'd spent time in New York before the war, put the POWs up in the family barn under the living quarters.¹² Ten-year-old Piero Secchia was sworn to secrecy about the strange fugitives stored with the family animals.

In 2012, aged ninety-nine, Frank's wife Nina regretted that she had little food to share with the POWs under her living room. But respite and compassion were enough to sustain Col's trust and gratitude, and he made a point of noting Frank's name and place in his notebook. To acknowledge 'assistance given to Allied soldiers during wartime that enabled them to evade recapture from the enemy', after the war Francesco 'Frank' Secchia received a certificate from Field Marshal General H.R. Alexander, commander of Allied troops.

Col was referred to Crevacoure, presumably by Frank or a contact. He walked for about 15 kilometres following the western side of the Sesia River, traversing Coggiola and Crevacuore on the Torrente Sessera. With no access road, his arduous climb was escorted by 'an organisation', as Col put it,¹³ on one of several trails from Coggiola, Ailoche and Postua, bringing him to buildings nestled in a saddle just below the peak of Gemovola near Mount Barone. The precise nature of the 'organisation' may not have been evident to young Australians like Col. Foreigners caught within an effective web of formal and informal networks were often not privy to subtle contexts of loyalties and resistance efforts that worked covertly to nudge escapers towards Switzerland.

2/32nd Battalion's John 'Ted' Faulkes was heading in the same direction, and on a close route to Col. He'd left Collobiano camp and followed the western side of the Sesia, walking the periphery of Buronzo, immediately south of Rovasenda, as well as Gattinara, to its north.¹⁴ Ted, from Kojonup north of Albany, had partnered with fellow West Australians Tom Bullock and 'Bill' Morgan. Continuing north as Col had done, Ted's trio 'stumbled across a large building ... much too big to be an ordinary family house so we decided to sit back and observe it. The only people we saw going in and out were a man and a woman working in the garden.

'After satisfying ourselves it was clear of Germans or Blackshirts, we approached them and said *buon giorno*.' Ted was stunned by the reply from the Italian man, 'who spoke with a pronounced American accent', asking the West Australians, 'You guys aren't Italians, who are you?'

Ted confirmed the Italian's suspicions: that they were former prisoners heading for Switzerland. The Italian looked warily at Bill Morgan's blonde hair and blue eyes. Once he was convinced that Bill was not Tedesco, German, he introduced himself as Angelo Zaninetti. His nickname was l'americano because he had lived for forty years in New York. He now sought to retire in Italy with his sister Clementina. Before the war, their hotel was frequented by Italians from the plains who climbed the trail for a holiday in the mountains. The Zaninetti siblings cared for their aged mother, who washed dishes as part of her contribution.[15]

Ted's trio accepted a 'very good meal' of polenta, bread, cheese and fruit, and were shown to their accommodation, an outbuilding with a bed of hay. In the morning, Angelo mentioned a fledgling band of partisans located a few hours' walk from the hotel, and that New Zealanders had joined them. These partisans, Angelo disclosed, were supporters of General Badoglio, who was now working with Italian forces who'd changed sides to support the Allies.

West Australian Lloyd 'Mick' Wilson had also found Monte Barone's hotel of resistance. 'At Noveis near Mount Barone we met with 200 or 300 alpini officers and OR's [other ranks] who were trying to organise a resistance movement. We remained with them for about six days. They tried to raid a small village. The raid was a failure, several of them were killed, after that several of them came up into the hills and the movement broke up.'[16] Peter Erickson alludes to similar activity: 'whilst with C. Zaninetti, I and other soldiers were going to join the rebels but they were raided on one or two occasions and disbanded.'[17] Bill Morgan reported spending twelve days with a 'guerilla band' near Postua, down the hill from Monte Barone.[18]

Angelo spoke to Ted Faulkes about the best route to reach the border, pointing out snow-capped Monte Rosa. 'Always keep that on your left, and Monte Moro is to the right of that. You must go over Monte Moro.' Ted memorised these instructions 'well and truly'. This advice soon came in handy.

During an evening with partisans in a building adjacent to the hotel, Ted Faulkes, Bill Morgan and Tom Bullock met New Zealander partisan recruits Roy Lunn and Lionel Hood, escapers from Salussola.[19] Machine-gun fire from a German ambush sent the five POWs sprinting towards the nearest rise. Bill Morgan lagged behind, losing sight of the others. The remaining four men fast-tracked north-west to Scopello, tucked in a Sesia River valley about six kilometres away, reaching Switzerland on 26 September. Bill Morgan caught up with them in Switzerland on 28 September.

On 19 September, before the Faulkes and Bosgard party fled Monte Barone, Col Booth, as well as Norm Freeberg and Paul Lavallee's mini-army checked in at the Zaninetti's hotel. Despite being made welcome and given food, Paul and Norm's party felt nervous about the place and about staying too long. They heard that guards had been increased on the frontier borders, and that in coming weeks the northern autumn would bring more snow and ice to the mountains, making the border increasingly difficult to traverse. They learned that the hotel was involved with contraband pre-war, and that all POWs in the area were being directed to the hotel base. They gleaned that some civilian-dressed men at the hotel were Italian officers and men of other ranks.

After dinner on the first night, Norm watched as POWs 'Nicol, Ferguson, Dawson and [Peter] Bosgard stepped inside accompanied by a dubious-looking character toting a luger in a hip holster. His intention of arming everyone with rifles made us realise we were among partisans. This fellow was trying to organise a rebel army to engage in raids on German troops and installations.' Paul and Norm wanted no part of it. As more men docked at the hotel, Norm estimated there were a 'hundred mouths to feed' including Italian officers and men of other ranks in mufti clothing who had come to join the rebels. Paul and Norm did not share Angelo Zaninetti's confident exclamations that on the following day, 'domani, domani', a guide would come.

On the following morning, Paul and Norm spoke with an alpine guide who was going to the border on a contraband route and offered to take them along, but after leaving the hotel, he didn't return. 'We had a suspicion that Zaninetti was behind it. He did not want us to leave the hotel.' On leaving their cabin, Paul and Norm's departing swelled to fourteen POWs, hearing that Switzerland was 'only three sleeps away'.

Ross Wycherley,[20] Col Booth and Peter Erickson stayed as hotel guests for another week. Considering Peter Erickson's head-count of eighty-seven POW at the Hotel Alpe Noveis and its out-buildings during their twelve-day respite, it could be considered an erstwhile army transit camp under the command of an ageing hotelier and resistance-fighter, and his sister. It is not known whether Clementina considered herself to be a resistance fighter, nor whether the escapers thought her so, but her efforts were a subtle and significant snub to the dominant occupying regimes.

At 100 years of age, Paul Lavallee rued his decision to allow other escaper groups to merge, swelling his party's ranks to a highly conspicuous column.

In his wartime memorabilia Paul retained a handwritten list of POW names and their service numbers, but more than seven decades later, he struggled to recall where the list was compiled. 'I worked in the farm camp's office. Perhaps it was there,' Paul presumed.[21]

Indeed, Paul's list details a subset of Campo 106 POWs. But, according to a number of their later reports, not all were stationed at the same camps. In addition to listing all fourteen men of Paul and Norm's escaper group combinations, Paul lists the names of Don Steele and Colin Gardner whom they encountered on route to the hotel. The list also contains Col, Peter, Ross, Ted, Mick, Don and New Zealanders Roy and Lionel. These POWs later reported convergence at or near the Hotel Alpe Noveis and Monte Barone's partisans.

Regardless of whether Paul's list was pulled together at the hotel or with partisans nearby, Angelo and Clementina could not convince Paul and Norm to stay in their refuge for longer than four days.

12
'A BLOODY GERMAN FRONTIER GUARD': COAL-SHUTTLE HELMETS AT THE BORDER

'In a litany familiar in accounts of the improvised battles of mid-1942 in the desert ... much went wrong. No daylight reconnaissance was allowed for fear of alerting the defenders ... the attacker's route was inadequately marked. At the last minute, orders were altered ... The July battle of Alamein has long been overshadowed by the larger and more decisive second battle in October. In July, however, Auchinleck's army had stopped the advance of Rommel's Panzerarmee Afrika ... The first battle saw both protagonists played out to exhaustion. Both had already fought for five months, moving for 300 miles at the height of the North African summer, usually in combat, beset by all the disruption of living and fighting in the desert.'

—Mark Johnston and Peter Stanley, 2006[1]

When prisoners cheekily walked out of prison camps in September 1943, less than a year had elapsed since the July 1942 battles and prisoner captures at Alamein's Sanyet el Miteiriya, dubbed Ruin Ridge. For troops ordered to surrender at Alamein by commanding officers, control was increasingly snatched from them during captivity.

With camp breakaways in 1943, escaped POWs formulated their own land-based fighting objectives and strategies, blundering into Italy's civil war, trekking into alpine landscapes antithetic to the North African desert, most with no commanding officers telling them what to do as they had done within the Italian theatre of war in North Africa. German militia remained salient to both, regardless of the official national alliances.

Veterans advanced forward and backwards, up and down hills and into an array of make-do shelters. Their regimental batteries and battalion companies scattered and dispersed, they were unable to communicate with men of their own units, even when they followed close to mates' heels. On snow-capped ridges of greater proportions than North African desert blimp Ruin Ridge, soldiers feared another defeat as they stealthily approached their objective of safe territory and Allied forces. As escapers, they had fought their way northward for weeks or months, fearful of alerting the enemy during daylight reconnaissance, beset by living in flight or fight readiness in the Italian high country.

In escaper accounts about surviving periods of evasion, there are parallels to their pre-captivity service. In the North African desert, soldiers made do with rations and rough bedding; in desert battles, troops were vigilant day and night for enemy ambush and capture. As hungry fugitives, the soldiers may have missed army-issue bully beef stew seasoned with desert-dust. Enemy attackers' locations were inadequately marked. POW protagonists played out the advance to the frontier to exhaustion.

Bob Ward was captured with many of his 2/28th Battalion on 27 July 1942, the morning following the Ruin Ridge Alamein battle, as was his POW companion Norm Woosnam. Bill Pannowitz, 2/32nd, was nabbed by Germans at Alamein on 17 July 1942.[2]

Following the Italian armistice, the men spent a fortnight staying close to Tronzano, then pushed on, lumbering to Santhia, two kilometres north of Tronzano.[3] A woman conversed with them in English. Her husband, Albert Macchieraldo, had lived in England for twenty years. Bob embraced the Macchieraldo hospitality: 'We had a royal time with them, living on roast chicken, potatoes and other such things that we hadn't tasted for over two years. As for grapes, we gorged ourselves. We never drank water, always wine.' Bob's quartet helped the couple to pick and make wine. In turn, Albert contacted friends who provided clothing and arrangements for train passage northward. Albert bought the tickets.[4]

On Monday 27 September at Brianco, several kilometres north-west of Santhia and Tronzano, the Australians farewelled Albert and embarked a train. Albert arranged the next link in the helper chain. The POWs followed his orders. At the first station, one of the POWs tried to make himself seen through the carriage window, to enable Albert's elderly contact to identify their carriage. In the darkness, it took several tries before she saw their signal.

Bob recalled: 'We were supposed to be Italians but were recognised as Aussies. It was a very humorous trip. Girls on the train expressed willingness to act as guides.' At Biella, the POWs mingled with the crowd, following their elderly guide to a block of flats. Locals flocked to meet them. Bob wrote that they 'were treated like lords'. Two girls visited; 'they had just finished a sentence of eighteen months in gaol for speaking too freely about the fascists'.

With haversacks loaded up with food, wine and liquor, the men readied for a stroll along the main street to board another train. Bill Pannowitz, fair-headed and standing at six feet,[5] was probably very recognisable as a foreigner. This train trip brought them within an hour's walking distance of the commune of Piedicavallo, within the Biella province, where they camped in a barn full of meadow hay. Next morning, they headed north on a mule path. *Alpini* told them that bad weather rendered the pass too treacherous. As September ended, they turned back south. At some point, they'd climbed to higher ground above the Santuario di Oropa north of Biella, and from that 'high perch' they observed German tanks cruising around. They opted not to descend to the Santuario and sought out a cow shed further uphill. Inside, Australian and New Zealander POWs sat tight, and Bob's gang settled in with them for three days.

According to Max Wills's POW report, he, and presumably this group, considered joining rebel forces but bustled on when the partisans were disbanded by Germans.

Len Holman from Warwick, Queensland, a 2/15th veteran captured at Derna in early 1941, also sampled the precarious comfort of a train.[6] Len departed San Germano on 12 September and stayed working for farmers for a week. He then travelled from Novara, south of Milan, to Varallo. To local passengers, foreign escapers in civilian clothes who sat or stood silently on trains stuck out like the proverbial sore thumb. Len stood at nearly six feet tall, and with his light-blue eyes is likely to have attracted passengers' stares.[7] A British escaper, Ian English, found that Italian train travellers rarely gave away the escapers.[8] German patrol troops on trains were less skilled than Italians in discerning Allied escapers, relying mostly on identification papers.

Len's train trip paid off. He stood at the edge of the alpine frontier on 21 September. Six other Queenslanders—Harry Watts, Clarence Reid, Fred Curtis, Harry Cox, Rae Johnston and Neville Lavaring—got there the same day.[9] Overall, it was a busy day for border patrol as twenty-six Australians stood ready for Swiss scrutiny on that day.

Bill Rudd was travelling alone, just behind these men, when he reached the town of Macugnaga on 22 September 1943.[10] He'd been warned by a trio of English soldiers wearing battledress not to go near the town; it was 'full of Germans'. The English soldiers wanted to hook up with partisans. Bill recalls their advice that he'd be 'mad to try and get to Switzerland via the "Monte Rosa" Pass'. One of them had confused Rosa with Moro pass. As Bill was keen to try to get to Switzerland, they shrugged and walked away. By this point, Bill knew he was close to the border.

When Bill began his climb up to Moro, he was probably unaware that fellow Victorians had got toes into Switzerland on the two previous days. Melburnians Max Judd and Jack Judd assembled at the border on 20 September, tailed by Mordialloc brothers Cyril and Claude Farrow and Allan Ward on 21 September.[11]

Through clear skies on 22 September, Bill Rudd glanced down to Macugnaga. 'It lay in the sunlight like a toy town, and the movement of military traffic was quite obvious. My supplies were running low, my boots had almost given up the ghost, and it was becoming increasingly cold. I saw what seemed to be a mountain-climber coming down towards the town. I decided to talk to him.'

Fortunately, this mountaineer was a smuggler who'd taken bicycle tyres into Switzerland, returning with coffee and cigarettes. Bill was unsure of the route, there was no clear marking. The mountaineer set Bill straight on the best route, insisting that he follow Monte Moro Pass rather than tackle the trepidatious Rosa. The smuggler suggested Bill follow his recent footprints, most likely still imprinted in the snow. 'After a few sorties I found his trail and followed it for almost an hour.'

As Bill climbed higher on 22 September, he felt colder. The afternoon waned quickly, and he feared failure so close to the border. Adding to his woe, snow fell and smothered the smuggler's footsteps. 'Finally, I lost them and began to panic. No option but to keep on climbing and then quite suddenly, I sensed the going becoming easier. I was no longer climbing. I was going downhill. There were no landmarks of any sort. The sun was sinking fast. It stopped snowing. The light was still reasonable but the utter silence a bit unnerving.

'Then I saw the coal-shuttle helmet and grey uniform suddenly appear from behind a rock, casually but firmly cradling a rifle in one arm. I almost burst into tears.' Flabbergasted, Bill panicked. 'All this way and a bloody German frontier guard!'

The guard beckoned Bill, tapping his chest with his free hand. Bill picked up a stone as weapon and slowly stepped forward. The buttons on the guard's uniform lit up Bill's eyes. 'He was a Swiss frontier guard and I had made it. My tears were those of joy!' Bill exhaled his inner relief: 'Thank God!' The guard responded, in English: 'Ah, English is it? I have been watching you for some time. You'd better come on down and have a cup of tea.'

Twenty minutes later, Bill entered a stone guard house where Swiss guards and civilian escapees sat around a roaring fire. A huge pot of stew bubbled in a corner. Next morning, Bill and several other escapers boarded a bus to the village of Saas-Fee, known as the 'Pearl of the Alps'. After a quick interrogation by a Swiss lieutenant, Bill and others were moved to Brig's railway station, about 40 kilometres down the valley.

Bill carted the cheesecloth package given to him by Nello all the way to the border. At Brig, Bill handed over the package, believing that it likely contained the locations of the Campo 106 detainments. He was transported on to Wil, a purpose-built camp awaiting British and colonial escapers for further interrogation.

Outfitted with British uniforms, Bill's batch relocated to the small village of Turbenthal. At a gymnasium commandeered for their accommodation, clean straw bedding covered the floor, a similar method used by Swiss soldiers when on manoeuvres. 'I was now definitely a guest of the Confederation of Switzerland,' Bill recognised.

He later learned that his POW mate Jock Smith's southward trip had paid off. Heading in the opposite direction, Jock's progress ran neck-and-neck with Bill; he announced himself to Allied forces about the same time as Bill made it to Switzerland.

West Australian Syd Shaw, who'd put up his age to enlist into the army, was close on Bill's heels.[12] Syd had been captured at Alamein on 22 July 1942 and ended up in Campo 106 barracks inside a Vercelli gymnasium after being moved there from Sali farm. Syd met a family who formerly lived in Roma, Queensland; he recalled their creative message dissemination: 'A tall blond fella used to walk past our billet and throw a message wrapped around a stone over the fence to give us the BBC news.'[13]

In readiness to flee, Syd added vegetables to the pockets of his greatcoat but, to his surprise, he noticed a lot of food growing at that time of year. 'I was chewing on almonds for days.' He aimed to stay out of sight, 'keeping low by day, moving by night', blundering through creeks, rivers and orchards.

Local people spotted his army boots and invited him to sit on the ground for a yarn, offering directions. On village outskirts, locals sent out food to his group, sometimes with requests for a written 'chit'—a testimonial note signed by POW to evidence assistance. 'Ned Kelly signed a few of those!' Syd chimed.

Along the way Syd's escaper group split. With remaining travel companions, he decided to have 'a crack' at the home stretch without a guide. They'd covered a lot of ground, about 83 kilometres from Vercelli, in thirteen days. There were no signposts to aid them. On one full day, 'we passed a wooden cross and thought it must be Switzerland but we ended up back three-quarters of a mile from where we started'. Eventually, they engaged guides. 'The *alpini* were like mountain goats.' Syd's group felt languid compared to their young, agile, fast-footed guides. Syd put the fast pace down to fears of being shot.

To keep up with the guides, on 22 September, Syd grudgingly decided to reduce weight by ditching his greatcoat; without it, he was dressed only in shorts.

In his ninety-third year in 2015, Syd recalled that two of his party of thirteen had dropped out of the running when confronted by the border ranges. One fellow 2/32nd POW, Morris Jackman, was recaptured on the road to Domodossola by a German motorcyclist. An older 2/28th POW gave himself up to Germans as he couldn't sustain the pace. Out of the eleven men pushing on, Syd recalled three of his companions who were from his battalion: Henry 'Harry' Meldrum from Katanning, corporal Norm 'Bill' Tripovich from Melbourne and corporal Dave King from Chinchilla, the group leader.

Syd acknowledged that escapers coming together on the run may not have known each other well, and not everyone clicked. Their shared fighting-on objective was survival, as it was for Italian alpine troops. 'We would never have made it,' Syd was certain, 'but for the alpine soldiers who guided us up the mountains. They stopped short of taking us to the Swiss border, mainly because of the smuggling that was going on at that time.'

Syd went on, 'After the guides left us a thick fog descended and we couldn't see a thing. We spent the night huddled under rocks, very, very cold.' Next morning, 23 September, dawned clear. Our landmark was a great heap of snow and ice,' Syd recalled. 'We made our way up over the border where there was a great brass bell mounted on a wooden stand. Some way down the mountain a sentry hailed, "Alt". We naturally assumed him to be German, our mutterings of grabbing him, but as we got closer, we could see the white cross—Swiss. You beaut,' Syd's eleven rejoiced, 'we were in Switzerland!' Norm 'Bill' Tripovich later reported that assistance to their party of thirteen men earned the guide 1400 *lire* and two watches.[14]

Wagin-born Syd Shaw knew a fellow 2/32nd Battalion soldier captured with him on 22 July 1942 as 'Pagey'. Frank 'Pagey' Page, like other escapers from outback flat country, was also put to the alpine test in terrain vastly different to his pre-war home. Pagey, an Aboriginal veteran from Winton, took about ten days to reach the frontier near Monte Moro after leaving his camp. Travelling on foot, he sought assistance from farmers. In his 1944 POW report, he summarised the trip: 'After leaving Vercelli [region] I came directly for Switzerland, keeping to the more unused roads passing near Biella, then through Legno [Alagna] and to the frontier at Monte Moro. I received no help from any organisation.'[15]

Tailing Syd, Pagey presented at the Swiss border on 24 September. According to George 'Bill' Thompson's escape notes, Pagey had left La Corte farm with him as well as George 'Bluey' Burton, John Oborne, 'Nip' Robinson (probably Alfred Robinson). Atop Monte Moro on 24 September, Bill Thompson wrote that those men still in his company 'had to crawl on hands and knees over steep ground and boulders', finding themselves lost for more than an hour until a line of posts indicated the border.[16]

Many early Australian arrivals to Italy's extremity faced a mountain range unlike anything seen in home regions. A number of these soldiers trained in the mountains of Lebanon, where many Ninth Division troops underwent ski training.

Raised in the Queensland outback, Frank Page was more accustomed to plains of scrub and sand. As his nephew, also named Frank Page, put it decades later, his uncle 'Brunz' was skilled in navigation without a compass and in bush survival.[17] Pagey's quick pace through the Piedmont ranges confirmed his battalion buddy Syd's expectations. Pagey 'was one bloke who could look after himself'.

13
'NORTH WAS THE GRIM LINE OF THE ALPS': CLIMBING TOWARDS THE FRONTIER

> *'Despite often quaint experiences of many men, their situation was always highly dangerous. The longer they remained at large the more people knew about them and, if caught, the less likely their status as prisoners-of-war was respected.'*
>
> —Susan Jacobs, 2003[1]

During the Second World War, Italian partisans referred to *sentieri della liberta,* the trails to freedom. These were medieval paths through mountains used by pilgrims and other travellers that became busy with the foot traffic of Allied servicemen, mostly escaped prisoners and downed airmen, fleeing Italy. Starting near Vercelli, one key route was to go north closely following the River Sesia along its curves to steer to the Hotel Alpe Noveis, or to continue as far as Alagna before diverting north through valleys and foothills heading to the Anzasca Valley. From Biella, one of these freedom trails climbs to the Santuario di Oropa and then down into the Cervo Valley. The trail rises again to traverse another pass and into the Sesia Valley before climbing once more to the Turlo Pass and dropping down into the Anzasca Valley. There, the freedom trails leading to Monte Moro and Mondelli passes begin.

On the same day that several escaper groups assembled at Hotel Alpe Noveis, to the east Ernie Sparnon, Henry 'Harry' Perrott and their companion known only as 'Stevo' assembled at Santuario di Oropa, at 1000 metres altitude, on 19 September, 'very tired and sore', acting on referral from a sympathetic Yank.[2]

For centuries the ensemble of courtyards and building comprising the Santuario di Oropa, sited within a natural amphitheatre, had welcomed travellers and pilgrims.[3] Like the Hotel Alpe Noveis, the religious sanctuary sat within the partisan radii of the Biellese region and provided a rendezvous base. War periods slowed down work on its eight-metre cupola.

'This place was run by priests and nuns,' Ernie summarised. 'They did not want us to stop on account of the Germans but the old Father took pity on us and set us up for the night. The nuns treated our feet for blisters and even said a little prayer. We must have looked terrible: tired, unshaven and old clothes.'

The tatty trio packed at 6.30 the next morning. They struck out north for Piedicavallo, on the western edge of Piedmont province bordering the Aosta, relieved that 'no Germans were about'. After a long day, they accepted offer of a hayloft. They plodded through Piedicavallo, ten kilometres north of Oropa, on 21 September. Although Harry was eleven years younger than Ernie's thirty-five years,[4] his legs were troublesome. As they set off on another cold morning, still 'tired, sore and very cold', Harry humbly asked Ernie to help him.

Col d'Olen at 2880 metres, south-east of Alagna, tested their tanks. At times Ernie closed his eyes to block out giddiness. The sight of another mountain over the rise nearly broke their hearts. On a ridgeline at 7pm, thick mist blocked visibility. A miserable night wrapped around them as they huddled together, 'cold, no cigs and only a few prunes we had in our pockets'. Without the nuns, it now fell to him to rub Harry Perrott's swollen legs.

Early on 23 September, the day that Syd Shaw's posse found Swiss sanctuary, Colin Weekes and companions Alan 'Blue' Neave, Eddie Scanlan and Jerry Neame woke in their warm hayloft sanctuary to dry clothing.[5] All going well, they expected this Italian host family would be their last before leaving the country. Breakfast offerings of hot milk, coffee and bread warmed them even more. Four little loaves of bread were given to them by their hosts as a parting gift. Their hostess reminded them that fascists patrolled the mountains. Colin's POWs decided to take the risk.

'We moved out into the damp morning air, leaving an unhappy crying household to do our worrying for us. It was a good start, with good visibility.' Colin was also buoyed that 'the correct track was found easily', and sooner than anticipated they stood plumb on top of a rocky bluff among little stone sheds, *baite*, made from rockfall. English voices fluttered from one shed. Inside, four British and a young Italian debated whether to descend back to the valley. They'd trekked close to the border but guides left them at 2am. 'We found them crowded around a little fire looking as miserable as I have seen any persons.' Their border descriptions unnerved Colin. 'Two hundred yards straight up,' they told him, crying about 'boulders and cliff-faces, snow and ice which could not be passed'. Some of their original group had become sick and already descended the mountain, while another three waited in huts further up. The Italian had lost his shoes so Colin handed over his handmade slippers.

Colin's crew gave farewells and propelled their hopes towards the next clutch of huts, agreeing that if they'd not reached their border objective by midday, and if weather was still bad, they'd return to the huts for a night. They doubted whether their boots were up to another trip.

Heading off, Colin's four steadily ascended, taking time to locate a 'foot-wide worn path' which they followed until it became less distinct. Discarded sardine tins amongst cow and goat dung gave clues of some sort of path. Increasingly sparse grass patches made the track harder to hold. Banks of dense cloud thwarted their vision to 'less than ten yards'. A natural staircase of flat stones awaited hikers. Higher up the slope, cairns of stones peeked through portals of skyline. As they stomped the incline, they gathered white stones to add to each cairn to help them identify this track in the event of a return trip.

Up 'into the unknown', Colin's column spread apart, with Blue as rearguard. When Blue's shape blurred, Jerry and Colin took brief smoko, snacking on bread and resting until the group reformed. By this point, vegetation was almost negligible; their dilapidated boots sloshed 'two inches deep in water'. Colin took in the scene: 'Ice and snow less than one thousand feet above us. Deep red rocks, black rocks, patches of ice and the fog cloud all around us.' A swathe of silence around them was overwhelming, jarred only by their footsteps until, out of nowhere, voices drifted within the clear air from an indiscernible distance or direction. The track faded as the slope flattened out. Boulders sat stern but Colin scrambled over a '29 foot' example while the other three crept upwards through a fissure between towering stone walls.

Up there, the clouds were lighter and the air clearer. A 'natural stone tile floor made up of hundreds of millions of small flat chips, all deep red and black' and a 'small grassy lake' unrippled by breeze created a surreal environment. Colin's description may refer to Lago Smeraldo on Moro's high terrain.

Beyond, the men saw that rock fell away to a small gully and to a black wooden hut with stone roof and chimney. Without thinking about possible dangers, they opened the door. The single-room hut was deserted. Bunkbeds had been broken up for fire fuel, empty tins and *grappa* bottles were strewn on the floor 'but not even a smell was left, so old were they'. They looked outside to check if anyone was near, and focused on fire and food. 'In our bags, we had two 3 oz. tins of egg powder,' remembered Colin. 'Eddie had a mess tin, I had a spoon and Blue had spotted a creek almost at the very doorstep.'

While Eddie and Blue whipped up a hot pot of scrambled eggs, Jerry Neame and Colin 'went out to see where Switzerland was'.

Within 200 metres they approached a ridge-top and, squinting through the thinning mist, they pondered a dark patch that, upon closer inspection, revealed a high cairn of stones surrounded by a granite post with a trig mark. They stood on top of the block. One side displayed an 'I' carving; the other side exhibited a large 'S'. Jerry and Colin, using a rock, scratched their names and numbers on the rusty iron discs to evidence their win. Looking towards Switzerland, it seemed as if the country was only snow, ice and cloud.

These minutes are etched in Colin's memory: 'Below we spotted a path of footsteps in the snow so we slid down the rocks to observe more closely. They were foot marks and large ones too. Some three or four pairs plus a very large pair of dog pads led across the snow from east to west. We passed over them to see what was ahead but almost immediately our keen senses became aware of a third person coming our way. We froze as the faint sound of crunching snow grew louder and louder. It came from dead ahead and as we waited the few seconds that were necessary for our third person to appear, our hearts pounded.

'The sharp metallic click of a rifle bolt sent a cold shock up our spines and immediately two hearts stopped while two pairs of eyes peered at the now ghostly soldier who stood a mere thirty feet from us. The muzzle of his upraised rifle became clear as he ordered us to "Alt". Two pairs of hands lifted skywards as a pair of hearts began to sink.'

As Colin's arms shot up above his head, his eyes scanned the frontier soldier for an indication of his intent. 'I could just make out an *alpini* hat above the rifle and tried my hardest to discern whether the usual feather projected from it. As the figure advanced, I saw the hat sported nothing in the bird line, but on the tunic arm, bright and clean, the Swiss white cross with white flower emblem of the frontier soldiers below it.

'Excitedly I spluttered out, "Are you Swiss?" in my best Italian. He said "Ja" or "Si". I just can't remember. With his rifle still cocked, he asked for identification papers and proceeded to search us for weapons. Finding none, he uncocked his rifle and, placing it on a rock, he began to unzip his rucksack. Out of it he took the largest piece of bread we had set eyes on for three years. A thermos flask followed the bread while our conversation continued apace, punctuated by large pieces of brown bread and rich vegetable soup from the thermos flask.'

Colin and Jerry scuttled back along the snow and ice to find Eddie and Blue sitting tight in the 'little black hut with its smoking chimney and stone roof'.

Colin diarised the significance of 11.30am on Thursday 23 September 1943. 'On the summit of Mount Moro, in cold damp clouds, four ragged soldiers stood with one single guard, with one single thought beating over and over in their hearts: we made it.' Their mountaineering crash-course was almost over.

The soldier guided them along a very steep and indistinct track, gingerly descending in tough terrain to traverse a snow-covered glacier. 'All was quiet in the pale grey clouds,' Colin recalled, 'except for the sharp click of the guards' heavy boots accompanied by the dull squelch of our worn wrecks. Each footstep had to be selected because one slip would mean, perhaps, death.' With little heel left on his boots, he could not follow the Swiss's technique of using 'his heels to catch the little edges of rock on the slippery surface'. Blue suddenly lost his shoe-hold and slid down onto Colin. Quick as a flash, the Swiss guard tended to Blue's cut hand and chin. Blue steadied his footing with a spiked walking stick.

Glancing back at the mountain, Colin noted, 'In its soft grey cloud shroud, like a strange giant whom we had defied, he no longer held any horrors for us.' After a 'goodly swig on grappa', Colin mused on the 'sorry sight' of fatigued Italian refugees lugging gear and offered to carry a suitcase.

Travelling a day behind Colin Weekes, Ernie Sparnon and his younger companions 'Stevo'[6] and Harry trod ground near Alagna.[7] Locals cautioned them about German patrols, telling them to move through quickly; this was reiterated by a sympathetic *carabinieri* officer who'd been instructed to take any prisoners coming through. Low on energy and strength, they went into a baker's shop to buy bread before their assault on Alpe Faller.[8]

'The battle with 'this mount nearly beat us', Ernie declared. 'We were resting every 200 yards. At 2pm, only halfway up, we had to give in as were all tired, hungry, and our condition was starting to tell on us.' They whiled away the remainder of 22 September in an old shed, consuming cheese and milk given by Italians. Ernie listened in to advice that escapers had already been caught in Macugnaga.

About 7.30pm their guide suggested it was time to commence climbing towards Monte Moro Pass. The night was clear and they climbed until 10.30pm where they divvied up small quantities of food and slept.

On 24 September they got away early and tackled another foothill. On the way down, an Italian who was helping prisoners to the farthest point told them there was only one more mountain to conquer before the border peaks: Tovo. 'It was our worst.' They aimed to get higher before daylight, to avoid alerting German defenders wearing binoculars. After reaching Macugnaga, they went into hiding until 7pm. 'A lot of our boys had been caught here by Germans,' Ernie understood.

Exactly twenty-four hours after Colin Weekes' party found asylum in Switzerland, Ernie Sparnon, Stevo and Harry clocked in, seven hours after leaving the Macugnaga valley. 'What a great sight it was to see the Swiss guards!' Ernie's trousers had clung to his legs for a fortnight, but now were without the seat and both knees. Harry's legs made it, sore but intact, thanks to the help of Ernie and Stevo.

West Australians Syd Shove, Fred Price and 'Newt' Moore of the 2/28th Battalion had followed the River Sesia northward through Borgosesia to Varallo, where they left the Sesia and were given food at a church in the Varallo hills, perhaps Sacro il Monte di Varallo.[9] After passing through Fobello, the trio caught up with other Australians, forming a party of twenty or so, and stayed overnight in Macugnaga. Trudging over Monte Moro on 23 September, Syd Shove acknowledged that the guide leading the large escaper party 'got us through allright. The last 500 metres was the hardest.'

Familial groups also crossed the Swiss terminus on 24 September. Pat O'Rafferty arrived safely that day.[10] Along the way he departed company with his brother Geoff, and was assisted by Giovanni Saviolo of Olcenengo. Pat travelled for seven days, firstly heading north-west to Fontainemore and Gressoney-Saint-Jean, before turning north-east for the Monto Moro trail. Also on 24 September, brothers Eddie and Bill Sincock, all of the 2/24th Battalion, stepped on Swiss earth.[11] A third Sincock brother, Herbert known as 'Harry', was still at large in Italy.[12] Bill Sincock gratefully acknowledged the leadership of 2/15th Battalion's Bill Bushnell, a former carpenter from Maryborough, as he 'spoke to Italians on the way and led us into Switzerland with the help of a guide from Monte Moro'.

All up, thirty-five Australians busted to pass border interrogation by the Swiss on 24 September.[13]

14
'NONE OF US WERE PREPARED TO ARGUE WITH TWO RIFLES': RE-CAPTURE AT THE FRONTIER

'By mid-November 1943 roughly 24,000 POWs had been transferred to Germany, a figure that rose to 50,000 by the end of the year. This meant there were still something in the region of 30,000 ex-prisoners at large in Italy. More would continue to be arrested by Germans and fascist forces, but by October 1944, 4000 prisoners had crossed the Swiss border, and a further 6500 reached Allied lines in the south. An unknown figure remained in hiding in Italy ...'

—Adrian Gilbert, 2006[1]

More than one-third of the Australian POW cohort at Campo 106 were recaptured by German patrols or handed to Germans by Italians, about 300 men, nabbed either at or near the farm camps or somewhere in the field after escape.[2] POWs, in their private memoirs, express feelings of humiliation similar to that of their initial capture experience. Recaptured POWs were transported out of Italy to German-controlled camps.

All escapers feared this fate. Mostly, outcomes came down to luck.

Paul Lavallee and Norm Freeberg were determined to stick together throughout their war. Their morale waxed and waned in the days after leaving the Hotel Alpe Noveis. Norm narrated subsequent events for his large party of escapers, leading to what he later described as 'one of the most formidable [days] of our lives.'[3]

As they departed the hotel, Monte Barone was wrapped in a blanket of dense fog, reducing visibility to five metres. Advancing single file, it was almost impossible to see the man in front unless one kept right on his heels. They lost bearings amongst black jagged rocks that seemed to stretch upwards to be swallowed by fog. Loose stones slid underfoot until they reached the valley floor, ready to review their plans and rest their legs. 'Ascending,' Norm explained, 'one's calves ache and breathing becomes laboured; descending, the knees, heels and thighs suffer. Either way is tortuous.'

As they debated whether Scopello would be their next target, three Italians came along, claiming to know the way. There was little choice for the Australians but to believe them. 'They led, we followed.' After some disheartening wrong turns, they aimed for the valley floor, via 'sharp rocks, thick moss and tufts of wet grass, slipping and sliding most of the way. Only to be lost once more. There was no sun, no compass and it was impossible to orient the map.'

With aching legs and backs, and feet bleeding from blisters, they challenged themselves to stagger higher towards a clump of shacks built from boulders and rusted sheets of iron. At the shacks, Paul vomited. Norm and a few others collapsed to the ground with exhaustion. The guide took a donkey and some rope to bring in Mick Wilson who became so unwell he had to stop on the trail. With Mick's stability secured by rope around his waist, Norm eyed the trip-worn mob: 'everyone, donkey included, stumbling along the uneven ground'. Norm felt sure that without their guide's recovery provisions of cheese, polenta, tea and a warm open fire, their trek towards Switzerland may have ended right there. Norm nestled within sleeping quarters on Monte Barone to the tinkling of cowbells on nearby slopes.

Dawn delivered a cloudless sky. Feeling refreshed and rested, they accomplished the next leg to Scopello. Norm revelled in the magnificent glimpse of the Alps 'with their peaks draped in perpetual snow. Monte Rosa stood among the surrounding crests like a queen watchful over her subjects.'

Scopello villagers eagerly offered transport with local truck drivers who went daily to work at ore mines near Alagna. 'We politely refused, saying we preferred to walk as it enabled cover to be taken quickly if any emergency arose.' In a hotel they re-fuelled with hot rice and retired to 'billets' in private homes for the night.

At nearby Piode on the southern bank of the River Sesia, locals unharnessed their hospitality. To reciprocate the escapers wrote 'chit' notes documenting the sharing of food and shelter at great risk, in the hope that these civilians would later receive compensation. Paul attested to assistance received: 'Rice farmers from Vercelli to Monte Rosa in the province of Piedmont, on either side of the Sesia River, were very kind in giving directions, food, map, compasses, lodgings and even civilian clothing to all POWs. [At] Piode, the wine saloon by the bridge in the town (west side), gave us food and drink for fourteen men, also in my case lodging in house on the east side of the same river.'[4] Locals, as many POWs discovered, kept tabs on German movements and communicated this valuable intelligence to escaper troops in the field. Norm described how a young lad rushed to the house, warning of a truck full of Germans coming up the valley road. Scurrying behind the boy, the POWs hid in a hayshed in the woods.

After a 'bitterly cold' rainy night, sunshine with 'a few cumulo-cirrus clouds skudding over the mountain peaks' was a welcome wake-up. The boy brought six tins of meat. With bellies loaded, their column wended north-west from Scopello towards Alagna, Norm was struck by the juxtaposition of a small roadside shrine alongside a monument to Hitler and Mussolini. The trail, they learned, was built in 1933 by an alpine regiment; in many places it had been cut through rock. Norm's description fits the Turlo Pass route. The winds from a nearby glacier chilled them to their core, exacerbated by their sweat-saturated clothes. For Norm, the massive field of glacial ice was a sight never forgotten.

Descending towards Macugnaga, Paul and Norm's infantry troops met a new guide, a young boy who offered to steer them to Macugnaga, 'passing a silver mine and the river'. On or about 26 September, the boy gave unhappy news to Paul and Norm's platoon. Sixteen Australians had been captured by fascists and handed to Germans.

In late 1943, a German garrison encamped at Macugnaga as a guarded gateway vigilant for prisoners of war yearning to cross the Alps in search of sanctuary in neutral Switzerland. The majestic Monte Rosa massif, marking the end of Anzasca valley, held ground as dominant overseer to a passing parade of prison escapers, refugees and smugglers crossing the valley and dodging German and fascist militia to make their freedom bids.

Leaving the group in the woods, the boy returned six hours later at 8pm to take them to his mother's house for 'a feast of hot boiled potatoes and cheese'. The boy offered to put them on their way but he would leave them to continue unaccompanied to the border. 'For some time in the subdued light from an old oil lamp', Norm's party pondered whether to wait until morning to make a move or do it right away. Consensus was to go. 'At ten o'clock, one at a time we quietly slipped from the house into the inkiness of the night.'

Their reconnaissance showed three streams on the south side of the Macugnaga village, each of which was spanned by old iron bridges. Torrente Anza, an alpine torrent, flows through the Anzasca Valley from Monte Rosa's glacial melt. 'It was imperative that all three bridges be crossed.' They scurried across two small bridges, untroubled. Paul and Norm understood their close proximity to the Swiss frontier, literally up the wooded mountain-slope before them. Their mini-army had safely got this far, in near sight of the finishing line.

The third bridge had longer span. In the dark, it was impossible to see whether the other end was guarded. 'Perhaps this one was also unguarded. We had to risk it.' With the last bridge tempting them to cross, and with little time to fiddle with imperfect choices, the snap decision was to expedite transit and cross as a group of fourteen men, rather than in spurts of two or three at a time. 'It was so dark we were probably within ten feet or so of the bridge's end before anyone realised that we were facing two heavily armed fascist soldiers.' Paul and Norm felt gutted. 'We were well and truly covered when the smaller of the two shouted "halt" and asked if were "Inglese". Both were carrying rifles, pistols and German-type stick grenades tucked into their belts. They began to count us and only ten were accounted for.'

Not looking back, Norm assumed that 'Wilson, Berg, Dawson and Collins' had lagged behind and found safe cover in the darkness. 'None of us were prepared to argue with the two rifles pointed in our direction, and before long we were at the fascist barracks above the village (at Pecetto). Our trek of over 200 miles along the Sesia to Switzerland was over.'

The bitter irony of being caught by Italians at the Macugnaga bridge, to be placed into German hands was not lost to them. Norm processed that 'the situation resembled a game of chess, and we undoubtedly were the pawns'. Adding to the irony, ten of their escaper pundits were soon transported by open truck down into the valley and across the work plains of the Piedmont and north to Intra on the shores of Lake Maggiore to be given to Germans and bound for southern Austria.

During their hair-raising ride down the mountains towards Lake Maggiore, the terrified POWs thought the truck would end up over the edge. Their German minders broke their journey at Bardonecchia, west of Turin, to enforce the recaptured prisoners to work on clearing a bomb-damaged tunnel through the Italian–French border. At a prison in Turin, Norm scavenged rubbish bins for cabbage and onions. Relocated via Spittal to Klagenfurt in Austria in November 1943, the deportees sat tightly in the enemy grip.

Many years later, Norm reflected on his sixteen days of freedom and their '350 kilometres laborious march' in northern Italy. Of their last day in Italy, he concluded that 'we deserved to get re-captured. It was in retrospect really ridiculous, fourteen men trudging through the mountains like an army on manoeuvres.'

There is a key disparity between Norm's account of the fateful bridge encounter and that written by Lloyd 'Mick' Wilson. Mick's recollections fill in a small grab of time, and exemplify that during peak stress, brief critical incidents may not be experienced or remembered the same by all persons involved. Mick's POW report of 1944 states that he was recaptured at the bridge with the wider group, albeit shortlived. 'In Macugnaga the Germans rounded up fourteen of us and took us to the *carabinieri* station for interrogation. Before going into the building, four of us ran from the escorted party. They fired some shots but no one was hit.' Mick reported that his getaways found help by Italians to cross to the Saas Valley.[5]

Mick Wilson along with Ernie Berg, Alfred Collins,[6] Neil Corke and 'Peter' Dawson, noted by Norm to be in their party, were amongst sixteen Australians who were relieved incomers to Switzerland on 28 September 1943.[7]

Col Booth and Peter Erickson were still at Hotel Alpe Noveis. Col's thoughts churned with worry about punitive action by fascist spies and the risk to Clementina Zaninetti: 'It was getting too dangerous for the woman.'[8]

Revived by the Zaninetti refuge, Col, probably with Peter, swaddled their gear at the end of September, readying to make their charge towards Macugnaga.

15
'FIRST TIME I HAD BEEN ON A BIKE FOR NEARLY THREE YEARS': LATE DEPARTURES

'Try to "collect" a bicycle. They proved invaluable ...'
—Foot and Langley, 1979[1]

Near the end of September, an approaching northern winter sent chilly calling cards to the plains. Soon, snowfall would dust mountainous areas to the north and douse crops and ground food sources. It dawned on POWs hanging about the farms and adjacent villages and wooded areas that it was now unlikely that Allies would soon liberate them.

For some, it still felt a jolt to leave the plains. Fraternising with farmers and civilians had created a paradigm shift for POWs interned at Campo 106 farms. *Ities* became individuals. Italians were a 'very temperamental race', thought Charles Warburton, 'but very kind-hearted—with of course exceptions—but generally they will share their last loaf of bread with you.'

In the third week of September 1943, Charles Warburton was downhearted when the sanctuary of the Montonero mill ended with a jolt.[2] Charles and his camp corporal were relaxing in the *osteria* on dusk with other prisoners and young Italians when a car abruptly halted outside. In a flash, someone screamed that *Jerries* were coming. Men scuttled into the garden and the trees. Through dusk haze, they saw someone charging towards them. In a panic, Charles visualised a German with a Tom gun.

'During those seconds,' before Charles realised it was an Italian, he 'realised how much freedom meant'.

Germans had come to ask the farm *padrone*, Bull, whether any prisoners were about. They demanded two of his cows, plus pigs and poultry. Juggling needs for labour and the risk of harbouring escapers, Bull hedged his bets. He asked that six men stay (two were ill) but offered good clothing and a map for the others. He understood the British were asking Italians to help and would pay for guides, and that organisations had arisen to assist escapers into Switzerland.

Two of the sick men were Charles's mates, so Charles decided to wait with them while others went ahead with Bull's food and money. In batches, the leavers went just before dawn. In the days that followed, word came that Germans had captured some POWs nearby.

Near the end of September, winter loomed. It was now unlikely that Allies would liberate them, Charles figured. 'In spite of the fact that we were living like hunted dogs, I still preferred now to times [in camp] as we were free and could—within reason—be our own bosses. I thought it best to remain as long as possible as, if we were to contact the organisation, it must be around Vercelli. We gained nothing by wandering about as practically every *padrone* was now too nervous to give us shelter and work. I had no intention—unless absolutely necessary—of attempting to cross the Alps without a guide. I knew food was non-existent there, and very soon we would be lost in that maze of soaring heights.'

Within days, another raid hit the mill. Outside the POWs' hayloft, German truck lights swept towards the Bull's courtyard. German soldiers spoke to Bull and his sister, and woke another man by sticking a Tom gun in his ribs and asking where the six prisoners slept. He told them the POWs had left. The Germans checked the stable under the lofts while nervous prisoners huddled and watched from above.

The following morning Charles was confronted by an Italian asking him where the prisoners slept. Charles replied vaguely with a wide sweep of his arm, hoping this Italian informer was none the wiser. Bull's sister was rattled by the raid and the Germans' warning that if they found prisoners, Bull would be shot. One *padrone* in the area had already been killed. Charles wished Bull had told him earlier, so he could've departed in darkness. 'I could see the game was up ... As before, we changed into uniform and packed our civilian clothes in haversacks, and collecting our meagre gear, we set off.' One of the Montonero POWs who'd headed north days earlier returned with negative news. 'Without aid, food was scarce; his guide cleared off. *Jerries* were around the foothills. He said what I'd guessed—without food and a guide, it was death from cold and exposure. Away from the road meant climbing row after row of mountains. This chap met chaps who had tried to get south. Some had got over the Po, but had to return as all roads were alive with Jerries and food was impossible to get.'

In early October, Charles's work gang straddled Montonero's precarious hospitality and the hideouts in nearby countryside. Villagers delivered bread and milk to the prisoners, in spite of fascist warnings. As if summoned by a click of fingers by the peckish POWs, three women were spotted on a nearby path, looking for them. The oldest woman secreted bread loaves in her apron; all three were upset. Uttering *'povero prigioneri'*, impoverished prisoners, she steadied a bottle of milk on the ground. Charles worried she gave up her dinner.

At times, the POWs had more milk and rice than needed, concerned civilians insisting they fill their dixies before they left. 'Rich today, poor tomorrow', Charles philosophised. One woman brought medicine to ease a face irritation caused from rice-blower dust. An elderly Italian waddled his bicycle towards them, sounding edgy, asking whether they desired to reach Switzerland. He knew Bull. Emphatically, the POW consensus was affirmative. This Italian urged them, for the time being, to hide in a big terraced drain outside Montonero until nightfall. Whether this man represented the enigmatic 'organisation' they'd heard about, they had no idea.

In buoyant moods, the men walked to Montonero after dusk, and sat on the canal bridge until an alert rang out: '*Tedesco, Tedesco*'. Clutching dixie bowls, they rushed to low willow trees. Touching the damp ground, they gathered armfuls of dry hay to buffer their bedding of blankets and overcoats against the cold. To their dismay, rain came down in sheets. Charles mused that the start to October was 'one of the dreariest nights of my existence'.

In the morning, wet twigs yielded to a small fire. Bread was toasted, tea was sipped. Shaves and washes refreshed their optimism. Their best Italian speaker went to the canal bank to meet their couriers, returning with bottled milk and instructions to return the bottles due to scarcity. The guide had heard that plans were afoot to move them and another group to Switzerland; the POWs must source civilian clothes and not return to Montonero's headquarters. Charles regretted that the mill was out of reach, and he was reluctant to plough on. 'North was the grim line of the Alps'. Some escapers had not made it across, they heard, and passes may have closed.

A POW returned the empty bottles to a designated spot the next morning. Charles was spotted by the tractor driver and his pregnant wife. She'd walked two kilometres to bring food on earlier days. They handed Charles a can of rice and broke some of their bread. Despite Charles's protestations, the driver waved away his concerns, patting him on the back.

A familiar lady 'in her sixties' working nearby with rice cutters, spotted Charles. She cried as she lifted her dinner from her apron, placing it in Charles's hands. He felt helpless. 'I could not speak the language enough to explain that we had sufficient.' Others brought meat and wine, insisting Charles and another POW drink it on the spot. They wouldn't leave without the recyclable bottle. Local contact Pedro met them on the canal bank, reminding them that if they needed to move during daylight to do so alone, pretending to be gathering rice. He chided them for walking with non-purposeful strides.

Another day dragged by. Snippets of information indicated that they'd travel in relays of six men, wearing civvies and hats, carrying limited gear. Charles, as nominated scribe, prepared a chit in case the Allies made an appearance. 'To any English or American officer whom it may concern, these people have been very kind and helpful, they have supplied us with food and money, and have done everything possible to aid our escape. We would be extremely grateful if you would show them every consideration.' POWs signed their names. They may not have heard that the US Fifth Army had by this time reached Naples. The chit was handed to the next visiting bearer of wine and cognac.

Readying to depart, and no longer part of the labour force, Charles memorised the sights of the farm and mill. The rice girls were still busy, and local men loaded drays ready to go to the mill. Another Montonero POW, Ronald Douglas,[3] reported that Italian efforts to usher them northward was prompted by an escaper-assistance organisation.

Two guides stood ready, Charles noticed, one dressed in a white overcoat. He was an officer, and inspected the unruly bunch of ex-prisoners. Hats were distributed. One POW confessed he couldn't ride a bicycle, so it was planned for others to double-dink him in relays. Through their interpreter, the officer listed instructions. He'd start first, with others to follow, at '100-yard intervals', watching his white coat. They'd cycle through Vercelli's outskirts for 16 kilometres, keeping vigilant watch of those in front. To settle nerves, he produced two bottles of wine, and one glass. Each POW swilled two full glasses. Most had not cycled for years. Charles scored the ladies' bike. He encapsulated the mixed emotions: 'At last we were on our way. It was glorious to realise that with luck, we might soon be clear of this wandering, hunted existence in beautiful Italy.' Although Charles thought it bizarre to be cycling a woman's bike on a winding path next to an irrigation canal heading towards a city base for enemy troops while following a white-coated officer, the spectacle and the wine charged Charles's spirits.

As the troupe neared Vercelli's outskirts, Charles sobered with thoughts of traffic and Germans. In front of him the 'double-dinking' pair wobbled. They pedalled past Germans and, to Charles's relief, none of them blinked an eyelid at his clothing ensemble. Traffic helped conceal them, but the busyness brought Charles to an unplanned halt. For several nervous moments, Charles lost sight of his white-coated leader. Catching up again, Charles and fellow cyclists pedalled onto the main road that led to Turin.

At a village, the pedalling prisoners dismounted, wheeling their bikes to a blacksmith's workshop where they silently waited while their guide examined the route. On his return, the group hustled onto a waiting bus. Civilians idly lined the street; Charles suspected they'd been deployed as look-outs. Passengers in the packed bus gawked at them in unspoken recognition of foreigners standing strap-hung, not speaking to each other. One elderly lady was annoyed when the men refused to tell her the time.

On a winding road the bus climbed and lurched. The standing men buffeted from side to side, without uttering a word for two and half hours until reaching Borgosesia, on the eastern banks of the Sesia River flowing south-west of the Italian northern lake district.

Charles doesn't indicate whether the bus's northward journey followed the western or eastern side of the Sesia. Either route traverses approximately 55 kilometres, Milan's outskirts 30 kilometres to the east.

Charles observed Borgosesia as a fair size, noting its cobblestone road as 'necessary in any town where there are steep rises, as in winter the ice would make it impossible for a horse to keep a foothold'. Charles checked out the form of the mountain girls. 'They are far different to ordinary girls and women of the plains. Living amongst the mountains naturally means much exercise—especially for the legs—and as their food seemed to consist of a simple diet eg. macaroni, rice, cider and apples and of course bread, they were very healthy, virile and had rosy complexions. They are immensely strong, wear big heavy mountain boots, and carry everything on their backs in big wicker baskets.'

At their Borgosesia shelter that night, an elderly woman in well-worn clothes cooked dinner in a pot suspended over a fire. A young male fiddled with a radio, trying to tune it to English news. The woman inquired about the Australians' ages and the duration of their captivity. Charles said he'd been a POW for about two years, being captured at Tobruk in September 1941. Her reply was unexpected. She considered him lucky. 'I've been a prisoner of the fascists for twenty-two years,' she spat. 'For half my life I've been under fascist rules. They came and got my brother seven years ago. He's been exiled on an island ever since. I have never heard whether he's alive or dead.'

After dinner, blankets were issued to each man. Lantern light illuminated a winding path uphill to a *baita*, a small wooden shed warmed by resident goats and fowls. Charles looked out in the morning, reassuring himself they were well and truly in the foothills. Some POWs braved a crisp wash in a spring while others cooked chestnuts inside the barn. Twelve other escapers paraded in to join their number, followed by eighteen South Africans with a guide.

Coming into the third week of October, the cold mountain air nipped through their clothes. Charles spotted a person climbing uphill to deliver food. Understanding that food was short in the area, they thanked the Italians for their small offerings. A German aeroplane roared overhead, presumably searching for escapers, reminding the ex-prisoners to keep as out of sight as practicable. German armoured patrols frequently visited Borgosesia.

In the morning an elderly man entered the crowded hut to wake them. 'The stars were still shining' as Charles's crew followed a tall lean elderly bearded man with a birthmark on his face. Heading upslope, the largest POW was entrusted to carry the copper. Two South Africans squirmed from injured ankles; their pace slowed as they carried their share of gear and food. The guides suggested that they wait until another group came through, but they preferred to continue.

Charles was not alone in craving a diet of greater variety. Apples abundantly brightened the trees, a beacon for a large group of supperless travellers who'd speedily strip a tree. Local cheese made from goats' milk was a treat for their POW bellies. Chestnut groves yielded important winter stores and Charles's agricultural eye studied the gathering of chestnuts into wicker baskets. 'These baskets are made of strong cane ... they have leather straps to put the arms through and, when inserting the arms, the person has to kneel. When walking, it is usual to have hands clasped in front.'

Charles recognised that these farmers were very poor, to his comparative experience. Wood-cutting gave supplementary livelihood. Pasture plots were only as big as the average garden plot in Charles's home town.

A nearby stream gave fresh water. Braving the chill, most did not come back for seconds. Brisk rubdowns with towels failed to bring warm glow to their skin. Their summer of farm work was behind them, an uncertain winter ahead. In contrast to the fit local girls, their tanned summer-laboured forearms had faded and thinned.

Ernie Sparnon
Courtesy Bruce Fellowes

John Laws
NAA B883 NX16597

Norm Freeberg
Courtesy Ann Plumb

Paul Lavallee
Courtesy Ann Plumb

Ernie Berg
NAA B883 QX5190

Thomas Anderson
NAA B883 VX34767

Lloyd Wilson
NAA B883 WX6100

Frank Jobson
NAA B883 QX3237

Bob Ward
NAA B883 WX5890

Norm Bailey
NAA B883 WX13384

Thomas Davis
NAA B883 VX47656

Frank Sharp
NAA B883 NX60017

Colin Weekes
NAA B883 NX38152

Charles Warburton
NAA B883 WX5299

Frank Page
NAA B883 QX1639

Bill Waller
NAA B883 VX47958

Ted Newbey
NAA B883 WX7406

Les Parker
Courtesy of Jean Beswick

> My dear, (post mark date)
> *(Data del timbro postale)*
>
> I am alright (I have not been wounded (or) I have
> Sto bene (non sono stato ferito (o) sono
> been slightly wounded). I am a prisoner of the Italians and
> stato ferito leggermente). Sono stato catturato dagli Italiani e
> I am being treated well.
> mi trovo bene.
> Shortly I shall be transferred to a prisoner's camp and
> Nei prossimi giorni sarò trasferito in un campo di
> I will let you have my new address.
> prigionieri del quale vi comunicherò l'indirizzo.
> Only then I will be able to receive letters from you
> Soltanto allora potrò ricevere la vostra corrispondenza
> and to reply.
> e rispondervi.
> With love (signature)
> Saluti affettuosi (firma)

1941 POW postcard advice to home.
Courtesy of Elaine Milbourne

1942, Bert, Bill and Harry Wilson
Courtesy of Harry Wilson

Harold Sanderson
Antonio Manfroi,
Il Soldato Harold

1941, Tel Aviv, (L to R) Harold Davis, unknown, Jack Nie, unknown POWs.
Courtesy of Jack Nie

1943, POWs at Salussola, Baraccone or nearby camp.
Courtesy of Bill Rudd

Baraccone or nearby farm, 1943. Bill Rudd in middle row fourth from left.
Courtesy of Bill Rudd

1943, Salussola or Baraccone POWs.
Courtesy of Bill Rudd

Carpeneto POWs, 1943.
Courtesy of Bob and Norma Kerr, Mat Sincock and Bruce Wilson

Carpeneto POWs, 1943.
Courtesy of Bob and Norma Kerr,
Mat Sincock and Bruce Wilson

*1943, Carpeneto, Brinley Jones and Titch
Messenger.*
Courtesy of Jones, Sincock and
Wilson collections

Carpeneto POWs, 1943.
Courtesy of Bob and Norma Kerr,
Mat Sincock and Bruce Wilson

*1943 Carpeneto; Brinley Jones (centre)
with Charles Stuart and Dudley Sedgwick.*
Courtesy of Bob and
Norma Kerr

Carpeneto POWs, 1943.
Courtesy of Bob and Norma Kerr, Mat Sincock and
Bruce Wilson

1943 probably at or near Tronzano, Don Radnell's POW group.
Courtesy of Daryl Radnell

Carpeneto farm buildings, not including wartime accommodation for POWs which has been demolished.
Courtesy of Carla Bonello and Lucia Vaccarino

Carla Bonello, Carpeneto, wearing a shirt she refashioned from a POW's shirt.
Courtesy of Carla Bonello
Lucia Vaccarino

Carpeneto tavern
Courtesy of Carla Bonello and
Lucia Vaccarino

Lachelle farm buildings, 2019.
Katrina Kittel

Santuario di Oropa postcard.
Col Booth collection

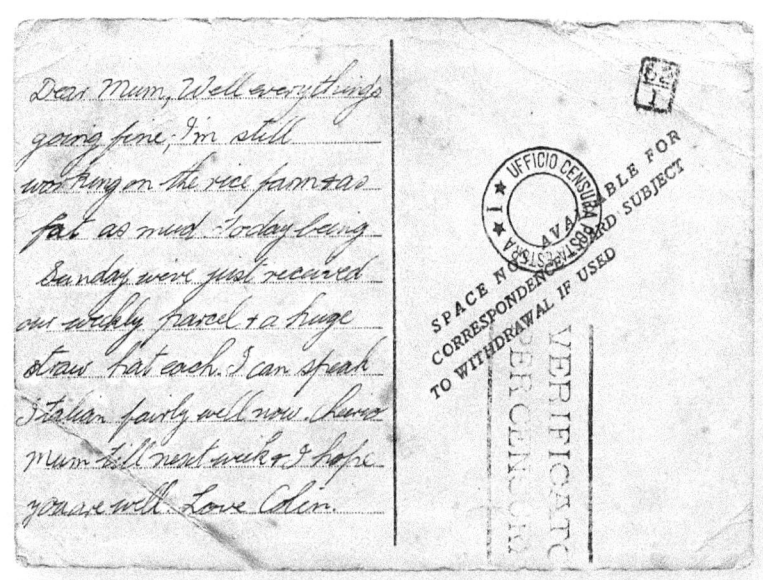

1943 POW Postcard from Col Booth at Campo 106 farm to his mother Ruby in Auburn (Sydney) hospital.
Col Booth collection

Col Booth's notebook page listing Italian placenames–some with phonetic spelling.
Col Booth collection

1943, Ted Price and a group of POWs. Photo taken in same location as Booth trio (see photo below), perhaps near Allodi or Cascina Gattesco. Ted Price notes in Bill Rudd collection

1943, Col Booth Peter Erickson with unidentified POW. Col Booth collection

Hotel Alpe Noveis, Monte Barone.
Courtesy of Liliana Cerruti

Hotel Alpe Noveis, Angelo Zaninetti in pointed hat.
Courtesy of Liliana Cerruti

Hotel Alpe Noveis proprietors Angelo and Clementina Zaninetti.
Courtesy of Liliana Cerruti

Frank and Nina Secchia, 1955.
Courtesy of Piero Secchia

Nick Lawrie, Jim Kinder, Dick Gill and Jack Duggan at the Ansaldi home, late 1943.
Port Lincoln News, June 1982

Saas-Fee Switzerland 1943 postcard.
Photo Klopfenstein Adelboden, Col Booth collection

Saas-Almagell Switzerland postcard, early 1940s.
Col Booth collection

Hotel Monte Moro, Saas Almagell, brochure.
Courtesy of Annette Andenmatten

1943, Monte Moro pass looking to Monte Rosa postcard.
Col Booth collection

Col Booth annotates this photo as, 'our first meal in Switzerland 4 Oct 1943'.
Peter Watson Bates, print in Col Booth collection, Alexander Turnbull Library (NZ) website displays an undamaged image

POWs, boots on arrival to Switzerland probably 4 October 1943, Nick Emery says shoes with bandages were the ones given to him by Italian helper.
Photograph by Peter Watson Bates, Col Booth collection

1943, Hotel Mattmark and sentries.
Peter Watson Bates, Col Booth collection

Mattmark Hotel 1943. Mattmark Dam, built 1960s, covers this site.
Peter Watson Bates, Col Booth collection

Macugnaga Pecetto postcard.
Giuseppe Oberto edition

Postcard of Varallo.

Rifugio Oberto Maroli, Monte Moro.
Katrina Kittel

Giuseppe Oberto, alpine guide Macugnaga
Photo by Paolo Zanzi in *Giuseppe Oberto, un Walser Guida Alpina.* 2011

Macugnaga. Alpe Pedriola. Rifugio Zamboni postcard.
Rip Vietata

Pecetto Macugnaga mountaineers cemetery and Monte Rosa.
Katrina Kittel

Pecetto Macugnaga postcard.
Courtesy of Ann Plumb

This group of happy cleaned up POWs were new arrivals to Switzerland, probably at Wil, 7 October 1943. Courtesy of Ron Maitland

No. _____

EMERGENCY CERTIFICATE.

THIS IS TO CERTIFY THAT

BOOTH. Colin.

is a British Subject by birth, having been born at

Sydney. Australia.

This Certificate is valid for the journey to the United Kingdom and residence in Switzerland.

(Signature of Bearer.)

The validity of this certificate expires TWO years from date of issue and must be surrendered to the Immigration Officer at the place of Arrival.

(Signed) His Majesty's Consul General
          His Majesty's Consul.

(Date) 23 DEC 1943

Col Booth's Swiss Emergency Certificate.
Col Booth collection

1944 Adelboden, L to R, John Shaw, Ross Wycherley, Col Booth, Peter Erickson and Dan Serfontein on skis.
Col Booth collection

1944 Switzerland, evadés band, Eddie Sincock on trumpet.
Courtesy of W and M Williams

Bob Ward, Bill Pannowitz, Norm Woosnam and Max Wills, probably Switzerland, 1944.
Courtesy Alma Ward

1944, Switzerland, (L to R) Harry Sibraa, Charlie Fraser and Roy Jenks.
Courtesy of Terry Sibraa

1944, POW group in Switzerland.
Courtesy of W and M Williams

1944, POWs gather in Switzerland.
Courtesy of W and M Williams

Adelboden Switzerland postcard 1944.
Col Booth collection

1944, Adelboden POW skiers, Nick Emery wears 13.
Courtesy of Nick Emery

Arona and Lago Maggiore postcard.
1935 Cesare Capello

1944, Ottenbach, Col Booth,
Frau Sidler and Fritz and
British POW Bernard Thompson.
Col Booth collection

1944 cartoon in POW newspaper Marking Time. *Purchases of Swiss watches were popular for souvenirs and gifts to take home.*

1944. Bombay. L to R, unknown, Vic Angrove, Norm Bailey, Jack Nie and Stan Bailey.
Courtesy of Jack Nie

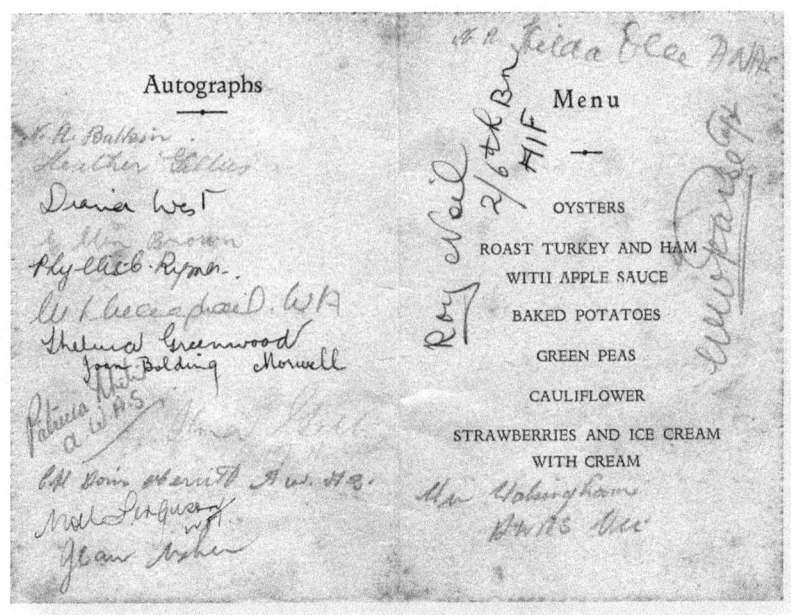

1944. Menu at reception for returning POWs, Melbourne 17 November 1944.
Mostly contains signatures by AWAS servicewomen. See Notes for list of AWAS names.
Col Booth collection

1943 or 1944, Propaganda leaflet dropped by planes.

Lloyd Moule (centre back) with POWs and others, in Switzerland.
Courtesy of Lloyd Moule

2018, Tavigliano monument to Smedley, Clark and Batt
Courtesy Luciano Guala

2018, Tavigliano monument includes Smedley, Clark and Batt.
Courtesy Luciano Guala

Jim Brennan
Jan James, *Forever Warriors*

Raleigh Hoy
NAA B883 WX2773

Arthur Fogg
NAA B883 WX6905

Douglas Smedley
NAA B883 VX42361

Eddie Albert
Trish Albert, Unsung Hero

Eva Cerruti
Courtesy of Cerruti family

*Trivero monument (at Ponte Babbiera) to Nicholls, Harvey, Blain, Liddell and Wolfe.
Note that the plaque has date of 5.5.1944.*
Claudio Martignon

Clive Liddell   *Ernie Wolfe*

COMMONWEALTH OF AUSTRALIA.

STATUTORY DECLARATION.

I, Stanley Eric PEEBLES (formerly VX31755) of 9 Hugh St., Footscray,

do solemnly and sincerely declare that the statement attributed to Pte. Black was made by me to an Intelligence Officer in Camp at Eastbourne and was corroborated by him.

The group including Pte. Miller, Cpl. Bowes, and about twelve Italians were captured in the hills above Vallimosso in North Italy in Province of Piemonte during an attack against the Partisans on the 20th February '44, and were shot the next day against the cemetery wall at Mosso Santa Maria.

The Partisan Commandant recovered Pay Books, personal papers, etc., from the bodies which were afterwards buried in the cemetery.

The Italian Lieutenant who had command of the forces quartered at Vallomosso for about 5 months and who was responsible for the execution could be easily identified by the fact that his right arm was severed above the elbow, and is well known by the community.

The Partisan Commandant who recovered pay books, etc., and whom I believe still has possession of these, was known as Attilio and was Commander of the Partisan police in the Biella area of Piedmonte.

And I make this solemn declaration by virtue of the *Statutory Declarations Act* 1911 conscientiously believing the statements contained therein to be true in every particular.

S. E. Peebles.

Declared at Melbourne the twentieth day of February 19 46, before me,

L. Legat

Capt. Aust. Military Forces.

NOTE.—Any person who wilfully makes a false statement in a Statutory Declaration is guilty of an indictable offence, and is liable to imprisonment, with or without hard labour, for four years.

Statutory Declaration by Stanley Peebles re death of Harry Miller.
(NAA B883 VX31755)

COMMONWEALTH OF AUSTRALIA

STATUTORY DECLARATION

[1] *Here insert name, address, and occupation of person making the declaration.*

I, [1] Frank William BLEWETT
WX9047
111 Brandon St
South Perth.

[2] *Here insert matter declared to. Where the matter is long it should be set out in numbered paragraphs*

declare [2]   , do solemnly and sincerely

(1) On the 8th May 1944 together with VX48203 Pte. R. McIntyre 2/32 Bn of 3 Johnson St., Ashburton Victoria I was loose in Italy in the Italian Alps.

(2) While there we knew that –
Pte W.O. Harvey WX10591   2/32 Bn
Pte E. Wolfe   2/32 Bn
Cpl.   Nicholls   2/28 Bn
Pte. Harold Blain   2/24 Bn
Pte Clive Liddell   A.A.S.C.
and an Englishman were living in a house about half a mile from us.

(3) About the end of the month (May 1944) we were told by civilians that the six had been killed and that they (the civilians) had buried them.

(4) We went to the house, located the graves.

(5) We removed some of the soil and were able to verify that at least 3 bodies were in the grave.

(6) We did not identify the bodies.

(7) We put a marble stone over the grave, had the names engraved on it.

(8) We then left the area and remained in Northern Italy until rescued by the 5th Army.

And I make this solemn declaration by virtue of the *Statutory Declarations Act*, 1911, conscientiously believing the statements contained therein to be true in every particular.

[3] *Signature of person making the declaration.*

[3] (Sgd.) F.W. Blewett

Declared at 109 Convalescent Depot,   the Fourteenth
day of   September,   1945 , before me,

[4] *Signature of person before whom the declaration is made.*

[4] (Sgd.) B.L. Grieve
WX6
Capt

[5] *Here insert title of person before whom the declaration is made.*

NOTE.—Any person who wilfully makes a false statement in a Statutory Declaration is guilty of an indictable offence, and is liable to imprisonment, with or without hard labour, for four years.

Statutory Declaration by Frank Blewett re murder of Liddell, Blain, Harvey, Wolfe and Nicholls.
(NAA B883 WX9047)

1945, Fred Tabram in partisan uniform. Courtesy Ray Tabram

Mariuccia (Maria) Olivero of Ronsecco sent this photo to Fred Tabram. Courtesy Ray Tabram

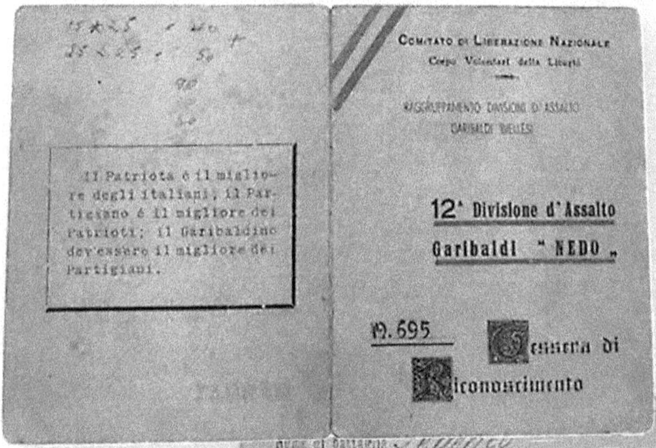

Front

Rear

Fred Tabram, partisan ID card. Courtesy Ray Tabram

Raimondo Febbrario's granddaughter with a POW, probably British.
Courtesy Amanda Girardi

Raimondo Febbrario's granddaughter with a POW, probably British.
Courtesy Amanda Girardi

Raimondo Febbrario with his wife and daughter. At Ronsecco the family sheltered Fred Tabram, Bernie Bruce and Jim Brennan for a time. These POWs left their names and addresses with Raimondo.
Courtesy of Amanda Girardi

1947, Col Booth and Peter Erickson with Pamela and Peter, probably at Braidwood.
Col Booth collection

1981, Snowy Drew and Jim Wilson.
Courtesy Mrs Wilson

1969, Col and Evelyn Booth.
Col Booth collection

Nick Emery at home, with wall of photos.
Katrina Kittel

2003, Tom Anderson and General Cosgrove.
Herald Sun 2003.

16
'Monte Moro was testing our resolve': From Turlo to Moro

> 'The fact that one had actually got out [of captivity] was an enormous stimulant to morale; it did not always last through to the end of an escaper's journey. Moreover, the closing stage of an escape or an evasion—traversing the battle front, or crossing into neutral territory ... was often as difficult as the original breakout ... and this final stage, when physical and emotional exhaustion were at their most intense, was a real test of endurance and of fieldcraft. Many, too many, attempts foundered just when success was in sight. This above all was the moment when a prisoner needed a sense of humour and a sense of proportion; needed not to take himself and his fate too tragically; and to be able, if he was hard-headed enough, to observe what errors he had made ...'
>
> —Foot and Langley, 1979[1]

At Macugnaga's village of Pecetto, the old mountaineer churchyard's bell-tower heralds the beginning of the summit-searching trails ascending towards Monte Moro on the Italian–Swiss border. At this closing stage of evasion, escapers dug into psychological and physical reserves to commence the final push to their objective: Swiss territory. By the beginning of October 1943, approximately 160 AIF POWs had stepped into Switzerland.[2] Many escapers had followed Italian tips to complete these last laps via the well-known Monte Moro Pass, well-guarded on both Italian and Swiss sides during wartime. Some escapers diverted, by choice or chance, to just north of Moro and the lesser-known Mondelli Pass favoured by wartime contraband operators.

Mondelli Pass has two saddles on top. The north-east saddle crosses the slopes of Galmen into Ofental. Down from the south-west saddle was a small glacier, Talliboden-Gletscher above Talliboden, or Saastal.[3]

On their journey through the villages in the far north, POWs were often hailed with cries of 'where are you going?' and best wishes for the journey. Women wept at their plight, planting kisses on their cheeks. Macugnaga was founded by the Walser, a Swiss German-speaking people who colonised some parts of northern Piedmont in the 13th century when they migrated from Switzerland into these valleys, taking their culture with them as they escaped persecution. They were an enterprising ethnic group who moulded their lifestyle to the mountains. Many village homes in traditional Walser style were built of wood over stonework capped by slate stone roofs. Along the roadsides and trails of these northern villages, little shrines populated with Madonna statuettes and patron saints bore silent witness to the parade of prisoners. Don Radnell quipped that 'they had more saints than you can poke a stick at.'[4]

Taking an old pilgrim path on their way towards the Swiss border, Queensland's Arthur and Tim Jobson with Joe Newbey stumbled upon the Santuario di Oropa sanctuary's architectural ensemble. Its monumental buildings contrasted to the simple peasant dwellings in the foothills, its dome a fundamental reference point for travellers and pilgrims.

Tim Jobson reported that later in September 1943, they 'met some people who took us to join the rebels at Oropa.'[5] They stayed with them for three days. Arthur wrote that their hosts wanted them to stay longer, but the offer was reconsidered the following morning, 29 September, when Germans began to fire from lower ground towards planes.[6] The power supply to the aerial railway was cut, putting it out of action. The Jobsons thought it best to clamber down to the valley, hearing that 'Switzerland was only three sleeps away'.

Invited into a café, discussion turned to Switzerland, and their rampaged boots. Their dinner host had boots left by another escaper days before. Arthur dismayed that these were far too small, but a solution was found: 'Joe was wearing a pair of nearly new size 9s and I normally wore 7s, so we were on our feet again.' Five-Miler's boots and feet were wrecks. He was the elder POW in their party and couldn't face going on. He was adopted by a family who promised to shelter him until war's end. Joe Newbey and the brothers Jobson resumed their 'safari' the next morning.

At Scopello, a village elder paraded his World War One medals. His son was missing on the Russian front. The POWs bedded down in a haystack.

Moving on, they were hailed by an elderly lady. She was picking apples and offered some to Arthur, inquiring about his health. She sobbed when Arthur told her that a bout of malaria was slowing him down.

Walking through villages that appeared to be unoccupied, they sensed they were being watched from behind windows and doors. To confirm it, a lady suddenly opened an upstairs window to inquire whether they'd eaten. Tim and Joe misunderstood the question, or the dialect, and replied with a polite 'Yes'. Arthur expressed his consternation. 'You blokes just talked us out of a meal. The lady asked us, "Have you eaten?" Not "Will you eat?!"' Residents alerted them to an approaching German patrol, and that a group of POWs was being accompanied by two guides to hike to the next range. The Jobsons aimed to catch up with these thirteen men.

'We started early next morning,' scribed Arthur. 'When the crest of the range was reached one of our guides pointed to a higher range across the valley and said, "There is Switzerland." For the first time in our safari it would have really hurt me if we'd been picked up by Germans.'

From the Turlo Pass Monte Rosa's face peered over the range, waiting for passersby.

Caught up in the waves of wandering escapers funnelling at Pecetto and other Macugnaga settlements at the alpine frontier, brothers Arthur and Tim Jobson with Joe Newbey descended from high ground to Macugnaga as October commenced. The Jobson field troops contemplated their next battle objective, to spear uphill to Monte Moro, with trepidation. On the previous day, a party of about nineteen prisoners was nabbed by German patrol. Arthur understood that POWs still in uniforms were chided by hosts to change into Italian threads.

The Jobson trekkers woke at 2am, and thirty minutes later they stepped outside. 'As dawn was breaking, we walked along a path about five feet wide, set in the face of the precipice.' To Arthur's summary, 'this seemed to extend over a thousand feet below and a long way above us to the top. We reached a place where the path came to a stop, and the rock face extended across the path.'

Rookie mountaineers were plunged into problem-solving. 'The method of overcoming this obstacle,' realised Arthur, 'was via holes sunk in the face of the rock at shoulder height, and one at toe level. The top hole was grasped with the right hand; the right foot was pushed into the bottom hole. Then one swung over nothing but air, and felt for similar holes on the other side of the rocky outcrop. Releasing the right hand and foot, one swung past the obstacle, and resumed his travels.'

Far down the slope, conifers resembled mushrooms touched by faint dawn light. Monte Rosa's long face began to glow; dawn light woke her highest serrated peaks first. The Jobsons' guide searched with binoculars every now and then for German activity in the village below. Up here, machine-gun fire could still reach them. Just before the snow-line, guides reminded the POWs to steer clear of the crest because of fascist patrols.

Mountain traffic increased to their left as numerous small groups of civilian and military refugees trod towards the sky. The Jobsons met a Jewish family who were fleeing with their teenage daughter and a son who had a bullet wound in his knee. The boy was carried to the top by one of their two Italian guides. Everyone hoped that the boy would survive this exodus.

As the Jobson journeymen reached the top of the Moro pass about midday on 2 October 1943, cloud-free skies beckoned their view down to Saastal and further down the Saas Valley into Switzerland. Three soldiers held sentinel at the bottom of the snow-line dressed in German-type uniforms, wearing coal-scuttle helmets. The POWs felt dread, but their stamina wouldn't sustain turning back. For eight hours, they proceeded downslope, helping each other to plough through snow until they faced the three unknown waiting soldiers. They struggled to envisage how they might dodge or fight them.

They need not have worried. With little formality, the guards hastened them to a reception depot. Soldiers requested them to show passports as identification. Taken aback by this demand, the Australians flashed their army paybooks. Arthur's account applauds their ease of entry to Switzerland. Unexpectedly, mates homed in just ahead of them and sidled up to Arthur and Tim for hearty greetings.

Arthur, Tim and Joe were invited to have a cup of tea of unusual taste, made from linden leaves. It went down a treat. They joked that they expected the teaspoons to stay upright, the Swiss had put so much sugar in their cups. Arthur was elated by the strong contrast of the Swiss 'grub' and treatment, as opposed to that dished out by Grupignano authorities earlier that year.

Arthur, on his Swiss entrée, spotted the daughter of the Jewish refugee family they'd encountered on the mountain. In celebratory gesture of the embrace by the Swiss, she offered lollies to the Australians. Arthur did not have the heart to accept one.

Vic Wills wallowed in the Swiss reception on the same day.[7] In all probability, he was brother to Max Wills of Bob Ward's group. Like the Jobsons, Vic had briefly engaged with rebels near Santuario di Oropa for a few days. Ron Strickland, without his brother Bill, also appreciated the welcome, as had about 60 other POWs.[8] Further east, Australian lieutenants Tom Elliott from Queensland and Ron Jones from Melbourne touched down on Swiss soil.⁹ They had leapt from the same train from which father and son Sharp had jumped on the night of 13/14 September.

While the 24 September arrivals slept in warm Swiss quarters, Ron Maitland and his Kiwi offsider 'Lofty' Johnson tussled with Monte Moro's indifferent moods.¹⁰ Their guide, too, had ended his shift, leaving Ron and Lofty to slowly navigate snow patches as deep as a metre. They struggled onto slippery ledges less than a metre wide, perching precariously over 1500-metre drops. Wearing escaper footwear, their boots were not up to it. Snow slop made them walk like awkward toddling infants. 'Our first night on the mountain was spent huddled under narrow shelves of rock, pressed against large, frozen boulders being ever mindful of the fall to certain death only feet away,' Ron jotted sixty years later.

'Our sense of self-preservation allowed limbs, chilled to the bone, and minds sapped of strength to snatch only shreds of restless sleep lest our exhausted bodies should roll too far out and over the edge.' Lofty, in his gravelly voice, told Ron that if they made it, they deserved a 'bloody army decoration'.

At early light they set off, 'upward and onward', Ron wrote. 'We were so far into the heavens I thought we must've reached the pinnacle. My heart sank when I saw we'd reached the highest point in the direction we were climbing, but a higher peak stood in the distance, offering us no access without retracing our steps, forcing us to try a different route. Monte Moro was testing our resolve. I admit that on more than one occasion I almost capitulated. Too many times we zigzagged through a steep icy labyrinth only to be blockaded by impassable terrain, crushing our spirits and dissipating our strength. Surging frustration and anger then became our driving force, bolstering our determination and pushing us on. Would this nightmare ever end? One concession was abundant, pristine water flowing through the rocks. We drank it, we bathed in it and used it so supplement our meagre rations of polenta.

'As we ascended the slopes, the snow lay thicker on the ground. Our light clothing offered no protection against blustering winds and frozen earth. Our extremities were completely numb and the effects of frostbite were becoming a serious concern. At least our faces were covered with heavy beards, barriers against the penetrating cold, relentless wind and piercing sunlight. Our bodies were spent and our spirits deflated. The reality that we would not be able to survive this torment indefinitely was becoming increasingly evident.

'Suddenly, almost unexpectedly, we were there! It seemed impossible that we had finally reached the summit. We were so excited we wasted no time getting over to the other side. Just as suddenly, our hopes were dashed. We could not believe our misfortune when we encountered soldiers on skis. This must be a German ski patrol, we thought. We watched and waited.'

The soldiers skied out of sight. On 3 October, Ron and Lofty washed their faces in a stream and approached a hut. A German-speaking Swiss officer listened to Ron nervously explain their position and replied: 'Welcome to Switzerland.' Not knowing what would happen next, Ron drew on his philosophy: 'Take every day as it comes.' His gut felt cautiously optimistic. 'I kept one eye open, half expecting the rug to be pulled from under my feet at any moment.'

Nick Emery seized his escape opportunity the same day, 11 September, as Bob Ward's group.[11] Nick also headed south to confront German-guarded bridges and retreated back north. Nick was frustrated he could not get word to his family after leaving camp, having 'nothing to write on, nothing to write with'.

In 1944, Nick reported that he travelled on foot to Arborio on the western banks of the River Sesia north of Vercelli, where he was sheltered and fed by Ida Constanza.[12] His group of six split into groups of two to be less conspicuous and to more easily score assistance. They chucked battle-dress in favour of Italian discards. Nick was pleased to be with a POW who spoke some Italian, Victorian Charlie Mills of 2/32 Battalion, a former butcher from Ashburton.[13] POWs who absorbed Italian in the Italian camps had an advantage, even amongst regional dialect variations. As another POW put it, prisoners put effort into learning 'proper' Italian but 'each village was a different dialect'.[14]

Nick and Charlie were in sync about several rules of evasion. They would avoid main towns; they'd keep moving, *sempre sul*. They'd be careful about female advances, particularly as one woman took 'more than a motherly interest' in Charlie. They agreed to eat what they found or were offered, including polenta, tomatoes, grapes and frogs. For a day or two, food to hand was a couple of teaspoons of sugar. Nick was aware that his fair hair startled some Italians who mistook him for a young German spy. As they scouted through a parade of hills and valleys, two shepherds took them in for one night, sharing lamb stew cooked in a large metal cauldron over a fire. Satiated, the Australians slept soundly on firm ground.

In his post-war report, Nick noted two persons in particular; each provided a week of food and shelter: Cabrino Elveziro of Pianceri Alto and the aforementioned Ida Constanzo of Arborio. Nick and Charlie accepted brief respite with a baker and his family, but whether this person is one of the above Italians is not known. The baker's children were anxious about the strange visitors and the baker felt wary about informers, so they requested the POWs to get moving. The baker escorted them uphill, advising they stay on the route, *sempre sul*.

Within Nick's report, and that of others, there are anomalies with the spelling of Italian placenames, due to limited signage of off-road routes and the phonetics of an unfamiliar language. Heading northward from Arborio, Nick's list of placenames indicates a string of hamlets—Pila, Piode, Riva, Campertogno and Scopello—located along stretches of the River Sesia. Nick and Charlie's flimsy boots splashed through waterways sweeping ice melt down from the Alps.

Reaching the base of the border-searching trails in Macugnaga, Nick and Charlie connected with two guides. Their party of nine men fleeing Italy comprised two Yugoslavian officers, three other Australians, one Italian and a New Zealander, probably Maori POW Robert 'Bob' Hohaia, ex-Baraccone prisoner.[15] The footwear of the group was as varied as their places of origin, but shabby condition was the point of commonality. Nick felt he'd drawn the short straw, wearing women's shoes that were falling apart, insecurely tied into place by cloth.

At 3am the party had begun their climb towards the mountain pass, taking detours over tricky terrain if there was concern of being spotted. They heard about a British escaper who fell down a crevasse, with no chance of rescue. Guides took them to the smugglers' route and departed, retreating to their home or base, perhaps readying the next batch of newcomers.

Close to the border and with no clear way ahead, the abandoned journeymen made their own decisions. Nick and Charlie shouted and waved towards the general direction of Switzerland. Their small party descended the slopes to the Saas Valley on 4 October 1943.

Swiss records list twenty Australians arriving on 2 October; twenty-four, mostly Victorians, on 3 October; and coming up solidly behind them, fourteen Australians, mostly New South Welshmen, entered via Switzerland's southern ranges on 4 October.[16]

A former farmhand from Ashley near Moree, Ron 'Fitzy' Fitzgerald enlisted into and remained in the 2/3rd Anti-Tank Regiment during his service in North Africa leading to his capture at Mechili on 8 April 1941.[17] From capture and throughout captivity, 'Fitzy' stuck with four regimental mates who'd travelled from the Moree plains to enlist. Interned in Italy in 1943, the five friends left quick as a flash from Selve situated three kilometres north of Veneria. Ron put it succinctly: 'I was not going to buggerise about.'[18]

On 11 September 1943, Fitzy, Carl and Paul Carrigan, Lloyd Ledingham and Ron McIntosh stole a restless sleep at nearby Cascina Tambarina.[19]

A week or so later, a *padrone* and an Italian officer associated with the resistance asked POWs to meet at nearby Selve farm. From there, three Italians escorted them during nine hours of walking through stormy rain to a meeting point. Fitzy diarised that they were 'dog tired, wet through, hungry and with boots full of blisters. We had nothing to eat since the raw eggs two days ago.' Pre-arranged, a green tie-wearing officer whistled 'Lilli Marlene' to attract their attention. They heard that another POW party was going through, around 140 with a horse and cart loaded with Breda machine-guns. Fifty men had rifles. Petro, the leader, was an ex-contraband runner. At Pista Nuova, just south of Biella, they were given polenta and milk for dinner.

According to Carl's notes, at daylight they camped south-west of Biella. The Moree five heard that 40,000 German troops were based there. 'We pulled up at a place; we ate all of their figs and grapes and nearly everything else they had,' remarked Fitzy. 'We found their potato patch, their winter supply. Not far out of Biella and 40,000 Gerry SS troops in Biella. And it's their tucker we're pinching!' Taking food from Italians was a different matter and weighed heavy on Fitzy's conscience.

About this time, while sheltering in a hayloft, the POWs were forewarned that Germans were approaching. In the rush to skedaddle from the raid, Ron McIntosh chose a different direction to run. The four others heard that Ron had been recaptured.[20] As an Italian officer and his American girlfriend spoke to the four POWs, Fitzy was astounded that in front of them, 'along came this blooming tram', a tram that ran from Biella to Oropa.

The Moree brigade tramped on the heels of the Jobson brothers to tackle the stiff incline of the Turlo Pass. On the Turlo Pass approaching the Anzasca Valley, they were directed onto a high trail to another mountain hut to camp the night. The trail was dotted with several stone summer shepherd huts. The Moree men carried macaroni and rice and set about gathering brushwood to fire up the copper. Fitzy later admitted that his enthusiastic stoking of the fire resulted in burnt rice and the shepherd hut engulfed by flames.

On 2 October, atop Monte Turlo, they took in a magnificent sunrise and descended to a Quazarra village. When the Moree men reached a destination, by their guesswork to be only a day from the border, they sought help. 'We struck a young bloke, a young kid,' Fitzy recounted. 'We said, "Where's Switzerland, will you help us?" and he said, "Up there, over that mountain."' The boy wanted the greatcoats, a valuable item on the black market. 'I want pay,' he told the POWs before taking them to a hut for the night.

Very early next morning he brought them each a boiled potato, followed by a drink. Although Fitzy did not give it a name, the firewater was probably *grappa*. In addition to hosts' beds, warm fires and cigarettes, a strong drop of *grappa* brought glow to escapers' cheeks. Arch Scott, a New Zealand escaper, was persuaded by an Italian host to carry *grappa* in case of remedial needs. '*Grappa*,' he vividly recalled, 'was a colourless, innocuous-looking liquid made from *sarpa*—the skin, stalks and seeds of the grapes after the juice had been pressed out of them. It was distilled by each family from its share of the grape harvest ... the theory was that *un po' di riscaldamento*, a little warmth, would remedy most minor ills.'[21] Eric Newby, a British escaper at large in the Apennines, wrote in his book that he considered *grappa* to be stronger than army rum.[22]

'We did not know what it was but by Jeez it was a GOOD drink!' quipped Fitzy. Warmed by the beverage, Fitzy's four set off at 2am with their young guide, up a steep incline, through stands of pine trees, steadying themselves in the dark by grasping at strands of grass. Reaching the top of a mountain, the boy announced he wouldn't go further; he needed to be back by daylight as the path was monitored by patrols below. His brother had been caught offering this type of assistance and was shot by the Germans.

These last days on the high country offered the Moree men sights of sunrise, prettier than Fitzy had ever seen. In weather that could turn on a pin, a blizzard suddenly blew up. They ploughed on, finding a smuggler trail. Negotiating the slippery trail, they had to slide down at one point, and one man was injured. After helping each other in a metre of snowfall, conditions eased. Tall, fair-headed Lloyd Ledingham and one of the others set off following a creek, finding a hillside hut with a light on. Soldiers with Swiss crosses on their shirts quickly responded. The Moree men sipped tea, caressed cigarettes and bunked down in straw.

17
'WHILST WE WERE EATING THE LAST OF OUR GRUB': MONTE MORO AND MONDELLI PASS

> *'... as the festival atmosphere of the early days was dissipated by the concrete evidences of the German presence and the Fascist resurrection, offers of help grew fewer and more guarded.'*
>
> —Roger Absalom, 1991[1]

Col Booth and Peter Erickson checked out of the Hotel Alpe Noveis at the end of September.[2] Like vulnerable hobos on alert for their next meal, they traversed remote villages heading to Domodossola, ten kilometres in direct distance from the Swiss border.

Some people, fearing for their safety, shut doors in the faces of foreigners who knocked. Depending on individual response to low food rations during captivity and periods of evasion, nutrition was a healthy obsession. New Zealander escaper Arch Scott echoed a commonly held anxiety: 'Food, a close second to water on the necessity list of all POWs, was adequate to sustain life—in the short term. More important than the content was the effect that the lack of sufficient food had upon us. Bread, truly in these circumstances 'the staff of life', meagre in terms of our need and longing for it, took on a new meaning, powerful enough to change a man's life, indeed to change the man himself ... Unless one has known gnawing hunger, together with the background thought that the condition may persist perhaps forever, one may not appreciate just how much such a ration of bread, the size of a roll or a bun, can affect one's morale and self-concept.'[3]

Col resorted to sucking eggs until dry and gnawing raw chicken.[4] Peter remembered raw potatoes and grapes[5]. If there was no food to kill or bandicoot when stomachs tightened, they tried demanding it, or begged.[6] At times the close bond within POW groups strained as they argued about what was best to do.[7]

'We went higher to Sabbia,' Col mentioned to a journalist, 'but everyone shut and locked their doors except one woman who fed and dried us. But we had to leave the village, people were too wary.' To travel from Monte Barone to the hamlet of Sabbia, two kilometres north of Varallo, the pair would've crossed the Sesia, flowing across their northward path, and the narrower Torrente Mastallone before climbing its banks to Sabbia, with green peaks all around.

'After Sabbia,' Col added, 'we met a Tom and a South [African] and set about getting enough food for our walk to Switzerland. Between us we had a bag of apples, six loaves of bread, three tins of meat and a small bag of rice.'[8] Not knowing how long they'd be at the frontier, rations had to be carefully measured.

They plunged on to Campello Monti,[9] a Walser village in the Verbano-Cusio-Osola province dominated by the high church steeple, then went further north to Bannio, on a flat area. On the other side of the Torrente Anza, the terrain turned upwards towards the border trails. One of the bridges here, Col and companions could not know, had a week earlier brought Paul Lavallee and Norm Freeberg to their knees. 'We climbed higher in the mountains and then it got hard. In fact, it was a nightmare. We had to demand food and directions.'[10]

Col's spirit sank, as flat and flimsy as the soles of his boots. To 'come a gutser' on the frontier's steep terrain was highly risky. Col, and probably Peter as both were in the same regimental battery, had felt the chill of snow during ski training near Cedars Chalet in the Lebanon mountains.

On the high Swiss Alps, with no army support or ski shoes, stress made the alpine scene surreal. Peaks pierced mercilessly through sliding clouds, mist flopped like dry ice on sunken shoulders. Some escapers, like Peter, suffered frostbite.[11] To keep warmth in their lower backs, the mates sat back to back, arms interlocked, and tried to rest.[12]

Feeling there was only a few days' strength left in his body, Col dragged his step like a dishevelled delinquent entering detention. Tangible help was at hand at this crucial juncture. 'We found a guide who had been running contraband and he took us within close distance of the border.'[13] Probably this was at or near Mondelli, a couple of kilometres west from Bannio, a hamlet below hillside stone slab *baite* on slopes rising steeply from the river valley and downhill from the Mondelli and Moro passes.[14] Whiffs of illicit coffee stashes wafted from the smugglers' huts, announcing its presence to the valley below. Intermittent crashes of rockfall, like nagging elders, reiterated warnings of mountain wrath to travellers in the valley.

One of Col's group relinquished their blanket to pay the smugglers like a gambler throwing down his last card. On 3 October, probably late at night, they approached the border on the back of a contraband truck. Presumably, the smugglers dropped the POWs on the Italian border edge and returned to Mondelli base. They were initially marched backwards because of their entry via a lesser-used trail. 'Swiss guards picked us up.' They surrendered themselves and their army paybooks for interrogation, panicking they'd be considered spies.

While October's changeable weather crept over high horizons, about 380 Australians were still on their way to Swiss sanctuary, and over half of these had made their home-run by 4 October 1943.[15]

On the reverse of a small crumpled black-and-white photo taken months later, Col's annotation reveals that he and the men pictured joined forces to cross the border on 4 October. Peter stands next to Col, along with John Shaw, a British anti-tank gunner from Lancashire; and South African Johannes

'Dan' Serfontein from Johannesburg. John, the 'Tom' Col mentioned who'd met them at Sabbia, had been interned at Campo 133 Grignasco, about 50 kilometres north of San Germano before being allocated to a farm.[16] On 24 September, *carabinieri* hunted out his POW cluster. Ten days later he met 'two Australians'– Col and Peter—on Monte Moro slopes.

Dan Serfontein decamped Castello d'Agogno, 12 kilometres south-east of Vercelli. A week later he boarded a northbound train at nearby Olevano, three hours later disembarking at Varallo to walk toward the frontier.[17] Victorian Ross Wycherley,[18] who had been at Hotel Alpe Noveis the same time as Col and Peter, brought their summit-searching party to five.

Coming behind Col's international infantrymen, Bob Ward's troop of Norm Woosnam, Bill Pannowitz and Max Wills had luck in finding hosts after moving to high country north of the Santuario di Oropa.[19] At one rest stop, Bob was charmed by a woman he described as 'the nicest, kindest and most sympathetic woman I met in Italy'. Bob showed her photos of his wife Alma and his young daughter Evelyn; three years had elapsed since he'd seen them. Tears welled in the lady's eyes as she took the four Australians into a spare room to share champagne and shortbread biscuits. To cheer them, her children carried in a gramophone and English records. A meal of tomato and lettuce salad with egg, potato and parsley fritters, followed by salmon and cheese, seemed too good to be true. Her husband was equally as attentive to their needs.

After everyone had eaten, the Italian couple tuned their radio to an American-controlled Algerian station. They heard about Italian resistance in Naples. At daybreak, Sunday 3 October, the satiated POWs revisited their travel plans, hearing that three good days would get them to Switzerland.

As Bob's troop headed north-east towards Mosso Santa Maria, about ten kilometres from Oropa depending on their chosen trail, people offered hot coffee, bread and yeast buns with cheese in the middle. Further along, their picnic supplies burgeoned with more bread, chocolate, sausages and 'three pounds of steak'. At Mosso, 'half the town was there to talk to us and give us advice'. Two *carabinieri* came forward, looking the Australians up and down. In the babble of the moment, the POWs were bustled inside a small covered utility. Hefty shouts of good luck from the crowd made them worry that their luck was about to extinguish. The rough-shod ride screeched to a halt at another village and they were hustled inside. As locals gathered to drink wine and throw *lire* on the table, they cautiously sensed all was well.

A guide led them to 'Micca', probably Sagliano Micco, bringing them west again to Oropa area, and motioned towards due north, to Alagna. On the way, they stoked a fire to grill the steak. Within a cow barn, they slept like contented calves.

The next morning, 4 October, Bob woke to a sore dry throat. His breathing laboured. By the time they reached Alagna, 19 kilometres north, Bob ached all over. Directed to the local priest for help, they were invited to rest at a wash-house, with a light meal of 'drained water' and small buns. This Alagna host grew nervous and showed them the door. German patrols were rife in Alagna, another Italian said; it was best to move north to Macugnaga.

Early on 5 October, they hiked a mule path along the Turlo Pass. The trail bends and zig-zags; it cuts through and around the geography to turn its travellers from steep drops. Bob counted nine gruelling hours to reach the top. Succumbing to strong thirst, they filled their mouths with snow, despite knowing it could make them sick. Bob wrote that they 'would've given anything for a drink'. Downhill strides quickened. The valley floor flattened after three hours' walking; one more hour brought them to Macugnaga's outskirts. His cold stealing more of his body's reserves, Bob found difficulty in tailing Bill Pannowitz, Norm Woosnam and Max Wills. They wanted to complete this leg before light dwindled, expecting it to be their last night before a final dash to Switzerland the next day.

Abruptly, an old man darted out of a doorway, running across the road, asking whether they were English. 'We told him we were Aussies. His toothless smile threatened his ears!' The man, eighty-two years of age, and his son-in-law proposed that they escort them. The men hankered to drift into asleep, but it was futile. 'It was so bitterly cold, no one could sleep, so our guides thought it would be best if we got going. At quarter past three, we commenced the last leg.' Bob's cold worsened into flu.

His fledgling mountaineering skills faltered in pitch-black darkness. 'My shoes kept slipping from under me' which added to Bob's woe. 'I had to pull myself up by my hands and they did get very cold. I thought I'd never make it, but after one particularly heavy fall on a nasty rock and sliding to within 50 or 60 feet of a 150-feet drop, I got savage, and literally scorched my way to the top. By this time, it was light enough to see things. I found out why my hands were so cold—everything was thick with frost.

'After such a gruelling climb we had a shock when our guide started down the mountainside. We silently battled on, about halfway down into a ravine and commenced to a climb again. It was stiff going. We had to cross this glacier before we could climb another mountain on the other side, what a picnic! We had to get ourselves to an almost sheer rock-face and edge our way across with nothing more than the small space where the glacier had melted away from the rock-face. It was about 150 yards across and one slip meant sliding about 800 yards to the piled-up boulders.'

While the younger Australian POWs battled the landscape's ferocity, Bob's descriptive notes make it clear that the older Italian guide took it all in his stride. 'Norm [Woosnam] who was next, had gone 30 to 40 yards when he slipped but he made a convulsive grab,' Bob startled, 'and in a more than thousand to one chance, he managed to get his hand wedged between the rock and the glacier. The rest of us were extra careful after that, although we freely managed it without incident. We commenced climbing the other peak, although we'd already climbed what we thought was the limit of man's effort; this was the daddy of them all. It was a tooth-and-nail climb over rocks and loose shale to finally reach the top of another peak, only to find that even our guides couldn't make further progress. It was heart-breaking. We had to work our way across to another peak, then down on the same side as we'd already climbed.

'By this time, I was beginning to wonder if I could carry on to the end. The going down was the hardest going I have ever experienced. At times I thought further progress was impossible. Several times I fell through sheer fatigue and it was all I could do to stop myself from going to the bottom. In one particularly bad patch, I fell heavily and slid and rolled some distance before I managed to grab hold of some jagged splinters of rock practically on the edge of a cliff. The young guide got to me just as I was about to fall. I was tired and aching in every bone and muscle. Then we had to work our way around the foot of the mountain over rocks and loose shale into a valley.'

Flu-ridden, Bob was floundering, and was the last to catch up. Looking to the next mountain, the highest they'd faced, he felt like lying down and staying there. 'I felt dead beat, but I thought of home and how everyone would worry about where I was. From Switzerland, my loved ones would be notified I was safe. I kept doggedly on, all the time plodding ahead, forcing myself to try and just get behind the old guide because something told me that climb was to the Swiss border. My heart was pounding so hard that I went "stone deaf"; as for my lungs, I thought they would burst. My legs felt like weak water. The last few yards seemed like miles.

'Somehow, by sheer force, I reached the top where I staggered a few yards and collapsed in the snow. I lay gasping for breath because of my flu and the thin air. I lay there for some time. It seemed hours.'

When Bob's dizziness eased and breathing steadied, he propped up to see a concrete post with 'I' and a 'S' marking. It was 11.30am. Bob absorbed the quiet reflection of his Italian and Australian companions. Glances to each other expressed more than words. 'After seven and three-quarter hours of constant slugging', Bob was glad for the downhill journey.

Handing the old guide all their money with thanks and goodbyes, the tired POWs, with four accompanying Italian soldiers, started off down the valley. The Australians stopped to change back into their army uniform as their civilian clothes hung in shreds. They retrieved their rations, realising they'd not eaten for six hours. 'Whilst we were eating the last of our grub, we spotted a Swiss frontier guard coming up the valley towards us. None of us felt too comfortable. We thought he might send us back. He first got onto the four Itie soldiers who were with us. Then he turned to us.'

On 6 October, Bob's posse nervously fielded interrogation questions by frontier guards. The guards 'wanted to know who we were, did we have a guide and what pass we came over. We told him we were Australians but made out we didn't understand any more for fear of getting our old guide into trouble. The name of the pass we didn't know then but learnt later that we had come over Monte Moro Pass. After a time, he told us to keep on down the valley, but the Ities had to go back. He escorted them to make sure they did.'

Bob Ward, Norm Woosnam, Max Wills and Bill Pannowitz were asked to wait until the first soldier returned from sending their Italian companions back onto the track. Relieved, the men heard the other solider say, in English, that cups of tea were being prepared. Bob thought it tasted like senna. But it was hot and they relished it.

A couple of hours later, their frontier soldier returned with two Kiwis. About 5pm Swiss took the Anzac POWs down the valley to the small village of Saas-Almagell. After more questioning, they waited in a room for dinner, filling in forms with their personal particulars. A medical orderly inquired whether they had anything wrong with their feet. Earlier arriving POWs suffered frostbite and other foot injuries.

The Swiss apologised because they had only soup, bread and cocoa. As soon as the ravenous POWs emptied their bowls, Swiss refilled them. The tea was so sugary the spoons stood up. Max, the comedian of their quartet, joked, 'That word "tea": I seemed to have heard that word before, what is it?!'

18
'QUIET RESORT EQUALLY SUITABLE FOR REST-SEEKERS AND MOUNTAINEERS': SAAS VALLEY

> *'To give some perspective to the enormity of the task of playing host to the human flotsam of war ... Marshall Badoglio of Italy signed an armistice with the Allied armies advancing northwards from Southern Italy, while the Germans decided to continue their resistance. The Swiss estimated that 40,000 of the 85,000 Allied POWs in Italy and the hundreds of thousands of Italian troops no longer willing to fight on, would try to enter their country.'*
>
> —Bill Rudd, 2012[1]

In peacetime, Italians and Swiss border inhabitants freely scaled the old Moro and Mondelli passes to trade and interact with family and contacts on the other side of the high Italian–Swiss ranges.

In wartime, Swiss sentries kept their eyes on Mondelli and Moro Pass areas into October 1943. The parade of Australian escapers coming down to the lower slopes' landmarks of Saastal's meadow, where the Moro and Mondelli trails converge, then funnelling a short distance downhill to Distelalp and the Mattmark Hotel was a recent phenomenon. The earliest rush of groups of ex-Campo 106 Australian POWs had turned up at the border thresholds on, or by, 19 September.[2]

There was no speedy means for the escapers to notify families of safe home-runs. By the time Lieutenant Colonel Thomas, officer in charge at the Records Office in Melbourne, wrote an official letter to Bill Pannowitz's family in Yanac on 28 October 1943 to advise that Bill had entered Switzerland from Italy,[3] Bob Ward and companion Bill Pannowitz had been in Switzerland for three weeks.

POW arrival to Switzerland, their families were instructed, was to be kept in strict confidence, and in the interest of the soldiers concerned, families were urged not to divulge this information beyond their own household. In the same way that Italian civilians passed on intelligence to trusted contacts about POWs, the Australian bush telegraph would not be silenced.

Swiss border patrollers used Mattmark Hotel as a base.[4] Joachim, a Saas-Almagell teenager in 1943, worked with Mattmark's border team, earning him a wage higher than what his family could afford to pay him at Almagell's Hotel Portjengrat during the wartime slump.[5]

From Mattmark's preliminary interrogation post, refuge-seekers deemed eligible to enter the country were led downhill to Saas Valley villages for further processing ahead of relocation to other areas of Switzerland.

New Zealand POW Peter Watson Bates, who'd reached Switzerland on 21 September 1943,[6] photographed the Mattmark reception scenario, presumably doing so on commission by the Swiss or British authorities to record the processing of the stream of Allied escapers. Souvenir print-sets of these small black-and-white images were distributed to some of the men entering Switzerland at the beginning of October.[7] To remind the escapers of the panorama from the border ridges, Bates's memorabilia included views of Monte Rosa and its ribbon glacial spectacle as viewed from Moro summit.

In Bates's images of the four-storey Mattmark Hotel and its armed sentries, a Swiss flag flutters atop the rundown hotel, wood piles lean against a wall. On a side wall facing down the valley, a 'Hotel' sign harks back to its peacetime function of accommodating tourists in search of mountain-fresh air and pretty alpine flowers.

During the late-1943 flood of first welcomes, Swiss sentries performed necessary checks of identification documents. Then, as erstwhile receptionists and waiters, served many Australian filthy hands shaking with cold; trembling with pleasure to sip thermos tea and cocoa, and to fondle cigarettes. On the back of Col Booth's copy of Bates's black-and-white image of the Mattmark Hotel is the inscription: 'Just over the border, the frontier guard house, had tea and cigarettes here, 4 October 1943'.[8]

Having recuperated, the arrivals proceeded to Saas-Fee or Saas-Almagell. Col Booth snapped up a souvenir postcard of Saas-Almagell. It depicts the tiny village's cluster of old barns, wooden and stone buildings wedged on the valley floor overseen by the church steeple and mountainside larch forest. Peter Watson Bates's camera snapped a scruffy, subdued group of hungry escapers bowed over a meal.[9] One man's head is bandaged. All have the dignity of a dinner plate and cutlery. Some sport untrimmed hair, longer than regulation army cut. Glances around the table hint at shared disbelief and relief. On the back of Col's photo of that group, he penned: 'Our first meal in Switzerland, 4 October 1943'.

Annette Andenmatten's grandparents owned Hotel Monte Moro in 1943, and they spoke to her about sourcing vegetables from local growers to feed the hungry asylum seekers.[10] In all likelihood, it is this hotel to which Col refers in his annotation on the postcard reverse: 'First bed, 4 October 1943'.

From Italian hillside *baite* to Swiss alpine hotels, the accommodation had hopped up a few notches from the crowded barracks at Grupignano and Vercelli camps.

The erstwhile Australian tourists embraced a hotel check-in for snacks or bed, which they did not forget. Without having to beg or barter, a blanket for each man was dished out. A guard was posted at their doors that night, but exhausted prisoners were in no hurry to get back on their feet.

Unlike his nervous night hours at Hotel Alpe Noveis at Monte Barone, on 4 October Col closed his eyes without shadowy fears of fascist night intrusions. In the previous twelve months, Col's war had exposed him to varied sleeping arrangements—from Grupignano's ninety-six men hut to a barn, an alpine hotel, shepherd hut to rocks and earth. Saas-Almagell was the pinnacle, true to promotional pamphlets of the era: 'Saas-Almagell is a quiet resort, equally suitable for rest-seekers and mountaineers.'[11]

One of Peter Watson Bates's photographs zooms in on four escapers' feet to capture their array of dilapidated footwear, of which Nick Emery's tatty tied-ons feature.

Through the post-war decades to the present day, Bates's important photographic record offers treasured glimpses into the finish line for many Campo 106 escapers who'd traversed this key freedom trail. Col Booth's souvenir set stayed within his Globite case; Nick Emery's copies shine through laminated plastic on his wall.

Colin Weekes beat his regimental mate Col Booth to the Saas Valley by eleven days. At Saas-Almagell, on 23 September, a smiling Swiss guard had handed Colin Weekes and Blue Neave—who'd been pipped to the border by seventy other Australians—to a tall solidly built sergeant who spoke very good English. 'The big fellow led us to a hotel lower down the road where we were to be fed. Into Hotel Monte-Moro we walked to find the lounge full of Aussies, Kiwis and Tommies, all from Italy.'[12]

As beer was served, Swiss soldiers and an officer spoke to them, interrogating them for identification. 'After another beer, food was mentioned', to Colin's peckish pleasure, 'so we all trooped out into a big mess room, where two long tables were set up with real soup plates and spoons, forks, knives, salt and sugar bowls. After the soup, which was soup, we were served meat stew and potatoes followed by as many cups of pure creamy milk cocoa as we could manage to soak into our overstretched insides.' It was the best meal the prisoners had eaten in years, Colin reckoned, particularly as rice was not on the menu.

Following brisk washes in the icy water of the creek for Colin and Bluey early the next morning, breakfasts were offered of coffee, bread and jam.

The men were marched further down the valley—an easy forty-minute walk, according to the hotel brochures— following the river to the next village of Saas-Grund. The valley widened; the clank of cow bells came from the pastures. While buses readied for their ongoing journey to Swiss camps, Colin sat on the steps of a new church, watching Swiss soldiers grooming a mule team.

On the following day, Ernie Sparnon was self-conscious about his appearance on arrival, thinking that he 'must have looked terrible to the people: old clothes, unshaven and still very tired. The clothes I started with and also finished with were one pair of worn boots, socks, light trousers, singlet, silk shirt and sweater, and tied to my belt my paybook, photos and diary.'[13]

As unruly, frightened-looking foreign men like Ernie hobbled through the Saas villages, locals did take notice. At first, they had no inkling of their origin. Augusta Venetz, as a young Saas-Grund girl, remembers her parents calling her from their garden to watch the unexpected parade, led in silence by Swiss guards.[14]

The tide of tired escapers kept coming, dipping into Swiss hospitality. All up, approximately one hundred Australian escapers made inroads into Switzerland between 1 and 7 October.[15]

The Jobson brothers' escaper group made their appearance in one of the Saas villages on the afternoon of 2 October.[16] A Swiss interpreter cordially announced dinner, as Arthur emphatically repeated: 'A meal has been prepared; however, owing to lack of space we cannot serve you all at once, so we would ask you to eat as quickly as you can. If you would like more, JUST ASK FOR IT.' Could the men believe their ears? The interpreter added, 'But think of your friends who are waiting to be served.'

Interrogation was next on the agenda, and Arthur shared other POWs' trepidation about internment in Switzerland. Arthur's interrogation, like many fellow escapers before him, was pleasant, brief and commenced with a cigarette. 'A few questions asked and that was it!' Arthur would have known his good fortune to find asylum with his brother Tim. Their sergeant, Joe Newbey, undoubtably wished that his brother Ted had had that chance. Joe still had the funeral pall ribbons from Ted's coffin securely tucked under his shirt.[17]

Bob Ward, after his first Swiss dinner on 6 October, was stunned that the venue-owner asked his thirsty mob what type of beverage they'd prefer—wine or beer.[18] They couldn't believe it. Max joked that in Australia nearly everyone drank beer. She brought out four bottles as starters, then another two. Bob kept the diary going, outlining the predominant transit route out of the Saas Valley: 'Next morning, we were joined by another forty-two. Some chaps we knew. After dinner and a couple bottles of beer per man, a train to Visp.' The men had been bussed down the valley through Stalden, on the Visp-Zermatt rail-line.

'After medical inspection, we were taken to our first shower. Four days in Visp, a very pretty little town.' The transiting POWs were 'then put on electric train for Brig' ten kilometres from Visp. 'Here we met a lot more of the boys, quite a few we knew.'

In Ron Maitland's post-war memorabilia, there is photographic documentation of further interest in the arriving POWs.[19] He prized a group photo of sixty or so Allied escapers, taken, to his memory, on 7 October at Wil. Ron does not mention the photographer's name, but the venue was probably school buildings used for temporary accommodation and as a Red Cross facility to record the arriving POWs' details. Nick Emery, Col Booth, Peter Erickson, the Moree four and Ron Maitland with about forty others posed in neat rows, resplendent in new uniforms, boots, deloused hair and clean-shaven faces.[20] Ron and Col, as well most of the others, grin widely.

From that stopover, smartened-up évadés—as they were known by the Swiss—entrained to the town of Wald in Canton Zurich where a key base for évadés was established. Already évadés deduced that in contrast to Australia, Swiss trains arrived dead on time.

While the sixty spruced-up évadés rested inside Swiss territory on 6 October, Bill Waller's wanderers were frazzled, stepping precariously onto a nearby border frontier, heading for another Swiss resort village.

A month earlier, Bill Waller had left Campo 106's Pettiva base with fellow 3LAA Regiment POWs including those who were from the nearby Tenuta Colombara work party: Tom Russell, Jack Nicholson, Tom James, Allan Young and Ernie Preiser.[21]

Contemplating an itinerary northward, a woman singled out Monte Rosa massif on a map to warn them to steer away from its hostile terrain: 'Go there you die'. Waller's party sampled guerrilla warfare with a partisan band under the name of an Italian colonel, Pietro. Near Biella, they were ambushed at dawn and cloistered by German armoured vehicles. At this time, they were unarmed. Bill Waller's diminished party of Ernie, Tom Russell and himself pressed on, foot-slogging west of Biella and into the Aosta Valley. The route traced Torrente Lys that flowed south from the border Alps, passing via Fontainemore, Issime, Gaby and Gressoney-Saint-Jean. Their objective was Zermatt—presumably via the Teodulo Pass—and sanctuary in Switzerland.

They had traipsed north into the foothills of the Alps, evading German patrols, but were finally surrounded by Germans in armoured vehicles who opened fire on them. 'Tom Russell, Ern Preiser and I ran diagonally up hills as Germans opened fire,' team narrator Bill Waller wrote. 'Called on to surrender, we hid in bushes, joined by Tasmanian Joe Turner. The Germans gave up as rain poured down. From our hiding place we saw them march off our captured mates—Jack [John] Nicholson, Alan Young and Tom James. An Italian woman gave us food. Asked why she helped, she replied: "I have a son in Montenegro (Yugoslavia). He might be hiding from Germans now. When I saw you I thought of him."'

In the dark they stumbled through creeks, striving forward. Guided to the valley of Aosta, they found that identifying as English solicited more help than Australian. Many people had never heard of Australia.

A man named Bruno congenially offered to help them to cross by a secret route which he and his father-in-law used for smuggling in peace time. They said it was a difficult route. 'We were joined by seven Australians and two Englishmen, Captain Fred Porter (RHA) and Captain Sir Julian Hall (Intelligence Corps). We made ourselves scarves and gloves out of an old blanket in readiness for the climb.

'Departing at night, we reached the snow-line roped together in three parties. The officers as POWs had not been required to work whereas we Australians had been working on farms for six months and were in better physical condition for the trial ahead. We reached the Monte Rosa wooden cabin and used the sticks of wood we all carried to boil water from snow. At dawn the peaks of Mont Blanc (Monte Bianco) and the Matterhorn showed over the clouds. Our guide Alberto said: "There are a few people who have done this climb by daylight. You are among the very few to do it by night".'

Glancing at the dawn panorama, Bill 'stared at the most incredible view. Most people, these days, have travelled in aeroplanes and are accustomed to looking down onto fleecy clouds. I had never done so.'

At 3600 metres up, the party was roped together for passage over solid ice in steps cut by their guide with an ice-pick. At 9.30am the guide left as he would be interned if he crossed the border. He reiterated the unsoundness of ice bridges over crevasses, and through binoculars he pointed out a beacon: a hut below at the end of the glacier. For the rookie mountaineers, progress down was hazardous as ropes were joined to lower one at a time over ice cliffs with a 20-foot drop into snow at the bottom. 'As the problems with ice cliffs and snow blindness reduced our party to despair that we would freeze to death after our hair-raising experiences, Swiss soldiers suddenly appeared below us roped together.'

The Waller crash-course mountaineers straggling to a resort welcome in Zermatt on 6 October 1943 included British escapers 'Captain Fred' Cheeseman and sapper William Croft. Victorian POW Ernie Preiser is also noted within Bill Waller's party. Ernie was almost forty years of age when undertaking their arduous mountaineering feat.[22]

Bill refers to his group merging, at some point, with other escaper parties on the same treacherous route. Coincidentally, one of those POWs, Ernie Hayes, tapped Swiss soil near Zermatt the same day. He was forty-three.[23]

19
'I'M SORRY MATE, WE'VE BUNGLED IT': LEADERSHIP AND LOSS OF BEARINGS

> *'... The Germans describe this as Fingerspitzengefühl, (literally, "finger-tip feeling"). Colloquially it means flair or a sixth sense that enables them [commanders], almost instinctively, to seize on the right thing to do, or to be in the right place at the right time, either to ensure victory or to stave off defeat.'*
>
> —David Miller, 2001[1]

The evasion phase of the POWs' war was an unconventional campaign of unpredictable duration and outcome. Within escaper units' fluctuating formations, it was important to maintain unit discipline and to motivate each other to undertake feats which, ordinarily, they might not wish to do.

At the mountainous frontier, individual escapers under their own command or within self-contained units grappled with a sense of isolation and disorientation. It was easy to lose track of time and place. Profound experiences gripped tired and emotional journeymen.

Waking alone on 6 October, 'stuck up here in the mountains', Cloncurry's Donald 'Duncan' Robertson remembered his decision to go under his own command, splitting with his travelling companion Jim Gardiner the day before. For the next few days he procured 'good feeds' from locals, building strength to start early on 12 October 'with the clouds still about the tops of the mountains'. Needing some orientation, a boy showed him the track to the pass from where he sighted 'a mile of snow and ice' and then a Swiss guard. With 'socks all worn out and my boots just about done', Duncan embraced hot tea and bread at the guardhouse.[2]

Jack Wauhop, also on his own, had made slow progress since leaving the crazed guard pinned by a pitchfork after their dramatic pre-armistice exchange at the prison camp.[3] Although Jack's early camp departure could have meant pole position to reach Switzerland, the obstacle race was tough and grinding, and it dug deep into psychological and physical reserves. Ethical dilemmas handicapped the journey as Jack's conscience prickled at having to thieve. He rationalised a different spin: 'Just borrowing things without putting a down payment on it—I would rather put it that way. Every crumb I had to eat from the day I escaped, I stole at night. Every bit of clothing I had on I exchanged along the way; I purloined it off sort-of clotheslines: hanging on a fence, on a gate, or as I plundered in the middle of the night these isolated farmhouses. I'd find a shirt on a tractor seat or some sort of clothing like a blanket which I stole and tore into strips to make some socks because I'd run out of footwear. I had to bind my feet with strips of blanket that I stole from a seat of a truck in a shed. That was my way of existing, of surviving.'

One night, as he trundled along a highway that carried traffic from France, Jack was only vaguely tuned to his surroundings. He did not hear an approaching German sidecar nor the troop-heavy convoy following it. Headlights were dimmed. By the time he realised, Jack thought he was a goner. The sidecar's wheel hit his leg, spinning him over.

Dusting himself off in the darkness, Jack reassessed his strategy and turned towards the Swiss Alps. After that, he travelled only by day, feeling reasonably safe as there were no people about. 'Over the foothills, the first sight of the Alps is one of awe,' he exclaimed. 'Suddenly there's a sheer wall of ice and snow, you hoped there was ground underneath it. I am sure God was sitting on top of the first mountain I saw, it was way up that high. I was either wet or soaking or half-drowned with the rain and the fog and everything else. I decided to head fast for the border, get lost on the way; get into the snow; give it a go.' Jack's mind flashed to a centuries-old legend. 'If Hannibal could cross it with some elephants, I will find a way to get over too.'

Jack didn't have a watch, and was uncertain about the month. He'd been tallying days by marking little sticks until he got to ten, then he'd make a Roman numeral for ten. But, at fifty-two days into his run, he'd lost count when he hit the mountains.

'I not only ran out of sticks and a sharp stone to scratch each day on it, I ran out of food also. There was no food, no change of clothing ... alone on the Alps, not a bird in sight, not even a St Bernard dog. I wondered why I was up there all by myself, no one else seemed to be.

'One day I got to the top of this particular mountain and there before me down in that beautiful valley lay one of the most comforting, endearing sights I have ever seen ... a village far below in a verdant patch of green on a flat bottom of the valley. Snow mountains all round. It was put in the shape of a cross. There was a whole village of some thirty, forty or fifty buildings in the shape of a proper crucifix where the all-white walls, red roofs and a church spire coming right from the centre of the cross. There must have been a couple of hundred people down there. Untouched by war, unsullied by any enemy or predator whatsoever. It was a most beautiful sight, and in my condition, in my circumstances, I would have been a zombie, I reckon, if I hadn't sat down in the snow and looked down at that beautiful picture ... I think I got nearer to God up there and it seemed to be a sacrilege as a little thought passed through my mind—wait until dark and go down and try to steal a loaf of bread. That was the day I went slithering down, unstoppable on the northern side of the Grand Saint Bernard Mountain.'

Jack had conquered the legendary trail of Hannibal's journey. Swiss officials may have informed him of the date and month: 20 October 1943.[4]

Following on their heels, trio Ronald 'Bones' Jones, Ted Kent and Gordon Putland entered Switzerland on 28 October.[5] A Biella merchant known as 'Fraser' arranged for them to be covered by hay in the back of a car, and secreted through northern Aosta region to Vollon, near Brusson, from where they walked to the border.

Like Jack Wauhop's description of his thoughts on the high country, other escaped prisoners felt peaks of emotion, tapping into their inner belief systems during times of great hardship. It had been something to draw on during intense soldiery in North African deserts and continued as they battled on in Italy.

British escapee Eric Newby wrote about an encounter with a 'superboy' in Italy in late 1943.[6] A boy had been assigned to escort him to a village meeting in the Apennines. 'The little boy was not more than eight years old, but he was as agile as a flea,' Eric wrote. 'He took me down along the edge of the cliff, hopping and skipping in front of me, and occasionally waiting for me to catch up ... as if I was an aged relative whom he'd taken out for an airing. He was a strange, very self-possessed, solemn little boy with a cropped head which looked as if it was covered in brown velvet.'

The boy didn't speak to Eric until the journey's end, but along the way he jabbered to himself 'pretty incessantly when he was trying to work out what was the best way around some insurmountable rock'.

Deepwater's Lloyd Moule recalled a similarly moving experience on the Alps.[7] Lloyd's group was approached by a young boy, about ten years of age with curly hair and piercing brown eyes. He told them which trails to follow, contrary to directions given by another Italian. Lloyd went on ahead with the boy to see if it looked clear, knowing that the boy was worried about *Tedeschi* in the area. The boy insisted on taking Lloyd to a house, introducing him to the occupant. She was sympathetic because one of her sons was interned as a POW in Australia and his letters informed her that he was treated well.[8]

Lloyd returned with the boy to his waiting mates, who included Wally Cook, Roy Scales and Charlie Stanley. When the other POWs 'jacked up' about the veracity of the boy's directions, Lloyd began to cry, profoundly moved by their child guide. To Lloyd, the boy was 'like a guardian angel' sent to help them. Even at ninety-six years of age, his memory of the solo child helper remained profound enough to bring him to tears.

Lloyd's companions were in accord with his gut feeling. The next morning they went with the boy's directions to Macugnaga. Later, the POWs heard that SS troops had invaded their original planned destination, executing local people for subversive actions.

Other boys and girls stepped forward to assist. They ran food to shelter, carried warnings and acted as guides in their high-country playground. In the forefront of his mind, Lloyd recalled the boy's tip to keep to the right of Rosa. While they contemplated the scenery, they had a little bit of salami and bread to munch on. 'We came into more snow and we came to the point of no return,' Lloyd narrated. 'It was sort of an ice front; there was no way to the right or left and we had to go down after that. I was frightened, I feared to take it on. I felt it, and I apparently didn't show it, I looked around to the guys and they were depending on me as their leader and maybe they were as frightened as I was. We had to accept the challenge and if we didn't, we failed, the hurts and the dangers and all the depuration and all that would be gone; we had to go on if we wanted to make freedom.'

The biggest man in the party became disoriented and hallucinated. At one point, Lloyd felt the pressure of maintaining his group's discipline to push on through fear and exhaustion. Lloyd struck one of his men, hoping to fire him up, to return him to his feet, to fight on.

Downhill they slogged, feeling there was no way back. Charlie Stanley hurt his back on the slide down and needed two men to help him along. 'We noticed the snow was becoming thinner until it was about a metre and then a little trickle. It was getting dark.' On 22 October, Lloyd was concerned but wanted the race to be over. Some of them developed frostbite to cuts under their fingernails from gripping rock walls. 'We had walked from early-morning daylight. I think it was fourteen hours. I said to a fellow [Roy Scales], "Come with me and we will go ahead and see" and it was downhill. Buoyed, we were descending. The adrenaline started to pump, we had a new lease on life. He and I were halfway down by this little stream and in the distance, we saw a light and made to it ... from the calling out, lights came on, and voices and peak caps ... We thought, "Oh no, we are in bloody Austria!"'

Lloyd's faith was shattered. He swung around to his nearest companion and gasped, 'I'm sorry mate, we've bungled it.'

'Imagine our joy when the figures moved into the light and we could see the white Swiss cross on their shoulder patches. I had difficulty trying to explain that more men in our party, one injured, were on their way. Eventually I was allowed to go to the edge of the lighted area. After much calling out that everything was OK, they limped in.'

The Swiss took them 'into a two-storey place', probably Mattmark Hotel. Still disoriented, Lloyd presumed they were in the middle of nowhere. 'They made us tea, where the hell they got the tea from I don't know, and gave us cigarettes and a bed of straw to sleep on.'

Ron Crellin was neck and neck with Lloyd Moule's battered runaways on that day, within cooee of the border range. Similarities in the accounts by Ron and Lloyd suggest that their groups had come together at the last leg.

Six weeks earlier, in a party of seven men, the first thing Ron Crellin did when he walked out of a San Germano farm was shed the POW uniforms and search for civilian clothing.[9] Taking shelter at a nearby house, he hoped for contact with partisans. It came in the form of a farm-owner's daughter aged in her early twenties who was working with an organised network. She had an escape plan and Ron went along with it.

Firstly, Ron met a man in a pre-arranged location. He led Ron's group to the Milan–Turin main road. The POWs hid in rushes until the 'all clear' was given and a similar strategy was used, with good timing, to cross the rail-lines. Soon afterwards, a rail trolley with six German soldiers rumbled by. They reached the shelter of a forest near a river after walking a couple of hours. Other POWs were there. Two girls rode bikes to their hideout, bringing food. Another partisan arranged for some of the POWs to depart at 4am the next morning.

They lumbered two hours in darkness to catch a 'workers' bus. It dimmed its headlights on approach to give the 'all clear'. The guide instructed them to sit at the back while he sat at the front. The bus filled with girls heading to work in the early morning.

Reaching a big town, the guide got up and, as planned, they followed without speaking to him, looking for their next contact. As expected, a man stood near the bus stop with his hat in his hands. When they eyed each other, he flipped his hat on his head and walked with the POWs, toddling not too closely behind. Turning into a side lane, he hid the men behind a wall and checked the surrounds before leading them to a house for a rest and a meal. Ron believed the town was Biella.

The next day they trekked into a 'big valley covered with trees and a good road'. Ron had been on the loose for two weeks, relying on one meal per day. As they penetrated higher into the hills, passing many tiny villages, they met an Italian teen boy who told them of Germans with dogs in his village. Their guide diverted their route and allocated the carrying of cases of ammunition to them until they reached a new base where a partisan leader asked them to leave.

Another guide assumed lead to Ron's party and led them higher, where 'timbered country was giving way to open rocky country'. There, a POW who Ron refers to as 'Ray' decided he'd go back. Ron later heard he was captured by Germans. Ron's remaining group reached the border summit area at night, cold and numb, 'seeing nothing but cloud and mountain peaks'.

Ron crossed the border at Monte Moro Pass, as had Lloyd Moule and on the same day, but neither knew the name of the pass and its glacial-ice obstacle course. Ron refers to descending into a valley after a hard climb of about eighteen hours, and at the end of the snow-line hesitantly approaching a building that looked like an old hotel—a similar account to Lloyd.

To Ron's account, 'We could see no sign of life and the door was locked. We decided to stay for the night. We were attempting to force our way in when, to our surprise, a voice called out from upstairs in German. Everybody froze. We thought we'd been misdirected and had finished up in Germany.' In all likelihood, the old hotel was Mattmark. To their relief, as for Lloyd Moule's party, Swiss soldiers told them they'd made it.

Neither Lloyd's or Ron's accounts list all men in their party. But as the Swiss registered only eight Australian arrivals on 22 October—including Lloyd, Charlie, Roy, Wally, Ron as well as Jim Dawes, John Oliver and Bill Rose—their groups probably merged during their step up to the frontier.

Ron wrote that his mob were given a room with straw on the floor. 'The guard went away briefly and came back with packets of smokes and a big pot of stew. Believe me, we had not had such a meal for weeks … It was a great feeling after eight weeks of sleeping with one eye open, waiting for the slightest noise or of someone coming around the corner, and not knowing where the next meal was coming from.'

They were taken to Saas-Fee village and to a home of a Swiss guard. His wife cooked them boiled potatoes with melted cheese. Instead of being moved down the valley through Stalden directly to Brig, Ron's batch were walked to Zermatt for two nights' stay and Red Cross provisions of clothes and haircuts. During a guided tour, they viewed 'the famous Matterhorn, through the public telescope in the town, where climbers could be watched making their ascent of the mountain'. Next day they travelled to Brig, Bern and Elgg. 'We were told we had been very lucky to have got over the mountains when we did as normally the first snow-falls come in November.'

20
'THE MOUNTAIN GAVE THE IMPRESSION OF BEING ALIVE': MOUNTAINEERING, LATE OCTOBER 1943

'... the time had come for Italians to declare their allegiances ... civilians either joined the partigiani (partisans) or other similarly motivated but mufti-clad resistance organisations. The great majority, however, simply chose not to declare themselves but to show by word and deed their total opposition to the Nazi and Fascist regimes.'

—Arch Scott, 1985[1]

From the rice-cultivation plains, the mountainous frontier of the northern Piedmont region stirred fear within POWs. While teeing up guidance at the Italian frontier, POWs' fear of recapture and mountaineering was intermixed with awe of the majestic mountains. Many POWs were still with familiar others and trusted mates; some fell in with other POWs at latter stages of evasion and may have had little opportunity to get to know each other well. Many POW parties had chopped and changed during the weeks of travel to reach the frontier. By the end of October 1943, three-quarters of the Australians to enter Swiss territory had pipped the Swiss border post, finally out of harm's way.[2]

Still scouting around in the Italian hills in October 1943, Charles Warburton gingerly opened a hayshed door.[3] Twenty sullen South African faces looked up, reluctant to share their bottom-storey digs. Directed to the top storey, the Australians complied with requests to use a specific pile of straw for bedding under their blankets. Three neat straw piles belonged to three *padrone* and were not to be mixed.

Fed up from being cocooned in the shed for eight days, and doubting the trustworthiness of their Italian host, the South Africans' nerves jangled with worry. Adding to their suspicions, the South Africans were told by two *Tommies* that if POWs signed certain documents and handed over money, they would receive food and arms. It sounded fishy.

Like a stage cue, an *alpini* wearing a distinctive *alpini* hat with feather on the side of the brim sauntered into the hayshed. Growing *alpini* forces were trying to stockpile arms and ammunition to shoot up German convoys. Some of the hayshed fugitives considered joining these rebel bands; others went with offers to sleep and eat in homes. But Charles was not seduced by the *alpini*'s words. He believed that Italian rebels would not have had army training and discipline to effectively engage in warfare tactics. Instead, he placed his trust in a guide who claimed that his services would be paid post-war by the British government for every man he assisted over the border. Charles's faith in him grew when he and his brother turned up at an agreed time the following day.

Charles's party of thirteen men gathered gear, each lugging a supply sack. Starting off on a path that traced the easiest gradient, they attained a steady pace, stopping to regain breath at a two-storey iron-roofed hut. Ferns lined the walls and floor of the loft, scalable by a ladder.

The men wangled their way in with eyes peeled for the 'four-foot-high' roof pitch and dangerous gaps in the rough-hewn plank floor. No mountaineer desired a broken leg or banged head so near to their target. Charles's account indicates their descent was into the Anzasca Valley: 'Even if the place lacked people, it was in no way short as regards scenery,' Charles gushed. 'Standing by our hut on high ground, I looked across a wide, deep valley surrounded by very high hills. To the right, at the farthest end, they were high enough to be called mountains, while on the left were mountains even higher.' Charles, like foreign tourists with enthusiasm for unexpected highlights, took in 'what must be one of the most impressive views of mountain grandeur in the world'.

While earlier Switzerland arrivals admired the scenery over the other side of the Alps, Charles's itinerary offered longer to gawk at the Italian side of the Alps. He notched ten spectacular sunrises while he bided time until guides were available. 'Rising from the edge of the valley was a rugged, high mountain range, with the clouds moving lazily around the top. Behind this, as far as the eye could see, rose range after range of mountains: each as it got further back seemed higher. As their tops were serrated and rugged, they gave the impression of a sombreness and grandeur impossible to describe. High and rugged as the peaks were on those mountains, they were dwarfed into insignificance by soaring ramparts of the mighty Monte Rosa. Her cliffs were covered in perpetual snow, she rose high above the highest peak about her and, as the base of her was almost always shrouded by clouds, her summit seemed to be suspended in air ...

'I never missed a morning the whole ten days we were there, but on every occasion except once, clouds floating about the summits spoilt the view. I was lucky once. It was then, as the light grew stronger, her snow-capped peaks swiftly changed from white to pink, and the whole made a sense of beauty which will take a long time to forget. Then, as the sun rose higher all along the summit turned gold.'

Amongst Rosa's cluster of peaks, Dufour Peak pricks the sky at 4600 metres. Rosa's long easterly face extends more than 2000 metres.

With flair, Italian woodcutters returned in the evenings by flying fox, stretching about '300 feet' above the valley floor. The woodmen, in groups of two or three, sat in a sling suspended from wire on a wheel, and the first two were pushed off. From a distance, the wire was invisible, giving the impression of woodcutters whizzing along with the wind. Charles marvelled at the speed. The last man to go always stood up, Charles deduced, because the last man had to launch himself. Wood wobbled along the fox, each bundle pounding into the tree holding the wire.

One evening, Charles's crew strolled to the village water-pump to wash. A woman, accompanied by a girl happily singing, approached them as they dried off. She offered apples, as many as they could eat. The bounty crop was stacked on the floor and beds of her house. Charles dodged an invitation to sleep at her home as he wasn't keen to bunk down near the goats under the house. Four of the others took up the offer. The men guessed that the woman and girl were having fun at their expense by switching to dialect to discuss them.

Grateful for accommodation and apples, some POWs put up their hand to help to carry apple baskets, not thinking it would be entirely uphill. Charles smirked that even the bigger men at over six feet tall found it hard-going, unaccustomed to the steep gradient.

Charles admired the physique of the singing girl, befitting the everyday training on mountain slopes: 'A typical mountain girl, legs on her which a footballer would envy, and a sturdy well-built figure, and a rosy complexion.' The women sustained a solid pace while two Australians stopped to rest. 'I have seen old women, easily over sixty, plodding along carrying huge loads on their backs, more often than not uphill, and they never raise a sweat.'

One day, Charles did offer to help carry rations into a nearby village. He yarned with a 'very good-looking and refined' girl to inquire whether Germans were about. She was also a visitor, staying with relatives because her home city Naples was in shambles and typhoid was a risk. 'Undoubtedly,' Charles pondered, 'it would have been our bombers, or the bombardment by the navy, which probably wrecked her home.' She rustled up a sack of cooked chestnuts and some pumpkins to share.'

Two of Charles's group helped to make cider. It was too sweet for Charles's liking. Exploring the local *chiesa*, church, the most impressive building in the village, Charles mused that Italians 'are very fond of painted scenes from the Bible'.

Despite the local sights and smells, many of the escapers became restless; snow would soon block the mountain passes. A young local professional guide dressed in *alpini* uniform had assisted climbers before the war. He marshalled guides, who'd be ready in late October. Other escapers drifted into the village, bringing their number to seventy men of mixed nationalities. Some POWs still had money and offered to pay for chocolate supplies. Six British POWs opted to stay put and work for the woodcutters. One Australian POW 'cleared off' to live with a woman whom he fancied.

While Charles watched Monte Rosa's tips glow with dawn rays in late October, ten Australians crossed the border on 28 October and five on 30 October. Still waiting in line on 2 November, about fourteen other Australians stepped into Swiss hands,[4] including a group of three men from Charles's 2/28th battalion, Bill Strickland, Frank 'Nugget' Leach and Jack Knight.[5]

Charles's turn was nigh. For those in his POW group plunging on, organisers distributed boots and blankets. POWs suspected the organisers' requests to swap their larger blankets for smaller ones. It could be profiteering but, on the other hand, Charles knew of a local woman remodelling army blankets into coats and trousers for her family.

Charles expected that in Switzerland, POWs would be detained behind barbed-wire. 'Even though fruitlessly wandering about, I had at least been free.'

In single file behind their guide, Charles's mini-troop was prepped to undertake mountaineer initiation. 'I had imagined the way to cross a mountain range was to go straight over top and down the other side. In my short time in the foothills I learnt the correct way, to go around everything possible. If it was necessary to go over the top, then use the easiest gradient possible, even if it meant hours walking. Also, to take a medium pace and never to climb on the toes, but always to place the foot down heel and toe together.'

The colourful POW parade donned felt hats of various shapes and colours. 'As our line wended its way through, some had civilian suits, still very smart and spruce; others like myself, in ordinary working clothes. Others had half civilian clothes and half military, while several had complete uniforms on, and in some cases even had packs and haversacks.'

The oldest guide was annoyed when he noticed a haversack was undone and a tin of puree was missing. He accused them of discarding the tin to lighten load. The outburst was rescinded when the tin turned up in another pack. POWs shot dark looks his way. Tempers tenderised. 'A man who has been craving for a smoke is not a man with patience.'

The gradient steepened. Ringing of woodcutters' axes reverberated through the pine trees. One guide chatted to locals, gesturing up to the next range where alpine huts, like tiny matchboxes, beckoned the walkers to begin the one-hour climb. Two figures squatting near the summit came into focus. Astounded, Charles recognised these armed *alpini* scouting ahead for fascist patrols as men he'd met at Borgosesia.

Charles's guides shared their mountaineer wisdom about altitude climbing. Regardless of thirst, water shouldn't be drunk. If one must drink, a mouthful of cognac or a sip of wine might be permitted. If one drank water, it would reduce strength in the legs and possibly cause stomach cramps. With limited time to eat before climbing, it was best to eat light meals. It was best to eat often but only a few mouthfuls of bread at a time. Chocolate was excellent; every mountaineer carried chocolate in his haversack. The rookie mountaineers fumbled with stout wooden sticks. Rice sacks made the climbing more arduous, particularly for those with sore feet. Carriers alternated. The men aimed for brief rest stops, keeping moving to maintain body warmth. One POW snapped, opening his pack and slinging away most contents. He offered his blanket to any punter. Another POW carried it for him. One famished POW ignored admonishments about large meals, tucking in to Canadian Red Cross tinned bully beef that he'd carted from Montonero.

Clouds drifted below them; cold started to bite. Conquering the summit climb, Charles took brief respite, feeling pleased with his progress.

Two other POWs had to be helped by their mates while guides went downhill to help others.

'We now had a peak to climb,' diarised Charles, 'and the path led nearly straight up: its height would be over 300 ft above us. The strugglers looked at it with apprehension.' Charles offered to carry rice for another POW. Downhill, a guide was practically carrying one man, while others rested frequently. Word passed forward for those ahead to keep going. Stragglers would be brought along later by the *alpini*.

As the path weaved to higher ground, their altitude workout pounded their stamina. One POW lay down on the earth. Guides gave blankets and brandy to the weakened and put on brave faces, reassuring the POWs that they'd assist any man to go further. Charles bent to pick up a rice sack. He heard a POW moan that 'he had trouble in making his legs obey him'. Like a shot, Charles felt the same. His match fitness had drained.

Like invisible shots of shrapnel, chill pierced the bodies of slipshod hikers. The fear of illness, injury or falling behind plagued all POWs' thoughts.

'From the waist down, I suddenly lost all strength.' Charles had dreaded this happening. 'My heart began to pound, I felt hollow and weak in the stomach. Curiously, my head was clear as a bell ... So cold was it that the sweat could not dry on my body. I had to force myself to put one foot in front of the other. I felt as weak as a baby, and seemed unable to control my movements. The one overwhelming desire was to stop, lie down and sleep. I forced the desire away. I could feel my legs moving but couldn't feel my feet treading the path ... I had to literally flog myself.

'After what seemed hours, I reached the hut where a few chaps were standing talking to another Aussie. Seeing me, he said, "You look in a bad way," and taking my blanket he wrapped it around my shoulders and told me to sit down.'

Four *alpini* beckoned the Australians to their barracks in a stone building perched atop levelled ground on a high range surrounded by enormous peaks. A deep ravine dropped from the front of the building; a flying-fox rope slung eerily into its depths. The *alpini* wore tunic uniforms with trousers made of rugs. To Charles, it looked odd but blissfully cosy.

Alpini ushered them to a large room with a cold concrete floor thinly concealed by leaves. In late October, the room felt like a refrigerator full of thin icy air. Charles was exhausted as they settled in. 'Three of us could get under one blanket. Putting one underneath, we put the other two over the top … my clothes, which were still wet from sweat, were icy cold. If at that moment the Jerries walked in,' Charles conceded, 'I could not for the life of me have moved.'

To thaw their frigid bodies, *alpini* served broth laced with brandy and cognac, hot rice and bread. A fire flickered in another room. Charles improved, despite intense thirst, listening to news that two of the POWs who'd stayed back with the other *alpini* had, somehow, 'done over a fascist'. *Alpini* briefed them about others who'd got over the border.

With current conditions of a foot of snow on the ground, they anticipated that three days of climbing was ahead. Two POWs announced they wanted to turn back. Those men not yet feeling ready opted to stay put, awaiting the next wave. The men's last issue of rations, rice sacks and bread loaves, were divided up. Surplus gear was turfed. Charles's mate with the bad feet opted to continue.

An early November sunrise sent golden splashes onto the mountain peaks. Charles gazed across the valley to Monte Rosa, the second-highest mountain in the Alps, entranced by the towering, ice-covered peaks off which wind whipped up flakes of snow. Echoes of ice crash in the distance pierced the silence. 'I could see why the natives regard mountains as gods. The mountain gave the impression of being alive.'

Charles's thirst intensified. He believed it was worse than ever experienced in the North African desert. He itched to cup his hands for large gulps of water, but heeded the guide's instructions to consume small quantities. Unsated, he sucked his wet handkerchief. Charles envied the female guide's boots: heavy, thick and watertight.

On 3 November, facing Moro's slope, Charles greeted autumn in wet cold boots. A South Africans' boot-sole was semi-detached, baring his soles to the snow. Guides raised fingers towards a freshly made track steeply rising towards the summit saddle. Farewelling their female guides, the men wrote names and addresses. The girls gladly accepted money, and with '*buono fortuna*' the girls, and their intimate familiarity with the frontier, were gone.

Despite the clear sky and warming sun, the day grew bleaker for Charles. 'The climb was going to be arduous and would take over an hour. There was always a chance of a Jerry patrol ... we lost no time in starting in foot-deep snow concealing loose rocks and gaps.' Their sticks gave scant support except on firm rock. 'Soon it got deeper, and the track became steeper, and now we were climbing with hands as well as feet.'

Vanguard pathfinders pressed the snow down firmly for those who followed. All men rested frequently. The South African 'with the weak heart' followed Charles. 'Half way up, the path turned right to avoid big rocks, then swung left again, and now was very steep. The chap with the bad knee was having a bad time. Snow gave way all the time and made climbing very hard. The speed of the hampered chaps became slower. I was going along very easily, though a little out of breath.'

Monte Moro rises to nearly 3000 metres above sea level. Chewing snow eased the hikers' rapacious thirst. Moro's boulder fields and its saddle with sides of high snow-covered peaks loomed ahead. Behind them, the grey bell-tower of the Pecetto churchyard in Macugnaga would soon don a snowy-white cap, like marzipan icing.

'We had practically a vertical climb of 100 foot.' The logistics of the task was memorised by Charles. 'Digging our feet sideways to get as good a grip as possible with our boots, and using hands as well, we commenced climbing. The chaps with the bad feet were toiling now, while the South African was gamely struggling on, resting every few yards. About 40 foot off the top, the three fittest chaps were practically at the summit. Then, a few minutes later, their voices came floating down to tell us they had made it.

The last 15 foot was practically vertical, and one of the chaps came down to assist the chap with the bad knee. At long last the entire eight of us were on top of Monte Moro.

'There was no sign of barbed-wire or Swiss soldiers. The only indication was a small pyramid-shaped cement post each side of the saddle, marked with the words of the country. To the left and right, peaks of the range rose many hundreds of feet above, very steep, covered in snow, the tops having ice on them.

'Looking over the Swiss side, I could see a huge snow-covered decline stretching for nearly a mile till it ended at the bottom of a deep narrow valley. From each side rose mountains sheer, their tops jagged and covered in snow, a white wilderness of snow and ice.'

Charles realised that although Italy had been his jail for nearly two years, the 'backwash of war' was not a true indication of Italy in peacetime. On Switzerland's threshold he indulged his propensity for nostalgia: 'I knew that as the passing of time would erase much of the bitterness of prison life, I would remember with pleasure the beautiful countryside, quaint villages, the glorious sunshine in May, and beautiful moonlight nights. I would remember the happy, laughing rice girls. I will always remember the simple, hardworking peasant women, and their equally kind-hearted men, to whom anyone in distress would never have to appeal more than once—if at all.'

Charles's heart sank when border guards fell in behind them, believing them to be German, and that his group would be placed in a barbed-wire compound. Charles declared his meagre possessions wrapped in a handkerchief suspended from his shoulder.

Charles warmed up with 'a decent feed of potatoes and bread' at a table with 'real tablecloths' while a Red Cross officer apologised about the food and another scurried about getting towels, soap and toothbrushes. They arranged cables to be sent to the Australians' families. When a doctor examined them, Charles appreciated his summation: 'You have been without food for a long time now and have had a hard time.' At the handling camp at Wil, English uniforms were issued.

By the time of Charles's arrival on 3 November 1943, the Swiss had processed approximately 340 Australian arrivals, many trickling in via Monte Moro Pass and the Mattmark Hotel.[6] On 3 November, other Australians making Swiss inroads, possibly within Charles's party, included Ronald Douglas as well as Harold Pack and Melvin Maynard.[7] Melvin was not his real name. Allen Maynard, Melvin's younger cousin, adopted Melvin's age and moniker in order to enlist into the 2/48th Battalion in 1941.[8] Adhering to army paybook documentation for arriving POWs, Swiss officials accepted the name of Melvin Maynard as entering their territory on 3 November.

21
'ALONG THE WAY WE LOST SNOWY': POW MATES SEPARATE

'Evaders were simply fugitives. Like other fugitives, they had to eat; and, after a few days, stealing or begging were likely to be their only sources of food, unless they were taken in by some local inhabitant who managed to put them in touch with an organised resistance movement—best of all, with an escape line.'

—Roger Absalom, 1991[1]

Along the way, escaper groups crossed paths, blended, thinned out, disbanded and changed direction. Even those who initially desired to stick together because of friendship or trust became separated by strategy or circumstance.

In the watershed that followed the promulgation of the armistice, Tom Anderson and Fred Tabram had escaped in separate groups, following their respective strategies to traipse north and south of the River Po.

During the early weeks of freedom, Fred Tabram and Frank 'Bluey' Blewett kept moving around between a familiar circuit of various shelters and people keen to assist.[2] Italians recognised them, and sourced clothes and supplies. Fred made the most of the hospitality of villagers at nearby Ronsecco, in particular the Olivero family, until 3 November 1943.[3]

'A few days here and a few days there, the same routine was followed, walking most of the day, asking for food and in the evenings asking if we could sleep in hay barns.'

Having crossed the Po River, travelling southward towards advancing Allied lines, Tom Anderson, Garvan 'Snowy' Drew and Joe Andrews moved through different regions like tourists on 'a rare culinary adventure', sampling regional staples. 'At a house we stayed at, they made a kind of porridge called *gestani* from chestnut flour. It wasn't served in individual bowls but poured onto the wooden table in one big round slab. When it set, everyone helped themselves.'[4]

On the outskirts of a village, Tom's trio met a farmer who invited them to his house for the night. Tom thought it amusing: 'Me and Snowy flanked by the Italian, his daughters and the donkey, as we walked into the village in broad daylight. In our civilian clothes and beards, we must have looked sufficiently like Italian peasants to fool the Germans. And we saw many Germans.

'The lady of the house welcomed us and gave us the evening meal. We all went to bed, then it seemed we'd only been asleep a couple of hours when we were woken by sounds of the family stirring. In the early hours, they were preparing breakfast. Apparently, breakfast was the big meal of the day, and it took them about four hours to prepare. They made pasta and hung it in the kitchen to dry. And there were potatoes.'

Food was not wasted by the Italian people, as exemplified by the sight of Italian men retrieving the body of a donkey which had fallen down a cliff. At the Oratory of San Pellegrino within the Italian province of L'Aquila, located approximately 60 kilometres east of Rome, a 'monk brought us bread and wine and then presented us with this big, round cheese', recalled Tom. 'They left us with it. We weren't sure how to approach this. It must have been a very old and precious cheese. It was crawling with jumpers. We could see them hopping. The whole thing was alive with them. We very gingerly cut off small pieces to taste. It was good. We'll have a bit more of this, and a bit more, and a bit more. This went on. Then, suddenly, our enjoyment was over. The monk came in and whisked it away. He reckoned we'd had enough of his precious cheese!'

Tom heard that a Victorian buddy, Mick Simmons,[5] was unfortunate to be handed over to Germans. In November, Tom Anderson's trio had a sudden split. 'The weather was getting colder as we got closer to our destination. Then, along the way we lost Snowy.' As the trio meandered through a large town, they'd briefly separated to minimise attracting attention. Tom and Joe took longer to get through the town and lost sight of their mate.

The duo proceeded on their quest to reach American forces in the south. They may have regretted ditching the shorter trek to the Alps for a considerably longer walk in the opposite direction.

As they approached Monte Greco, east of Rome, they met up with an American. Together they trudged uphill until they reached a shepherd's hut. A sign on the door read 'MORTE'. The trio were freezing and their boots had that many holes that the slush was going in one side and out the other. On Thursday 25 November, Thanksgiving Day, 'we entered the hut', Tom narrated, 'and there, laid out on a table, was a dead Italian. The cold had been too much for him, apparently.'

Not wanting the same fate, a fire was prepared. The American was the only one with food, and he shared tins of coffee and raspberry jam. For water, snow was boiled and coffee and jam stirred into it. 'Delicious,' Tom enthused, happy to boost energy reserves to keep moving. 'After three months of hiking we were anxious to be with our own men again ... only the Sangro River was between us.' Tom and Joe roughly guessed they were within eight kilometres of the front-line and freedom: they could hear artillery fire.

They held fast at what appeared to be a suitable place to cross the lines and kept watch until darkness fell. As they waded across, ex-jockey Joe, shorter in stature than Tom, and a non-swimmer, struggled to keep his head above water. A rifle shot shrilled above their wet heads. As they crawled onto the riverbank, guards popped up. Their much-anticipated reunion with Allied forces was thwarted.

Tom's trio stood up with rifles trained on their dripping bodies. 'Captured for the third time in this war, we were prisoners again.' The only consolation was receiving their first food in three days.

Tom and Joe stewed in a prison camp near the Umbrian city of Spoleto, about 70 kilometres north of Rome. German guards nudged them onto a train bound for Moosburg, Germany.

Back 'in the bag' Stalag 7A, Tom continued to get into strife. One night he stepped out of his tent to piss. Guards had neglected to inform him that it was forbidden to leave the tent after dark and a bullet whistled past his ear. Reflexively, he hit the ground, then yelled, 'Missed, you bastard!'

A brief entry in Fred's notebook refers to a brief excursion to Trino and crossing a River Po bridge. 'Neatly dressed' in an Italian friend Gianni's best clothes, and accompanied by 'Josephina and her brother', Fred relaxed. In contrast to Tom's reasons for going south, Fred was pleasurably derailed to help harvest grapes. The Italian family recorded the day out on camera, with Fred posing with bunches of white grapes.

Back to the reality of his itinerant life on the northern side of the Po River, the weather was getting cold. Wide-eyed and war-ripped after three months of 'wandering the plains' with winter drawing closer, Fred and Bluey headed higher into the foothills. Fred's notes inform that from late 1943 to late 1944, he circuited villages located within a triangle west of the Sesia River, south of Monte Barone and east of Biella.

For some periods, 'the days were always long and monotonous. Usually when I had no definite plans to go at night, I went to bed at around 7 o'clock when it was dark. To move about in the darkness was always dangerous.'

Breaking the lonely spells, Fred crossed paths with other POW swagmen including Jim Brennan and Bernie Bruce, 'Wally and Chick', and Geoff O'Rafferty, a fellow Albury boy, whose brother Pat had reached Swiss territory in late September. Fred took pride in his increasing understanding of Italian language, but was challenged by dialect variations. Roaming about, ever-watchful for *carabinieri* and fascist spies, he grew familiar with Piedmont hills, valleys and friendly tavern and shop proprietors.

During several months of hiding in the hills, Fred and Bluey were generously assisted in most upper Valsesia villages they entered. An Italian advised Fred to dye his blond hair black. 'Our men adopted various disguises ... Those with feminine faces dressed as girls; some posed as old men and one masqueraded as a priest.'

In late autumn 1943, Fred and Bluey received a tip-off about a hotel north of Postua at Noveis, Monte Barone, about 25 kilometres north-east of Biella—Hotel Alpe Noveis. He was informed that the hotel was acting as a collection point for transfer of POWs to Switzerland. The only access to the hotel was by a mountain track.

In his notebook, Fred makes abbreviated reference to the Italian–American proprietors as 'C and A', presumably due to concerns about enemy reprisals if his notebook was discovered. He noted that several POWs were received at the hotel every day during one of his visits. On one visit Fred mentions seven POWs there: British, Scottish, New Zealanders and Australian escapers. Clementina offered for them to stay until the English arrived.

Fred earned his keep by working around the hotel grounds, chopping trees, sawing wood and carrying piles up steep slopes to a shed. He heard that a group of 52 POWs had departed for Switzerland three days before his arrival.

After heavy snowfalls at the beginning of winter, Fred helped clear the steep, narrow mule trail so the donkey could bring supplies of food and wine. Fred's notebook indicates that he and Bluey stayed at Noveis for several weeks in November until a guide showed up at the hotel in early December. Fred knew that raids had been made by German SS and fascist Blackshirts. Clementina and Angelo Zaninetti were 'two of the best and they helped every prisoner'.

Ian Knight and his New Zealander companion probably were at the hotel the same time as Fred.[6] Before he was directed to the hotel, Ian's duo expanded when other escapers tacked on. A small armed force raided a village's outskirts where they slept. In the entanglement of machine-gun fire and 'split-second decisions to run for thick forest', Ian could not discern who was recaptured or killed. 'This experience convinced me to never again travel with more than one mate.'

At Zaninetti's hotel, Ian augmented the POW labour force. 'We cut wood for the fires and to store under the sundecks for the coming winter. Fruit and vegetables were also stored there, packed in thick layers of mountain moss to prevent them from freezing. Chestnut and other large leaves were stored for animal bedding during the severe freeze.'

By late 1944, partisan bands were loaded up by arms drops from British planes, but Ian declined involvement with some, disagreeing with their methods and political views. He accepted invitation by communist partisans, 'reds', but feared that their presence would be discovered by fascists in nearby Crevacuore.

On Christmas Day 1943, Fred was introduced to local 'rebels' who celebrated with cannons, mortar, rifles and machine-guns. 'The whole mountain came alive.' After being searched and interviewed by the rebel leader, Fred 'spent time with this mob, about twenty of them, some only fifteen years of age. Rifles and weapons were toys to them.' Disenchanted with their inaction and 'long distance talk' about 'doing over fascists and Germans', Fred forged on, eager to meet up with other Australians and to aim for the mountains of Saint Bernard.

Clementina made arrangements for Fred and several POWs to be shepherded to another guide near Borgosesia who would hand them to another guide. 'C gave us a very good supper before we set off and an emergency supply of her own cookies.' Waiting for five hours in the cold, it was evident to Fred that the second guide was unavailable to assist. Fred learned he'd gone into hiding after a partisan skirmish.

Each day in December 1943, 'the reins were being held tighter', Fred feared. The Allies were still only one-third in occupied Italy. Fred and Bluey parted company to increase chances of travelling unnoticed and to 'be adopted' for a night or two.

'Being on your own, for days and nights, no one to talk to you, dodging fascists and Germans was not always pleasant; in fact, it was terrifying,' Fred exclaimed. 'I was determined never to be taken prisoner again, this kept me going.'

For the new year of 1944, Fred resolved to have another shot for neutral Switzerland. 'Five of us stayed at one place, five at another. Guides had a price on their heads and left. Again, that was the end of our chances of going to Switzerland.'

It was not Clementina's fault, Fred recognised, that plans had fallen down. She had more pressing matters to contend with. 'Fascists were forever with their eyes on this place. She received more than one friendly note to get rid of us.'

In his diary, Ian recorded that 'one fine morning, shortly after Christmas and beginning of 1944, carrying wood back for storage, we heard mortar fire down at the lower village—within seconds the shell exploded in the mountain side. We hiked higher to Monte Barone, and safety ... A couple of days later, fascists came up from Crevacuore, they laid waste everywhere, completely burning the albergo [hotel], shot our milking cow, took the sheep and gentle donkeys, arrested Angelo and Clementina who were, I imagine, sheltering either in the cellar or the under the sundeck storeroom.'

'I wandered about the Val Sesia for a day or two until I was able to meet up with my New Zealand mate. We took a quick cautious journey back to the albergo to find the above shocking scene.' Others witnessed Angelo and Clementina being taken away to a political prison.

In late April 1944, Ian and POW companion known as 'Blackie' made a last-ditch effort to cross the high Alps. Thwarted by 'glasslike ice fields' and no gear to aid them, the duo retreated to familiar topography, with plans to retry the higher Alps later. Keeping to alpine footpaths on slopes and ridges, rather than the easy path of the valley roads, had proved a safe travel strategy for seven months. On the morning of their second stab at the high Alps, they diverted in haste to meet Italian friends, taking the valley track near the river. It led into the path of a fascist patrol.

'We were exhibited to the village inhabitants on the village green, some of whom we knew very well, but of course neither we nor they, on this sad occasion, recognised each other for obvious reasons.' In early June, Ian and Blackie sat, sealed within a windowless cattle-truck, on a train speeding towards the Brenner Pass.

In July 1944, Nazi forces pursued partisans on Alpe Noveis's pastures. Seven partisans were captured and executed.[7] Clementina and Angelo paid dearly for their support to the resistance, according to Italian friends who remembered them in their later years. Thrust into a difficult period of detention after the 1944 raid and beaten in prison, Clementina and Angelo Zaninetti's kickback against fascism had 'stolen even their smiles'.[8]

22
'The last station in Italy': Hidden help by escape organisations

'Most of the Australians who fell in with partisans did so serendipitously... [Johnny] Peck, in contrast, had sought contact with oppositional elements in Vercelli from the moment of his release from jail. His motivation to organise a helping hand for men who had little idea where to turn next ... that humanitarian impulse was shared by the Italian men and women who placed themselves at Peck's disposal and, through selfless acts of kindness, thumbed their noses at a new regime.'

—Peter Monteath, 2017[1]

For fortunate train-riders, it was the quickest way to reach the goal of the Italian–Swiss frontier. Some bought their own tickets. Others discovered that civilian arrangers of train tickets did so out of spontaneous compassion, or because they were embedded in escaper assistance organisations. It was not always possible for escapers to discern where a helper sat on the spectrum of resistance and subversion. Moreover, escapers may not have known when it was one of their fold, an Australian escaper called Johnny Peck, pulling the sympathetic strings.

For many escaped POWs, their inability to decipher the differences and crossovers between the complex interplay of informal and organised networks is testimony to the cunning and careful planning by civilians acting on their own initiative as well as by those swept into Peck's slipstream.

Peck, as a key planner of staging points, secret routes and safe houses, faced the same risks as the Italians with whom he collaborated. The dangers inherent in Peck's labours stemmed not just from the occupying German forces but also from the fascists and their sympathisers who waged a kind of civil war against partisans of northern Italy.[2] Guided escapers travelled to within short distances of the border, including Domodossola, Luino or Ponte Tresa, aiming to avoid border inspections.[3] From their drop-off points, they'd continue on arduous but short walks to Switzerland.[4]

The main 'resistance organization', the Milan-based *Ufficio Assistenza Prigionieri di Guerra Alleati* (Allied prisoners of war assistance service) had started several weeks before either German frontier guards or Allied agents were in place. The main task of organising the assistance was entrusted to Giuseppe Bacciagaluppi who, with his English wife Audrey, had homes in Milan and near Lake Maggiore, perfectly located to assist transit of escapers with the help of their assistants.[5]

Crete veteran Clifford Chard's group was assisted by civilians to reach Novara to catch a train for Luino, on the eastern side of Lake Maggiore, within several kilometres of Swiss territory to his east or north, and arrived 28 September 1943.[6] Alamein veteran Len Boskell presented the same day, and reported the same itinerary of help. 'Met organisation near Novara, train to Luino, entered Switzerland at Agno.'[7] Horace Tyrie and a mate, having spent three weeks post-armistice at Casalrosso, just east of Vercelli city, after walking there from Tronzano camp, had also decided to try for Switzerland. They took a train from Santhia northwards and disembarked close to the border at Villadossola, just before Domodossola. They walked towards Antrona and the border but were diverted towards Gondo, in the vicinity of the Simplon Pass, by Italian soldiers on 2 October.[8]

Alfred 'Ray' Cotterell and Cecil Nott's group took their seats on a train heading north.[9] After the armistice, Ray had exchanged his uniform for civvy clothes. At a mountain monastery, a monk proffered monk's habits for the Cotterell party. Fearing that the monks could be in peril due to this gesture, the men declined the offer. They decided to catch a train bound for Switzerland, regardless of German patrol.

Ray practised his basic Italian and purchased tickets. Seated opposite Ray and Cecil were two young Italian girls who kept pointing to their feet, dropping firm hints that their British army boots were a giveaway. Conversation was conducted in mixed English and Italian, with vigorous hand-gesturing. The girls, the POWs discovered, were part of an underground organisation's arrangement with the train driver to give three whistle blasts as signal to jump. On cue, Ray's group jumped the rattler and dived for cover. The girls boldly called out *'buona fortuna, Aussie'*. Worried that the girls may have been heard by patrols, the men laid low but no volley of bullets shot from the train chuffing away.

Having escaped late August, Ray's group took thirty-eight days to reach the border frontier. Ray, Cecil and nine others were clear to traipse with their English boots into Switzerland on 7 October 1943.[10] As a group photo was taken at Gondo, on the Swiss frontier, on 8 October 1943—including Cecil Nott, 'Ned' Inglis, Bill Doig, Ken Calder, Norm Colson, all listed as having arrived 7 Oct—there is indication of a wider group merging near the Simplon, or close on heels, and the day afterwards posing for a celebratory photograph.[11]

Other Australians were indeed on the same route on the same day, desperate not to bungle the last phase of the trek out of Italy. On 7 October Arthur 'Caff' Caffrey, aged forty-two years, also reached Gondo, presumably having made use of part of a hiking trail from Domodossola to Gondo.[12] Arthur does not state more detail about his path but smugglers used nearby Monscera Pass during the war.

Jim Hyland's account lists 'Caff' in his escaper party, as well as 'Ray', Norm Colson, 'Mick' (probably Mick Gillies or Frank Dalton) and a 'Bluey'.[13] Jim Hyland recalled their journey to Domodossola.

Around the beginning of October, Jim's group sheltered at San Nazzaro, six kilometres north of Vercelli. A French reporter, 'Froggie', from the newspaper *La Stampa* commenced arrangements for northward passage. Plans stalled briefly because General Rommel was believed to be in Novara. On 5 October, a car, secreted in the haystack, began to shuttle the POWs, conspicuously underdressed on a cold day, on the first leg to a train station. A *carabiniere* turned his back to avoid seeing them; the ticket inspector did not blink an eyelid at their tickets. Their *padrone* made arrangements for a whistle-blast signal to jump before Domodossola, within shouting distance of the alpine frontier.

The *padrone* accompanying them went ahead to source a guide. At 5am on 7 October, the climbing and pathfinding began. The going was tough. 'We have only had one loaf of bread between two for two days.' As their guide advanced, they became subsumed within a larger traveller party totalling about thirty-five, comprising eleven Australians, Italian officers and soldiers, one sailor and three airforce. Jim was informed that he was amongst the first Australians to present to border near the Simplon area.

All up, twenty-three Australians had hit a home-run to Switzerland on Thursday 7 October 1943.[14]

On the day after these Australians' arrival in the land of cuckoo clocks, Queenslander Bob McClelland stepped onto a train at or near Vercelli with two Italians bound for Como. 'I was handed to another guide who conducted me to the frontier.'[15]

As the weather started to cool off into the early days of November 1943, Jim Wilson initially followed advice to head south by an inland route, and to catch a train only for short distances.[16] He'd walk between stations to break up the length of travel. There were many German and Italian troops about, and he had difficulty getting information. He avoided larger towns and slept in haystacks, lofts and barns. He decided to turn back and head northward.

'When I got back into the Vercelli area, an Italian, himself trying to avoid Germans, helped me build a dug-out in the side of a canal …a tremendous canal system through this area, from the Po River.

'One day I heard Aussie speech and found three Aussies on the far side of the canal. They wanted to go to Carpanetto [Carpeneto] so I went along to show them the way. Some distance on, two Italian provosts jumped from behind a hedge, each with a revolver and rifle aimed at us. They let us go but advised us to give ourselves up to the Germans. This, of course, we weren't prepared to do.'

Jim raised the issue of heading to Switzerland with the friendly manager at Carpeneto farm and his wife. After dinner, they gave Jim money and two letters of introduction for their contacts. The manager's brother offered money towards a train fare.

On 4 November 1943, Jim 'caught a train that night from Vercelli to Domodossola'.[17] Reaching Domodossola, the railway junction between Italy and Switzerland, within cooee of the Swiss border, he 'talked with fellow passengers, mostly folks down from the mountain area for rice and grains'. Their advice, freely proffered, was to 'be careful on the mountains, to keep my hands off the snow and to keep my face away from the wind'. After he disembarked at Domodossola, he crossed the road to a hotel.

Possibly the hotel was the Eurossola Hotel, across the road from the train station. Clutching a letter of introduction, he stepped into the hotel's dining room, noticing half a dozen dining German officers. Jim carried a revolver and a newspaper which he flipped open, pretending to be absorbed. 'No one bothered me,' Jim was blessedly relieved to note. For extra reassurance, he rummaged his room, noting the distance to the ground if he needed to jump.

At first light, 'not even waiting for breakfast', he hopped on the first northbound train. Jim followed the farmer's directions and stepped off the train at the recommended station near the Swiss border. He presented the second letter of introduction at the village's hotel desk.

'The proprietor whisked me out the back and cared for me, sending his son to purchase my train ticket for that afternoon. I left the train at the last station in Italy (next stop would have been Switzerland and there would have been German guards at the border). It was mid-afternoon as I walked out of the village and commenced my trek over the Alps.'

Jim walked along a small bitumen track, peering downslope to see vehicles 'no bigger than match-boxes'. Moonlight assisted his walk to a small tunnel with a narrow-gauge trolley line. A man stood in a pill-box, 'something like our telephone boxes', reading by candlelight. Jim watched and waited. To his relief, he couldn't see a guard's silhouette at the other end. He sneaked quietly past the candle-lit box and through the tunnel. The track passed a small village where people were singing and dancing but Jim did not approach them.

Jim kept moving until early morning, when he found a shelter at a farmhouse. 'I made use of one [shed] to burn some leaves and twigs for warmth and had forty winks.' Daylight brought a little old lady, very annoyed because of the fire. 'She directed me to the track up the mountain. Soon I could look down on a 50 or 60-acre flat and what appeared to be a guesthouse.'

There, a man eagerly pointed towards Switzerland, by two mountains, although it did not look that far. The day dribbled by before he touched the snow-line. A herd of goats gave silent welcome, allowing their glorious milk to flow into a jar that Jim carried in his kit.

At the guesthouse, he was instructed to follow the left part of a narrow, forked track. 'One slip could've taken me down thousands of feet. I did slide about 20 feet down when making my way across to the second mountain—rubbed a hole through my pants and removed a piece of skin.' Moonlight, kindly, offered visibility. Cement crosses marked the Swiss border. Jim's excitement tempered as he observed a log-cabin, checking for human movement. Deeming it safe, he 'dossed down' in the straw to sleep, woken when the straw wriggled with fleas.

On 17 November, out of food, he trod downslope in morning light to be confronted by a guard with an Alsatian dog. At first, the uniform appeared to be German. Jim's anxiety dropped when he spotted a white cross on his cap. 'He asked if I was Italian. When I said Australian, he thought I said "Austrian". When I said British, he understood.' Jim gulped coffee, an apple and a sandwich.

When the guard set off in his strong spiked boots, Jim had trouble keeping up. He'd entered near Gondo. Like Monte Moro Pass, for centuries this area had been used by Roman legions crossing the alpine trading route between Switzerland and Italy.

Jim reported that the Italian guides were part of a 'proper organisation'. He does not disclose companions in his account but in his 1944 report, Jim declared that 'two Italians came to the farm' after the armistice and it was arranged that he 'go to Switzerland with three other Australians—Ptes Davis, Green, McKelvery'. Swiss records note the arrival of John 'Brian' Green and George McKelvie on the same day as Jim, 17 November 1943.[18]

New Zealand-born Australian, Albert Grimsey, touched down on Swiss slopes the same day, according to Swiss record-keeping.[19] At thirty-six years of age Albert was one of the older POWs.[20] After hanging about farms near his Vettigne camp for about ten days, he and fifty-five others went into hills near the tiny village of Zubiena, between Ivrea and Biella.[21] Chased by Germans, fourteen POWs returned to Vettigne, Campo 106/3, staying put until 25 October, given food, clothing and money by Benedetto Francese. He and eleven others left when fascists and Germans combed the farms. He spent three days sitting tight at Monte Barone, 'eight other POWs were there,' and he left with others for Switzerland and crossed Monte Moro Pass. In contrast to the Swiss record, his POW report lists 7 November.

'Most Italians were on our side,' Stan Bailey wrote, echoing Albert's experience, 'but the *fascista* were always around so we kept moving.'[22] As escapers, Porongurup's Stan Bailey and Jarrahdale's Vic Angove, both from Albert Grimsey's 2/28 Battalion, were nudged onto a train.[23]

The concerted decision was to head north for Switzerland but for a few days during the post-armistice upheaval, they roamed the countryside near the farm. An Italian offered to guide them for a 2am kick-off to the border, but at first the duo worried it was a trap. With his help, and with that of a local doctor, their train rides were paid for.

'This sounded pretty good, so our train ride began. The train stopped at Arona, a large town.' Arona, approximately 70 kilometres north-west of Milan, straddles the Swiss–Italian border on the western banks of Lake Maggiore. The guide left Stan and Vic to renew their train tickets, presumably to continue towards the Swiss border, but didn't return. 'We sat on the station waiting, but the town was under curfew so we decided to head for the mountains.' Vic had blue eyes and stood over six-feet tall; his appearance would've attracted glances by Italian passengers.

'We found a small cow shed; inside were a couple of milking cows and some hay. It felt warm so we decided to bed down for the night. You can well imagine the look on the cocky's face when he came next morning and saw us. He was a good bloke, gave us breakfast and directed us on our journey.'

Stan and Vic scouted on foot. 'I remember coming to a fast-flowing river with a bridge under the watchful eyes of a sentry post. The only crossing was across the bridge. The whole area seemed to have people moving around, so we decided to join the mob and stroll confidently across. All seemed well until a couple of small children spotted our boots, *"Inglese scarpa"* (English boot) they yelled.' Stan was relieved that the sentries didn't hear or react to the innocent children's comment.

He need not have worried; the sentries were Swiss. On 13 November 1943, Stan scribbled his details on a slip that had a pre-printed declaration of being been taken to Switzerland with his consent and that all necessary assistance has been provided. As this slip was in Italian, and different format to Swiss arrival cards, it was presumably for the purposes of the organisation that helped them. Vic also signed a slip.

Lismore's Ross Mudge, a stretcher-bearer in the 2/3rd Pioneer Battalion,[24] was at a farmhouse near Donato when a German/fascist *rastrallamento* round-up hit on 13 November. He was shot in the leg by a German soldier to slow him down for recapture, but the soldier added a shot to Ross's abdomen. It was reported that the soldier also kicked and spat at Ross, and left him in agony for over two hours before an Italian soldier helped him.[25] Taken to hospital in Ivrea, Ross died. He was just twenty-three years of age. Ross's grave, until re-interment in Milan's Commonwealth War Graves Commission cemetery, was tended to by Ivrea woman—acknowledged by Ted Peachey as a 'Number 1 underground worker'–Selina Roffino.[26] In a painful irony, Ross's service and casualty record states that 'stretcher-bearers were declared protected personnel under the Geneva Convention.'[27]

On 27 November 1943, Alfred Griffiths made his run.[28] He left a three-week billet with Rita Perazzo at Salasco, the woman to whom Lloyd Moule also felt gratitude. Alfred reported that Rita put him in touch with an escape organisation run by Australian POW Johnny Peck on 20 September. Affiliates spurred Alfred onto a train at Vercelli bound for Novara, thence to Luino. On foot he continued from Luino on a short sprint to cross the Swiss finishing post on 1 December.

Alamein survivor Doug Le-Fevre put the evasion period in a nutshell: 'Escape was simple but the thing was to stay escaped.'[29] In January 1944, Doug worried about Germans cracking down and destroying villages where POWs had been 'lying doggo' (hiding). 'Enough is enough,' thought Doug. He and Norm Terrell decided better late than never on Switzerland. 'We did it the easy way,' Doug exclaimed, 'mainly by train.' Clutching money given to them by partisans, they headed to Vercelli, along the way teaming up with George Rea and Jack Dodd, other ex-POWs of La Corte. They too had feared endangering Italian lives as well as their own. They bought train tickets at Vercelli, going as far as they dared, before bailing out and walking over border mountains. Doug, the self-confessed 'snotty-nosed and very insecure young man' and his 'muto' mate Norm Terrell were safely ushered deeper into Swiss territory.

Jack Dodd, when in Ronsecco farm area several weeks earlier, had touched base with an 'organisation'.[30] Jack had some idea about its founder and modus operandi: 'There was a guy doing a bit of organising ... this guy's name was Johnny Peck. I never knew him. Only knew him when he came into the train ... just saw him briefly ... I think he went to sleep and was supposed to get off with us and didn't.'

POW trafficking had thinned by December.

'Doug [Le-Fevre] and Norm [Terrell] were going to go one way and George [Rea] and I were going to go another way,' narrated Jack Dodd, but as they were about to split, circumstances changed in an instant. Jack added that '... a guy comes tearing along on a pushbike and says, "Come on quick, quick, you've got to catch a tram, a man will walk through with a black hat on and he'll take his hat off when you get to Vercelli, you follow him". So, when the tram pulled up, we went and just dawdled around and followed him into an old church and then the activity went on—there was clothes being thrown everywhere and then we had to catch a train out of Vercelli then to go right up to Lake Maggiore. I forget the name of the town but it was where that big lake that's half in Italy and half in Switzerland [is] and the train stopped right on the edge of that, never went into the station. I believe it was all pre-planned.'

The four escapers had been hustled along together, likely to have fallen softly into Peck's web. 'It was things that you would see in films, almost, and we were in the middle of it.'

The four Australians walked over the mountains on an old contraband route for three days, crossing into Switzerland at Brissago on 5 January 1944. In his 1989 interview for Keith Murdoch Sound Archive, Jack Dodd reflected on 'areas of our life that are really precious times to us, that bring out real character in men. I saw circumstances change strong men. I've seen strong men that I looked up to weaken when they're short of food and they would pinch the last biscuit you had.'

Speaking about Italian womenfolk, Jack Dodd said, 'They were so good to us. Invited us to their homes. The problem we had was not having a big enough capacity for their wine.' Former enemies collided, and colluded.

Train travel did not gift Don Radnell with a safe home-run.[31]

Don had stuck with his POW offsider, twenty-three-year-old Norm King, who was in a bit of strife with a bullet in his leg. In December, Don sensed that after two months of aid by Italians, it was time to shoot through. 'As Italians couldn't safely take Norm to a doctor, arrangements were made for him and I to get to Switzerland. This was going to cost money and we had none but if we left a "to whom it may concern" letter for the Yanks or British when they got there, this would cover everything. Norm wrote out a letter saying how much these people had helped us, we left a letter at each of the two farms then they gave us more clothing and more money. We hid the money, about 300 *lira* each, in our coat collars.'

Fortunate to have hooked up with a guide who purchased a family train ticket, Don and Norm embarked on a journey from Vercelli station, heading north. Whether the guide was part of an organised network, Don did not know, or did not disclose.

Fascist troops boarded the train, checking passengers. Scrutinising their tickets, the troops pulled their guns. The Victorians passed into German hands and were slammed into a civilian jail in town.

A large snowfall overnight blocked the view from the cell window the next morning. Handcuffed, the two Victorians were marched to the railway station. Protecting themselves and their guide, the POWs denied any knowledge of being helped on the train. At Milan, Don and Norm we were given over to other German troops. 'We'd been handcuffed all this time,' Don recounted, 'but I have a very small hand and was able to pull a hand out to stretch my arms then put my hand back again. About the third time I did this the guard saw me, and nearly shit himself.' Under closer scrutiny, they were relocated to Trento, 60 kilometres south of Bolzano, destined for Austria via the Brenner Pass.

Inspection and interrogation by Germans 'was an experience', Don understated. 'You would think that we were the whole of the British army. Norm having a bullet still in his leg and being with the partisans didn't make it any easier.' Norm, six feet in stockinged feet, probably looked imposing to their captors.

'We were put in separate rooms for interrogation. First, they searched us stripped naked, and made us stand in the centre of a room. Our clothing was searched and they found money in our coat collars. We told different stories, but still maintained we had been together and Norm was shot by a German soldier while walking through a village. They searched each of us still naked, looked through our hair and bent us over and looked up. They still kept us apart and repeated this search each day and sometimes twice a day, the reason being that our stories didn't match up. This went on for seven days, then they put us together again.

'One morning they marched us to the interpreter who spoke perfect English. He placed a large map of Italy in front of me and asked just where I had been. I placed my open hand on top of north Italy and said "around about there". Norm followed suit, acting vague.' The interpreter, they reckoned, had hoped that they'd spill the beans about partisan activities.

Three days later, Boxing Day 1943, the Australians shivered at a railway station, awaiting their transfer to German-controlled camps. There was one consolation. At some point during their transits, a German doctor removed the bullet from Norm's leg.

In the last days of 1943, 'We were put with a lot of political POWs and loaded into railway trucks, eighty men each truck,' Don Radnell lamented, 'packed in so tight that no one sat down, we all had to stand. These trucks had only a small barred window about two-feet square, the only light and air we could get. We were sent to Germany in these conditions. We were given bread before we left and travelled through Austria into Germany which took three days and nights. In some of these trucks people died. At one stage I rested one foot by lifting it up. I didn't get it back on the floor for about an hour. Things looked bloody bad for those three days.

'We got somewhere in Germany when the train stopped to let us out. You can imagine the sweet smell of fresh air. All we had in the train truck for a toilet was a large bucket that was never emptied until now.' Don recalled that the Allied troops were separated and sent to Stalag IVB at Muhlberg between Dresden and Berlin. A further sixteen months of captivity was ahead for the former furnace worker and his tall storeman mate.[32]

23
'The easy way to Switzerland': Border lake crossings

'Despite the upheavals of World War Two, Italy was a patriarchal, rural society that was still steeped in traditional notions of gender relations. Young girls were cloistered at home under vigilant family supervision ... Most Italian women were the central forces of their households and, to the eye of a casual observer, seemed to do all the work while the menfolk just hung around. The majority of fit young Italian men were absent. Thousands were prisoners of war in Allied countries, while others had been rounded up to join the Fascist militia or had been deported to Germany to provide manpower in German war industries. A sizeable portion joined partisan formations fighting in the mountains.'

—Susan Jacobs, 2012[1]

Autumn deepened into October 1943 for the dwindling numbers of runaways who still roamed the Italian countryside. Monte Moro and Teodulo passes became less of an option for making inroads into Switzerland. Border lakes provided a viable alternative, despite being awash with their own dangers. As many weeks had passed since the armistice and German patrols increased, it became more difficult to move north without assistance.

After escaping Tronzano Vercellese camp, Queenslander David Todd, 2/15th, and Victorian Alan Nicholson, 2/24th, bagged a train journey north. 'Three Italians offered to take us to Switzerland. They did not belong to any organisation. They took us by train to Milan, then train to Cantua. We continued on without their help to Como.'[2] Alan, who was ex-officer at Campo 106/2 Tronzano, added that on the way they'd been 'bivouaced and whacked up by partisans', and Germans recaptured most of their initial party of 150 men.[3]

'We hired a boat to cross the lake,' continued David, crossing at or near Lake Como, about 25 kilometres east of Lake Maggiore. They climbed the mountains with a blackmarket Italian who carted rice and went to an Italian frontier post where they stayed the night. David and Alan had crossed the mountains. Their home-run on the morning of 13 October 1943 was facilitated by a marshall at the frontier post who sent them 'through the gate'.

Meanwhile West Australians Jack Nie and Norm Bailey, brother to Stan, were sitting tight amongst the rice farms. They had left Pettiva camp after the armistice, to wander about for a week or so, then reverted back to Salasco, a hamlet adjoining Pettiva farmlands. An older couple whose son was a POW in West Australia took them in. In his POW report, Norm acknowledged 'Luigi Chisio' of Salasco for providing food, clothing and lodging from 19 September to 1 December. Luigi also gave them 200 *lire*.[4]

The POWs absconded from Luigi's orbit when it became 'too hot' with fascist snoops. Jack and Norm navigated their way by a coloured map of Vercelli province on which Jack blue-lined their northbound trajectory. The blue pen marks a six-day journey spearing due north, keeping a few kilometres west of the Sesia River while passing through rice areas of Vettigne, Palestro to Balocco and Rovasenda. Seeking to cross the Sesia, the pen-line turns sharply in an easterly line towards Ghislarengo on Sesia's western banks. Blue ink traces their smooth crossing of the Sesia north of Gattinara, perhaps at a bridge leading to Romagnano Sesia, and scrawls on north-east, drawing closer to Lake Maggiore which lies beyond the map's parameters.

Jack and Norm passed through Borgomanero to Sesto Calende to see Maggiore's southernmost waters flowing into the Ticino River, east of its parallel river, the Sesia. Tributaries of the Po River, both the Sesia and Ticino rivers originate in the Swiss Alps.

During their six-day marathon, what Jack considered to be 'the easy way to Switzerland', they kipped in haystacks, most of which, they discovered, were kept undercover in Italy.[5] Jack was boosted by the welcome by local folk. Decades after their wartime flight, Jack recalled in his nineties that they were 'only knocked back for help once'. A chap they got talking to said 'hop in here', gesturing to his rowboat. Giving their legs a reprieve, he ferried them across the lake.

Jack recalls a major obstacle blocking their inroads, a '12-foot fence with bells on it' alongside the rail-line. Unable to 'make a dent in it' with their knife, they mounted the fence, boot toes stuck into fence gaps and hands stretching for the top, and slumped down to a rapidly flowing creek. But as Jack said, there was 'not a soul there'. Norm got wet first. To enact a swiftwater rescue, Jack hurled out a stick to him to get him back to the bank. Soaking wet, they went back over the fence to cross a bridge.

Whereas Jack's blue-penned route ends abruptly at the map's edge, Norm's report takes them on to Luino, and east to the shores of Lake Lugano on 6 December, to enter Switzerland at a border village, Ponte Tresa. At this village, one of Johnny Peck's staging points, Jack's army boots still held, providing quality carriage. Approaching a house, the occupants made contact with Swiss patrol.

Dick Gill and Jack Duggan were still biding time, just south of the River Po in the province of Alessandria, with their Brusaschetto abettors. Spending most of their time indoors, they were keen spectators as a Brusaschetto host, Rosa Bianco, cooked with a large circular cauldron suspended by chains over an open fireplace.[6] Rosa sliced pasta dough, made from wheat grown on the farm, into strips and hung it to dry. Dick savoured her spaghetti with 'perfect' mushrooms and boiled eggs. Rosa prepared polenta from maize or chestnut flour, served with rabbit smothered with mushrooms. The Australians chipped in to thrash rice in a barrel using a round pole to remove husks. Despite the unavailability of butter, they welcomed dried bread with juicy apples. Appetites sated, the Australians slept with the household's animals in the loft.

The Bianco family brought Dick in contact with the Ansaldi family and escaper Nicol Lawrie. Pre-war, Scottish-born Nicol Lawrie worked as a farmer in South Australia's Tumby Bay district.[7] Nicol was captured at Alamein on 1 November 1942, eighteen months after Dick and Jack were nabbed at Mechili.

Although Nicol had been a prisoner of war for less than a year, he was keen to try to meet Allied forces in the south.[8] He'd worked at several farms before arriving near Brusaschetto. There, he'd encountered other POWs sheltered in a stone building in receipt of advice about safe houses, one of which belonged to Aldo Ansaldi. On break from medical studies, Aldo took the escapers to his widowed mother's small home on a little wine farm.

Aldo's mother welcomed them with 'a beautiful rice meal and a bed of straw in the loft which we made our home for three weeks'. Neighbours took turns to bring meals, boosting the POWs' body weight and strength. During evenings of songs around the piano, Nicol was invited to play. He was an accomplished schoolboy pianist under Miss Vera Schrieber's tuition. Nicol and Dick exercised their beginners' Italian to enjoy conversation and to talk about their Australian lives. Their hosts wanted to leave war-torn Italy and migrate to Australia for a new life. Radio news reminded the POWs that war continued around their safe-house location. Allies were advancing further from the south; the Russians were advancing on all fronts. The Allies had difficulties, they heard, to push Germans back through the mud.

POW plodders, Dick, Jack, Nicol and Jim Kinder, would have been unaware of the number of men who'd reached Switzerland in October 1943. They were cognisant of increasing danger to themselves and the Italians.

Winter whistled closer, and dews dampened their clothes, making them wonder whether they ought to have mobilised earlier. The quartet jotted letters for their helpers to give to Allied forces to document eligibility for compensation for food, clothing and shelter.

Their three-week stay snapped to an end when Nato Ansaldi, Aldo's brother, gave fair warning that German guards were in neighbouring areas. The escapers stashed away their uniforms for the time being, but later heard these were found by the patrols. Nato hatched his plan. The quartet split into two parties, one allocated to Nato and the other to his friend. A train ride was part of the plot. 'We were dressed as peasants and spoke enough Italian to pass German guards on the stations and on the trains where we mingled with the crowds.'[9]

With each day, risks increased for the Bianco, Bruscara and Evasio families. On 3 December 1943, Michail Bruscara remarked that he'd contacted his brother at Intra, on Maggiore's shores, who in turn contacted two smugglers plying their trade between Italy and Switzerland. The smuggler's fee was 7000 *lire* to transfer four men.

The following day, the villagers made the POWs emotional as they 'gathered in full force to farewell us with numerous glasses of wine, embraces and with many a face full of tears.'[10] With Guiseppe and Maria, the POWs headed north past Trino, 'over-run by German troops', and to a depot to catch a tram to Vercelli, about 20 kilometres away. On dusk, they reached the city. Guiseppe bought torch batteries.

At Vercelli station, they hoped to blend with travellers, but eyes pierced their disguise. Germans patrolled. Without incident, they stepped onto a train with Nato bound for Novara, the first train leg. On the second journey, the train tracks led directly to *Lago* (Lake) Maggiore straddling the Swiss–Italian border, the second largest lake in Italy.

The Australians were astounded that Nato found a boat-owner willing to take them to Intra. 'Patrol boats were everywhere,' Nicol worried, 'but the man who rowed our boat sang all the way across and I never heard anything so beautiful as his voice as it echoed across the lake.' The decoy was perfect. Patrolling boat skippers ignored them, perhaps believing they were workers returning home after a party. Crowded into the small vessel, the men took turns to row, showering each other with splash. The boat tossed and bucked as if they were adrift on a rough wide sea. Maria's brother-in-law and sister waited to fetch them all. They'd already drummed up two smugglers to escort them from the hotel to a trail used for border contraband.

With more farewells to abettors, the Australians became uneasy. Feeling like exiles, they regretted they could not scram underground to hide until Allied forces liberated them. Nicol clutched an envelope to give to the smugglers, containing 7000 *lire* rustled together from Brusaschetto villagers' donations.

With bread in their pockets, they made headway with their guides towards a winding mountain shepherd-and-goat track. Early on, the POWs laboured with the climbing as they'd been accustomed to low-lying country and were not in army-training fitness. Several hours of strength-searching brought them to a small village, Scareno, about ten kilometres due north of Intra. Venturing northward on the western side of Lake Maggiore, tough terrain dictated a four-hour hike to reach Socraggio, approximately ten kilometres from the border. There, two South African POWs, accompanied by a Jewish woman, met them. The POWs convinced the woman that it would be difficult to proceed with them.

Before setting off again, the men shared dinner and slept in front of a log-fire, disturbed by intermittent howling of the timber wolves. The next day they warred with the slopes Mount 'Pao Darla', rising to 3900 feet. On the other side of the valley, Dick said they were told that 'Mount Lunedario'—probably Monte Limidario straddling the Swiss–Italian border overlooking Brissago—stood at more than 6500 feet.

The valley crossing in 1943 was precarious, patrolled by German troops. Nicol lamented that 'for every three steps up, we slipped back two, even though we helped each other. Unfit, we were all exhausted. Our clothes and shoes were not meant for mountain climbing.' In spite of an urge to find a warm log-fire, they closely circumvented the next village's houses by crawling low on hands and knees through bushes, whipping those behind with the sting of branches on faces and shoulders. The obstacle course threw in a rocky cliff with a 'foot-wide goat track' covered by ice and water. Gingerly, the men edged along sideways, facing outwards. Dick resisted looking down the rocky gorge. 'One slip of the foot would mean certain death,' he proclaimed. 'Should one be inflicted only with an injury, rescue would be impossible.' Brief rest stops helped to reduce cramps, but on a plateau knee-deep in snow, one South African developed leg cramps. He pleaded to be left behind to unburden the others, but the others shored him up, using free hands to clutch sticks to probe the snow for crevasses.

A deserted hut, used in summer by shepherds, signalled refuge. Even without firewood, the crude bare interior beckoned them for an overnighter. With no blankets or overcoats, the squatters huddled for warmth. They set out at daybreak. It seemed they walked through clouds, saturating their clothing during the hours required to climb Monte Limidario.

In the North African desert, the sight of the enemy and the search or digging for shelter was limited by dust. In the Alps, the mist was kinder on the eyes but cruel on their nerves.

The Italian *contrabandieri* drew their attention forward. All eyes stared at a tin-can propped high on a two-metre stick, humbly announcing the Swiss–Italian border. Tentative shouts of joy echoed from rocks as the POWs chucked snow at each other. Nicol gladly handed the guides the envelope with the 7000 *lire*.

Creeping into Swiss territory, they stammered towards a cluster of huts. A soldier seemingly stepped out of the blue, cocking his rifle towards them. Feeling cold dread, the POWs thought he was an Austrian soldier. Nicol and the others fathomed that if they ran they'd be shot like rabbits. 'We thought we'd had it,' Nicol recalled.

The soldier spoke in French and Jim was able to reply. The soldier was Swiss and listened to Jim explain that they were prisoners of war. The guard held out a cigarette for each man before escorting them downslope to his headquarters.

Despite their first-hand accounts saying the four men stepped up to border patrol at the same time, 5 December according to Dick's recollection, the Swiss ledger held varying entry dates for this group: 7 December for Nicol, 6 December for Jim Kinder and 1 December for Jack and Dick.[11] Dick later reported arrival date of 5 December.[12]

Soldiers cheerfully greeted the POWs with hot milk and more cigarettes which they smoked in front of a huge fire. A doctor checked their sore feet. After sleeping under cosy blankets, they refuelled with bread and hot milk courtesy of a bell-collared goat housed under the building.

The men were escorted downhill to Brissago on the Swiss edge of Lake Maggiore, followed by 'motor' to Locarno and train to Bellinzona. Feeling like army men again, they happily submitted to close clipper haircuts and delousing. They delighted in hot soapy showers and a stroll through brightly lit shops selling Christmas goods. Bellinzona, the men realised, was also first point of respite for Jewish refugees who'd paid thousands of *lire* to get there. Dick voiced his fellow POWs' sentiments about the Jewish people: 'For the way they were treated, being hounded and hunted and thousands of them murdered. They were without a country to call their own, whereas we were soldiers, fighting a war and expecting to kill or be killed.'

Lake Maggiore's threshold on Swiss territory attracted other late 1943 runners, the tail-enders of the Australian charge on the northern frontier.

The 2/3 Anti-Tank Regiment's Claude Gibson's transit had commenced with a jump from a train bound for Germany. He hooked up with an organisation to be 'given a pistol and a guide' assisting him to entrain to Varese on the eastern side of Lake Maggiore, then on to Cittiglio to rest from his injuries for three weeks. He was chauffeured by another by bicycle to her house and stayed until a party was assembled for escort across the border on 3 December 1943.[13]

The 2/15th's Bill Pritchard would have felt relief to make it the same day.[14] At some point during his months on the run, he witnessed 'throat-slitting stuff' when men he had encountered, nationality undisclosed, were gunned down. Bill survived by hiding in a thorny bush. In another critical incident, which gave him angina attacks and anxiety when recollected post-war, he killed a young German soldier who confronted Bill in high country snow. The soldier looked only sixteen or seventeen years of age, but in life and death decisions, Bill realised 'it was him or me'.[15]

Victorians, 2/24th Battalion's Richard Wilson and Edward 'Ted' Bracken left a lengthy period of post-armistice shelter at Tronzano camp and left for Switzerland. As their 1944 POW reports converge in dates, they were probably together, leaving on 11 November for Varallo to be subsumed into a partisan band until broken up by German troops on 15 January 1944. 'We were fed by partisans on way to the border,' Richard reported. On 23 January, west of Lake Maggiore, the pair sneaked into Switzerland's Spruga located within the Italian-speaking Swiss canton of Ticino.[16]

In his 1944 POW report, Bill Blair, 2/17th, credited 'Johnny Peck and Claude Webb [who] were working with an organisation for getting escaped prisoners to Switzerland', but also that their network miscarried in his particular case. Peck and fellow POWs under his command were at constant risk of betrayal and summary trial leading to execution. What the local people had to offer within informal networks and organisation, Peck facilitated through his knowledge of routes, Italian fluency and an organised movement of escapers.[17] As escapers were assisted, not all were privy to the motives or organisation behind the assistance. Touching down in March 1944, Bill Blair was one of the last Australians in the race to freedom in Switzerland.[18]

Bill mentions help from a 'Davis organisation'. A British escaper, Ian English, referred to this network being under command of a lieutenant 'Arca' who transferred 'two hundred and fifty' POWs into Switzerland.[19] 'Arca' was the adopted battle name of Armando Calzavara.[20] Ian English also found that a café proprietor in Cannobio, on the western shores of Lake Maggiore, suggested suitable *contrabandieri* guides.

Reaching Intra on the western shores of Maggiore, Bill Blair advanced across mountains to reach Chiasso, located within a nipple of Switzerland extending into Italy on the western shore of Lake Como.

Freedom trails out of Italy had been well-trodden through the late months of 1943 and into 1944. Partisans, with whom they had fought for months, ushered late-runners, Victorians Les Dower and Thomas Davis, from Valtournenche to arrive at Arolla in Switzerland on 31 July 1944.[21] They were accompanied by Luciano Beltrami to their freedom trail, a high mountain pass via Col Collon in the central Pennines, west of the Mattherhorn and the Teodulo Pass.[22]

Late runners to Switzerland were lucky to get out of Italy. Spring 1944 reawakened active searches by German and fascist troops for POW stragglers; being on the run within northern Italy became increasingly perilous.

English-born Australian escaper Harry Miller, using an alias of Kenneth Osborne, was shot on 21 February 1944 alongside New Zealander Frank Bowes and Italian partisans with whom they'd fought,[23] ten days before Bill Blair stepped over Switzerland's doorstep. Jim 'Mick' McCracken from Ararat was shot on 15 April 1944.[24] Italian observer Gianni Nascimbene's comment about Mick has potent meaning for the POWs who did not reach Swiss sanctuary: 'The Australian will remain in my memory as a sad and taciturn fellow traveller, one you could never forget, and never will I be able to forgive myself for not having been able to help as I wanted. The Australian had wandered through half the world, into the whirlwind of the biggest of events that were too strong for him. He had been overwhelmed unintentionally and, inevitably, was no longer able to get out.'[25]

24
'THROUGH GERMAN LINES': SOUTH TO ALLIED LINES

'Lucky ones soared through difficulties that ought to have kept them pent ...'

'Some hundreds were left at large, drifting south-eastwards along the Apennine foothills, in effect begging food from the peasantry; lending a hand with the wine harvest, or any other odd job about the farm.'

—Foot and Langley, 1979[1]

Alone in a hut in late November 1943, Garvan 'Snowy' Drew moped. Since his sudden parting of ways with Tom Anderson and Joe Andrews east of Rome, Snowy had pursued the same objective as other southward landlopers: keep drifting southwards in the hope of encountering advancing Allied lines. After their separation, Snowy could have no idea that Tom and Joe were unfortunate to be recaptured while trying to meet the same objective.

'Making my way through this foreign enemy-occupied country and with my fair complexion, I didn't blend in with these southern Italians,' Snowy worried. 'I can tell you I was very lonely.'[2]

He understood that Allied lines were close by. Snowy cooked potatoes in the ashes of a fire burning in a large fireplace. He relented to share his bread and potatoes with two other escapees, a 'Pommie called George, and the Algerian, who we called Ali'.

Deciding to no longer travel alone, Snowy joined forces for the next leg with these two new escaper companions to set off about sundown to descend to lower ground. They followed directions to cross a river, two roads and a railway line before walking down into a gully to an adjacent track. As darkness crept in early under cloudy skies, they slowed their pace, walking in single file and keeping apart by about 'four yards'. George took the lead.

The dim light offered no clue what was ahead. Like a scythe cutting the clear night, a German voice snared them to halt. Snowy stood frozen against the bank on their left, aware that George was also rock steady, standing before a German. In the rear, Ali bumped into Snowy as Snowy whispered the distress signal: 'Tedeschi'. Rigid as statues, they saw George march close by. Neither George nor the German soldiers behind him glanced their way.

As Snowy and Ali quietly walked on, flashes of light pulsated the darkness at regular intervals. Snowy deduced it was a large British gun, and he quietly complimented the 'Pommies' for a light source that steered him around several German encampments. In chest-high water, the Australian and Algerian safely waded across a river. Snowy, a poor swimmer, sighed relief. A swamp served up another hurdle. Waist-high water lapped at the men for 'two hundred yards' before they darted across a road and rail-lines. Rain drizzled unrelentingly, making them cold and tired. A bough offered a place to crouch and sleep.

On waking, Snowy and Ali busied to keep moving before they froze to death. They conversed in Italian. Before they had gone 50 yards, and barely beginning to thaw, voices floated in from a distance. Ali seized Snowy's arm. Snowy chided him to 'get down, maybe Tedeski (sic)'. Ali disagreed, thinking it was English slang. Snowy soaked up the sweet words he reckoned he would remember forever. 'For fuck sake bring that fucking tea up here.'

With hands raised, Snowy and Ali tentatively approached the men who held British rifles trained on them. Snowy looked down at himself, alarmed at how rugged he now appeared. He proudly produced his paybook, glad it had survived the rough-sleeping, a river and the swamp.

'I was able to identify myself and vouch for my friend,' he delighted. 'They gave us a cup of hot tea and a packet of Wild Woodbine cigarettes and put us between a pile of blankets in a two-man tent. We lay back puffing our Wild Woodbines. Ali kept nudging me and saying, "We made it, we made it." The long trek was over.

'I didn't see much of him after that. As we were sent back through the lines, he went one way to his home in Algiers no doubt, and I to mine in Aussie via Alexandria in Egypt. No doubt he thinks of me and says, "We made it, we made it." I often think of him.'

In a reverse order to his original journey across the Mediterranean from Benghazi to Italy, Snowy departed Italy's shores with thirty Allied recovered POWs on a cargo ship heading to Alexandria. Evading a German submarine, the trip took seven days. The ship's captain requested them to parade before him, and apologised for the lack of proper quarters and mess facilities. Rations were ready for all of them but they had to prepare food themselves. Army blowers and dixie food bowls provided cooking facilities on the deck. A meeting was held to elect a cook. Snowy, the former POW camp cook, was swift to volunteer.

Snowy was back in Alexandria camp for Christmas 1943. 'With two and a half years' pay in our paybooks, you can imagine what a time we had in Cairo with our Kiwi friends. We had plenty of Australian bottled beer to drink.' There, Snowy caught up with Jock Smith who had also headed south from the rice farms and crossed paths with Snowy on their 'walk through Italy'. Over a year earlier, at Salussola, Jock had wanted to head south, and declined Bill Rudd's suggestion to head north with him.[3] Both Bill Rudd and Jock Smith scored home-runs at the opposite ends of Italy, arriving within days of each other.

After clearing out of camp in September, Bert Lockie's lads from four different Australian states had also flipped their choice to head south. But 'Fraser' (James Fraser of 2/23rd and 'Dixie' Johnson (probably Charles Johnson) left the group at Tricerro, three kilometres east of Ronsecco and immediately north of Trino on the northern banks of the Po River.[4]

The remaining quartet—Snowy, Fred Vardy, Jack Fullarton and Matt Knight—had navigated the Po River crossing during the third week of September. A well-dressed Italian with 'a flurry of hand-waving' ushered them across a bridge. To Matt Knight's recollection, on 24 September they left Brusaschetto and walked south about 14 kilometres, passing by Castelletto Merli to Moncalvo, a pretty medieval town in the province of Alessandria. At Moncalvo they stayed put, picking grapes, from 27 September to 28 October 1943.[5] Moving further south, the wine-growing area around Asti was invisible to them as they skimmed the city fringe late at night.[6]

A few days later, at Acqui Terme in the province of Alessandria, they took in first sight of the Apennines. They reached Castelletto d'Erro, just south-east of the small town Acqui Terme, on 1 November. They were now at the southern area of the Piedmont region. Genoa, on the coast, was about 40 kilometres to the south-east. It was about here that Matt Knight left the group and proceeded alone to the small medieval town Lucignana, fifty kilometres south of Florence. He stayed there from 17 November 1943 to October 1944, falling in with partisans such as Bruno Stefani to help fight against German troops.[7]

Lockie's remaining trio had gone further south than most Australian escaper groups by late autumn of 1943. In a village known as 'the Protestant village', a Scottish woman welcomed them into her English-style home, offering a cup of tea and real beds. Bert thought his unsettled stomach was due to the dominant menu of polenta and other meals made from chestnut flour. To some Australian palates, chestnut bread and cakes seemed stodgy, unpalatable and not easily digested.

They came down from high Apennines to the hilly Tuscan countryside. Farmers tooted the horn about any fascist people or villages to avoid. Edging the ancient city of Pistoia between Lucca and Florence, they steered clear of German troops. A secondary defence line was under construction near Florence.

A wealthy English woman took them in for a few days, along with other Allied escapers. Like the River Po further north, the Arno was considered a formidable barrier, but Lockie's lads were rowed across by a friendly local and given instructions on how to proceed.

The Chianti Hills south of Florence, renowned for their famous wines, gave the Australians ample opportunities to sample their varieties. In the higher mountains, teenage shepherds were generous with food and cigarettes. The trio met charcoal burners near their small huts. Bert Lockie, Fred Vardy and Jack Fullarton were invited by an elderly Italian for Christmas dinner. Despite their poverty, a feast was celebrated. Although winter encroached on food supplies, wine remained plentiful and was drunk more than water. Fred Vardy wrote that they stayed six weeks, and that seventeen other POWs were there.[8] By this point in their trekking trip, Fred Vardy hobbled with one boot and one shoe, both dilapidated from squelching through ice and snow. Fred paid 450 *lire* for a second-hand pair of boots.

Better equipped, in early months of 1944 they approached Subiaco, about 30 kilometres east of Rome. Germans were about in large numbers. Locals became cautious about inviting the trio inside during daylight hours. After dark, they'd be welcomed to sit around a fire for a meal, and to sleep in haylofts and stables. Germans had burnt houses and removed families for hiding escaped Allied POW.

At Subiaco, they were taken to a cave. To their surprise, two Australians and a couple of British POWs nested there. Village couriers trafficked supplies and appraised the POWs about German movements. One day in the hills, the trio was approached by a well-dressed Italian who said he had access to the Vatican, a neutral area. A rendezvous was planned for a few days' time and he'd bring money and food. 'Although we took no risks in case of betrayal, he kept his word.' Bert Lockie learnt 'he was a courier for the Irish priest in the Vatican, Monsignor Hugh O'Flaherty, who had organised an underground to help escaping POWs, Jews and others, right under the noses of the Germans'. British historian Roger Absalom depicted him thus: 'O'Flaherty was a golf-playing, pipe-smoking quintessential Irishman' who was a tireless campaigner for better conditions for prisoners of war.'[9]

When Germans burnt down a nearby house and took the family away, betrayed by fascists, the trio charged on. News of the Allied landing at Anzio had reached their ears in February 1944. The trio estimated they were about 30 kilometres from the beach head. But as the German army's line was a static barrier before them, their sights turned to Allied lines at Cassino, between Rome and Naples.

By mid-March 1944, the weather had improved enough for Lockie's lads to head to the mountain tracks. 'It was obvious now that we were heading into areas thickly populated with German troops and materials dumps,' Bert Lockie chronicled. 'The people were visibly afraid, but where safe, they continued to help us.'

By early April 1944, Lockie's lads approached the German secondary defence line across the hills at the Sora Valley. It was the last time they could move by day. One village proved extraordinary as it was pro-German and angry villagers made it clear to the ostracised POWs that they were not welcome. In contrast, a village perched on a hilltop to the west, Filettino, welcomed them for twenty days. An American parachutist had been dropped in the thickly wooded hills to distribute boots, clothes and food to escaped prisoners. Wondering if it was too good to be true, the POWs took a calculated risk and cautiously followed his directions to a well-camouflaged cave where he said he was based. There, the American greeted them. They eyed the stash of footwear and a radio transmitter.

The American's role was to map routes through enemy lines to Cassino for escapers, and accordingly, the Australians sighted and memorised the maps. The following day the three Australians cut and ran.

The date was 8 May 1944. Little could they know that in the northern mountains of Italy, 700 kilometres from their location, five Australian escapers were executed by fascists that day: Clive Liddell, William Harvey, Harold 'Butcher' Blain, John 'Ticker' Nicholls and Ernie Wolfe.[10]

Bert Lockie, Jack Fullarton and Fred Vardy joined with two escaping Gurkha soldiers, dressed as farmers. As they approached the high hamlet of Terelle, within eight kilometres of Cassino, evacuating Italians carted their possessions on mules. At the front-line, Terelle, six kilometres north of Cassino, Germans were everywhere. The trio suddenly split. Bert, one Gurkha and Fred remained together.

In ghostly light, the Australians ripped up their remaining blanket to wrap their feet, muffling the sounds of their boots. The approach of two Germans sent them scurrying to ground in a gully, close enough to touch the legs of the passing soldiers and a mule. They spotted the bombed-out monastery at Cassino under light of the rising moon. At a cliff-face, they searched and found a parachute cord planted as a guide-line by the cave-dwelling American and followed a gorge. Machine-gun fire from German and Allied forces crossed the river. On this front-line, 'Nerves by now were pretty tight.'

They eyed a German work party busily laying land mines. With only two hours to daylight, time to reach Allied lines was slipping from the POWs' sweaty palms. They whispered to each other. Fred, partially deaf since bombardment at Tobruk, keenly watched for hand signals. They crept to a rapid-flowing creek and 'in a final fling for freedom' they plunged into chest-high water, 'flitting from boulder to boulder'. Their compass directed them south. Communication wires, unsure whether these were 'theirs or ours', dangled like an unwelcome obstacle course.

Having successfully navigated the creek, the dripping soldiers melted into the cold shadows near a makeshift steel bridge. A jeep and trailer rollicked towards the bridge. In the half-light they saw the 'very welcome sight of the familiar British battle helmet' on the driver's head. As the jeep slowed, Fred, Bert and the Ghurka bounded out of the river and onto the trailer. Fred crawled over the vehicle to sit in the front with the startled driver, prattling to him that they were escapers. A non-British guttural accent replied. Aghast, Bert turned to the others and exclaimed, 'We're in the bag again! This fellow is a German!' To make it worse, two men popped up from foxholes at the road edge, vigorously indicating with machine-guns for hands to be placed on heads. When Fred asked if they were *Tedeschi*, Germans, they replied with forceful spits to the ground. Bert shakily held out his paybook. In broken English, the recipient blurted, 'Me, Tobruk!' He was a Pole who'd fought alongside Australians at Tobruk. The POWs had stumbled upon a Polish military police traffic post.

Feeling at ease, the Gurkha shirked off the peasant farmer garb, under which he was wearing his full Gurkha uniform.

Within an hour, at about 2am, an English officer greeted Fred Vardy and Bert Lockie. Soaking wet and in old rags, they felt triumphant to have crossed German lines into Allied territory. It was 11 May 1944.

Following issue of new clothes and toiletries, they felt civilised for the first time in months. They requested to be taken to a New Zealand artillery unit nearby, which welcomed them 'like long-lost brothers'. Jack and the second Gurkha later made Allied lines.

In March 1944, Herbert 'Harry' Sincock reached the countryside around Bardi and Reggio Nell'Emilia, northwest of Bologna, keeping to his plan to safely cross Allied lines. Thwarted on several tries, he bided time near Bardi from July to October, coming safely through the lines on 5 October.[11]

Ron Bryant had escaped as he turned twenty-nine years of age.[12] Initially with Doug Le-Fevre and Norm Terrell, he soon left their company when it was decided to split into smaller groups.[13]

'Many of my companions were recaptured, tortured by fascists.'[14] Ron chose the southward strategy but stalled at Italy's coast in the hands of Allied sympathisers. His substantive shelter base for the rest of the European war was at the home of the family Bione at Sestri in the coastal port of Genoa.[15]

Elda and Guglielmo Bione could not turn away four young escapers—two British, one South African and Ron, the only Australian—who were hungry and frightened. The Bione family were anti-fascist and had helped over one hundred escaped prisoners with their efforts to reach the northern border. Ron engaged with patriot bands. Elda believed that as a man to shelter, Ron was 'perfect', enhanced by his acquisition of dialect, his jet-black hair and olive complexion. Refining his Italian accent would add to the new identity.

It was more nerve-wracking than being in a POW camp, Ron believed, to be constantly ready to hide when visitors came to the home. From his early captivity days at Benghazi, Ron's body remained on high alert to unexpected touches, re-triggering a reflex to kick a gun out of a guard's hand, or that of an ambusher, should they come too close. One day at the Bione home, as police or fascists banged on the door, Elda spurred Ron to creep under a bed. The intruders searched the apartment but Ron remained undetected. Under a high bed, Ron hoisted himself up, clinging underneath to the bed springs by his fingers and toes, gripping tightly until the coast was clear. If discovered, Elda had a back-up story ready, and claim that the hiding man was a nervous lover.

Elda arranged identification papers for him to use in an emergency. When on trains, they would never sit together but Elda would watch from a distance. On one occasion, Germans stopped a train while crossing a ravine. Ron clicked, sharply, that the game they were playing was no longer a game. As Ron looked to Elda, she leant forward and crossed herself. A German requested Ron's identity papers. Ron stood and handed over his papers.

Whether it was pre-planned or a reflex moment, Ron abruptly burst into song: an Italian patriot tune. The German threw his papers back at Ron, pushed him in the chest with a rifle, calling him an 'Italian pig' and walked out of the carriage. Ron's tenor singing voice and command of Italian had saved his life.

Ron remained out of harm's way, under close watch of the Bione family, until 1945.

By late 1944, the number of Australians entering Switzerland dwindled. Due to circumstance or choice, or swings of both, no less than forty Australians formerly of Campo 106 remained at large in Italy.[16]

Harold Davis, an Aboriginal man from West Australia stayed in Italy until liberation in mid-1945.[17] Jack Nie recalled how he and newly captured 2/32nd colleagues needed to back up Harold's claim to enemy authorities that he was an Australian.[18] Harold had been incorrectly placed into a transit camp compound containing black South African prisoners. Harold's 1945 statement by a repatriated prisoner of war says that he stayed on the loose from escape to 1945. He'd fought on with partisans, and his substantive base was in Gaby, in Aosta Valley, where the locals kept him in food, clothes and lodging. He singled out a Russian woman, Vera Wolff.

Harold was reluctant to leave Italy. If a grapevine in Aosta is correct, a Russian noblewoman, probably a refugee, bore Harold's child. Harold's eventual return to Australia caused him great sadness and he became a recluse.[19]

25
'Marking time': A year in Switzerland and coming home

> *'Scheming Mussolini and raving Hitler were very clear and certainly correct in their assumption that the Swiss sympathised to an extraordinary extent with Great Britain.'*
>
> —Jurg Stussi-Lauterburg, 2004[1]

Despite being surrounded by German occupiers, Switzerland extended hospitality to many thousands of refugees and prisoners of war during wartime. The country was 'bulging with people from all over, every different country', as Jack Dodd put it. A Swiss officer spoke to him soon after he stepped into Switzerland, saying that 'we're surrounded by Germans and all our troops are on the borders. The moment that there's any border open we will get you out to your own lines. But he said at present we just have to keep you here. We had to stay about three weeks in quarantine.'[2]

In overhauling the barrack accommodation and the medical and sanitary facilities, the Swiss divided their country into sectors where Italians, British, German and Americans could be housed in separate groups. East Switzerland was allotted to the Allied évadés. It was known as Secteur Sitter or Sitten and included eight hotels taken over in Adelboden for British and American évadés and internees.[3]

During the months of September to November 1943 in particular, the arrival of Allied prisoners of war provided a steady flow. The majority of Australians who entered Switzerland arrived by the end of November.[4] Bill Rudd estimates that 108 New Zealanders secured safe transit into Switzerland. After initial processing, prisoners were corralled away from the border areas without delay, en route to large camps for the Allied prisoners at Wald. In transit or at Wald, new uniforms were issued, and a general clean-up of hair and body. The ordeals of previous years—from desert battles, capture and confinement in Italian prisoner of war camps, to weeks or months of evasion to reach the Italian–Swiss frontier—had taxed the men.

The Swiss employed creative solutions to manage large numbers of Allied soldiers within their borders. According to Bill Rudd, it suited the Swiss to put them up in 'hotel camps'. The lack of tourists meant many of the popular resort hotels were empty, so a deal was struck between the Brits and Swiss to get rental paid by the Allies in exchange for putting up their POW in Switzerland. With large numbers of ex-POWs fiddling with time in Switzerland, authorities in early 1944 thought it wise to 'recondition them as soldiers after long periods of captivity in close confinement with lack of food and exercise'. As a means of providing training and activity for all ranks, senior British officers organised winter sports under skilled supervision in all billeting areas. A ski battalion began to form at the ski resort village of Adelboden in Bernese Oberland where the largest number of escapers was quartered, with arrangements made with the UK government to provide 700 skis.[5]

Early in 1944, Adelboden offered its hotels to assist in the accommodation options for the Australians, including the Hotel Beau Site and the Grand Hotel. In a batch of about 200 men of Allied nations, Ron Crellin with mates Bill Mitchell, Neil Collyer and Wal Parker travelled by train and bus to Adelboden, which was blanketed in snow. Hotel Beau Site was Ron's group's home until May 1944. Each hotel had its own skating rink.

Once they got the hang of skis on the flats, rookies tried the slopes below the ski run, later learning to ride the T-bar lift that extended about three kilometres.⁶

On first ride, 'I didn't think I was ever coming to the top,' Ron Crellin exclaimed. He wondered whether they were being trained as ski troops to be deployed as needed. 'As we became more skilled, we were involved in races down the hill with civilians.' Large-print competitor numbers were sewn to évadés' jumpers. Ron fell and broke an ankle bone, and after resting in plaster for five weeks, he was keen to try out for the highly prized Swiss Silver Medal testing. When he passed the test, his night of celebration in a restaurant went past 10pm curfew. Military police greeted Ron and mates at their hotel door.

POWs also came in from camp at Wald to take ski lessons and to enjoy recreation leave. Attendance at ski training was considered compulsory for many évadés, to occupy them and to maintain fitness. Some trained as ski instructors, and excelled in competitive ski events. During Arthur Jobson's four-week Adelboden stay, 'the ski sergeant in charge of our operation was our sapper, Bill Rudd, a damn good skier in his own right.'⁷ Col Booth enjoyed skiing at night in a long line of skiers holding flame torches, singing as they enjoyed the beauty of the alpine sanctuary.⁸

At first, locals were wary of the influx of large numbers of young ex-POWs flooding their small village and ski resorts. But soon, Adelboden came to embrace the men. Their presence was a welcome boon to local businesses. Silleren and Hahnenmoos, at higher slopes above Adelboden, were easily reached and offered access to the snow runs. Ice-skating championships with costumed Swiss skaters were held in the village. A number of Australian and American airmen constructed a stone archway at the entrance to Adelboden's church, as expression of gratitude for village hospitality.

In late 1943, Syd Shaw spent his twenty-first birthday in a bit of Swiss strife. Syd was living in Adelboden's Kulm Hotel, whereas his mate 'Newt' Moore was living in a nearby chalet. A biff broke out and Newt was hit by a chair. 'Five of us walked off and encountered a big Swiss sergeant at 1am. Court-martialled at Lausanne, we were locked up in a local jail at Frutigen for 33 days with a dirty Alsatian dog guarding the door.' Syd conceded that despite the time in the cell, the Swiss looked after them.[9]

When billeted in a school house in Elsau near Winterthur, Jack Nie was sent to an Arosa holiday hotel where he skied, tobogganed and ice-skated. He was also drafted for soccer, although he'd never played it. His penchant for Australian football inspired him to try marking the soccer ball with his hands, rendering a sharp whistle blast from the referee.[10] Dances were held, with POW bands performing, including a band ensemble around the Sincock brothers, Eddie and Bill.

Ron Crellin put his name down for a ten-day excursion to the city of Basel in north-west Switzerland. As Basel's districts tip the borders with France and Germany, the men were forewarned to steer away from the German railway station. They knew that the Allies had landed in France, so a list of 'dos and don'ts' were given to the twenty Australian tourists. Ron soaked up the vibe of the Krafft Hotel along the banks of the Rhine, meeting local girls and visiting local sights. He befriended a hairdresser working next door to the hotel, Helena Schwartz.

In early spring 1944, opportunities to work were extended to the men, in occupations as diverse as farmhand, peat-digger and watchmaker. It was a bonus to local Swiss communities as some of their men were deployed elsewhere, in war-related activities.

John Morish assisted the Red Cross to pack parcels for distribution to German-controlled POW camps. Jack Dodd and Col Booth worked on farms.[11] Col lent a hand at the Sidler and Muff family farms outside Zurich, at Ottenbach, working alongside British escaper Bernard Thompson.[12] Arthur Jobson volunteered to help a dairy farmer. Herr Schmidt gave Arthur a detailed demonstration of milking a cow. 'I was milking more cows than he was,' Arthur boasted. 'One evening I mentioned that my first job in Australia was on a dairy farm where we milked two hundred cows in summer.'

When progress in the wider war provided opportunity to move large groups of internees out of Switzerland in September 1944, the villagers of Adelboden lined their main street to farewell them. In Adelboden and other locations in Switzerland, some of the 1944 romances between servicemen and local women resulted in marriages, and accordingly, a small group of Swiss brides later followed their husbands to Australia. Bill Rudd met his wife in Switzerland, Dutch-born Caty. Ron Maitland met his future bride, Ella, while he was at camp Wald, and their courtship continued after Ron's move to Cauz where he was billetted in Hotel Regina.

Word filtered that the Allied push on the continent was gaining momentum; 'it seemed the enemy opposition was crumbling', Ron Crellin delighted. The Australians expected that their Swiss sojourn might soon end, but in the meantime Ron went back to work as a woodcutter in Bendel, and a peat-digger at Schwarzenbach. Helena came by train to see him on the weekends.

Most of the Australians—more than 400 AIF and RAAF men—stayed in Switzerland for twelve months.[13] In September 1944 the majority were released from internment. 'At the end of the twelve months we wanted to get out,' Ron Crellin stated. 'We knew the invasion was on for June 5 or 6. We watched the progress of the invasion, and in a few weeks, we were taken out of Switzerland to a French port and then shipped to Australia.'

During a trip to Lausanne, Charles Warburton heard that 'the frontier is open, just across the lake, at Geneva'.[14] Earlier, on 2 August 1944, Charles was requested by authorities to fill in answers on the two-page 'POW report' form to summarise his dates and locations in Italy, and journey to Switzerland. Most of the approximately 400 Australians interned in Switzerland were interrogated during July and August 1944.

On 13 September 1944, Col Booth was at Bornhausen, completing his POW report, making a point to acknowledge Clementina Zaninetti in the assistance column as did Peter Erickson on his report given at Wald camp on 31 August.[15] Most Australians who were interrogated opted for brief reports—perhaps due to the rush to prepare to leave, or because they believed that detail would not interest report readers and analysts.

Ahead of being prepped to leave in the third week of September 1944, the men were brought in from their areas of employment. Col Booth was working on the farm of Alois Muff, at Ottenbach, outside Zurich. Alois had an arm injury so Col was allocated to help out. As he prepared to leave the farm, Col asked Alois's wife to take him to the village to do some shopping. He said his farewells to the family Muff with several shiny new Swiss watches swinging under his coat.[16] POWs spent their remaining Swiss francs, to Ron Crellin's recollection, on Swiss watches.

At Geneva customs, the Australians exceeded the maximum of two watches. Jack Dodd was bemused that 'everyone had walked through customs like a ticking time bomb... they had them up their arms and up their legs'.[17]

Paris was liberated by Free French troops on 25 August; Marseilles was freed on 26 August 1944.

The border with France had become safer, and the time had come for most POWs in Switzerland to be repatriated to Australia. Ron Crellin recalled being told that the Americans had reached the Swiss border near Geneva and that they would be moved out the next week. At Wil on the Sunday before, Helena and Ron spent most of the day together. 'It was a sad day for both of us,' Ron recalled. 'Her friendship had meant so much to me.'

John 'Brian' Green busied with preparing and printing the final issue of the POW broadsheet, *Marking Time*, at its Sirnach's camp for évadés.[18] POWs valued the newspaper, informed by war communiqués and delighted by bold cartoons interspersed with seductive adverts for American toasted cigarettes, Johnnie Walker and watches. The 28 July issue announced the engagement of Harold Digwood 'who has spent nine months in hospital' to his nurse Margrit. 1 September's issue included a photo and caption: 'The évadé band goes to town with St Louis blues', of which the Sincock brothers played their part. An article about a swimming carnival held at Arosa also featured, accompanied by a photo of men doing battle on the greasy pole.

Syd 'Bluey' Shaw tied with Eddie Aitken, according to the report, whereas Syd Shaw, in his nineties, was adamant that he won that contest.

The 1 September issue was the last for *Marking Time*, and included a glossy souvenir lift-out offering farewell words blended with Swiss national pride:

'Well, the long period of "marking time" is nearly over. Soon the enforced idleness, the tedium and restraint, the nostalgia and general feeling of being "left out of things" will be swept away in the joy of home-coming and the exigencies of the new tasks that lie ahead. But long after the less congenial aspects of évadé life have been forgotten, certain memories of Switzerland will come to life again as a reminder of people you had grown to like, of things you had enjoyed for their own sake, and of places that would have made a deep impression on you—as they have made upon thousands of your compatriots—had you visited them under more normal circumstances.'

'One day, perhaps, when you start telling the folks at home of your escape and subsequent adventures, of your enforced stay in Switzerland, of your first attempts at ski-ing, of your efforts to speak the outlandish lingo called Schwyzerdutsch, of your trips to town (legitimate and otherwise) and the hospitality of strangers who soon became friends: one day all these memories will revive and you will see Switzerland in the real perspective, and without the hated tedium of "marking time". And then, perhaps, pictures such as these will pass through your mind like a film and you will feel the urge to renew acquaintance with these friends and places over here—this time in "civvies". So Long!'

Adelboden villagers lined the narrow streets to tearfully farewell the évadés. Letters were sent to next of kin to say it was confidential information that the soldiers were coming home, no newspapers were to be informed. The request was not to divulge the exciting scoop outside one's household.

Receiving very short notice to be ready to leave Wald camp, Arthur Jobson and those with him were instructed not to tell their Swiss friends of that evening's departure.

As dawn broke, the train carrying men based at camp Wald crept into Geneva. Most men had not slept, Ron Crellin observed, and they disembarked to wait in a park for orders. Ron felt the quiet mood of those around him. With orders to stand, the men filed to the French side of the station, receiving an American army ration pack, and boarded a French train, settling into a third-class carriage. Arthur noted the official request not to eat at stations as people were short of food, but he did not need the reminder: 'We had learned how it felt.'

Heading into French territory, soldiers stood near the tracks with machine-guns slung over their backs, as if to remind the passengers that war was not yet over. Trains had been fired on by German troops scattered in nearby hills.

At the border at Saint-Julien-en-Genevois, there was a delay, diarised Arthur, due to commotion on the platform. 'We were saluted by a guard of honour comprising local French partisans.'

Much of the trip south was in darkness, mountains and hills looming over them. Upon arrival in Lyon, they saw the devastation caused by aerial bombings. The train snailed into a makeshift rail-line in the war mess of what remained of Lyon's rail marshalling yards. The rails had only just been pegged down, Jack Dodd remembered, and they were not pegged properly.

At the station, a German uniform stuffed with straw was hung by its neck, swinging sinisterly. People waved and cheered the train at every village and town they passed, including Grenoble. Perhaps they thought the entrained soldiers were Americans, Ron Crellin wondered.

The third-class wooden seats with no cushions grew harder and more uncomfortable. At Orange, the men were permitted to step off the train to stretch their legs. Ted Kent recalled witnessing the effects of the European war: 'Knocked-out tanks, crashed aeroplanes and blown-up towns.' He added that 'the French were happy they'd just got rid of the Germans'.[19] Avignon was burning. At one station a locomotive lay in a huge bomb crater alongside their rail-line. Two rail bridges had collapsed behind them, Arthur later heard. Ron Crellin's journal noted a week's stay at Marseilles before boarding a tank-transporter craft, 'little more than an enormous hollow shell' anchored in the bay, a ship-to-shore amphibious craft.

This leg to Naples was the worst, Ron Crellin reckoned. Wild storms and tossing seas sent Nick Emery chucking up over the landing barge edges.[20] A smoky Mount Etna was also chucking up, another recalled. An American crew member said it was one of the roughest Mediterranean seas he'd experienced. Ted Kent wrote, 'It was one of those flat-bottomed ships in the rough sea, just like a cork in the water.' Arthur Jobson, mentioning two craft 'LST 495 and 496', was told by a mate watching from the second craft that they didn't think Arthur's vessel would make it. They watched as it plunged from a high wave crest into the trough, staying still 'for a few moments then a bulge ran through the steel deck and the bows began to rise'. Later in the day they passed through the strait between Corsica and Sardinia into calmer waters.

At Naples, they were housed in a British army camp for a week. Ron recalls being taken to see the landing beaches at Salerno. Matt Knight, who'd been hiding out in the north of Florence, was on his way south after making contact with 'Brazilian forces' at Bagni di Lucca, to be guided into Allied hands on 6 or 7 October 1944 with Roy Harris and Richard 'Dick' Smith.[21] The transit was timely as they caught up with the ex-Switzerland repatriated POWs at Naples.[22]

The POWs received updated paybooks brought by staff from London. There was time for the Australians to be tourists. Jack Nie, at ninety-eight years, had not forgotten the artwork he spotted in the Pompeii brothel. Arthur Jobson, with a mate and a guide, remembered that 'amongst the highlights were the mosaics in the mansions of ill-fame, many of them depicting such outrageous acts that they were shielded from public view under lock and key, but opened by the guide to all male parties'.

The cohort sailed for Alexandria's Port Said. To Bill Blair's recollection, the ship was *Queen of the Pacific*.[23] At Port Said, AIF uniforms and slouch hats were issued. Rested for a night, the cohort was trucked overland along the canal to Port Suez. Arthur Jobson takes up the narration: 'When we berthed in Alexandria the wife of an Australian diplomat in Cairo came aboard to give a rundown on current conditions in Australia,' including 'Lord Haw Haw's propaganda regarding Americans taking over our place with the ladies. I really began to worry.'

At Port Tewfik, Suez Canal, the next day, they boarded a liner turned troop-ship, *Orontes*. POW escapers liberated from other parts of Europe who had been waiting at Alexandria for transport also embarked, including POW partisans, Australian Ralph Churches and New Zealander Harold Sanderson, both liberated from Slovenia.[24] Also readied to join with the large repatriation cohort, West Australian Patrick 'Paddy' Maher enplaned from Italy to the Middle East in late September, presumably having presented to Allied lines after a year at large in Italy.[25]

The men stayed at a hot dusty Suez camp for a day or two before sailing south through the Red Sea, India-bound via Aden. They berthed at Aden for twelve hours without shore leave, Arthur Jobson diarised. The cohort included large numbers of airmen.

On the *Orontes*, sailing in convoy with the *Orion*, there was more paperwork for the returning prisoners to complete, to respond to questions on a two-page 'Statement by Repatriated Prisoners of War'. 398 Australians completed their statements.[26] Many, again, kept these statements brief, despite having much to say. Harry Sibraa was warned by Ted Paul 'not to mention names and to alter and change dates, presumably due to the fifth column activity and other Allied POWs in the north of Italy'.[27] This may account for the brevity of these reports.

The Australian repatriates stayed in Bombay until 3 November. 'We went up to British barracks,' Ted Kent recalled. 'We let loose in Bombay. Red Cross ladies had a marquee there, lots of fruit and soft drink for us. We had a great time.'

They embarked *General AE Anderson*, an American liberty ship. Ron Crellin bemoaned: 'There was nowhere to sleep except on deck.' Ralph Churches also noted the sharp contrast of the former cruise ship *Orontes* with the austere steel liberty ship, but applauded the American crew 'who went out of their way to keep us entertained with movies, magazines, cards, board games and table tennis'.

Ron noted the distressing sight of a row of barred cages containing American soldiers. 'For these unfortunates the war had proved too much and they were held this way for their own safety.' One day, one of these men jumped overboard. Then another, but nothing could be done to rescue them. Sharing concern for the psychologically wounded soldiers, some POWs visited the tormented caged men to speak to them.[28]

Thinking that the ship was heading to West Australia, Ron was surprised that Port Philip Heads loomed in the morning haze. 'A band was on the wharf to welcome us and beyond a convoy of cars lined up. Three to a car, we were conveyed to Royal Park.' Australian Army Women's Service (AWAS) servicewomen acted as drivers. One driver expressed disappointment at the low-level fanfare of this homecoming to the docks. 'The lady in the car I was in remarked that she thought it disgraceful that we were being treated like criminals sneaked home,' Arthur Jobson remembered. 'We were contented with the situation.' Wal Cooke wound down his car window and his wife half-jumped into the vehicle, hanging there until the driver stopped. Ernie Sparnon's wife jumped a barricade fence when she saw him approaching, but military police plonked her back over the fence to wait with other relatives.[29]

That night, 17 November 1944, after being allotted their sleeping accommodation, a dinner was laid on by AMF commander-in-chief General Thomas Blamey at Royal Park, Melbourne[30]—although Arthur recalled that General Blamey apologised for being unable to attend. To welcome them home, Blamey's menu offered a spread of oysters, turkey and ham with apple sauce, baked potatoes, cauliflower, strawberries and ice-cream. It was a long way from bully beef, watery soup, macaroni and Populare cigarettes. AWAS servicewomen served as waitresses. Col's menu was signed by twenty AWAS women of corporal, driver and private rank, outnumbering the men's signatures.[31] Sapper Arthur Jobson heard a fellow soldier call to him, 'Have you ever seen a lady sapper before? Well, here's one,' referring to Diana West who was assisting with waitering duties.

Ron Crellin noted that it was almost exactly four years since sailing for overseas service with 2/24 on 16 November 1940. Despite the excitement, there were sad notes in the homecoming. Ron recalled, 'Not all of us were Victorians. The following day our interstate mates would leave to return to their own states. As we said goodbye and wished them well, we realised we would probably never be seeing some of them again.'

The following day, men lined up for parade and for their leave pay, and were sorted for their respective rail journeys towards home towns across the country.

Echoing Ron Crellin's sentiment about the rushed homecomings, James Maddern found the swift departures from Melbourne to lack some detail. James wrote to the Red Cross a week after disembarking *General AE Anderson*: 'On arriving home on Friday last, the reunion with our people and the speed which the organisation was carried out was a wonderful effort. Please except [sic] my warmest thanks for all that has been done for me and my pals overseas and at home,' he told them. 'At the same time,' James politely pointed out, 'it left the country soldiers no time to make inquiries as to our own colour patches, chevrons and little details that I would like to know. Could you let me know what are my colour patches and how many chevrons we are entitled to wear?'[32]

Most POWs had been away for over four years and had experienced events and locations they would not have predicted when they left Australian shores. Switzerland had played a significant part, and they did not need the clink of souvenir Swiss watches swinging under their coats to remind them. Lives and attitudes had changed.

Most men who disembarked on 17 November 1944 looked healthy. They were not the skeletal remains of men who were seen on the news reels arriving home from Japanese captivity; nevertheless, psychologically each carried baggage that needed to be unpacked and sorted, or left unopened. 'I went away,' Doug Le-Fevre declared, 'a snotty-nosed kid and I came back a man.'[33]

Most of the ex-Switzerland POWs were home in Australia with families for Christmas 1944. A minority were delayed due to various adventures or misadventures. Jack Dodd, one of Doug's escaper companions, had to leave the large cohort at Naples when he became sick. Jack ended up back in Cairo at the Maadi convalescent camp for New Zealand troops, embarking transport ship, *Ranchi* on 23 November to continue to Bombay. At Bombay, Jack Dodd embarked the *General Pope*.

Ex-Carpeneto POW Jim Wilson also embarked the *General Pope* in Bombay, packed with American troops and some Australians and New Zealanders. Jim had taken ill, vomiting blood, when he and Herbert 'Harry' Sincock were in Marseilles, wandered to the dockyards. Hospitalised with a suspect ulcer, Jim was transferred by hospital ship to Naples, then entrained to Bari where he fell in with RAAF ground staff heading home. After ten days of billets by Red Cross personnel, Jim was informed of the docking of the *General Pope*.[34]

The *General Pope* cohort was on schedule to be home on Christmas Day but a Japanese submarine scare scooted the boat further out to sea. They docked at Melbourne on 29 December 1944.

A small number of POWs coming out of Switzerland, including Brinley Jones, were repatriated via Eastbourne reception camp in England.[35] Instead of coming straight home, Bill Rudd and Fred 'Eggie' Eggleston stayed on in Switzerland with further duties. Fred, a pre-war graduate with Master of Science from the University of Melbourne, was detailed to the British Legation in Bern, alluded to as 'shady administrative work with the Secret Service'.[36] He left Switzerland on 25 January 1945, married to his Swiss bride, Heidi.[37]

Bill, also a University of Melbourne graduate, was snuffled by the consulate general in Geneva for his French and German language proficiency, experience in land surveying and skills in interpretation of aerial photographs.[38] Special duties awaited him under British command as part of a plain-clothed team of mixed nationals. He reported to station chief of SIS (Secret Intelligence Services) Count Major Frederick 'Fanny' van den Heuvel, 'the epitome of a perfect old-time diplomat'. Switzerland swarmed with spies; it had become a major collection point for intelligence about Axis war plans in Europe. To those who asked, Bill's work involved checking visas, but his role had more strategic contribution to the war than he let on. On 23 February 1945, Lt Col Cameron-Cooke reported on Corporal Rudd: 'Since 31 July 1944, Cpl WAC Rudd has been in employ of the British Consulate, Geneva, engaged in confidential work. He has fulfilled his duties to my entire satisfaction, showing consideration, intelligence, initiative and discretion.'[39]

Bill's Melbourne-based mother Ivy was sick of waiting: 'You have been away for five years. It's time to come home.' With his wife, Dutch-born Caty whom he met in Switzerland, he left Switzerland on 8 February 1945 and was released through liberated France to London. Discharged from the AIF in London, Bill went with Caty to her liberated Holland with the United Nations Relief and Rehabilitation Authority (UNNRA) to run a refugee camp in southern Holland until he and Caty travelled to Australia in 1946. Bill was one of the last Australian POWs, if not the last, to leave Switzerland, but bound to the Secrecy Act for fifty years.

Private Pat O'Rafferty had expected to leave Switzerland and return to his Australian wife Eileen and daughter Maureen in Yackandandah.[40] But on 26 August 1944, the day Marseilles was freed, Pat fell out of a second-floor hotel window in Adelboden. He sustained a compound fracture to the base of his skull and died. A court of inquiry found it to be an accidental death, with blame attached to no one.[41] Fellow prisoners and the people of the village arranged a full military funeral with large floral wreaths. Photographs were posted to his widow and young daughter. He was buried at Vevy Kanton Vaud.

Syd Shaw had heard, or surmised along with other POWs, that Pat 'had got out of bed sleepy, went to have a pee and the light coming into the open window attracted him'.

26
'CONTRIBUTION TOWARDS THE FINAL COLLAPSE OF GERMAN ARMIES IN ITALY': POW-PARTISANS AND SOE

'... a fighting man remains a fighting man, whether in enemy hands or not, and his duty to continue fighting overrides everything else.'
—Norman Crockatt cited in Foot and Langley, 1979[1]

POWs, cloistered in prison camps and later cooped away in hideouts, tussled with the frustration of being trained soldiers taken out of the fight. In late 1944, some were pulled back into the action.

On the same day that the Royal Park reception dinner in Melbourne for the *General AE Anderson* passengers was in full swing, Special Operations Executive (SOE) operatives jumped from a plane and parachuted to their landing target near Ivrea in Italy's Piedmont.[2] While the majority of Australians holed up in Switzerland adjusted to home soil, a number of their POW peers still on the ground in Italy faced a return to active service.

The SOE men dusted themselves off and commenced their mission to co-ordinate action against the enemy by means of subversion and sabotage on behalf of the Allied war effort. Their landing target of partisan-controlled areas was premised on a need to co-ordinate and direct attacks and sabotage operations, and to bring in supplies and munitions. It had first to identify, train, supply and co-ordinate the efforts of resistance groups in occupied Europe, to raise secret armies to fight in concert with the eventual

Allied invasion.³ Under command of Major Alastair Macdonald, the British operatives included Captain Pat Amoore, as well as explosives and sabotage expert Captain Jim Bell and radio operator Corporal Tony Birch.⁴ British escaper George Evans came into their fold.⁵ Cargo comprising a container of explosives, fuses and arms to be distributed among the partisans was loaded onto mule carts.

The mission began its search for POW-partisan stragglers who were at large in northern Italy: young, army-trained, partisan-savvy soldiers ready to have 'another crack at Jerry' and fascist regimes. Major Macdonald drew on various means to contact escapers. Young Italian women carried letters; priests distributed messages. The British mission, dubbed 'Cherokee', absorbed a number of Australians: Fred Tabram, Gordon Dare, Alex Campbell, Ted Peachey, Keith Jones, Roy Jackson, Ted Price and Edward 'Big Bill' Smith. Darcy Henderson and Syd McFarlane were two of the New Zealander connections. Before too long, the initial training by the Cherokee demolition experts to partisans led to frequent attacks on the upper Piedmont rail networks.⁶

In contrast to the regularity of their former POW camps, the POW-partisans battled on in a context of unpredictability and high-level vigilance. SOE's clandestine military actions operated outside the protection of the Geneva Convention. To the Germans, SOE agents were saboteurs, and those caught were handed over to the Gestapo where they faced brutal interrogation and a death sentence. These brave men and women had few illusions about their fate if captured, and many carried cyanide pills for such an eventuality.⁷ On one occasion, Alex Campbell fell into fascist hands.⁸ Partisans plotted his swift, safe retrieval.

After three months of wandering the plains after his Campo 106 escape, Fred Tabram had headed for the foothills. Despite many people nervous about the 'retaliatory grip' by the fascists and Germans, Fred sought warm shelter as November 1943 brought wintery conditions, moving from place to place for assistance, 'always threatened by spies who were out for a reward of 1800 *lire*'.[9] The Olivero family of Ronsecco provided a welcome hearth, on and off, from September to November 1943. Strona residents Placida Monti and Maria Bocchia-Monti 'succoured' Fred from 3 January to 10 August 1944.[10]

Along the Italian countryside's grapevines, word of fellow escaped prisoners would filter to others. Australians Malcolm Webster and Bill Wrigglesworth 'lay doggo' (in hiding) for three months near Mezzana, directly north of Vercelli, contemplating a dash for Switzerland.[11] Ever vigilant, the men were well aware of the sadistic treatment meted out by the German SS and the Fascist Black Brigade. Torture was used to force captives to reveal names of those helping escaped prisoners.

By April 1944, men of Mussolini's Republican National Guard (GNR) had moved to activity around Biella, and their efforts were intensified to capture evading POWs whether they were associating with partisan bands or simply hiding in the hillsides or among the hamlets and villages. Malcolm and Bill received communications in May 1944 that Australians and an Englishman had been caught by a detachment from the Fascist Militia Legion 'Tagliamento' at Piancone on the Sessera River, near an old Roman stone bridge. They heard that, despite these men being unarmed and not members of underground forces, they were summarily executed on the spot.

Frank Blewett, who'd been in Fred Tabram's company earlier, was at this time lying doggo with Ron McIntyre when they heard the same disturbing message about Australians who'd been living about half a mile away. Word of the execution of the five Australians disseminated to neighbouring villages.

Once they considered it safe to venture to the site a few weeks after the murders, Frank 'Blue' Blewett, who had spent months walking the plains with Fred, and Ron McIntyre located the graves. Ron and Blue cleared soil to verify that bodies were indeed buried there. To ensure that the location of their bodies would be identifiable, they marked the communal gravesite with a marble stone engraved with the names of the deceased.[12]

Fred Tabram heard the same dispatch from a trattoria owner whom he later reported as Angelina Cattella Guido, of Coggiola. She had witnessed the burial, and later exhumation, of the bodies at nearby Trivero. Fred listed the names of the murdered Australians on his June 1945 liberation questionnaire as: John 'Ticker' Nicholls, Ernie Wolfe, William 'Stan' Harvey, Clive Liddell and Harold 'Butcher' Blain'.[13] Butcher was from Fred's battalion. Ernie Wolfe's twenty-third birthday was the day of his murder.[14] Malcolm Webster visited Italy post-war and located a plaque erected by Italians that carries their names.

Frank Blewett and Ron McIntyre later joined Mission Cherokee to flush out other escaped prisoners who were 'lying doggo'. By the end of December 1944, the Nazis were offering a reward of one million *lire* for the capture of Mission Cherokee, dead or alive. For escaped prisoners who had engaged in sabotage on the rice farms of the Piedmont plain, the level of sabotage raids was notched to a more dangerous game of blowing up train-lines, bridges, shooting trucks and raiding farms of fascist followers.

Fred Tabram had joined a partisan band in early 1944, thinking it his duty to do so. 'I stayed with them and we waged a war of ambush against the enemy, we sabotaged whenever possible. During a large-scale fascist raking in high Italy, while I was with the partisans, I volunteered with four others (English) and two Italians to escort a British mission officer, Captain Amoore, through the mountains. His major, Major McDonald, was captured [in January 1945] so it was vital that the captain had to escape at all costs as he was the direct collaborator with the major who was in charge of the British mission in the mountains. I helped to escort him for more than a month then I went back with the partisans.' On his 1945 questionnaire for repatriated POW, Fred noted that he assisted partisans to blow up a bridge at Crevacoure, and to blow up a fascist armoured car with explosives at Valle Mosso. Later on, Fred was asked to join Mission Cherokee. 'I readily did so until American troops entered the town we operated in.'[15]

Fred's notebook entries cease in August 1944. He may have been worried about the notebook being read by the enemy if captured during the Mission Cherokee phase; he may have lost or secreted a subsequent notebook; he may have no longer wished to keep a record.

On 18 November 1944, the day after the parachutists dropped into northern Italy, an interrogation report was prepared regarding the escape from Italy into France by Private Ian Sproule, 2/32 Battalion. Ian reported that after he deserted a working camp following the Italian armistice announcement, he went to Santuario di Graglia.[16]

Ian upped sticks in September 1943 with Jack 'China' Powling, with an aim to hook up with partisans in the mountains. The duo encountered a woman gathering chestnuts, and met her daughter Elda. Shelter in a barn was offered by this *contadini* family. Ian was infatuated with Elda. Daily, Elda brought food and supplies and tutored Ian in Italian language.[17]

With increasing worry of retributions, the POWs again considered what to do. Thoughts returned to finding a guerrilla force and carrying on the war behind the lines. 'No one knew for sure who was friend or foe,' Ian recalled. 'Our ignorance of the language and the country meant we could not by ourselves make a single step in that direction.' Elda introduced them to an Italian army officer.

An Australian POW 'Happy' Hungerford was also a new arrival to Ian's hideout. Happy expressed doubts about the partisan group's organisational ability because they had no weapons or military tactics and little food. The overall leader of the group, a communist nicknamed by the POWs as 'Stalin', barred contact between the Italian officer and the POWS. 'Stalin' removed the officer and several other partisans and 'eliminated' them.

According to Ian, this 'shocked us to our back teeth ... in bewilderment we wondered who we were opposing—Germans? Fascists? And now Communists?' Ian witnessed 'Stalin' shooting a fascist youth as he bent down to pull on his boots. 'We had joined a partisan group, even though it was politically the "wrong" group,' Ian recalled.

Ian intended to stay because of his romantic attachment to Elda, and China planned to stay with Ian. Privates 'Big Bill' Smith, Ray Vigar, Norm Willacott and Bert Wainewright joined them. Soon after Christmas 1943, privates Les Parker, Scottie and two other POWs brought the Australian group to nine.

On one occasion the POWs were instructed to be part of a firing squad. As the condemned spy attempted escape, one of the POW partisans shot him, muttering, 'Someone has to do it.'

The POWs found different ways of coping. For Ian, it was his romance with Elda. The POWs listened nightly to the 'gasbag Stalin' but they could not understand him. 'You couldn't trust anybody because you did not know where they were coming from ... The irony of it all was that I and the other men had to show loyalty to a group whose basic presuppositions and mode of operating we thoroughly despised.' Ian alluded to considerable ethical dilemmas as they weighed up how to 'keep their skin intact', keep faith within the group, and maintain individual integrity. They engaged frequently in nuisance raids. They stayed because no other viable alternative had yet presented itself, and, as Ian noted, 'all of us loved the Piedmontese area and its warm-hearted people ... none of us wished to run the gauntlet of German and fascist soldiers to seek another partisan band.'

British drops of ammunition yielded a variety of welcome weapons to the POWs. Edward 'Big Bill' Smith, a former powder monkey from West Australia, led the POWs to blow up a train with plastic explosives. As summer 1944 arrived, the POWs were cognisant of Germans planning large round-ups. 'Stalin' was still the leader, and his band averaged thirty men. During an ambush of a German convoy, China was captured.

In August 1944, Private Les Parker's partisan episode struck a dark note during a raid involving thirty Italian communist partisans and five Australian POWs near Lillianes in the Aosta Valley. Les sustained shrapnel wounds when in action. His fellow partisan-POW Ian Sproule turned him over and noted he was 'badly cut across the throat, one wrist was smashed and there were wounds all over him'. Comparing their wounds, and noting he was lying partly across his legs, Ian concluded that Les had flung himself on to him to take the brunt.

A team of POWs lugged Les down mountains on a stretcher made from bush timber and a ladder. Changing to fresh carriers, led by partisans with machine-guns, Les's seventeen-hour bumpy downhill journey dragged on. At Torrazzo, doctors Francesco Ansaldi and Anna Marengo gave what they could. Finding refuge in a church-tower, the partisans bluntly briefed the caretaker priest that if he disclosed Les's whereabouts to the enemy, fascists or Germans, he would be killed.[18] But Les soon succumbed to his injuries.

Ian Sproule wrote in his published memoir that more than a dozen escapers, probably Australian and New Zealanders, came out of hiding to pay respects to Les, who was encased by a zinc-lined coffin arranged by Ray Vigar. To Ian and others who had spent almost a year underground in Italy with him, 'Les's death knocked the stuffing out of us.'

Les Parker's name is listed with thirteen Italians, one eighteen years-old, on a bronze plaque in northern Italy to honour the combatants who took up arms against Nazi and fascist regimes.[19]

A visitor came to the partisan camp with an official letter from the American forces in France, offering paid guides to escort the POWs out of Italy. Bill and Norm decided to stay put in Italy. In a snap, Ian made a decision 'which I have regretted for the rest of my life'. Ian 'walked out into the night and headed for the Aosta', leaving behind his beloved Elda. He would never reconcile how his abrupt departure affected them both.

The journey to cross into France near Mount Blanc took nine days. When he was safely in Allied hands, Ian spoke of what they had been up to in Italy: 'Keeping the Hun on the run in the alpine foothills. We have been with a partisan band for fourteen months giving Fritz something to write home about.' Ian was eventually evacuated to Naples for repatriation.

Happy Hungerford and Ray Vigar were interrogated on the same day as Ian Sproule on 18 November 1944. Happy and Ray's joint narrative confirmed their partisan connection in the Monte Mucrone area, and that they raided fascist houses and ambushed German trucks until October 1944. Fed up with shooting through someone else's war, they decided to leave the band due to internal political strife, as well as the intensified effort by Germans to destroy the partisan movement.[20]

POW partisans within Mission Cherokee were noted of significance to the socio-historical context of Italy's response to oppression under a foreign regime. Fred Tabram had played his role, as described by Captain Pat Amoore, OC Biella Sub-Mission in a report dated 22 May 1945: 'He joined the Biella Partizans on 5 July 1944 and fought together with them against the German and Fascist troops and thus effectively harassed the enemy rear lines of communication in Northern Italy. Joined the British Military Mission for Upper Piedmont early in Jan 1945 and formed part of a Squad of British ex-PW commanded by me during the two months of continual enemy attacks during very severe conditions of deep snow and cold. His personal contribution towards the final and complete collapse of the German Armies in Italy has been considerable both in actions fought against enemy rear areas including sabotage actions and in the training of Italian Partizans in the use of British weapons and equipment dropped by them by this Mission. The fighting conditions during the period can be judged as extremely difficult due to the peculiar conditions of this type of Partizan warfare. I have found him a reliable and willing worker.'[21]

Amoore added that Fred 'has since been of great assistance to us by serving in an administrative and general duties capacity within the mission organisation'.

Accordingly, Fred 'Federico' Tabram had documentation, postwar, to prove eligibility for the Italy Star medal. For a budding pre-war football player of talent, his war medal was akin to a 'Best and Fairest' in a different league.

In his application for the Italy Star, John 'Jack' Rowe summarised his experiences: 'When Italy capitulated, I escaped my Vercelli hospital and having malaria for some months was unable to escape to Switzerland. It was necessary to join the Italian partisans and I faced danger and death as many times with this crowd as in Tobruk and El Alamein where taken prisoner. I carried rifle (sometimes machine or Sten gun) and ammunition, and on more than one occasion actually engaged the enemy. The Major (McDonald) and Captain (Bell) made me in charge of a party of four Australians.'[22]

Jack Rowe eventually reached Swiss authorities on 20 January 1945.[23] He was one of the last, if not the last, Australian escaper to make it.

Benito Mussolini was captured and killed by Italian communist partisans on 28 April 1945.[24] Hitler shot himself on 30 April 1945 and German troops surrendered in Italy 2 May 1945. Europe's war officially ended on 8 May 1945.

On that day Ted Peachey and Jimmy Dean's war ended with a frightening event. They'd made it through nineteen months on the loose in northern Italy. Ted pitched in with Cherokee Mission's anti-scorch activities, and like his fellow Australian mission operatives, got through.

On 8 May 1945, Ted and Jimmy stewed in a prison cell. Sitting side-by-side with backs rigid against the door below a tiny window, without warning the window flung open. Machine-gun fire shot above their heads and killed three other internees sitting on a bunk.[25]

During their post-war years, to commemorate their lucky dodge of death and subsequent liberation by Allied troops, on 8 May Ted and Jimmy shot off telegrams to each other.

27
'Don't shoot, we're English': Ambush in the hills

'It is amazing that, overall, so few Italians engaged in spying despite the incentives.

The financial rewards for providing information leading to the capture of escaped prisoners of war could lift a struggling family out of poverty.'

—Susan Jacobs, 2003[1]

In addition to John Laws and Ross Mudge killed in late 1943, ten ex-Campo 106 Australian POW escapers were killed in northern Italy in 1944.[2] Most were executed.

Despite persistent subversive acts by civilians of northern Piedmont to host and assist escaped prisoners to reach safety, misfortune befell others.

The winter of 1943–44 had been particularly severe and drove many escapers to ground who might otherwise have tried to journey on, perhaps to aim for Switzerland. Some were lucky to make late entrance to Switzerland, but enemy patrols and inhospitable weather thwarted others. When spring's milder weather came, fascist and German patrols crawled the countryside. By April 1944, forty Australians remained on the loose in Italy.[3] They swung between periods of harassing the enemy, engaging in sabotage and subversion with partisans and special missions, and lying low with Italian hosts.

Amongst the stragglers who remained in northern Italy were two Aboriginal POWs who hailed from opposite sides of Australia, and from different military units: Jim Brennan, 2/28th, from Laverton in Western Australia and Eddie Albert, 2/15th from north Queensland.[4] At Campo 106, or soon after escape, Jim and Eddie teamed up. At or near Biella, the duo encountered New Zealanders John 'Jack' Clark and Leslie 'George' Batt, who had also escaped Campo 106.[5]

In January 1944, the four POWs as well as British escaper Eric Hamblin secured refuge in a farmhouse hideout in the wooded hills near hamlet San Giuseppe di Castro north-east of Andorno Micca village, and three kilometres north of Biella. The men were aided by Italian women Eva Cerruti and Elma Acquadro.

Due to threats from fascists, Eva moved the POWs around on the hills. From her home at San Giuseppe di Castro, she walked one hour to reach one of the hideouts. She carried food to them almost nightly. 'My financial conditions were not so good,' Eva pointed out, 'five of them lived with me for a long time, and I had to ask some neighbours to help me.'[6]

Referring to her dedication and connection to the escaped POWs, 'our boys', Eva documented that the two New Zealanders (Clark and Batt) lived in her house for thirty-four days, 'hiding away and clothed and fed by me as their conditions were pitiful. One of them was sick with malaria fever. I cured him just as though he was my brother. I gave him medicines and injections, giving him all that I could.'

Eva Cerruti welcomed three new POW wayfarers in April: Australians Arthur Fogg, Raleigh Hoy and Douglas Smedley, whom she presumed had come from Vincenza 'Cino' Moscatelli's partisan detachment to visit their friends. In his report, Raleigh stated he had mixed with partisans since escape. He met Douglas at Coggiola, sharing the goal of hiding in the mountains and awaiting favourable opportunity to cross the Alps.

Elma Acquadro attested that most evenings the POWs came to her home. 'Hamblin usually slept at my home.' On 22 April 1944, as they walked towards an adjacent hamlet of San Giuseppe, Elma and her sister Eda brought Eric Hamblin's attention to a woman loitering nearby, a suspected informer. 'We knew her to be a fascist spy,' Elma stated, 'and we warned the prisoners to leave the area and scatter.'[7]

On 23 April, the three POWs from the Moscatelli partisan group came to Tavigliano for food, and that night Eva took food to all eight men at the Cascine dei Canisei, a clump of unoccupied farm buildings near San Giuseppe in Castro. On 24 April, Eric Hamblin left to sleep alone in the hills, in a secluded place that he and Elma had prepared a few days earlier.

The area was relentlessly combed by fascist spies, informers and bounty-hunters. From February 1944 to April 1945, GNR (Montobello National Republican Guard) troops were stationed in and around Biella.[8] Although the POW group were warned to leave the area and to scatter, they chose to stay near their Italian helpers. Whether they did not heed the warnings, or were planning to move on soon, or were feeling helpless to move into unknown territory, is not known.

Early morning on 24 or 25 April 1944, an armed search party of the local fascist Montebello Battalion of the GNR left their base at 4:30 hours under instruction from Major Manfredi. Manfredi had been informed by a civilian on 23 April of the hideout in which escapers were hidden. The soldiers arrived at Canisei in early light for its *rastrallamento* of the site. Fifteen to twenty men stationed their guns around the hut.[9]

To Jim Brennan's recollection, the date was 25 April 1944—Anzac Day.

'Clark, Batt and Smedley slept in one part of the hut and Hoy, Fogg, Albert and myself slept in another part thereof,' Jim later recalled. 'At dawn on 25 April 1944, I was awakened by the sound of machine-gun fire. I got up and cautiously looked outside and saw Italian fascist soldiers all around the hut. Then the soldiers broke open the door of the hut which gave access to the part that Hoy, Fogg, Albert and myself were occupying and told us to march out of the hut, which we did and when we came out, we were lined up against the wall of the hut.

'I then saw that Clark, Batt and Smedley were lying near the said wall. They were dead, shot right across their chests with machine-gun fire. They had their boots off. They were dressed in civilian clothing. Right in front of us were two Italian fascist soldiers with a Breda machine-gun and there were Italian fascist soldiers on either side of us to prevent us escaping. There was an Italian sub-lieutenant standing about eighty yards away who was in charge of the Italian troops.

'I cried out "We are English!" and the officer then directed the machine-gunners not to fire. My idea of calling out as aforesaid was that I thought we were being taken for Italian anti-fascist rebels. We were searched by some of the Italian soldiers and the sub-lieutenant told us that if there were any arms in the hut we would be shot.'[10]

A war crimes investigating officer, Sergeant Rondel, documented that the slain men had come out of the farmhouse door shortly after three of the Montobello Battalion search party—Settimo, Pietro and Arturo—entered the cottage. One of the searchers waiting outside, Luigi, fired a burst of machine gunfire at them. They were all hit and dropped into crouching positions near the wall. The three searchers came out of the farmhouse and fired on the already wounded men.[11]

Raleigh Hoy reported that as he, Albert and Brennan were marched away, they noticed the bodies of their comrades with their heads to the wall of the hut. 'As we were not fully dressed,' Raleigh said, 'we requested that we be allowed to collect the remainder of our clothing and boots. Fogg was allowed to return with the fascist sergeant to collect our clothes. As he returned to the kitchen, which was on the ground floor of the hut, he looked at the three bodies which were beside the door. He noticed that the body of Smedley, which was nearest to the door, had a bullet wound through the forehead. He did not notice the bullet wounds on the other two bodies. We were then marched away to Andorno Micca.'[12]

Rifle fire had also woken Eva Cerruti, as well as Eric Hamblin in his hiding place uphill. Eric watched in horror from his vantage point as four of the prisoners were led from the farm by fifteen soldiers. The farmhouse was on fire. There was no intervention he could take, he realised. He estimated that two platoons of fascist troops had combed the hut, inside and out, for two hours before setting the stone building alight. He wondered, with alarm, where the other POWs were.

When he deemed it safe to come out, Eric scrambled downslope. In a moment of brain-numbing terror, he saw the bodies of Douglas, John and George lying on the threshold of their burning quarters. In his witness statement, Eric documented the condition of his colleagues' bodies. The soldiers had disembowelled the men with daggers and filled their insides with stones, leaving the fire to scorch their buckled bodies. He attested that he dragged the bodies from the fire's reach.

Eric thought back to the informer pointed out days before. He felt convinced that the POWs' whereabouts had been betrayed by an Italian farmer and his sister.[13] Both were known to have fascist leanings. They'd led the troops to Canisei for a reward of 5000 *lire* per escaper head.

Elma also went to the bodies. She covered them up. George Batt had been shot in the face and chest; Jack was shot in the head, his head split wide open and his feet burnt. The one she knew as 'David', Douglas, had been shot in the face, the bottom of which was missing. His fist was clenched as if ready to punch, or defend. To her memory or observation, it was John Clark whom she knew as 'Giacomo', who was wearing only a vest.[14]

All the protagonists and victims in the events around Anzac Day 1944 were indubitably entangled in the tragic event and its flow-on effects. Escaped prisoners, peasants and partisans, and those caught in fascist madness were in desperate and unpredictable times. All were in survival mode. Post-war war crimes investigators found there were no independent witnesses to this event. Indeed, all had personal agendas of survival and allegiances. Their affidavits, inevitably, reveal individual perspectives and biases.

Sergio Virgulto of Tavigliano reported on the parade of the captured group including Jim, Eddie, Arthur and Raleigh and accompanying soldiers through Tavigliano's streets towards Andorno Micca. One of the captives, 'black', was in chains. He looked beaten and unsteady.[15] In a reversal of their initial capture by Germans and being handed to the Italians, it was now a case of Italians handing them back to the Germans.

Elma saw the POWs and one civilian crossing the piazza, encased by two dozen National Republican Guard troops. She observed that, to her horror, 'the two blacks' were tied. Locals spoke quietly to each other, wondering whether the captives would be transferred to Germany or shot in Vercelli.

After being taken to Biella, Jim Brennan spoke with the two Italian soldiers who had executed his fellow POWs. The soldiers asserted that they shot the three men while they were escaping. Jim was incredulous. He knew Clark and Batt were too ill with malaria to make a run. When Jim revisited that morning's events to frame his affidavit for war-crime investigations, he recalled that the position of the bodies indicated that they had been shot while lined up against the hut wall. Jim formed the opinion that they had been mistaken for Italian anti-fascist rebels because they were dressed in civilian clothes. Jim contemplated that, if the three men had the presence of mind to utter 'English' as he had done, they may have been spared. One report verified that no weapons were found in the hut.

After the bodies were moved to the Tavigliano cemetery, a retired doctor Oreste Meliga was called upon late that evening, 26 April, to go to the cemetery where *carabinieri* awaited his examination of the bodies. He determined that all three POWs had fractured skulls caused by blows from a blunt instrument. One, identified as Batt days later, had a firearm wound on the left side of his head. Another, identified as Douglas, had a 'superficial' wound extending from lower lip to larynx, but profuse bleeding indicated he'd been struck while alive. Doctor Meliga noted no other mutilations to the bodies. The doctor was ordered by the lieutenant who commanded the squadron to alter his original report to make it appear that the sole cause of death was by shooting.[16]

On 27 April, *carabinieri* instructed photographer Luciano Avignone of Andorno Micca to photograph the bodies. 'The bodies were dressed in civilian clothing, none wore shoes or boots, one was clad only in an undervest.' Luciano added that in the course of his work he heard extra information from members of the National Republican Guard. 'It appears that the biggest man, in an attempt to escape, punched [Arturo] in the face. This action provoked the killings.'

Luciano Avignone inspected the bodies. One, he said, was 'about thirty years, normal build, shot in chest, what appeared to be a bayonet wound had split the head open. Another, aged about thirty-two years, with freckled face, red hair and Roman nose, badly shot in face especially forehead and nose, and shot in chest.' The third description, fitting that of Douglas Smedley, was of a man very strongly built, tall, fair hair, with what Luciano thought to be a tattoo of a woman on his left arm. 'He'd been shot in the chest and stomach, with what appeared to be a bayonet wound across the side of his mouth, leaving his lower jaw hanging.'[17]

Eva's observation of the half-naked body was that 'his skull had been blown off, the head completely empty'. All three men, she claimed, were 'cruelly cut up with daggers'. Following the identification of the bodies, parish priest Don Enrico officiated over the burials in Tavigliano cemetery.

On 27 April 1944, the fascist paper *La Provincia Lavoratrice* published its spin of the incident. 'Conflict between legionaries (Fascist Blackshirts) and Australian POWs—three dead and four arrested. For some time, notification of movements of rebels and of enemy prisoners in the district of Andorno Micca has been received by the command of the 115 Btn "Montobello" stationed at Biella. Last Monday a squad of "M" legionaries, led by an officer, laid in wait near the Montecasco (Andorno) dairy and surprised seven individuals—who turned out to be Australian prisoners—who on seeing the militia took flight under fire. The militia acted promptly, mortally wounding three of them and arresting the other four, who turned out to be Edward Albert aged 26; James Brennan aged 26; Raleigh Ebmure [Hoy] aged 24; and Arthur Enright [Fogg] aged 29.'

Two years later, 27 April 1946, Luigi, one of the Blackshirt soldiers, gave his version of the Canisei incident. Luigi stated that after he and three others had taken up position at the farmhouse rear, he heard the voice of his sergeant shout, 'Stop, halt!' which was followed by some small arms fire and a lieutenant, probably Orlando, shouting 'Stop, stop, don't fire!' The sergeant, Luigi heard, said that some prisoners had tried to get away. On arriving at the front of the farmhouse Luigi saw three bodies, and that four prisoners had been captured. 'We escorted the four prisoners to the barracks. They were fed and later sent by lorry to Biella.'[18]

A fortnight later, on 10 May 1946, Luigi made a second statement. 'I forgot to say in my previous statement that whilst I was at the back of the house, I heard some firing at the front and I fired my automatic weapon. I did not fire it at anyone but fired it into the air.' He claimed he was summoned to the side of the house by Sgt/Major Settimo where he could see the front, and was told to cover the front by his machine-gun. When he saw the bodies, he fired his weapon again.[19]

Luigi made a third statement. 'I remember now that as soon as I got to the side of the house [Settimo] fired one shot from his musket into the house. At the same time, I fired another burst from my machine-gun into the air. The three prisoners were already dead. I fired this second burst from my gun to frighten any prisoners who were in the house.'[20]

Pietro, a marble labourer and member of Montobello battalion from August 1943 to October 1944, gave his 1946 statement about 'the men killed by our party on 24 April 1944'. The search party of about twenty men, with machine-guns, were divided into several groups around the farmhouse. With an officer, Lieutenant Orlando, and the civilian spy, he was about '200 yards' from the farmhouse between the machine-gun positions.

'After about fifteen minutes I heard about fifteen shots which sounded like musket and rifle fire. The shots only lasted an instant and came from the front of the house. Orlando and I ran to the front of the house. Orlando shouted and asked why the shooting had taken place. I saw three bodies on the ground, two dead and one dying. About five minutes after the first shooting I heard the two machine-guns fire bursts of about five or six shots each. I never heard who killed them. I had a revolver in my pocket but did not fire it.'

One of the Blackshirt soldiers Nello shouted that there were other prisoners inside. Orlando ordered Pietro inside, and he found three prisoners sitting on their bunks. They were ordered outside. Two machine-gun parties had by this time come to the front of the farmhouse. 'After the shooting I saw Arturo reloading his rifle,' Pietro declared.

'Orlando noticed the prisoners had no footwear and allowed one to go back into the farmhouse to fetch shoes for all of them. One prisoner was black, one blond and one very bronzed.' Pietro said they arrived at Andorno Micca barracks at 10:00 hours, and later to Biella headquarters.[21] The recaptured POWs were prepared for transportation to German Stalag 7A.

Reporting in early 1946, Captain Fowles of the Missing Personnel Searcher Party heard that a captain in the fascist squad, then in Biella prison awaiting trial, claimed that the POWs were the first to open fire. Fowles believed he was too afraid to say more. He added that it was possible the three new POW arrivals were armed but it was well known by local people that the other five POWs never carried arms and had often said they would not resist arrest.[22] In the opinion of Captain R. Masters of the Special Investigation section corps of Military Police, Luigi did fire but Clark, Batt and Smedley were 'finished off' by Settimo, Arturo and Pietro. Doug Smedley had punched Arturo in the face.[23]

Captain Masters paid tribute to Eva Cerruti for assistance to a number of escaped prisoners. The women of Andorno Micca had also given assistance to Australians Leo Walker and Arthur Wilbrey, and New Zealanders William Martin and Thomas Hodgson. Hodgson later attested that the POWs' location was betrayed by an Italian girl, and that for ten days fascists blocked civilians wishing to view the bodies held in the church.[24]

Luigi was given a twelve-year gaol sentence. Pietro was executed as an Italian war criminal. Arturo and the informant siblings were arraigned and executed by partisans before the trial. Eric Hamblin left Canisei and entered Switzerland in transit for repatriation on 2 December 1944.[25] Ironically, Douglas Smedley's escaper companion George Brown found safe harbour in Switzerland[26] on or before the day of Douglas's execution, 24 April 1944. In 1974, a plaque was erected at the Tavigliano cemetery[27]. It includes the names of the three executed POWs and reads: '*non importa se il vento del tempo sbiadira, i nostri nomi dei morti partigiani scritti sul marmo: resti—ben inciso nei vostri cuori—oggi domani e sempre l'amore per la liberta.*' In English: 'It does not matter if the wind of time fades, our names of the partisan dead written on the marble remains—well engraved in our hearts—today tomorrow and always love for freedom.'[28]

28
'Never, ever heard us speak about it': Repatriation, resilience

> *'It is well known that the overwhelming majority of servicemen spoke little about the war to their families. One of the reasons for this was the complete strangeness of the experience in relation to all they had known before, and the absence of its continuity when they returned home ... soldiers were often suspected of exaggerating their experiences and were disbelieved. The world was tired of war. It was generally expected that men would make a clean break with that period and slot into 'normal life'.*
>
> —Susan Jacobs, 2012[1]

It is not easy to discern when being a POW ended.

Nick Emery's narrations took his listeners to the times, as if his POW years had never left him. Nick told his wife Enid of his experiences on the loose in Italy, and that he envied POW mates incarcerated in German camps. He fantasised about their regular issue of food, predictability of routine and comparative safety behind barbed-wire. He was worn thin by constant uncertainty, looking over his shoulder and grovelling to provide his basic needs. Sitting alongside him, well into his nineties, the prisoner was still very much inside the old man. At his advanced age, words flowed about aspects of his service, but stalled for others.[2]

Words never flowed at all for the POWs who remained clammed up.

Syd Shaw, in 2017, believed it is difficult to discern a point in their service when it did end.[3] Yet some thought this phase was done with when they stepped off the boat.

In 2017, Bill Rudd commented that it never has ended. It permeates his present-day. He refers to his retirement home complex as a 'hut', alluding to POW barracks. At one hundred years-old, he still researches the experiences of escapers who survived or died, referring to all as 'free men'.[4]

Bill Rudd and Gordon Dare, who cared for Bill after his arrival to Campo 57, became lifelong friends. Years after Gordon Dare's death in 1971, his widow Joan requested Bill to tell her and their four children something about the men's time in Italy as she 'never, ever heard us speak about it'.[5]

Joan Dare's request to re-enter the past led Bill to many years of research resulting in anzacpow.com, his extensive website publication, and which earned him an OAM honour in 2009. He speaks mostly about the stories of other POWs, and needs some encouragement to delve into his own. Understandably, his summary of the *Nino Bixio* attack is outlined on a second website,[6] but it is one of the entrenched memories he steers from speaking about. He and New Zealander Charles Watkins were instrumental in installing a memorial wall inside the restored chapel at the former Grupignano camp. The site draws descendants and relatives of former Anzac POWs interned there.

Fellow Alamein and Campo 57 veteran Col Booth had settled back into life in NSW's Southern Highlands. He was successful in a 1951 ballot to secure 1100 acres of soldier settlement property at Young, New South Wales, and became a sheep grazier.[7]

He still remembered Swiss woman Eva, who continued a postcard correspondence. Eva wrote to Col to practise her English and to tell him about excursions with guides that took her to high mountain areas where she reflected on the experiences of her Australian friend. Her postcards also sought to know how he was faring. On one postcard reverse, Eva wrote of her frustration at the lack of replies from Australia: 'Now that I know your address I will write from time to time even if I don't get an answer—If I am not quite wrong, you came to join us over the Monte Moro Pass or does my memory fail? But I will not awaken those bad remembrances.'

She sent another postcard soon after, this one depicting Monte Rosa photographed from Monte Moro Pass: 'I only wish you could spend some months in Switzerland without wearing khaki. You would look at our country quite otherwise. I fear that you nearly will remember all that was disagreeable and difficult for you. You surely will remember to have seen this mountain—the Monte Rosa—so you must have a picture to show your family.'

Jean Stauffer of Thun also wished to receive letters from Col: 'I have wrote you two letters and two cards. But never received an answer.' Col would have received Jean's postcard soon after the birth of his first son Peter, named to honour Peter Erickson. Another card followed in November 1948 which would have arrived as Col and his wife Evelyn awaited the birth of their second son, Brian: 'I ask every day what you are doing and where you are???? You has [sic] promised me, here in Switzerland, to give good news from your country?!'

Col's lack of replies may have been due to his courtship of Evelyn and subsequent marriage in July 1945. Nevertheless, he kept Eva's postcards in a shoebox. He spoke fondly of Switzerland for many years to come but family, farms and finances dictated he could never return. 'A man gets older,' he told a journalist in 1967.[8]

In 1957 Paul Lavallee drew a soldier settlement block of 1100 acres at Yallaroi, located between North Star and Warialda in north-western NSW. He found it a struggle to make the farm succeed through many years of drought. None of his four children showed interest in taking on the farm. He sold up in 1974, returned to Sydney and worked for the Water Board.[9]

In late 1950, the Prisoners of War Trust Fund opened to former POWs. The fund purported to consider the special hardships suffered by POWs, but there was vigorous vetting of applicants, lack of accountability for decisions made by assessors, no transparency in the logic they employed.[10]

Paul Lavallee and Charles Warburton submitted applications to the fund. Charles Warburton had tried to work his family's dairy farm at Brunswick Junction in Western Australia, but his love of farming became a burden by the early 1960s—'my health was not too special'—and he gave up that farm. He had a stint in a repatriation hospital.

In 1959, he applied through the prisoner of war trust fund for financial assistance to help him on his current one-acre property, to buy a rotary hoe and erect a fence. He was granted 155 pounds.[11]

By 1963, Charles struggled with a condition affecting both hands, an injury to his left eye and, in his words, 'a mental condition due to head wounds'. He reminded the fund assessors of his war service, and that at Tobruk he'd 'received machine-gun bullets in left arm and neck, grenade splinters in side of head'. On his application he stated that he lived alone, with no wife or dependants. He declared income from odd jobs and asserted that his case was worthy of support.

The investigating officer denied him the grant, pointing to 'cash in bank, 200 pounds. He hasn't saved that on his pension.'

Veterans were not always applauded—and nor could the RSL be counted on as a haven. When Len Holman returned to his Queensland RSL, he confronted an unexpected sentiment. Some members considered being a POW in Europe, and of the Italians, an inferior POW experience compared to prisoners of the Japanese and of the Germans. The reaction made Len clam up and he never went back. He did not march on Anzac Day.[12]

Paul Lavallee and Col Booth chose to march on Anzac Day. Although both were granted soldier settlement properties, not all of their fellow ex-POWs were equally compensated. Aboriginal returned servicemen faced barriers to soldier settlement opportunities due to societal and systemic prejudices. Not a lot had changed since the First World War when Aboriginal servicemen were denied full citizenship rights on their return, and few gained access to land made available through soldier settlement schemes, including land taken from Aboriginal communities to be given to white ex-servicemen.[13]

Jim Brennan returned to the goldfields of West Australia in 1945 and married Myrtle. Aboriginal voting rights were still twenty years away. Despite serving his country for five years and earning five medals, Jim had to fight to mix with white people. Aborigines were banned from the town centre from 6pm to 6am, and they were not allowed into RSLs or pubs; hence they could not talk about their experiences with fellow soldiers. In 1960, Eddie and his wife Nellie went to a RSL club in Tully, Queensland, but were turned away at the door.

In 1965, Jim founded the Eastern Goldfields Aboriginal Council. After rattling tins in the street and selling cakes, funds were raised for premises in town. At a young age, Jim was snatched from his family and taken to a government run settlement, Moore River Native Settlement. Both Myrtle and Jim were driven to work tirelessly for the betterment of Aboriginal people in their community. Jim's work was honoured with the award of Order of Australia in 1984 for services to Aboriginal welfare.[14] Eddie Albert's mother Nora, a Yidinji woman, lost the right to keep Eddie and his brother Fred.[15] According to Len Watson's observations, the war 'made some white Australians say: "Look, these blokes are just as good as us, they fought beside us in the war, they proved themselves." This change in outlook is terribly important—revolutionary in a way. It has laid the basis for all the other changes that have occurred in the post-war years.'[16]

On 31 March 2015, a memorial to honour Aboriginal servicemen and women was unveiled in Hyde Park, Sydney. Named Yininmadyemi (Thou didst let fall), the memorial is situated in a place of historical significance as ritual contest ground, a crossroads for traditional walking trails and an important site for Aboriginal ceremony, gathering and camping. Created by Indigenous war artist Tony Albert, the monument depicts 'four standing bullets representing those who survived, and three fallen shells to remember those who made the ultimate sacrifice'.[17] It draws on the story of seven escapers in northern Italy in April 1944. One of the seven escapers represented by one of the standing bullet sculptures is Tony's grandfather and POW mate to Jim Brennan, Eddie Albert.

Eddie's family recalls an unexpected visit to their home by a German man, as told by Stan Albert: 'I remember a young man coming to our house looking for an Eddie Albert. Mum answered the door telling the stranger he was at work and wouldn't be home until later that afternoon. The man spoke with a foreign accent and returned later that evening. It turned out he was the young German guard from Stalag 7A who befriended Dad in the camp. They used to play cards and he would smuggle Dad cigarettes. Dad always spoke of Australia and the German guard said to Dad if he ever survived the war he would go to Australia and find him. This he did and the two men hugged and I think they both shed a tear. I recall they went for a beer not long after.'[18]

Eddie Albert was taken prisoner at Derna the day before Frank Sharp and his son Keith were captured at the old fort of Mechili on 8 April 1941. 'I am sorry to be taking prisoner a man of your age,' a German officer stated to Frank, to his surprise. Frank was quick to reply: 'When we win this bloody war, you come to Australia and I'll buy you a beer.'

Years later, while working as a manager of a hotel on the New South Wales north coast, Frank received a telegram from a mayoral office in Melbourne. A visiting German had called in, looking for 'Sergeant Frank Sharp'. He was ready to share the promised beer. Frank tossed the keys to his pub over the counter and announced that he was off to have a beer with a mate.[19]

Some Australians returned to Italy, as did Matt Knight in 1969 during a business trip. He slept in the same room and on same bed-frame as in 1944. On return home, a letter from villager Modestino Damiani arrived to tell him that when Matt left, his father cried, 'because he considers you as a brother'. A news clipping arrived to Matt and his wife Hester, telling the story of Matt's reception by villagers he knew well, and others who wondered why the well-dressed Australian tourist's face was familiar. Translated, the article closed with his departure: 'Hugs and handshakes in remembrance, of gratitude as if to emphasise that feelings of goodness and affection have no limits in this world, even if there is between vast oceans, or foreign languages, or different religions. He left his greetings for those villagers whom he didn't have a chance to meet. He had tears in his eyes, like in all partings where there is no return.'[20]

While many returned soldiers succeeded in their chosen occupations and raised their families, others struggled with substance abuse, restlessness and psychological problems after the war, some committing suicide. No doubt, experiences of captivity, escape and evasion would linger into their lives long after they got off the boat back home.

However, the interplay of war experience and individual post-war resilience is complex. Post-war events and health issues cannot be solely attributed to war. Col Booth may have smoked anyhow and his anxiety about food may have started in his childhood. It is a complex cause and effect. For all returned ex-prisoners, their war, like any intense experience, was always kicking around in their heads, interjecting into daytime lives and night-time sleep in different ways. But, as Christina Twomey concludes, 'Disadvantage in the post-war world was woven from many threads; it is difficult but important to recognise war experience as one element in the complexity of veterans' life histories.'[21]

Carl Carrigan returned from his war to raise ten children. His brother Paul's war closely paralleled that of Carl through battle, captivity, escape and evasion. But their post-war outcomes followed opposing trajectories. Carl's daughter Cate Carrigan explains: 'Like most veterans, Dad wasn't keen on talking about his experiences but over the years pieces of the puzzle had been falling into place and their amazing feat of getting over those soaring mountains in northern Italy and into Switzerland enthralled us.

'There is also a very tragic side to the story. Dad's younger brother Paul suffered what we believe must have been Post Traumatic Stress Syndrome when he returned from the war—much like many soldiers returning from modern-day conflicts. In his case, although receiving some treatment and institutionalised for a time due to his behaviour, Paul became increasingly erratic. In late October 1948, he shot and killed his sister Joan while she was sitting in a car alongside her infant daughter, husband and mother Amy Carrigan outside the Max Hotel, Moree. After his trial in 1949 and just months before our parents married, he was sentenced to life in prison in a facility for the criminally insane.'[22]

Ex-POWs from the Carrigan brothers' regiment, Lloyd Moule remembered, wanted to help Paul, regardless of the crime committed. They chipped in buy him a television as their gesture of empathy for a soldier they'd trained and served with.

In addition to respect for his regimental mates, Lloyd spoke of empathy and respect for Italians who helped him, particularly Rita Perazzo. He talked about a German man he met in 1972, a former German soldier who opposed the Carrigan brothers and Lloyd in battle at Mechili. 'After battle, he gave assistance to Vince Rayner and Eddie Howe, my mates.' Eddie died of wounds that day. Importantly, Lloyd followed a doctor's advice three decades after the war to lift some of his memories from his chest, to begin to talk about it.[23]

During one of my chats with Lloyd, his wife Billie stole a chance when he left the room to comment about him. Billie cautioned me that his memory is not as reliable as it once was. Lloyd was slipping on a couple of place names and dates, I replied, but his gist, expression and emotion about key events echoed that of other veteran accounts.

Of their time in the camps, many POWs harboured negative memories of vindictiveness, pettiness and brutality. They often spoke in generic, disparaging terms about their enemies; German troops like Hubertus became 'Jerry', Italians like Rita became 'Ities'.

Yet opinions formed outside the wire often brought a new perspective on the Italian people, and were tinged with respect and love. A country with a reputation for disorganised chaos had, in times of poverty, successfully shuttled large numbers of escaped prisoners of war through enemy lines to safety. In their POW reports, most escapers from Campo 106 acknowledged the hardworking, war-suffering, honest Italian civilians who risked their modest homes and their fascism-crushed bodies to help foreign soldiers at their lowest ebb. Remembering Montonero's Paolo Prando, Charles Warburton wrote: 'Though I have said a few harsh words about you, looking back I am deeply indebted and thankful. When the tide of war has passed, I wish you many happy and prosperous years in the fields of the rich beautiful plains.'[24]

Former POWs who could do so returned to Italy post-war to meet with people who had become friends during times of shelter. Ron Bryant's relationship with the Bione family became so close that Ron helped them to migrate to Victoria after the war.[25]

For Italians in Italy, war resonates to the present day. 'The partisans who survive suffer the trauma,' Cesare Romano Stefanato wrote about young Italian men who took up arms to fight for Italy. 'We think that we have forgotten about the horrors and then without any warning, the nightmares return. The torment and anguish is hard to bear. It is hard to live with knowing that we killed and were killed, often not knowing what we were doing and often doing these things to save ourselves. Many of us were uneducated kids, and many of the killings were in retaliation for what had been done to us.'[26]

Carpeneto's Carla Bonello was one of the young teens who has not forgotten the nuances of alliance and prejudice that deepened when POWs arrived in her locality in 1943. Regarding the shooting of John 'Paddles' Laws, Carla in 2017 replayed events in her mind. Carla, in her nineties, released re-processed memories to her grand-daughter Lucia. 'Sometimes I still pray for John. It was actually another guard who pushed him to shoot.

[That guard] Nino always disliked him.' Another local girl, Laura, said that Nino reprimanded John for every minor infraction, 'like picking a cabbage destined for the animal's forage'. Although another POW, one of the Rose brothers,[27] stood up for John, Nino maintained his grudge.

Carla was told by the guard who shot John that he did not want to do it, but the burden could not be shaken. Seventy-five years on, Carla reflects on possibilities: 'He may have been tricked by a guard to climb the fence. It was his birthday and he was at a low point.'

Carla recalls another tragedy for Carpeneto. 'Mario, one of the guards, had a heart of gold, he was a corporal. He let us go and talk to the prisoners. Many years after, I heard he left his shoes near a well and jumped into the water. He committed suicide.'

In the same way that ex-POWs may choose to explain their post-war processing of peak experiences, Carla implores her grand-daughter Lucia to think about what she has told her, to consider poignant examples of the complexity and volatility of one small village in the thick of war-torn Italy: 'See how bad it became?'[28]

Epilogue:
'I am now ready to meet my father'

'...their time in captivity alone does not define who they are. But it shaped them, and it shaped those around them. To know what they have been through helps us to understand them, and ourselves.'

—Peter Monteath, 2011[1]

Twenty-five years after my father Col Booth's war officially concluded, at a wedding in Young, I thudded onto a slippery RSL Club dancefloor. Dad turned his head, abruptly twanged to attention, shifting his inner gears to army training. Without saying a word, he scooped his eleven-year-old daughter into his trustworthy arms; the pain of my dislocated left knee roared as he bumpily stretched me from the scene of the wounding to ease me onto the soft grey cushions of the RSL foyer's couch. Emergency response done with, he stepped back, a silent sentinel awaiting support troops with medical training.

In 1984, more than four decades after Col's war, the ripples of wartime Italy rose again. Sharing dinner with Dad in 1984, I playfully reached for a morsel on his plate. He seized my arm like a shot, a reflexive grasp shocking him more than me. 'I won't do that again Dad,' I whispered. Without saying a word, he recoiled into his usual quiet gentle self.

This was the moment, as an adult observer, to ask him about his war. I did not. Living with my parents during my early university studies of modern history, I neglected to research Col: a man of history I lived with.

During his 1945 medical assessment for discharge from the army, 'PTE', post-traumatic event, was noted. Col had clammy palms, the assessor noticed, and was 'nervy'.[2]

Both his sons, my older brothers, thought Col a tough father who worked them hard during the fifties and sixties on his 1100 acre soldier settlement farm.

He was forty-one years of age by the time I, his adopted 'Doll', crawled on the small lawn at the farm while my brothers absconded from farm duties to pound billycarts and scrape their knees on the rutted dirt lane beyond the homestead's gates.

I loved my gentle father who relished a good feed and long smoko after shearing sheep, weekend lawn bowls or just for the hell of it. At smoko break, Col feasted on Evelyn's cakes and biscuits, nodding with a full mouth in a gesture of content.

Tougher years came, drought; his boys left as soon as they secured apprenticeships. We moved into town, planning the family's relocation to the coast. Col and Ev slapped loud words around, shouting about leaving and blaming, slanging the words off the kitchen walls. Into the 1970s, these storms again built up force, and then subsided.

During the coast-life years, Col coped well as a proprietor of holiday flats, cleaner, doorman, local council road-worker. He was a champion at lawn bowls. Evelyn cleaned flats and shaved poodles, but at times her mood slumped very low, and her behavioural idiosyncrasies worried us. Throughout her battles, until his death, Col remained steady, remained loyal and quiet, and their marriage was mostly happy.

In the 1980s, Col and Ev lived with my husband and me. Col equated weight-loss with dying; he continued to draw comfort from a well-padded midriff. Seven decades after Col's discharge, on compassionate grounds as a POW, I discovered his handwritten statement on his army personnel dossier which reiterates that at Campo 57 'food was highly prized'.

In 1989, at seventy-one years of age, Col's heart gave up. His body thudded to the floor next to his bed. I was home, I saw him minutes later. In a dent in his left temple is congealed blood. By accident or by design, Col's temple presumably collided with the corner of the bedside drawers. 'We put suffering animals out of their misery,' he would say.

Evelyn died ten years later. She was also aged seventy-one.

Col's younger brother, Keith, revealed that their father, Albert, a Castle Hill grower and miller of herbal concoctions for WH Comstocks, was abusive. His force-feeding of his experimental potions may have given Col anxiety around access to good food. When Col's mother, Ruby, was hospitalised with Parkinson's Disease, Albert turfed the teen brothers out of home.

Which aspects of Col's life rendered him stronger or weaker?

I can only guess.

Like many war veterans, Col had his nerves rattled as POWs in a foreign war-torn country. Individual ex-POWs processed their memories in individual ways; all veterans carried their war into post-war life. They battled nightmares, as did their wives who heard them. Their families and those closest to them wondered about their secrets, snaps, sleep disturbances and stomach disorders. Conversations with veterans' families and friends inform me that we share the struggle to grasp their resonances and expressions; collectively we yearn to peel back the layers of our veteran's experiences as glimpsed within reports, statements, interviews, diaries and memoirs. We inquire together, we share what we learn and what we have heard; together we find that our conjectures and our discoveries can contribute to the written histories, that what we reveal broadens the historical evidence and interpretations of POWs in Italy.

To their non-combatant descendants, POWs did what seemed like extraordinary things; but they saw themselves as ordinary soldiers who were forced to do whatever it took to survive, to get home, to cope.

As with Col's wartime documents, postcards and photos, spread and aired on his old kitchen table, snippets of events converge but do not yield a precise narration. Alas, to date, there is no revelation to illuminate the event that Col spoke of, the reason he named his first-born son after Peter. Some things remain persistently mysterious.

To further follow the hints left in my father's notebook, my husband Brett and I travel to Europe in 2013, to experience the local knowledge, referral networks and village hospitality of the Italians and Swiss. Albeit succinct, Col's notebook entry of 'Frank Secchia, Rovasenda' suffices for Italian historian Marco Soggetto to find Piero Secchia, Frank's son[3]. Frank and his wife Nina had welcomed Col and probably Peter into their home at Rovasenda, allowing them to hide in the family barn under their living quarters. Piero was ten years old at the time.[4]

A brief train trip from Milan takes us to Novara train station to meet Piero. Brett and I sip aperitifs with Piero and his wife, Iva. They point out a partisan memorial in Novara on which a long list of names honours those killed in wartime for resistance and subversive actions. Perhaps this is an unspoken reminder that Frank and Nina's names could have ended up thereon.

Piero drives us to Rovasenda, where his parents had lived, a town that had been a stepping stone for a number of escapers following the Sesia northward route. At his parents' house on a lane in the town, Piero proudly unbolts the barn's wooden doors to reveal the walls that cocooned Col and probably Peter with the Secchia livestock.

I later realise, when I uncover more memoirs, reports and accounts in the following years and meet more families and veterans, that our 2013 trail traces routes of hundreds of Australian POWs in search of respite within Italian homes or freedom beyond Italy.

Preparing to leave northern Italy, my husband and I clamber onto a narrow-gauge railway at Domodossola, and with no fear of armed sentries we take in the view of the majestic Alps leading to our arrival at Brig and Visp, key transport interchanges for travellers in 1943 and 2013. We are backtracking on Col's 1943 tracks.

In Saas Valley, within coo-ee of the border passes, our guide Bernhard accosts elders with questions. I proffer crumpled prints of Col's black-and-white wartime photos.

In our pre-trip email exchanges, I sent Bernhard the photo of Mattmark Hotel's sentry base as held in my father's collection, and he, in turn, forwards it to Jurg, a senior Swiss army archivist. Neither of these Swiss men had heard of Mattmark Hotel. Checking with colleagues in their mountaineering enthusiast group, they learn that the hotel's foundations lie buried at the bottom of Mattmark Dam, the largest earthen dam in Europe, constructed during the 1960s.

We begin our ascent towards Saastal, up from the dam's flat-trail perimeter. Grazing black cows jingle their cowbells; small alpine flowers peep from crevices of rock slabs. Stones slide and crunch underfoot. Light rain cools our skin. A signpost informs us that in good conditions, the passes of Moro and Mondelli are reachable within one hour from this juncture. Jurg deepens the context beyond the POW stories to talk about Switzerland's wartime context and strategies.

Later, in Bern, Bernhard locates Col's friend Eva and he accompanies us to meet her. 'Did you consider my father a handsome man?' I inquire, wishing to ask more. 'Yes, he was a special older friend who helped me to learn English,' she replies. I thought about Eva's postcard messages of 1944, and the anecdotes of sitting amongst alpine flowers, and of a teen girl who seemed to have more than a crush on a foreign soldier. As she sits alongside her husband, whom she married in her fifties, I choose not to pry further.

Touched by this beautiful woman who met my father as a twentysomething, we compensate for Col's negligence as a correspondent and send each other postcards. In one, she sweetly says that she is writing on an anniversary date, the last day she saw Colin in Zurich. 'We kissed goodbye and I had my second cigarette.'

Bernhard's diligence also tracks the families Sidler and Muff for whom Col worked as a farmhand. As we approach the village Ottenbach near Zurich, I spot the Sidler home depicted in Col's photo taken in September 1944.

Brett and I learn about an annual event in Vace, thirty kilometres east of Ljubljana in Slovenia, that commemorates partisan history and the active involvement of Allied POW escapers. We decide to ditch a visit to Venice and go there instead. On the Italian–Slovenian border we board a train for Gorizia to meet our contact Leigh Thompson, a recently retired Melbourne QC. Leigh and his Slovenian-born wife Katja are in Slovenia for several months. Leigh is hooked on uncovering Slovenian, Australian and New Zealand shared partisan history.

On a remote Slovenian hilltop at Vace, a three-hour ceremony unfolds like an Anzac Day commemoration on steroids. French, Austrian and Slovenian speakers, singers, dancers and artists thrill the international crowd. A French dramatist oozes fake bullet-wound blood. A Slovenian flag-bearer faints. It is a glorious afternoon, even though we cannot understand one word. Leigh steps up to the microphone to introduce the sons of New Zealand POW escaper Harold Sanderson, Paul and his Italian half-brother Antonio, as well as myself, to the crowd. As descendants of Australian and New Zealand escapers, it is clear to the three of us that to varying extents, our fathers' private wars had played out within public and historical theatres of deep undertones that reverberate and resound to the present day.

At a celebratory feast following the formal proceedings, I tail an elder as he leaves the gathering. I wish to shake his hand. As a teen, this Slovenian risked his life to row a boat carrying Australian escaper Ralph 'The Crow' Churches[5] and others across a river to freedom. Later, I write to Ralph in Adelaide to tell him of our Vace adventure. He is delighted; his respect for Slovenian partisans remains strong. Reciprocally, before Ralph died, a medal of honour from Slovenia was bestowed on him.

The ceremony attendees head uphill to a B&B. At the celebratory feast, we share stories with Leigh, Paul Sanderson, Antonio and Antonio's researcher friend Paola. In 1943, Antonio and Paul's father Harold Sanderson broke away from Torviscosa work camp, Campo 107, located not far from Grupignano. He found long-time shelter with the family of Maria Corona in Erto, about 60 kilometres north-west of Udine.

As our bellies fill with food and wine and night falls around the hills, we realise it would be unsafe to drive back to our hotel, a three-hour trip, on the other side of Slovenia. With the B&B fully accommodated by the ceremony's performers, our group is invited to bunk down side-by-side in the bottom level of the host's home. We snuggle under blankets like giggly schoolchildren exhausted from a modern history excursion—or, like our forefathers, dossing down in safe refuge.

Antonio returns to his home in Italy, to write a book about his father Harold, his mother Maria, and the hot-bed of civil strife within Italy during wartime.[6] Harold had joined with Slovenian partisans.

After Harold's liberation in Italy, he was interrogated by repatriation officials. He acknowledged Maria as one of the people who'd helped him in Erto and Casso. Accordingly, Maria was visited by an officer of the 'Commission of Verification' on behalf of the Allied authorities and granted compensation of 12,000 *lire*. She was also awarded the Alexander Certificate. It was during this meeting that she informed the officer that Harold was the father of her child Antonio.

Harold returned home to New Zealand, to meet and marry Doreen. On return from their honeymoon, Harold received a letter from the 'Verifying Commission of the General Headquarters of the Italian Allies' indicating that Maria had borne a child and that Harold was the father. When Harold left Erto and Casso, he did not know Maria was pregnant.

As a newlywed man, Harold could not find the right words to reply to Maria. He wrote a poem, held captive in New Zealand, to express his emotion and his circumstance: 'Twas too Late'.

Growing up in New Zealand, Paul Sanderson, the youngest of Harold and Doreen's children, was unaware of an older brother born in Italy. After Harold died, Doreen and her children found the letter, and they decided to contact Maria and Antonio. In 1983, Maria received a letter from the Sandersons, signed by Doreen. Antonio, profoundly struck with emotion, could not sleep for many nights. He was keen to visit his New Zealand family and in six months he learned to speak basic English.

He flew to New Zealand in November 1984 with his wife Marisa. Paul Sanderson treasures his memory of that visit. 'I will never forget that day, especially the next morning as we were getting ready to visit Dad's grave at the Maunu Cemetery. Antonio and Marisa appeared from the guest room, Antonio in a very smart suit and Marisa dressed completely in black with lace covering her face.' In beautifully spoken English, he told his New Zealand family: 'I am now ready to meet my father.'[7]

Rustling amongst the war books in Berkelouw Book Barn in Berrima in 2016, I strike up a conversation with the man alongside me, a major in the Australian army. I tell him of a POW's concern and frustration about a dominant paradigm: a perceived hierarchy of POW suffering that laddered POWs of the Japanese at the top, Germans in the middle rung and Italians at the other end.

I share the major's belief that such a hierarchy is simplistic. The major emphasises that for every soldier, for every POW, there are individually felt privations and suffering.

In contrast to wartime images of emaciated POWs coming home to Australia from other theatres, Col and most of the ex-Switzerland cohort disembarking at Port Melbourne in November 1944 displayed physical fitness. This image may have contributed to the perception of low suffering. Stepping off the *General AE Anderson* in 1944 to a return to civilian life, Col was the strongest, physically, he would be during most of his post-war decades. Switzerland was good for him and his fellow POWs, but war neuroses ticked under the surface.

Seventy-five years after my father Col worked the Ottenbach farms, Brett and I conclude our European travels in July 2019 with our adult son and daughter in Switzerland and northern Italy. With Bernhard's guidance, Brett and Aden walk from Mattmark Dam to tackle Monto Moro Pass and descend into Italy. Talia and I hike lower slopes and ride up to Monte Moro in the cable car. I know of two other Australian families soon to begin their trek of the Turlo and Moro passes. Dario, of Alice Castello located on the western edge of the Campo 106 farms, invites me to speak with the assistance of translator Olga to a meeting of ANPI Associazone Nazionale Partigiani d'italia, an association founded in 1944 by participants in the Italian resistance. A descendant of a Ronsecco fisherman called Raimondo shows me notes written by three Australian escapers and the photos of two British escapers. The Italian group burst with questions and comments about their partisans and civilians who embraced escaped POWs. They seek to share and increase understandings of their relatives' resistance efforts within a spectrum of covert and overt actions during their war.

Digging towards an understanding of Col's POW years, revealed to me mostly by archival record and the glimpses of collective memory as diarised and reported by his cohort POWs, I came to an unexpected, illuminating revelation about his time as a POW, and that of his cohort.

One or more of Col's escapes, and the breakouts of most of his Campo 106 colleagues, did not play to the tune of dramatic 'great escape' narratives. Escape, for most, was easy.

But the evasion phase of Col's war—the month on the loose, foot-slogging to the frontier, identifying friend from foe, scraping up a feed, weighing up his need for shelter with the safety of his hosts—in all likelihood was more taxing and nagging on post-war resilience than his thirteen-month phase of captivity.

Col, like Nick, may have opened up to me about some of this, shaking his head in brief hesitation—if I'd piped up.

Acknowledgments

Research for this book has brought me into contact with many families of ex-POWs and to all of you, my heartfelt thanks for the trust placed in me to work with material held in private collection. Since 2011, I have been wonderfully embraced by Australian networks of veterans and their families. There are too many names to list. In particular I am indebted to the ex-POWs' relatives with whom I have met, chatted by phone, and exchanged letters and emails over many years in relation to this book: Stan Albert, Keith Anderson, Pauline Anderson, Edgar Bione, Kathy Bridson, Gwen Bryant, Neil Campbell, Cate Carrigan, Bruce Fellowes, Gavin Fitzgerald, Nancy Hill, Bob and Norma Kerr, Antonio Manfroi, Trish Munro, Annette Nelson and Janice, Alan Newbey, Frank Page, Rob Peachey, Ted Peachey, Ann Plumb, Shanthi Premananda, Daryl Radnell, Paul Sanderson, Terry Sibraa, Mat Sincock, Margaret Smith, Josh Sproule, Ray Tabram, Ian Waller, Alma Ward, Nigel Webster, Martin Weekes, Vanessa West, Bob Wilson, Harry Wilson, Kathleen Wilson. I am thankful for our chats too, Pamela.

To the ex-POW Italy veterans and their wives whom I have met, my deepest thanks for generous conversations: Nick and Enid Emery, Doug Frame, Paul and Doreen Lavallee, Ron Maitland, Lloyd and Billie Moule, Bill and Caty Rudd, Bob Wood. I'm privileged to have had phone chats and letters with Jack Bell, Ernie Brough, Jack Caldwell, Ralph Churches, Alan Nicholson, Jack Nie and Syd Shaw.

My huge respect and gratitude to all volunteers and committees across Australia that have supported veterans and their relatives by maintaining unit associations' newsletters and activities. To mention just a few: Alastair Davison and Roland Nicholson (2/24 Bn), David Laurie (2/15 Bn), Phil McWilliams, Graham McEwan and David Warren (2/28 Bn), Barry Willoughby (2/3 Anti-tank), David McDonald and Malcolm Wrigglesworth (3LAA). My thanks for incorporating my writing or research findings within your print and online publications. Thanks also to Olwyn Jones (*Barbed Wire and Bamboo*), Department of Veterans' Affairs (Our Mob Serving Country), Dennis Hill, and Paul Skrebels, former editor of *Sabretache*, journal of Military Historical Society of Australia. To Nigel Webster and to Warren Farmer, thank you for sharing your experience in active army service. At Red Cross Australia, I thank Moira Drew; at Melbourne's Shrine of Remembrance, I thank Neil Sharkey. Tony Rudd, thank you for your assistance with regard to Bill Rudd's print and web-based collections.

I am particularly grateful for the encouragement and research advice extended by Peter Monteath. Other Australian historians and researchers to thank include Kristen Alexander, Kate Ariotti, Margaret Geddes, Lachlan Grant, Jan 'Kabarli' James, Philippa Scarlett, Michelle Scott Tucker, Neil and Sylvie Smith, Peter Stanley, Louise Wilson. To Leigh Thompson, we will never forget our 48 hours with you in Slovenia. From the other side of the Tasman ditch, Ken Fenton, Susan Jacobs and Rosanne Robertson have been generous in information-sharing and advice. I miss email chats and the sharing of source information with UK-based Brian Sims. Until his death, Brian generously shared documents he'd sourced from The National Archives, particularly POW escaper reports which contribute greatly to identifying camp locations, escape routes and names of Italian helpers. The assistance given by staff at National Archives of Australia (Canberra and Melbourne), Australian War Memorial and National Library of Australia also made my research journey much easier.

It has been a wonderful privilege to collaborate with, and to be assisted by, Italian researchers and ANPI (Associazione Nazionale Partigiani d'Italia) members. Many thanks for your information-sharing and research support, and for coping with my fledgling Italian: Liliana Cerruti, Claretta Coda, Maria Elena Coha, Dario Franciscono and ANPI Alice Castello, Rino Furno, Luciano Guala and ANPI Vallecervo, Claudio Martignon, Gabriele Salussolia, Marco Soggetto and Simon Tancred (Hidden Italy Walking tours). Olga Strikha generously offered translation assistance in 2019, as did Maryann McCoy in 2013. Italians have shared their stories, and those by relatives who extended help to POWs. For giving me this perspective, I thank Carla Bonello, Amanda Girardi, Vivian McDonald, Pietro Milano, Piero and Iva Secchia, Lucia Vaccarino. In Switzerland, my thanks extend to Eva, Muff and Sidler families, Rita Ackerman, Kurt Weber, Barbara and Jurg Stussi-Lauterburg. To our friend and guide Bernhard Banzhaf, thank you for sharing *jenepi* and your wit, as well as an unflinching patience with my hiking pace.

Feedback from Sophia Barnes and Jacinta di Mase regarding early chapter drafts helped me to progress. During the ACT Writers Centre's Hardcopy non-fiction program of 2017, feedback from writer peers assisted me to reshape focus in order to complete the book. Nigel Featherstone, thank you for your generous advice, and your role in creating Hardcopy's active network. To the Echo Books team, Peter, Ian, Cathy and my publisher Georgia, my gratitude for your guidance and patience.

As editor for *Shooting Through*, Nadine Davidoff's sensitive and insightful editing brought out my best. My deepest thanks, Nadine, for sharing this process.

Bill Rudd, my favourite email correspondent, it's my heartfelt privilege to receive your 'Demonic' Sherrin kickstart into this history and your research networks. I deeply value your ongoing mentoring and friendship.

My husband Brett never lost faith in me to complete this book, giving me innumerable hours of support. To our children Talia and Aden, much love for all the ways you have boosted me.

I welcome communications regarding the book and this history.
Email: katrinakittel9@gmail.com

Notes

Chapter 1: 'The war is over for you': Capture and captivity

1. Mark Johnston, *Fighting the enemy: Australian soldiers and their adversaries in World War II*, Cambridge University Press, 2000, p. 3 and pp. 9–10.
2. NX56333 Herbert 'Nick' Emery, memoir in private collection; NAA B883 NX56333, Emery, Herbert.
3. Nick Emery, personal communication.
4. TNA (The National Archives UK) WO 392, The War Office, Directorate of Prisoners of war, Prisoner of War Lists – Second World War. Sub-series WO 392/21: Imperial prisoners of war held in Italy. August 1943. Section 2: Australian Army. Units with high numbers of AIF POWs in Italy included 2/28, 2/24, 2/15, 2/32 battalions and the 2/3 Anti-Tank Regiment. Units with smaller numbers of POWs in Italy included 3LAA Regiment, 2/43, 2/48 and 2/17 battalions, 2/8 Field Ambulance, and Supply Corps. Most POWs were captured in North Africa campaigns; a minority captured during Greece and Crete campaigns.
5. NX23801 Paul Lavallee interview by Ben Langford, *Illawarra Mercury*, 24 April 2017.
6. Maitland, Ron & Christine Makella, *No Mountain too high: a life's journey*, Brookvale: self-published, 2006, p. 20.
7. Johnston, *Fighting the enemy*, pp. 9–10.
8. NAA (National Archives of Australia) B883, NX24360 Clarke, George, includes Statement by a Repatriated Navy, Army or Air Force Prisoners of War, 19 October 1944.

9. TNA WO 208, POW Report by James Wilson QX5417, Switzerland, undated 1944, courtesy Brian Sims. Most WO 208 reports by Australian escapers are held The National Archives, TNA, in UK. A small number of reports are held in National Archives of Australia (NAA) B883 Army personnel files.
10. NAA B883, NX3778 Gardner, Colin. File includes Statement by a Repatriated Navy, Army or Air Force Prisoners of War, 21 October 1944.
11. See Appendix 1, nominal roll of Australian POWs at Campo 106.
12. NX23801 Lavallee, memoir in private collection, courtesy Ann Plumb.
13. Paul Lavallee cited by Ben Langford, *Illawarra Mercury*, 2017.
14. Raymond Binns cited in Peter Monteath, *P. O.W.: Australian prisoners in Hitler's Reich,* Pan Macmillan Australia, 2011, p. 49.
15. For 2/15th Battalion accounts of capture at Derna see Austin, R.J., *Let enemies beware! 'Caveant hostes': The history of the 2/15th battalion, 1940–1945,* Slouch Hat Publications, McCrae Australia, 2008.
16. NAA B883, SX9123 Binns, Raymond.
17. TNA WO 208, POW Report by Gunner Carl Carrigan NX51288, Arosa Switzerland, 4 August 1944, courtesy Brian Sims. Refers to Campo 106/11 Selve.
18. See Alex Barnett, *Hitler's Digger Slaves: Caught in the web of Axis labour camps,* Australian Military History Publications, 2001, for his account of POW transit camps: Benghazi, Sabratha, Naples, Capua, Sulmona, Prato al Isarco, Grupignano.
19. TNA WO 208, POW Report by Lance Bombardier Lloyd Moule NX40603, Switzerland, undated 1944, courtesy Brian Sims.
20. NAA B883, VX48180 Sincock, Edward. File includes Statement by a Repatriated Navy, Army or Air Force Prisoners of War, 22 October 1944.
21. See Appendix 1.
22. VX34767 Tom Anderson, memoir, courtesy Keith Anderson.
23. Johnston, 2000, p. 53.
24. Anecdote told by POW Bill Kelly SX9027 in Kelly, William, *Journeys of a Restless Spirit: collected memories of Bill Kelly,* Adelaide: Van Gastel Printing, 2001, pp. 142–143. Also, WX5299 Charles Warburton, memoir.
25. Liddell Hart, B.H., (Ed.), *The Rommel Papers,* Arrow Books Ltd, London, 1984, pp. 261–262.
26. AWM 057024, AWM 057025, Bill Waller, *Go there you die,* 1989. Permission to cite, Ian Waller.

27. Refer Appendix 1.
28. WX9723 Jack Wauhop, Private, 2/32nd Battalion and a prisoner of war, interviewed by Brian Wall for Keith Murdoch Sound Archive in Australia in the war of 1939–45, S00512, 12 January 1989, p. 7.
29. Refer Appendix 1.
30. For Australian accounts of the Alamein battles, see Johnston, Mark and Stanley, Peter, *Alamein: The Australian Story*, Oxford University Press, 2006, and also Masel, Philip, *The Second 28th: the story of the 2/28th Australian Infantry Battalion in World War II*, PK Print, Perth, 2017, 3rd edition.
31. NAA B883, VX39694 Rudd, William; NAA B883, NX38152 Weekes, Colin; NAA B883, NX56333 Emery, Herbert.
32. NX38152 Colin Weekes, memoir, courtesy Martin Weekes.
33. See Appendix 1.
34. See Appendix 1.
35. NX56333 Herbert 'Nick' Emery, personal communication. Nick was also known as 'Harry' in the army.
36. For VX39694 Bill Rudd's account of Nino Bixio, see his Campo 57 website, <http://www.campo57.com/products.html> last accessed 19 May 2019, and also Jim Paterson, *Partisans, peasants and P.O.W.s: a soldier's story of escape WWII*, Optima Press, Perth, 2008.
37. VX39694 Bill Rudd, personal communication.
38. Gruppignano (double p) spelling was more commonly used in wartime whereas Grupignano (single p) is more common nowadays. Site of Campo 57 is in Premariacco, eight kilometres east of Udine.
39. Bill Rudd's website publication, <http://www.anzacpow.com/> last accessed 19 May 2019.
40. AWM54 779/1/22, Reports and Statements by Major R.J. Binns 2/8 Field Ambulance and Capt. E.W. Levings RMO 2/3 Anti-Tank Regiment AIF on Gruppignano POW Camp Italy. 1943.
41. NAA B883, NX60337 Booth Colin, Statement by a Repatriated Navy, Army or Air Force Prisoners of War, 22 October 1944.
42. Missing, wounded and prisoner of war enquiry cards, Red Cross, digitised, at University of Melbourne, contain dates of transfer from campo 57 to campo 106 for respective POWs: <https://digitised-collections.unimelb.edu.au/handle/11343/190446> last accessed 19 May 2019.
43. VX34773 Ian Knight, memoir in private collection, courtesy Janice and Annette.
44. Estimates by WX5933 Doug Le-Fevre 1989 p. 15, and by other veterans, refer to more than twice that amount of POW in transit. See Appendix 1 notes.

45. VX46243 Fred Tabram, memoir in private collection, courtesy Ray Tabram.
46. Ray Tabram, personal communication.
47. WX5933 Douglas Le-Fevre, as a Private, 2/28th Battalion and POW in Italy, interviewed by Brian Wall for Keith Murdoch Sound Archive in Australia in the war of 1939-45, S00517, 10 January 1989, p. 15.

Chapter 2: Smoko

1. Gilbert, Adrian, *POW: Allied prisoners in Europe 1939–1945*, John Murray (Publishers) London, 2006, p. 237.
2. Fred Tabram, memoir.
3. Weekes, memoir. See also NAA B883, NX38152 Weekes, Colin. Also, Red Cross Missing, wounded and prisoner of war enquiry card for NX38152 Weekes.
4. TNA WO 208, POW Report by Gunner Colin Weekes NX38152, 12 July 1944, Adelboden (Switzerland), courtesy Brian Sims. Refers to Campo 106/20 Salussola. POW Report by WX11913 Edward Winfield refers to number 106/20 for [Cascina] Pista Nuova. Report by NX1206 Frederick Sing refers to 106/3Arro, also near to Salussola.
5. Bill Rudd, a POW at Baraccone, personal communication.
6. Fred Tabram, memoir.
7. VX34693 Don Radnell, memoir entitled *I enlisted*, 1986, courtesy Daryl Radnell and Alastair Davison, 2/24th Association. Don's memoir serialised in 2014 and 2015 issues of *Furphy Flyer*, 2/24 Btn Association.
8. NAA B883, VX34693 Radnell, Donald.
9. Douglas Le-Fevre, S00517, 1989.
10. TNA WO 392: The War Office, Directorate of Prisoners of war, Prisoner of War Lists – Second World War. Sub-series WO 392/21: Imperial prisoners of war held in Italy. August 1943, include two Australian POWs with surname Hanson: TX722 Private Bernard Hanson and VX44187. Red Cross POW card for TX722 Private Bernard Hanson lists 106. He is likely to be Popeye.
11. Weekes, memoir.
12. NAA B883, NX60337 Colin Booth.
13. POW Reports indicate this cluster for Campo 106/1.
14. Bill Rudd, personal communication.
15. Col Booth cited by Tom Barrass, 'Swiss tour for war prisoners', *Newcastle Herald*, 14 October 1967.
16. Bill Rudd, personal communication.
17. NAA B883, QX5417 Wilson, James.

18. QX5417 James 'Jim' Wilson, memoir.
19. Affidavit by QX5417 James Wilson within TNA WO 311/1219, Murder of Pte. J.E. Law (NX16597) at Campo 106 Vercelli.
20. Carla Bonello, personal communication via grand-daughter Lucia, 2017.
21. NAA B883, VX37427 Jones, Brinley Jones, and WO 208 POW Report for Lance Sergeant Brinley Jones, Wil (Switzerland), 5 July 1944.
22. Murder of a POW called 'Paddles' at Carpeneto is recounted by several ex-POW. Spelling of surname varies across sources: his service file (NAA B883, NX16597) refers to Laws; Milan's Commonwealth War Graves Commission (CWGC) cemetery refers to Law: <https://www.cwgc.org/find-war-dead/casualty/2816908/law,-john-ernest/> last accessed 16 June 2019.
23. In AWM PR88/185, NX23800, Norman Freeberg, *A synopsis of prisoner of war camps*, cited with permission from Shanthi Premananda, Freeberg refers to news of shooting of 'JL'.

Chapter 3: Go grey thinking about it

1. Midge Gillies, 2012, *The barbed-wire university: the real lives of Allied prisoners of war in the second world war*, Aurum Press, London, p. 49.
2. Gilbert, *POW*, p. 117.
3. Paul Lavallee, memoir.
4. Don Radnell, memoir.
5. Gilbert, *POW*, p. 238.
6. Charles Warburton, memoir.
7. Bill Rudd cited regarding tobacco in Geddes, Margaret, *Blood, Sweat and Tears: Australia's WWII remembered by the men and women who lived it*, Penguin, 2004, p. 141.
8. Le-Fevre, S00517, 1989.
9. Carla Bonello, personal communication via her grand-daughter Lucia.
10. Col Booth, POW letter postcard, *poste Italiane cartolina postale per prigionieri de Guerra*, private collection.
11. Tom Anderson, memoir.
12. Cascina Veneria, according to Tom Anderson, was a location for the movie *Riso Amaro*, Bitter Rice, which portrayed life for *mondine*. Cascina Veneria estate <http://www.agricolaveneria.it/> was acquired in 1939 by an institute chaired by Giovanni Agnelli, founder of Fiat manufacturing. Agnelli's goal was to transform the estate into an exemplary farming model for the surrounding territory. Some POWs walked to Veneria from Oschiena, administered by brothers Giuseppe and Michele Michelone.

13. NX53017 Richard 'Dick' Gill, memoir.
14. Maitland, Ron & Christine Makella, 2006. *No Mountain too high: a life's journey,* Brookvale: self-published, 2006, p. 14.

Chapter 4: Keep calm and stay put

1. Charles Rollings, 2008, *Prisoner of war: voices from behind the wire in the Second World War,* Ebury Publishing, United Kingdom, p. 5.
2. Warburton, memoir.
3. Turin Museum summary of July 1943 bombardment: http://www.museotorino.it/view/s/acb7d7d49d6147e188377fb9e9c491ef
4. 'We Italians to you British regarding our art', *POW News,* Switzerland, 1944.
5. Herbert Lockie (QX6577), 'Bert Lockie's Story', *Caveant Hostes: The Journal of the 2/15 Infantry Battalion Remembrance Club,* March 1985, Vol. 1, No.38.
6. VX32109 Ernie Sparnon, memoir, courtesy Margaret and Bruce. TNA WO 208, POW Report by Gunner Ernest Sparnon VX32109, Arosa Switzerland, 14 August 1944, courtesy Brian Sims, refers to Campo 106/1 San Germano.
7. Carla Bonello, personal communication via Lucia.
8. Doug Le-Fevre, S00517, 1989.
9. Gilbert, *POW,* p. 282.
10. Jack Wauhop, S00512, 1989.
11. Ray Tabram, personal communication.
12. Robert 'Bob' Ward, memoir, courtesy Alma Ward.
13. Ted Peachey (Jnr) Peachey and Rob Peachey, personal communication.
14. Gordon Dare lists escape companions in liberation report – TNA, WO 344 series, War Office: Directorate of Military Intelligence: Liberated Prisoner of War Interrogation Questionnaires, General Questionnaire for British/American ex-prisoners of war for Private Gordon Dare VX38610, 4 June 1945.
15. Jock McCaffery, the SOE's man in Switzerland, used code name 'Rossi', as cited by Peter Monteath, *Escape Artist,* p. 204. He may be 'Dr Rossi' or a relative. Roger Absalom, *A Strange Alliance: aspects of escape and survival in Italy 1943–45,* Leo S. Olschki Editore, Florence, 1991, p. 39, refers to key organiser of assistance to POWs, Giuseppe Bacciagaluppi, as known as 'Rossi', married to Englishwoman, Audrey Smith.

Chapter 5: That's when our war started

1. Bill Rudd, <http://www.anzacpow.com/welcome_letter> last accessed 7 May 2019.
2. Absalom, Roger, *A Strange Alliance,* p. 12.

3. QX3237 Arthur Jobson's account is included in Ken Ward-Harvey, *The Sapper's war: with ninth division engineers 1939–1945,* Sagoka Pty Ltd in association with 9th Division RAE Association NSW, 1992, pp. 97–107.
4. TNA WO 208, POW Reports by Ian Jobson QX21217, 22 July 1944, Caux, Switzerland, and by Arthur Jobson QX3237, 28 August 1944, Wald (Zurich), Switzerland.
5. Alan Newbey, personal communication. When Alamein veteran WX7406 Ted Newbey reached Campo 57, his brother Joe barely recognised Ted due to physical decline. POW Syd Shaw recalled, in his late 90s, Ted dying in an adjacent bunk.
6. NAA B883, WX7406 Newbey, Edward. Postwar, Edward 'Ted' Newbey's remains were relocated to Udine's Commonwealth War Graves Commission cemetery.
7. NAA B883, VX34777 Knight, Ewen.
8. Ian Knight, memoir.
9. Anecdote re tryst told to Laurie Quinn, a soldier settler neighbour to Col.
10. TNA WO 208, POW Report by Gunner Colin Booth, NX60337, Bornhausen (Switzerland), 19 September 1944, courtesy Brian Sims. Refers to 106/1.
11. Interview with Col Booth by Tom Barrass, 'Swiss tour for war prisoners,' *Newcastle Herald,* 14 October 1967. In his notebook, placenames in chronological order included 'Balsola' [Balzola] and 'Cassala' [likely, Casale Monferatto].
12. TNA WO 344 series, War Office: Directorate of Military Intelligence: Liberated Prisoner of War Interrogation Questionnaires, General Questionnaire for British/American ex-prisoners of war for Private Havaland Park WX14265, 29 May 1945. Park refers to Col Booth, Peter Erickson and Edwin 'Ted' Price amongst others with him at Cascina Gattesco until fascists caused them to disperse. Possibly, this was locality for Peter's act to save Col's life. With reference to POW Jack Nie's 1940's map, Cascina Gattesco and Allodi were in close proximity, perhaps same farmhouse cluster. Peter refers to 'Allodi, 14 September' at top of his notebook's placename list. Col acknowledges 'Mario Michelone, D'allodi' in his notebook. Ted Price's memoir, in Bill Rudd collection, refers to a tryst. Photos of uniformed POWs (held in Price and Booth collections) that include Ted, Col and Peter were taken at same canal, river bank or most probably flooded fields.
13. Carla Bonello.
14. Susan Jacobs, *Fighting with the enemy: New Zealand POWs and the Italian Resistance,* Penguin, Auckland, 2003, p. 96.

15. Advice to British medical officer cited in Gilbert, POW, p. 280.
16. Le-Fevre, S00517, 1989.
17. Bill Rudd, Australians at War Film Archive, interview 20 May 2003: http://australiansatwarfilmarchive.unsw.edu.au/archive/200-william-rudd last accessed 29 May 2019.
18. WX11748 Albert 'Bert' Wilson, diary extracts, courtesy Harry Wilson.
19. Weekes, memoir.
20. Bill Rudd regarding package, personal communication.

Chapter 6: The familiar rice mill

1. Peter Monteath, 2017, *Escape Artist: the incredible second world war of Johnny Peck,* 2017, p. 142.
2. Gilbert, *POW*, p. 287.
3. Refer Appendix 1 and Appendix 2–New Zealander POWs who reached Switzerland.
4. Absalom, *A Strange Alliance,* p. 31.
5. Warburton, memoir.
6. Carla Bonello.
7. Absalom, *A Strange Alliance*, p. 21.
8. Gilbert, *POW*, p. 288, refers to the 'final warning' being as early as 19 September.
9. Colin Weekes, memoir.
10. NAA B883, NX40603 Moule, Lloyd.
11. Lloyd Moule's interview by Australians at War Film Archive, Archive 1285, p. 52. <http://australiansatwarfilmarchive.unsw.edu.au/archive/1285-lloyd-moule> last accessed 24 May 2019.
12. TNA WO 208, POW Report by Lance Bombardier Lloyd Moule NX40603, Switzerland, undated 1944, courtesy Brian Sims.
13. Lloyd Moule, personal communication.
14. Giorgio Nascimbene, *Prigionieri di Guerra: L'anabasi dei prigionieri alleati che nel 1943 fecero parte dei campi di lavoro nelle risaie vercellesi e dintorni,* Societa Operaia di Mutuo Soccorso Villata, Vercelli, 2004, p. 137, translation by Katrina Kittel.

Chapter 7: South to the River Po

1. Ken Fenton, *Alamein to the Alps: war in the Piedmont with Mission Cherokee and the lost Anzacs 1943–4,* 2011, p. 32.
2. NAA B883, NX53017 Gill, Richard; NAA B883, NX50270 Duggan, John.

3. Dick Gill, memoir.
4. Argent, J.N.L. ('Silver John'), *Target Tank: the history of the 2/3rd Australian anti-tank regiment, 9th Division A.I.F,* Parramatta, 1957, pp. 66–67, lists Gill, Duggan and battery colleagues captured 8 April 1941, Mechili.
5. See <http://www.agricolaveneria.com/our-history/> for Agricola Veneria Agricultural Society, last accessed 24 May 2019.
6. With reference to Appendix 1, the men mentioned by Gill were Leo Armitage and Ernie Berg. 'Baker' and 'Wilson' may be any of those surnames listed.
7. Nick Lawrie's interview in 'Escaped to Switzerland from Italian P. O.W. camp', *Port Lincoln Times,* 16 June 1982, p. 4. Lawrie was captured late October at Alamein, amongst the last Australians captured in North Africa.
8. Don Radnell, memoir.
9. Bert Lockie's story.
10. NAA B883, VX34393 Knight, Matthew.
11. Tom Anderson's interview with Neil Wilson in 'From Geelong to Munich', *Herald Sun*, 24 April 2004, p. 27.
12. Fred Tabram, memoir.
13. Absalom, *A Strange Alliance*, p. 19.
14. Tom Anderson, memoir.
15. NAA B2458, 1900210, QX6959 Garvan Henry Drew.
16. QX6577, Lockie, Herbert, 'Bert Lockie's Story', *Caveant Hostes*: *The Journal of the 2/15 Infantry Battalion Remembrance Club*, March 1985, Vol. 1, No.38.
17. Jim Wilson, memoir.

Chapter 8: Our train ride began

1. Peter Monteath, *P. O.W.: Australian prisoners in Hitler's Reich,* Pan Macmillan, 2011, p. 117.
2. TNA, WO 392/21: Imperial prisoners of war held in Italy. August 1943. Section 2: Australian Army; Section 8: Air Forces.
3. Keith Sharp, 'Escape to Switzerland', *Stand To,* January 1952.
4. NAA B883, NX60017 Sharp, Frank; NAA B883, QX10358 Sharp, Keith.
5. Don Sharp, personal communication.
6. NAA B883, NX60017 Sharp, Frank.
7. Argent, J.N.L., *Target Tank*, pp. 66–67.
8. Don Sharp, personal communication.
9. Lloyd Moule's interview by Australians at War Film Archive, Archive 1285, p. 28. <http://australiansatwarfilmarchive.unsw.edu.au/archive/1285-lloyd-moule> last accessed 24 May 2019.

10. Keith Sharp, 'Escape to Switzerland'.
11. NAA B883, QX6017 Elliott, Tom, letter from Elliott to War Medals, 8 March 1954.
12. 252761, Frederic 'Fred' Eggleston, *Fred Eggleston's escapades Part 2*. <http://www.3squadron.org.au/subpages/Eggleston2.htm> last accessed 24 May 2019.
13. Australian arrivals to Switzerland recorded within Final Report of the Swiss Commission for 19/20 September 1943 include men mentioned by Keith and Fred: Donald 'Don' MacDonald, Robert 'Bob' Donnan, Robert Sydney 'Bob' Jones, Fred Eggleston, Gordon Reneau, John 'Sandy' Mair. Donnan's POW Report, courtesy Brian Sims.
14. Fred Eggleston's memoir refers to ex-Bologna British POWs Guy Greville, Richard Dennis and Peter McDowall (probably the three British mentioned by Keith Sharp) arriving Switzerland same day as him.
15. Summary of the Swiss list for Australian arrivals to Switzerland by date order as held within *Bill Rudd's AIF in Switzerland Vol. 1,* Australian War Memorial, Canberra, indicate that the Sharp and Eggleston groups were beaten to Switzerland by only three Australians: NX3653 John Parker, NX54410 Jack Walker, VX53572 Robert Esler. On 20 September, same day as Sharp duo, other early Anzac POW gate-crashers to Switzerland included seven New Zealanders (John Bonner, Percy Bremner, David Conlon, Henry Harrison, Adam Heka, Leslie Holemby, Harold Pattinson) as well as Australians NX23324 Ronald Cameron, QX15357 Roy Richardson, QX7025 Donald Fleming, VX33895 Alfred Bennett, WX9065 Bramwell Holmes, WX14235 Keith Cunningham.

Chapter 9: Coffee plonk

1. Roger Absalom, 'Allied escapers and the contadini in occupied Italy (1943–5)', *Journal of Modern Italian Studies,* 10:4, 2005, pp. 421–22, and pp. 413–425.
2. Foot, M.R.D. and Langley, J.M., *MI9: Escape and evasion 1939–1945,* The Bodley Head, London, 1979, p. 73.
3. English, Ian, *Home by Christmas,* privately published, UK, 1997, p. 43.
4. Colin Weekes, memoir.
5. NAA B883, WX12688 Neave, Alan.
6. TNA WO 208, POW Report by Private Alan Neave WX12688, Adelboden (Switzerland), 10 July 1944. Refers to 106/19 Baraccone.
7. TNA WO 208, POW report by Private Alan Neave.
8. Turlo Pass (Passo del Turlo): <https://www.neveitalia.it/ski/macugnaga/video/passo-del-turlo-un-confine-che-unisce> last accessed 24 May 2019. See also: <https://www.alagna.it/en/summer/routes-walks-trekking-monterosa/the-turlo-pass/> last accessed 24 May 2019.

9. TNA WO 208, POW Report by 40159 Private Edward Scanlan, 25 Bn NZEF, Wil (Switzerland), 6 September 1944. Refers to Campo 106/20 Arborio near Salussola.
10. TNA WO 208, POW Report by 11278 Private Gerald Neame, 26 Bn NZEF, Bornhausen (Switzerland), 28 August 1944. Refers to Campo 106/20 Salussola.

Chapter 10: Charlie did the talking

1. Gilbert, *POW*, p. 292.
2. WX11748 Albert 'Bert' Wilson's brothers were WX7185 William 'Bill' Wilson and WX2743 Harry Wilson.
3. TNA WO 208, POW Reports by Driver Albert Wilson WX11748, Turbenthal (Switzerland), 11 August 1944, and Driver William Wilson WX7185, Schwarzenbach (Switzerland), 1 September 1944. Both reports courtesy Brian Sims. Bert's report refers to Campo 106/20 Salussola.
4. Identification of New Zealander POWs Stanley Avery, 40427, and Norman Allen, 23862, sourced from Bill Rudd's website's Nominal Roll of Free Men: <http://www.anzacpow.com/__data/assets/pdf_file/0015/22740/3853_Anzac_European_Freemen_10-4-14.pdf> last accessed 24 May 2019.
5. Bert Wilson, diary extracts, courtesy Harry Wilson.
6. Patsy Adam-Smith, *Prisoners of war: from Gallipoli to Korea*, Ken Fin, Victoria, 1992, p. 122, includes reference by Campo 106 POW Colin Horman [VX46543] to 'a red-headed sergeant, Charlie Fraser, who could speak Italian like nobody's business.' Patricia Fraser, personal communication, also added to Charlie's story.
7. Bert Wilson, diary extracts.
8. Theodul (Teodulo) Pass history <https://www.ultratourmonterosa.com/interesting-information/> last accessed 24 May 2019.
9. Henry 'Harry' Sibraa's story was published as 'Three AIF prisoners crossed Alps to freedom', *Daily Mirror*, 20 January 1964, pp. 15–16. Terry Sibraa, personal communication, added to Harry's story.
10. NAA B883, NX35515 Sibraa, Henry.
11. Harry Sibraa, letter to Medals Section, undated, held on NAA B883, NX35515. Permission to cite courtesy Terry Sibraa.
12. Harry Sibraa, letter to Medals Section.
13. TNA WO 208, POW Report by Corporal Henry Sibraa, Turbenthal (Switzerland), 15 July 1944, courtesy of Brian Sims. Refers to 106/2 Tronzano Vercellese.
14. Harry Sibraa's story in 'Three AIF prisoners crossed Alps to freedom', 1964.

15. Arrivals to Switzerland listed within The Final Report of the Swiss Commission for the Internment and Hospitalisation of foreign Military Personnel 1940–45. In addition to 23 September arrivals mentioned in *Shooting Through*, the Swiss recorded: TX383 John Moore, VX34643 Ernest Underwood, WX6695 John Keenan, and VX40089 Claude Edmondson.
16. The mention of Charlie Fraser by Bert Wilson and Harry Sibraa indicate the two POW groups converged, or were close on each other heels, prior or during their arrival to border area. In all likelihood, at the Italian guard's outpost Charlie was already there, and assisted the Wilsons' encounter with Italian guards by acting as interpreter.

Chapter 11: The Italian man with an American accent

1. Absalom, *A Strange Alliance*, p. 33.
2. Absalom, *A Strange Alliance*, p. 17.
3. Paul Lavallee, memoir extracts courtesy of Paul Lavallee and Ann Plumb; and conversations between Paul Lavallee and author, 2016. Red Cross POW cards confirm respective dates of transit to Campo 106 for Paul and Norm Freeberg.
4. Cervetto, Vercelli, is encircled by Via A. Stoppani, Via Leon Battista Alberti and Via Antonio Pacinotti, according to Google maps last accessed 24 May 2019.
5. Norm Freeberg's memoir, *A Synopsis of prisoner of war camps*, AWM, PR88/185.
6. Andrew Campbell VX43960 is listed on a list created by Paul Lavallee while POW.
7. TNA WO 208, POW Report by Gunner Neil Corke VX45906, Wil (Switzerland), 13 July 1944. Neil refers to 4-day stay at Noveis.
8. Norm Freeberg, memoir.
9. Nick Emery, personal communication.
10. TNA WO 208, POW Report by Herbert Emery, Adelboden (Switzerland), 22 July 1944.
11. Col Booth wrote Frank Secchia and Clementina Zaninetti's names in a POW notebook, as issued to Campo 57 POWS on behalf of Pope Pius XII. Col also listed placenames passed on way to Rovasenda and on to Noveis, some in phonetic spelling: 'Billaloy [probably Brillaloio near to Olcenengo], D'Allodi [Allodi, Cascina Dallodi], Casa Nova [possibly Casa Nuova near Gattesco, or Casanova Elvo, both within his route net], Casa del Bosco [between Rovasenda and Crevacuore], Calasca [Calasca Castiglione near to Bannio, Macugnaga].' Peter Erickson's notebook entries are similar. In his TNA WO 208 POW Report, Col refers to Noveis stay from 19th to last day of September; Peter reports 12-day stay.

12. Piero Secchia, personal communication.
13. Col Booth cited by Tom Barrass, 'Swiss tour for war prisoners', *Newcastle Herald*, 14 October 1967.
14. Ted Faulkes, memoir, courtesy Bill Rudd and with permission to cite by Carol Faulkes. Ted refers leaving Collobiano. WX1462 Harold Digwood refers to a 106/21 camp near Collobiano.
15. Liliana Cerruti, '*L'Americano di Noveis*', date unknown, provided by Liliana. Claudio Martignon, personal communication, and quoting a document by Edovilio Hunt, added to background of Angello and Clementina Zaninetti.
16. TNA WO 208, POW Report by Lance Corporal Lloyd Wilson, WX6100, Caux (Switzerland), 20 July 1944, courtesy Brian Sims. Refers to 106/1 San Germano.
17. TNA WO 208, POW Report by Gunner Peter Erickson, NX33357, Wald Zurich (Switzerland), 31 August 1944, courtesy Brian Sims. Refers to 12-days at Noveis.
18. TNA WO 208, POW Report by Private William Morgan, WX7965, Caux (Switzerland), 18 August 1944, courtesy Brian Sims.
19. TNA WO 208, POW Reports by Sapper Lionel Hood, 28201, Wald (Switzerland), 15 July 1944, and Lance Corporal Roy Lunn, 32520, 18 July 1944, both courtesy Brian Sims. Both refers to 106/20 Salussola.
20. TNA WO 208, POW Report by Private Rossett Wycherley, VX28988, Adelboden (Switzerland), 24 July 1944, courtesy Brian Sims. Refers to 106/1 San Germano.
21. Paul Lavallee, personal communication.

Chapter 12: A bloody German frontier guard

1. Mark Johnston and Peter Stanley, *Alamein: The Australian story*, pp. 106 and 115.
2. NAA B883 files, WX5890 Robert Ward, WX6058 Norman Woosnam, VX38325 William Pannowitz.
3. Bob Ward, memoir.
4. TNA WO 344 series, War Office: Directorate of Military Intelligence: Liberated Prisoner of War Interrogation Questionnaires, General Questionnaire for British/American ex-prisoners of war for Private Gilbert Keats, SX12776, 20 June 1945. South Australian POW Gilbert Keats attested to help by Alberto Machieraldo/ Macchieraldo (Cascina Nicola in Cavaglia), Giovanni Machieraldo/ Macchieraldo (Cascina Caglieri, Cavaglia), Giuseppe Machieraldo/ Macchieraldo (Cascina Brianco, Salussola). Claude and Cyril Farrow reported in respective WO 208 POW Reports the same string of travel: stayed near camp for several days, train travel to Romagnano Sesia, on foot to Varallo and Ceppo Morelli, Macugnaga, Monte Moro.

5. NAA B883, VX38325 Pannowitz William.
6. TNA WO 208, POW Report by Private Leonard Holman, QX11027, Arosa (Switzerland), 9 August 1944, courtesy Brian Sims. Refers to 106/1 San Germano.
7. NAA B883, QX11027 Holman, Leonard.
8. Ian English, *Home by Christmas*, p. 62.
9. The Final Report of the Swiss Commission.
10. Bill Rudd, Australians at War Film Archive, interview 20 May 2003.
11. The Final Report of the Swiss Commission.
12. NAA B2458, WX12267 Shaw, Sydney; personal communication Syd Shaw.
13. Syd Shaw, personal communication, and correspondence to Bill Rudd, 15 September 1999, in which he details events of his companions and route.
14. TNA WO 208, POW Report by Private Norman Tripovich, VX14918, Arosa (Switzerland), 9 August 1944, courtesy Brian Sims.
15. TNA WO 208, POW Report by Private Frank Page, QX1639, Bornhausen (Switzerland), 24 August 1944, courtesy Brian Sims.
16. George 'Bill' Thompson account, courtesy Bill Rudd. Thompson is probably WX10398 who reported being at 106/2 La Corte.
17. Frank Page (veteran's nephew), personal communication. Frank Page is the only Aboriginal escaper identified by author's research to have reached Switzerland. See Katrina Kittel, 2015, 'QX1639 Frank Page 2/32 Battalion', *Our Mob; Serving Country 100 years and beyond*, DVA online. <http://www.dva.gov.au/i-am/aboriginal-andor-torres-strait-islander/our-mob-serving-country-100-years-and-beyond/qx1639> last accessed 25 May 2019.

Chapter 13. North was the grim line of the Alps

1. Susan Jacobs, *Fighting with the enemy*, p. 74.
2. Ernie Sparnon, memoir.
3. Santuario di Oropa: <http://www.santuariodioropa.it/db/en/history-culture/history-of-the-sanctuary> last accessed 25 May 2019.
4. NAA B883, VX32109 Sparnon, Ernest; NAA B883, NX19056 Perrott, Henry.
5. Colin Weekes, memoir.
6. With reference to Appendix 1 and to The Final Report of the Swiss Commission, Stevo is probably Harry Stephenson NX19374 who arrived same day as Sparnon.
7. Ernie Sparnon, memoir. Sparnon refers to Harry Perrott. Swiss record his arrival as 1 October, a discrepancy perhaps due to a late group split, or wrong name recalled.

8. Ernie Sparnon's notes read 'Alpe Fuller' and 'Togo', likely Alpe Faller and Tovo.
9. Account of WX6937 Sydney Shove, WX7860 Newton 'Newt' Moore and WX4462 Fred Price included in self-published booklet by Phillip Loffman, *POW*, pp. 57–58.
10. TNA WO 208, POW Report by VX34508 Private Patrick O'Rafferty, Adelboden (Switzerland), 12 July 1944. Refers to 106/2 Tronzano.
11. TNA WO 208, POW Reports by VX48180 Private Edward Sincock, Arosa (Switzerland), 4 August 1944; and VX26596 Private William Sincock, Arosa (Switzerland), 15 August 1944.
12. Bill Rudd, <http://www.anzacpow.com/__data/assets/pdf_file/0015/22740/3853_Anzac_European_Freemen_10-4-14.pdf> last accessed 25 May 2019.
13. The Final Report of the Swiss Commission, summarised in Bill Rudd, *AIF in Switzerland*, 2000.

Chapter 14: None of us were prepared to argue with two rifles

1. Gilbert, *POW*, pp. 287–288.
2. See Appendix 1 notes. Campo 106 POW deaths and arrivals to Switzerland are marked. Campo 106 POWs who also are on German lists allow for estimates of recaptured POWs.
3. Norman Freeberg, AWM PR PR88/185.
4. Questionnaire for British/American ex-prisoners of war for Lance Corporal Paul Lavallee, NX23801, 15 May 1945, TNA WO 344 series, War Office: Directorate of Military Intelligence: Liberated Prisoner of War Interrogation Questionnaires.
5. TNA WO 208, POW Report by WX6100 Lance Corporal Lloyd Wilson, Caux (Switzerland), 20 July 1944, courtesy Brian Sims. Wilson reports 28 September arrival to Switzerland, but Swiss guards registered him as 29 September 1943.
6. There were two Alfred Collins at campo 106: VX2053 and QX8213, but VX20153 best fits Norm's reference to his unit being 'AASC'.
7. According to summary details mentioned in Freeberg's memoir, and with reference to archive sources, the ten recaptured were: Paul Lavallee, Norm Freeberg, Peter Bosgard, Ian Barker, Robert Ferguson, Andrew Campbell, Ray Crook, Bill Nicol, B. Jones (probably Bryce Jones) and British POW G. Brien. Seven New Zealander POWs on Paul's list reached Switzerland, as did two British and one South African.
8. Col Booth, interview with Barrass, 1967.

Chapter 15: First time I had been on a bike for nearly three years

1. Foot and Langley, *M19: Escape and evasion 1939–1945*, p. 62.
2. Warburton, memoir.
3. TNA WO 208, POW Report by SX6310 Private Ronald Douglas, Caux (Switzerland), 3 August 1944 refers to Montonero as well as evasion details similar to Charles Warburton's account, indicating Ron was probably in Charles's group.

Chapter 16: Monte Moro was testing our resolve

1. Foot and Langley, *M19: Escape and evasion 1939–1945*, pp. 27–28.
2. The Final Report of the Swiss Commission.
3. Bernhard Banzhaf, 2012, advice re Monte Moro and Mondelli routes.
4. Don Radnell, memoir.
5. TNA WO 208, POW Report by QX21217 Private Ian Jobson, 22 July 1944, Caux (Switzerland).
6. Arthur Jobson's account is included in Ken Ward-Harvey, *The Sapper's war*.
7. TNA WO 208, POW Report by WX5534 Private Victor Wills, 18 July 1944, Wald (Switzerland), courtesy Brian Sims. Report refers to 106/19 Baraccone.
8. Ronald Strickland and Bert Wainewright escaped ambush near Oropa, believing many of the sixty POWs were recaptured. Ron went to Switzerland; Bert connected with partisans. Cited by Bill Rudd: <http://www.anzacpow.com/part_4__nominal_roll_all_evades/chapter_4__ninth_division/24th_brigade> last accessed 31 May 2019.
9. NAA B883, QX6017 Elliott, Tom, letter from Elliott to War Medals, 8 March 1954. Tom Elliott refers to cutting way out of a cattle truck with R.H Jones (VX 4360) and jumping near Trento on night of 13/14 September 1943.
10. Ron Maitland and Christine Makella, *No mountain too high*, pp. 25–26.
11. Nick Emery, personal communication.
12. WO 208 POW Report by Emery.
13. NAA B883, VX48196 Mills, Charles.
14. Tabram, memoir.
15. TNA WO 208, POW Report by Private Robert Hohaia, 924 (Maori Btn), Adelboden (Switzerland), 12 July 1944. Refers to 106/3 as Vettigne, and to Baraccone farm as provider of clothing and guide. Swiss Final Report, refer to Hohaia's arrival as 4 October 1943, the only NZPOW listed on the Swiss report to arrive that day.

16. The Final Report of the Swiss Commission.
17. NAA B883, NX51323 Fitzgerald, Francis Ronald.
18. Ron Fitzgerald, oral recording of Ron, with permission Gavin Fitzgerald.
19. Carl Carrigan's summary *Wartime Odyssey* by Cate Carrigan. Cate Carrigan's blog following his evasion route, 'Italy to the Alps': <http://italytothealps.blogspot.com.au/2013/09/to-monte-moro-conquering-alps.html?view=sidebar> last accessed 30 May 2019.
20. Lloyd Moule, interview by Australians at War Film Archive, Archive 1285, p.52, refers to Fitzy's conscience. In his memoir, Moule recalled that when Ron McIntosh was recaptured, 'Jim' Tasker [NX30450] was with him. Robert 'Bob' Noble NX52624 as well as the Carrigan brothers, Ledingham and Fitzgerald got away (all 3A Tank regiment). Noble, separated from the Carrigan group, arrives Switzerland (Swiss list) on 24 October 1943. Moule heard rumour that Tasker was felled by German bullets during this attack, but his chance encounter post-war with Tasker on Elizabeth Street, Sydney, reassured Moule he survived recapture.
21. Arch Scott, *Dark side of the moon: the unusual story of one Kiwi's war*, 1985, p. 110.
22. Eric Newby, *Love and war in the Apennines*, 2010, p. 213.

Chapter 17: Whilst we were eating the last of our grub

1. Absalom, *A Strange Alliance*, p. 20.
2. TNA WO 208, POW Report by Gunner Colin Booth, NX60337, Bornhausen (Switzerland), 19 September 1944; TNA WO 208, POW Report by Gunner Peter Erickson, NX33357, Wald Zurich (Switzerland), 31 August 1944. Both reports courtesy Brian Sims.
3. Arch Scott, *Dark side of the moon*, p. 41.
4. Laurie Quinn, soldier settlement neighbour to Booth at Young NSW, 1950s–60s.
5. Pauline Anderson, personal communication.
6. Col Booth's interview with Tom Barrass, 1967.
7. Lloyd Moule's memoir, for example, discusses this tension.
8. Col Booth's interview with Tom Barrass, 1967.
9. Col Booth's notebook's placenames in Italy include 'Mount Campello (Campello Monti), as well as 'Bannia' (Bannio), within Anzasca Valley.
10. Col Booth's interview with Tom Barrass, 1967.
11. Pauline Anderson.
12. Laurie Quinn, soldier settlement farmer to Col Booth at Young NSW, 1950s–60s.

13. Col Booth's interview with Tom Barrass, 1967.
14. Bernhard Banzhaf, Swiss guide, regarding Monte Moro and Mondelli passes.
15. The Final Report of the Swiss Commission.
16. TNA WO 208, POW Report by Gunner John Shaw, Arosa (Switzerland), 14 August 1944, courtesy Brian Sims. Refers to Campo 133/13 Grignasco. A photo taken in Switzerland 1944 (Booth's collection) is annotated 'five of us who got to Switzerland together' and the names of Erickson, Wycherley, Shaw and Serfontein.
17. TNA WO 208, POW Report by Signaller Johannes Serfontein, Adelboden (Switzerland), 12 July 1944, courtesy Brian Sims. Serfontein acknowledges help by Pavia residents Luigi Serafini for providing food and clothes for 10 days, and Piero Gallina for clothes and guides on train for nine men.
18. In TNA WO 208, POW Report by Private Rossett Wycherley, Ross refers to Noveis stay dates '17 September to 29 September'.
19. Bob Ward, memoir.

Chapter 18: Quiet resort equally suitable for rest-seekers and mountaineers

1. Bill Rudd, <http://www.anzacpow.com/part_2__escape_from_italian_camps/chapter_2__confederatio_helvetica> last accessed 31 May 2019.
2. The Final Report of the Swiss Commission.
3. NAA B883 WX38325, Letter from Lieutenant Colonel Thomas, Records Office, Melbourne, to family of Bill Pannowitz, 28 October 1943.
4. Mattmark Hotel ruins were submerged under Mattmark Dam built in the 1960s.
5. Joachim, in conversation September 2013 at Hotel Portjengrat, Saas-Almagell.
6. The Final Report of the Swiss Commission lists arrival date for Peter Watson Bates.
7. Booth and Emery collections. Both men arrived 4 October 1943 to Mattmark.
8. Col Booth's collection.
9. First meal in Switzerland photo by Peter Watson Bates, Alexander Turnbull Library: https://natlib.govt.nz/records/22689898 Prints of this photograph are held in private collections Booth and Emery, presumably distributed to arrivals on or about 4 October 1943.
10. Annette Andenmatten.
11. Promotional pamphlet, courtesy Astrid, Proprietor, Hotel Portjengrat, Saas-Almagell.
12. Colin Weekes, memoir.
13. Ernie Sparnon, memoir.

14. Augusta Venetz, personal communication.
15. The Final Report of the Swiss Commission.
16. TNA WO 208, POW Reports by Ian Jobson QX21217, 22 July 1944, Caux, Switzerland; Arthur Jobson QX3237, 28 August 1944, Wald (Zurich), Switzerland. Both refer to 106/2 Tronzano.
17. Alan Newbey, personal communication.
18. Bob Ward, memoir.
19. POW group photo included in Maitland p.43, courtesy Ron Maitland.
20. Identification of several POWs in Maitland's group made by families.
21. AWM 057024 and AWM 057025, Bill Waller, *Go there you die*. Waller refers to joining with other Australians to cross, 6 October, most likely Albert Barndon WX15376, Brian Smith VX33912, George Rhodes VX33373, Stuart Lauder QX9995, Thomas Kelly VX36598 and Ronald Irwin SX7858, according to Marco Soggetto in *Braccati*.
22. World War Two Nominal Roll <http://www.ww2roll.gov.au/> VX32728 Preiser, Ernest, 3LAA Regiment. George Rhodes recalled, according to son Kevin, that the British had money to pay for assistance.
23. <http://www.ww2roll.gov.au/> VX34562 Hayes, Ernest, 2/24 Bn. In his WO 208 POW Report of 10 July 1944, Adelboden, Hayes refers to Campo 106/2 Tronzano.

Chapter 19: I'm sorry mate, we've bungled it

1. David Miller, *Commanding Officers*, 2001, p. 13.
2. QX11222 Donald 'Duncan' Robertson, diary extracts, courtesy of Don Robertson.
3. Jack Wauhop, S00512, 1989. East of Saint Bernard, Robert Noble crossed Fenetre del Durand Pass, 24/10/43
4. The Final Report of the Swiss Commission.
5. In TNA WO 208, POW Report by NX15573 Corporal Ronald B. Jones, Adelboden (Switzerland), 20 July 1944, Jones acknowledges assistance at Cascina Forresto (Ronsecco) and by teacher Clara Verdoia at Parogno near Zubiena who provided clothes, shelter, food and money. Report refers to Campo 106, Sali. See Ted Kent interview by Megan Neil, 'Camp escapee recalls his years at war' ('La Trobe Valley Remembers), *The Express*, 15 August 1995.
6. Eric Newby, *Love and war in the Apennines*, pp. 217–18.
7. Lloyd Moule, Australians at War Film Archive, Archive 1285; TNA WO 208, POW Report by Lance Bombardier Lloyd Moule NX40603, Switzerland, undated 1944, courtesy Brian Sims. Also, Moule's personal communication with author.

8. Australia held nearly 18,500 Italian prisoners of war from May 1941 until December 1947. See Alan Fitzgerald, *The Italian farming soldiers: prisoner of war in Australia 1941–1947*, Melbourne University Press, 1981 and Bill Bunbury, *Rabbits and Spaghetti: Captives and comrades, Australians, Italians and the war 1939–1945*, Fremantle Arts Centre Press, 1995.
9. Ron Crellin, *Freedom at last*, Bendigo: self-published, 1994.

Chapter 20: The mountain gave the impression of being alive

1. Arch Scott, *Dark side of the moon*, p. 66.
2. The Final Report of the Swiss Commission.
3. Warburton, memoir.
4. Summary of The Final Report by Bill Rudd, *AIF in Switzerland Vol.1*.
5. Loffman, *POW*, pp. 71–72. Knight, Leach and Strickland took the Sesia route, via San Nazzaro Sesia, Rovasenda, Sostegno, Vrevacuore, Borgosesia, Varallo, Sabbia Monte Capio, Ceppo Morelli, Bannio, Monte Moro Pass, arriving 2 November according to Swiss Final Report except for John Knight recorded arriving 17 November 1943, presumably a delay in processing.
6. The Final Report of the Swiss Commission, and Rudd's *AIF in Switzerland Vol.1*.
7. The Final Report of the Swiss Commission, and Rudd's *AIF in Switzerland Vol.1*.
8. NAA B883, SX13037 Maynard, Melvin; personal communication with family.

Chapter 21: Along the way we lost Snowy

1. Roger Absalom, *A Strange Alliance*, p. 22.
2. Tabram, memoir. Fred kept a letter and photo from Mariuccia 'Maria' Olivero, Ronsecco. The circuit of helpers included 'Ronsecco fisherman Raymond', probably Raimondo Febbrario who kept names of Jim Brennan, Bernie Bruce and Fred Tabram according to descendant Amanda. Fred acknowledges his provision of news to POWs, and his tool shed with wooden bunks to Fred and Blue.
3. Questionnaire for British/American ex-prisoners of war for Private Frederick Tabram VX46243, 1 June 1945, TNA, WO 344 series, War Office: Directorate of Military Intelligence: Liberated Prisoner of War Interrogation Questionnaires.
4. Tom Anderson, memoir.
5. See Appendix 1. Mick Simmons was probably VX35945 Michael Simmons.
6. Ian Knight, memoir.

7. Ken Fenton, *Alamein to the Alps*, p. 342.
8. Claudio Martignon and Liliana Cerruti, personal communication.

Chapter 22: The last station in Italy

1. Peter Monteath, *Escape Artist*, p. 176.
2. Peter Monteath, *POW*, p. 367.
3. Peter Monteath, *Escape Artist*, pp. 154–156.
4. Gilbert, *POW*, pp. 290–292.
5. Absalom, *A Strange Alliance*, pp. 39–40.
6. TNA WO 208, POW Report by NX11450 Private Clifford Chard, 31 September 1944, Heiden (Switzerland). Refers to 106/8 Casalrosso.
7. TNA WO 208, POW Report by WX8857 Private Leonard Boskell, 12 July 1944, Adelboden (Switzerland). Refers, with question mark, to 106 'Pomerana?'
8. TNA WO 208, POW Report by NX23782 Horace Tyrie, 1944, Switzerland, courtesy Brian Sims.
9. For Nott and Cotterell, see Austin, R.J., 2008, *Let enemies beware! "Caveant hostes": The history of the 2/15th Battalion, 1940–1945,* Slouch Hat Publications, McCrae Australia, pp. 202–203. Eileen Cotterell added extra detail.
10. The Final Report of the Swiss Commission.
11. Photo of POWs at Gondo, in Hood collection, courtesy Dulcie Hood.
12. TNA WO 208, POW Report by VX32489 Bombardier Arthur Joseph Caffrey, Arosa (Switzerland), 1 September 1944.
13. Hyland, memoir extracts held in Ray Hood collection, courtesy Ducie Hood.
14. The Final Report of the Swiss Commission.
15. TNA WO 208, Report by QX2232 Gunner McClelland, Robert, 18 September 1944, Wil (Switzerland). Refers to 106/2 Tronzano.
16. Jim Wilson, memoir.
17. TNA WO 208, POW Report by QX5417 James Wilson, undated, Switzerland. His report is annotated to refer to Carpeneto as Campo 106/25.
18. The Final Report of the Swiss Commission.
19. The Final Report of the Swiss Commission.
20. NAA B883, WX15431 Grimsey, Albert.
21. TNA WO 208, POW Report by WX15431 Private Albert Grimsey, 27 July 1944, Sirnach (Switzerland). Refers to 106/3 Vettigne.

22. Stanley Bailey's notes courtesy of Raeleen Sounness.
23. NAA B883, WX5508 Bailey, Stanley; NAA B883 WX6803 Angove, Victor.
24. NAA B883, NX54257 Mudge, Ross.
25. Notes within Bill Rudd's collection.
26. NAA B883, VX2556 Peachey, Edward. File contains letter Peachey to Commanding Officer, 14 October 1957, re Ross Mudge and Italian woman Selina Roffino. Ted Peachey Jnr advises that a school was named to honour Selina's resistance efforts.
27. NAA B883, NX54257 Mudge, Ross.
28. TNA WO 208, POW Report by VX32516 Gunner Alfred Griffiths, Wald (Zurich, Switerland), 17 July 1944. Refers to 106/1 San Germano. In his 1944 POW Report, NX24177 Noel Sealy states help by Antonio Perazzo, Salasco.
29. Le-Fevre, S00517.
30. WX10009 Dodd, John (Jack), transcript of oral history recording John William 'Jack' Dodd, as a Private, 2/28th Battalion and POW in Italy, interviewed by Bill Bunbury for Keith Murdoch Sound Archive in Australia in the war of 1939–45, S00544, 1989. <https://www.awm.gov.au/collection/C87920> last accessed 7 May 2019. In his TNA WO 208 POW Report, he refers to Tronzano.
31. Don Radnell, memoir.
32. NAA B883, VX34693 Radnell, Donald; NAA B883, VX34642 King, Norman.

Chapter 23: The easy way to Switzerland

1. Susan Jacobs, *In Love and War: Kiwi soldier's romantic encounters in wartime Italy*, Penguin, Auckland, 2012, pp. 38–39.
2. TNA WO 208, POW Report by QX6922 Private David Todd, Arosa (Switzerland), 25 July 1944. Refers to 106/2 Tronzano. Absalom, *A Strange Alliance*, refers to Todd, p. 93.
3. TNA WO 208, POW Report by VX31699 Corporal Alan Nicholson, Switzerland, 17 July 1944. Alan Nicholson, personal communication. Alan was a senior officer at 106/2 Tronzano.
4. TNA WO 208, POW Report by WX13384 Private Norman Bailey, Caux (Switzerland), 2 August 1944, courtesy Brian Sims. Refers to 106/1 San Germano.
5. Jack Nie, personal communication.
6. Dick Gill, memoir.

7. NAA B883, SX11230, Lawrie, Nicol.
8. Nick Lawrie's interview in 'Escaped to Switzerland from Italian P. O.W. camp', *Port Lincoln Times,* 16 June 1982, p. 4.
9. Nick Lawrie's interview in 'Escaped to Switzerland from Italian P. O.W. camp'.
10. Dick Gill, memoir. See also Arthur 'Jim' Kinder, *A Long Time: a thrilling story of an ordinary soldier who escaped from a prison camp with romantic fiction intervention,* Book House, Sydney, 2001. Although written as fiction, it has similarities to Lawrie and Gill accounts.
11. The Final Report of the Swiss Commission.
12. TNA WO 208, POW Report by Gunner Richard Gill, Caux (Switzerland), 30 August 1944.
13. TNA WO 208, POW Report by Gunner Claude Gibson, Bornhausen (Switzerland), 31 August 1944. Refers to 106/2 Tronzano.
14. The Final Report lists arrival of QX6908 William 'Bill' Pritchard.
15. Bill Pritchard anecdote, courtesy of Alison Curtin, 10 December 2015.
16. TNA WO 208, POW Report by VX34368 Driver Richard Wilson, Turbenthal (Switzerland), 11 August 1944; TNA WO 208 POW Report by VX47713 Private Edward Bracken, Adelboden (Switzerland), 10 July 1944.
17. Monteath, *POW,* pp. 366–367.
18. TNA WO 208, POW Report by NX21419 Private William Blair, Adelboden (Switzerland), 25 July 1944. Refers to 106/1 San Germano.
19. Ian English, *Home by Christmas,* p.60.
20. Monteath, *Escape Artist,* p. 161; and personal communication with Paola Vozza.
21. TNA WO 208, POW Reports by VX40994 Private Leslie Dower, Wil (Switzerland), 18 September 1944, and VX47656 Private Thomas Davis, Wil (Switzerland), 22 August 1944. Davis refers to 106/2 Tronzano.
22. Luciano Beltrami worked at Ivrea's Olivetti Company, and friend to engineer Adriano Olivetti. The company assisted large numbers of POWs, Jews and anti-fascists.
23. Susan Jacobs, *Fighting with the enemy,* p. 125. Franklin Bowes 12626 and WX11952 Harry Miller shot at entrance church, Santa Liberata cemetery, a kilometre north-west of Mosso Santa Maria. Post-war, buried Milan's CWGC cemetery.
24. NAA B883, VX45756 McCracken, James.
25. Giorgio Nascimbene, *Prigionieri di Guerra: L'anabasi dei prigionieri alleati che nel 1943 fecero parte dei campi di lavoro nelle risaie vercellesi e dintorni,* Societa Operaia di Mutuo Soccorso Villata, Vercelli, 2004, p. 187.

Chapter 24: Through German Lines

1. Foot and Langley, *M19: Escape and evasion 1939–1945*, pp. 25 & 162.
2. Garvan Drew, 'Escape from Italy', *Barbed Wire and Bamboo: official organ ex-prisoners of war Association of Australia*, 35:4, August 1984, pp. 10–11; and Garvan Drew, 'To Redbank and Return'.
3. Bill Rudd, personal communication.
4. Bert Lockie's story, pp. 329–337. VX47635 James Fraser; WX7111 Roy Harris.
5. Fred Vardy cited in Loffman, *POW*, p. 42.
6. Lockie's story.
7. AWM54, 781/6/7, Interrogation Reports of Escaped Prisoner of War by Allied Interrogation Service CMF 1944, Interrogation Report on VX34393 Knight, Matthew October 1944. Hester Knight, personal communication regarding partisan Bruno Stefani. Patsy Adams-Smith, 1998, p. 138, refers to Matthew Knight mixing with partisans.
8. Fred Vardy cited in Loffman, *POW*, p. 42.
9. Absalom, *A Strange Alliance*, p. 279.
10. Harold Blain VX46586, William Harvey WX10591, Clive Liddell VX1664, John Nicholls WX7090, Ernest Wolfe WX14978.
11. AWM54, 781/6/7, Interrogation Report on VX48171 Private Sincock, Herbert, 18 October 1944.
12. NAA B883, VX34058 Bryant, Ronald.
13. Le-Fevre, S00517.
14. TNA WO 344, War Office: Directorate of Military Intelligence: Liberated Prisoner of War Interrogation Questionnaires, General Questionnaire for British/American ex-prisoners of war for Private Ronald Bryant VX34058, 21 May 1945.
15. Gwenda Bryant and Edgar Bione, personal communication.
16. The Final Report of the Swiss Commission.
17. NAA B883, WX14427 Davis, Harold includes his Statement by a Repatriated Navy, Army or Air Force Prisoners of War, 2 June 1945 at Eastbourne.
18. Jack Nie, personal communication.
19. Soggetto, Marco, *Braccati: Prigionieri di guerra alleati in piemonte e valle d'Aosta*, Aviani and Avaini Editori, Udine, 2013, pp. 205–206. Verification is difficult, according to Marco. Due to valley elders remaining tight-lipped about the war.

Chapter 25: Marking time

1. Jurg Stussi-Lauterberg in Stamm, L., Frey, S., Greminger, A., & Wanner, L. (Eds.), *Dignity and Coolness*, 2004, p. 7.
2. Jack Dodd, S00544.
3. Bill Rudd, <http://www.anzacpow.com/part_2__escape_from_italian_camps/chapter_2__confederatio_helvetica> last accessed 26 May 2019.
4. The Final Report of the Swiss Commission.
5. Memo for Prime Minister's Department, Canberra, from R. Whitelaw, Official Secretary, Australia House in London, 4 April 1944, in Bill Rudd collection.
6. Ron Crellin, *Freedom at last*, p. 55.
7. Arthur Jobson's account is included in Ken Ward-Harvey, *The Sapper's war*.
8. Laurie Quinn, personal communication.
9. Syd Shaw, personal communication.
10. Jack Nie, personal communication.
11. Col Booth's notebook; communication with Muff and Sidler families. Jack Dodd, S00544.
12. TNA WO 208 Report by Gunner Bernard Thompson refers to escape Camp 146/15, Rosasco [SE of Vercelli]. Report dated 23 September 1944 at Wald.
13. Dates for both arrival and departure from Switzerland within The Final Report of the Swiss Commission.
14. Warburton memoir, and TNA WO 208 POW Report by WX5299 Private Charles Warburton, Arosa (Switzerland), 2 August 1944. Refers to 106/7 Montonero.
15. TNA WO 208 POW Report by Gunner Colin Booth, NX60337, Bornhausen (Switzerland), 19 September 1944; TNA WO 208 POW Report by Gunner Peter Erickson, NX33357, Wald Zurich (Switzerland), 31 August 1944. Both reports courtesy of Brian Sims research.
16. Muff family.
17. Jack Dodd, S00544.
18. John 'Brian' Green reached Switzerland on 17 November 1943.
19. Ted Kent,1995, notes shared with Bill Rudd for publication on his website.
20. Nick Emery, personal communication.
21. Interrogation Report on VX34393 Knight, Matthew in AWM54 781/6/7. Foot and Langley, *M19: Escape and evasion 1939-1945*, p. 204, indicate that a Brazilian division fought with Allied armies in Italy from September 1944.
22. Hester Knight advised re Roy Harris and Dick Smith; NAA B883 Harris,

Roy confirms 17/11/44 arrival to Melbourne via General AE Anderson. VX26317 Richard Charles Smith's return date is not verifiable via currently accessible NAA records. See also Salvatico, Maria, 1999, 'The story of a Knight', University of Melbourne research project.

23. TNA WO 208, POW Report by NX21419 Private William Blair.

24. See Ralph Churches, *A hundred miles as the crow flies,* 1996, Adelaide: self-published, and book by son of Harold Sanderson, Antonio Manfroi, *il Soldato Harold: un neozelandese a Erto,* 2014, Edizioni L'Omino Rosso.

25. Patrick Maher WX10252. One account indicates Maher may be an Aboriginal veteran.

26. NAA B3856, 144/14/23 Statements made by Repatriated Prisoners of War Nominal Roll of POW [Prisoners of War] and Statements [mainly concerns prisoners of war in Europe]. This file states that 398 men (other than officers) did statements: Qld 63, NSW 72, Vic 137, SA 15, Tas 7, WA 104. Arthur Jobson's estimate in his memoir closely matches this report.

27. Harry Sibraa's story.

28. Col Booth.

29. Ernie Sparnon's memoir and personal communication with Margaret.

30. Souvenir menu of dinner 17/11/1944 in Col Booth's collection.

31. AWAS signatures on Booth's menu (service numbers accessed by name searches at DVA online nominal roll): Win Walsingham [VF509891], Hilda Olle [VF513791], Diana West [VFX129059], Heather Gillies [VF509551], Phyllis Rymer [VF396291], Joan Bolding [VF516099], Patricia White [either VF396358, VF396078, VFX64870], Ilma Gill [VF397148], Doris Merritt [VF396975], Moll Ferguson [perhaps Margaret, VF345415], Jean Usher [probably Isla Jean,VF513888], Ellen Brown [probably VF514277], Monica Balkin [VF396160], Helen Arnold [probably VF513574], Phyllis Garrett [V387975], Joyce Skinner [?], ? Pearse [probably VFX128396], Mae ? Kerr [perhaps Margaret VF518304], Joyce Winchester [QF272662] as well as Australian Women's Land Army servicewoman Thelma Greenwood. NAA Two New Zealander men signed Col's menu George London and (Bill Rudd's camp mate) Lou Moir, as well as Australian Roy Neil probably VX50923.

32. James Maddern's letter to Red Cross Australia 24/11/1944, NAA B883, VX3100.

33. Doug Le-Fevre, S00517.

34. Jim Wilson memoir, and NAA MP742/1 W/4/2540 Wilson James Arthur Private ex-Prisoner of War.

35. NAA B883, VX37427 Jones, Brinley.

36. Fred Eggleston, *Fred Eggleston's escapades Part 2*.
37. Date that Eggleston left Switzerland, from The Final Report.
38. Bill Rudd, personal communication re 'Fanny' van den Heuvel, and at: <http://www.aifpow.com/part_2__escape_from_italian_camps/chapter_10__the_soe_in_switzerland> last accessed 2 June 2019.
39. Bill Rudd's collection.
40. Maureen, daughter of Pat O'Rafferty, personal communication.
41. NAA B883, VX 34508 O'Rafferty, Patrick.

Chapter 26: Contribution towards the final collapse of German armies in Italy

1. Foot and Langley, *M19: Escape and evasion 1939–1945*, p. 24.
2. Fenton, *Alamein to the Alps*, pp. 325–326.
3. Fowler, William, *The secret war in Italy: special forces, partisans and covert operations 1943–45*, Ian Allan Publishing, Surrey, 2010, p. 75.
4. Fenton, *Alamein to the Alps*, p. 456.
5. George Evans, *A British POW becomes a partisan* accessed 29 May 2019 at: <http://www.bbc.co.uk/history/ww2peopleswar/stories/41/a2001141.shtml>
6. Fenton, *Alamein to the Alps,* p. 488.
7. Gilbert, *POW*, p. 60.
8. Neil Campbell cited in Fenton, *Alamein to the Alps,* p. 325–326.
9. Tabram, memoir.
10. Questionnaire for British/American ex-prisoners of war for Private Frederick Tabram VX46243, 1 June 1945, TNA WO 344 series, War Office: Directorate of Military Intelligence: Liberated Prisoner of War Interrogation Questionnaires.
11. Webster, Malcolm, *An Italian experience,* Wheelers Hill, Victoria, 1995, held National Library of Australia, cited with permission from Nigel Webster. Webster, Malcolm, 'Vagabonds Rest', *Italian Historical Society Journal*, 11, 1, Jan/June 2003.
12. NAA B883, WX9047, Blewett, Frank. Statutory Declaration by Blewett, 14 September 1945 re murder of Harvey, Wolfe, Nicholls, Liddell and Blain.
13. Questionnaire for British/American ex-prisoners of war for Private Frederick Tabram. Spelling varies for Angelina Catella Guido across other POW reports (Angelo Catilla Guido). Lived or worked at Frazione Zuccaro di Coggiola.
14. Ernest Wolfe: <http://www.ww2roll.gov.au/Veteran.aspx?serviceId=A&veteranId=751795>

15. Questionnaire for British/American ex-prisoners of war, Private Frederick Tabram.
16. NAA B883, VX38618 Sproule, Ian. This file contains extracts of POW Statements.
17. Ian Sproule with Lynette Oates, *Australian Partisan: a true story of love and conflict*, Australian Military History Publications, 1997.
18. Jean Beswick, personal communication.
19. Luciano Guala advised of plaque's location.
20. AWM54, 781/6/7, Interrogation Reports of Escaped Prisoner of War by Allied Interrogation Service CMF 1944, Interrogation Report on QX10626 Francis Hungerford and WX13239 Raymond Vigar. Refers to Val-d'isere as entry point.
21. Fred Tabram, private collection, courtesy Ray Tabram.
22. NAA B883, WX5292 Rowe, John.
23. The Final Report of the Swiss Commission.
24. Christopher Herbert, *Benito Mussolini: a biography*, The Reprint Society London, 1963, pp. 319–320, 352.
25. Ted Peachey (Jnr) and Rob Peachey, personal communication.

Chapter 27: Don't shoot, we're English

1. Jacobs, *Fighting with the enemy*, p. 74.
2. Les Parker, Mick McCracken, Harry Miller, Douglas Smedley, Jack Wilson, Harold Blain, William Harvey, John Nicholls, Clive Liddell and Ernie Wolfe.
3. Unpublished compilation by Bill Rudd and Katrina Kittel of Australian POWs in Italy.
4. NAA B883 respectively for QX7639 Albert, Edward and WX7128 Brennan, James.
5. TNA, WO 310/65, Shooting of Pte Batt, L.G., Clark, J.L., Smedley, J.D. at Biella, province of Novara contains affidavit by WX7128 James Brennan, 7 January 1946.
6. TNA, WO 310/65, Statements by Eva Cerruti, 25 August 1945 and 23 November 1945.
7. TNA, WO 310/65, Affidavit by Elma Acquadro, 10 April 1946.
8. War Crime summary by investigator Sergeant E. Rondel, 23 May 1946.
9. War Crime summary by investigator Sergeant E. Rondel, 23 May 1946.
10. TNA, WO 310/65, Affidavit by WX7128 James Brennan.
11. TNA, 310/65, War Crime Summary, Sergeant Rondel, 23 May 1946.

12. TNA, WO 310/65, Affidavit by Raleigh Hoy NX27773, 17 January 1946. NAA B883, NX27773 service file for Hoy indicates he also used a false name 'John Edwards'. General Questionnaire for British/American ex-prisoners of war for NX27773 Raleigh Hoy, 14 May 1945.
13. TNA, WO 310/65, Affidavit by Eric Hamblin, 8 March 1946.
14. TNA, WO 310/65, Affidavit by Elma Acquadro, 10 April 1946.
15. Sergio Virgulto, Tavigliano, undated. Text courtesy of Luciano Guala.
16. TNA, WO 310/65, Affidavit by Oreste Meliga, 10 April 1946.
17. TNA, WO 310/65, Affidavit by Luciano Avignone, 10 April 1946.
18. TNA, WO 310/65, Affidavit by Luigi Musetti, 27 April 1946.
19. TNA, WO 310/65, Affidavit by Luigi Musetti, 10 May 1946.
20. TNA, WO 310/65, Affidavit by Luigi Musetti, 11 May 1946.
21. TNA, WO 310/65, Affidavit by Pietro Musetti.
22. TNA, WO 310/65, Captain Fowles, Investigator, 22 February 1946.
23. TNA, WO 310/65, Captain Masters signed off on summary by Rondel.
24. Statement by 32867 Private T. Hodgson (32867, 2NZEF), 5 June 1945.
25. Australian arrivals to Switzerland listed in Final Report.
26. Australian arrivals to Switzerland listed in Final Report.
27. Memorial plaque information courtesy of Luciano Guala.
28. The bodies were exhumed after the war and reburied CWGC cemetery in Milan.

Chapter 28: Never, ever heard us speak about it

1. Jacobs, *In Love and war*, p. 19.
2. Nick Emery, personal communication.
3. Syd Shaw, personal communication.
4. Bill Rudd, personal communication.
5. Joan Dare cited by Bill Rudd, last accessed 7 May 2019: <http://www.anzacpow.com/welcome_letter>
6. Bill Rudd's Campo 57 website, last accessed 7 May 2019: <http://www.campo57.com/products.html>
7. Col Booth, author's private collection.
8. Col Booth, interviewed by Tom Barrass.
9. Ann Plumb, personal communication.
10. Christina Twomey, *The Battle Within: POWs in postwar Australia,* NewSouth Publishing, 2018, pp. 76–77, p. 86.

11. NAA B503, WX5299 Charles Warburton. Separate POW Trust Fund applications of 14 May 1959 and 4 September 1963.
12. Sue Baird, personal communication.
13. Joan Beaumont and Allison Cadzow, Eds., *Serving our country: Indigenous Australians, war, defence and citizenship*, 2018, NewSouth Publishing, Sydney, 2018. Soldier settlement issues for Aboriginal servicemen discussed in Chapter 5 by Samuel Furphy, pp. 109–111.
14. Tula, Haydn, 'Veteran reflects on fight against injustice', *Bunbury Herald*, 20 April, 2010; See also 'James Brennan: fight for justice', *Kalgoorlie Miner*, 13 January 2001. p. 17. Katrina Kittel's summary of Private James Brennan, Department of Veterans Affairs, Our Mob Serving Country: <http://www.dva.gov.au/i-am/aboriginal-andor-torres-strait-islander/our-mob-serving-country-100-years-and-beyond/wx7218> last accessed 3 June 2019.
15. Albert, Trish, 2010, *Unsung Hero*, Pearson Rigby, Melbourne, p. 15–16.
16. Len Watson, cited in Hall, Robert, *Black Diggers: Aborigines and Torres Strait Islanders in the Second World War*, 1989, Hall, p. 191.
17. Yininmadyemi Memorial, City of Sydney, last accessed 7 May 2019: <https://whatson.cityofsydney.nsw.gov.au/events/yininmadyemi-thou-didst-let-fall> last accessed 3 June 2019.
18. Stan Albert, personal communication.
19. Don Sharp, personal communication.
20. Hester Knight; undated news clip re Matt's return to Italy in Knight's collection.
21. Christina Twomey, *The Battle Within*, p. 106.
22. Cate Carrigan, personal communications further to: <http://italytothealps.blogspot.com/2013/09/following-our-fathers-world-war-11.html>
23. Lloyd Moule, personal communication. DVA nominal roll states that Vincent Rayner NX33853 was awarded Military Medal. Edward Howe was NX40662.
24. Charles Warburton, memoir.
25. Gwen Bryant, personal communication.
26. Cesare Romano Stefanato, *Boccia*, Little Red Apple Publishing, 2000.
27. Three POWs with surname Rose listed in Appendix 1.
28. Carla Bonello.

Epilogue
1. Monteath, *POW*, p. 430.
2. NAA B883, NX60337 Booth Colin.

3. Italian researcher Marco Soggetto includes stories of Australian escapers and Italian helpers in *Braccati: Prigionieri di guerra alleati in piemonte e valle d'Aosta.*
4. Piero Secchia, personal communication.
5. Ralph Churches wrote his story in *A Hundred Miles As The Crow Flies*, 1996.
6. Antonio Manfroi wrote his father's story in *il Soldato Harold*, 2014.
7. Paul Sanderson, personal communication; permission to cite Harold's poem.

Bibliography

Australians at War Film Archive (AAWFA), University of New South Wales, Canberra
Lloyd Moule, Archive 1285, interviewed 22 April 2004.
William Rudd, Archive 200, interviewed 20 May 2003.

Australian War Memorial (AWM)
AWM, 057024, AWM 057025, Bill Waller, *Go there you die*, 1989.
AWM54, 781/6/7, Interrogation Reports of Escaped Prisoner of War by Allied Interrogation Service CMF 1944.
AWM, PR88/185, NX23800, Norman Freeberg, *A synopsis of prisoner of war camps*.
SP459/1 573/1/53, War Crimes Investigation (NX70155 EW Levings).
SP459/1 573/1/54, War Crimes Investigation (NX70155 EW Levings).

National Archives of Australia (NAA)
Files from the following series:
NAA B2458 series: Army Personnel Files, multiple number series.
NAA B3856, 144/14/23 Statements made by Repatriated Prisoners of War Nominal Roll of POW [Prisoners of War] and Statements [mainly concerns prisoners of war in Europe].
NAA B503 series: Application forms for grants and associated documents, single number series with alphabetical prefixes [Prisoner of War Trust Fund].
NAA B883 series: Second Australian Imperial Force Personnel Dossiers, 1939-1947.

Primary sources - Articles
Drew, Garvan, 'Escape from Italy', *Barbed Wire and Bamboo: official organ ex-prisoners of war Association of Australia*, 35:4, August 1984.
Lockie, Herbert, 'Bert Lockie's Story', *Caveant Hostes: The Journal of the 2/15 Infantry Battalion Remembrance Club*, March 1985, Vol. 1, No.38.

Radnell, Don, diary serialised 2014 to 2015 issues of *Furphy Flyer*, 2/24 Btn Association.
Sharp, Keith, 'Escape to Switzerland', *Stand To*, January 1952.
Webster, Malcolm, 'Vagabonds Rest', Italian Historical Society Journal, 11, 1, January/June 2003, p.7-11.
Webster, Malcolm, 'An Italian Experience', Italian Historical Society Journal, 11, 1, January/June 2003, p.4-6.

Primary sources - Books
Barnett, Alex, 2001, *Hitler's Digger Slaves: Caught in the web of Axis labour camps*, Australian Military History Publications.
Broomhead, Edwin N, 1944, *Barbed wire in the sunset*, the author, The Book Depot, Melbourne.
Crellin, Ron, 1994, *Freedom at last*, the author, Bendigo.
Churches, Ralph, 1996, *A Hundred Miles As The Crow Flies*, the author, Adelaide.
English, Ian, *Home by Christmas*, the author, United Kingdom, 1997.
Kelly, William, 2001, *Journeys of a Restless Spirit: collected memories of Bill Kelly*, the author, Adelaide: Van Gastel Printing, 2001.
Kinder, Arthur, 2001, *A Long Time: a thrilling story of an ordinary soldier who escaped from a prison camp with romantic fiction intervention*, the author, Book House, Sydney.
Maitland, Ronald and Makella, Christine, 2006, *No Mountain too high: a life's journey*, the author, Brookvale.
Miller, John, 1989, *Friends and Romans on the run in wartime Italy*, Grafton Books, London.
Newby, Eric, 2010, *Love and war in the Apennines*, Harper Press, London
Paterson, Jim, 2008, *Partisans, peasants and P.O.W.s: a soldier's story of escape WWII*, the author, Optima Press, Perth.
Sproule, Ian with Oates, Lynette, 1997, *Australian Partisan: a true story of love and conflict*, Australian Military History Publications.
Webster, Malcolm, 1995, *An Italian experience*, the author, Wheelers Hill, Victoria.

Primary sources - interviews and correspondence with veterans
Nick Emery, Paul Lavallee, Ron Maitland, Lloyd Moule, Jack Nie, Laurie Quinn, Bill Rudd, Syd Shaw.

Secondary sources - Articles
Absalom, Roger, 2005, 'Allied escapers and the contadini in occupied Italy (1943-5)', *Journal of Modern Italian Studies*, 10:4, pp.413-425.
Barrass, Tom 'Swiss tour for war prisoners', *Newcastle Herald*, 14 October 1967.
Cerruti, Liliana, 1993, 'L'Americano di Noveis', *Vita Postuese*, Comune di Postua.
Langford, Ben, 'World War II through the eyes of a POW', *Illawarra Mercury*, 24 April 2017.

Marking Time: produced by and for British escaped prisoners of war, 1944, Switzerland.

Newman, P.H., 1944, 'The Prisoner of war mentality: its effects after repatriation', *British Medical Journal*, 1, 4330, pp.8-10.

Sweeney, Peter, (1993), 'A mate keeps a promise', *Sunday Times*, December 5, p.85.

Tula, Haydn, 'Veteran reflects on fight against injustice', *Bunbury Herald*, 20 April, 2010.

Wilson, Neil, 'From Geelong to Munich', *Herald Sun*, 24 April 2004.

--'Three AIF prisoners crossed Alps to freedom'. *Daily Mirror*, 20 January 1964, pp 15-16.

--'Escaped to Switzerland from Italian P.O.W. camp', *Port Lincoln News*, 16 June 1982, p.4.

--'James Brennan: fight for justice', *Kalgoorlie Miner*, 13 January 2001. P.17.

--'We Italians to you British regarding our art', *POW News*, Switzerland, 1944.

Secondary sources - Books

Absalom, Roger, 1991, *A Strange Alliance: aspects of escape and survival in Italy 1943-45*, Leo S. Olschki Editore, Florence.

Accati, Elena, 2014, *Infanzia di Guerra in Valle Cervo: un giardino di ricordi*, L'artistica Editrice, Savigliano.

Adam-Smith, Patsy, 1992, *Prisoners of war: from Gallipoli to Korea*, Ken Fin, Victoria.

Albert, Trish, 2010, *Unsung Hero*, Pearson Rigby, Melbourne.

Argent, J.N.L. ("Silver John"), 1957, *Target Tank: the history of the 2/3rd Australian anti-tank regiment, 9th Division A.I.F*, Parramatta.

Austin, R.J., 2008, *Let enemies beware! "Caveant hostes": The history of the 2/15th battalion, 1940-1945*, Slouch Hat Publications, McCrae Australia.

Bailey, Roderick, 2014, *Target Italy: The secret war against Mussolini 1940-1943: the official history of SOE operations in Fascist Italy*, Faber and Faber, London.

Battaglia, Roberto, 1957, *The Story of the Italian Resistance*, translated and edited by P.D. Cummins, Odhams Press, London.

Beaumont, Joan and Cadzow, Allison (Eds.), 2018, *Serving our country: Indigenous Australians, war, defence and citizenship*, 2018, NewSouth Publishing, Sydney.

Bunbury, Bill, 1995, *Rabbits and Spaghetti: Captives and comrades, Australians, Italians and the war 1939-1945*, Fremantle Arts Centre Press.

Clarke, Hugh and Burgess, Colin, 1992, *Barbed wire and bamboo: Australian POWs in Europe, North Africa, Singapore, Thailand and Japan*, Allen & Unwin, St Leonards.

Fenton, Ken, 2011, *Alamein to the Alps: war in the Piedmont with Mission Cherokee and the lost Anzacs 143-45*, the author, Blenheim Print, New Zealand.

Fenton, Ken, 2014, *At the Italian frontiers: episodes and recollections: wartime Italy 1941-1945*, the author, Blenheim Press, New Zealand.

Fitzgerald, Alan, 1981, *The Italian farming soldiers: prisoner of war in Australia 1941-1947*, Melbourne University Press, pp.1-2

Foot, M.R.D. and Langley, J.M., 1979, *M19: Escape and evasion 1939-1945*, The Bodley Head, London.

Fowler, William, 2010, *The secret war in Italy: special forces, partisans and covert operations 1943-45*, Ian Allan Publishing, Surrey.

Geddes, Margaret, 2004, *Blood, Sweat and Tears*: Australia's *WWII remembered by the men and women who lived it,* Penguin.

Gilbert, Adrian, 2006, POW: *Allied prisoners in Europe 1939-1945*, John Murray (Publishers) London.

Gillies, Midge, 2012, *The barbed-wire university: the real lives of Allied prisoners of war in the second world war*, Aurum Press, London.

Hall, Robert A., 1989, *The Black Diggers: Aborigines and Torres Strait Islanders in the Second World War*, Allen & Unwin, Sydney.

Christopher Herbert, 1963, *Benito Mussolini: a biography*, The Reprint Society London.

Jacobs, Susan, 2003, *Fighting with the enemy: New Zealand POWs and the Italian Resistance,* Penguin, Auckland.

Jacobs, Susan, 2012, *In Love and War: Kiwi soldier's romantic encounters in wartime Italy,* Penguin, Auckland.

James, Jan 'Kabarli', 2010, *Forever Warriors: this book honours all West Australian Indigenous men and women who served in all conflicts*, Northam.

Johnston, Mark, 2000, *Fighting the enemy: Australian soldiers and their adversaries in World War II*, Cambridge University Press.

Johnston, Mark and Stanley, Peter, 2006, *Alamein: The Australian Story*, Oxford University Press.

Liddell Hart, B.H., (Ed.), *The Rommel Papers*, Arrow Books Ltd, London, 1984.

Loffman, Phil, 1995, *P.O.W.: 2/28 AIF Btn prisoners of war,* the author.

Manfroi, Antonio, 2014, *il Soldato Harold: un neozelandese a Erto,* Edizioni L'Omino Rosso.

Masel, Philip, 2017, 3rd edition, *The Second 28th: the story of the 2/28th Australian Infantry Battalion in World War II,* PK Print, Perth.

Miller, David, 2001, *Commanding officers,* John Murray (Publishers) Ltd, London.

Peter Monteath, 2017, *Escape Artist: The incredible second world war of Johnny Peck,* NewSouth Publishing, Sydney.

Monteath, Peter, 2011, *P.O.W.: Australian prisoners of war in Hitler's Reich,* Pan Macmillan, Sydney.

Nascimbene, Giorgio, 2004, *Prigionieri di Guerra: L'anabasi dei prigionieri alleati che nel 1943 fecero parte dei campi di lavoro nelle risaie vercellesi e dintorni,* Societa Operaia di Mutuo Soccorso Villata, Vercelli.

Rollings, Charles, 2008, Prisoner of war: voices from behind the wire in the Second World War, Ebury Publishing, United Kingdom.

Scott, Arch, 1985, *Dark side of the moon*, Cresset Books, Auckland.

Soggetto, Marco, 2013, *Braccati: Prigionieri di guerra alleati in piemonte e valle d'Aosta*, Aviani and Avaini Editori, Udine.

Stamm, L., Frey, S., Greminger, A., & Wanner, L., (eds.), 2004, *Dignity and coolness: this small but energetic and highly educated nation has conducted itself with dignity and coolness*, Verlag Merker im Effingerhof, Brugg.

Stefanato, Cesare Romano, 2000, *Boccia: Bocia Cesarin*, Little Red Apple Publishing.

Ward-Harvey, Ken, 1992, *The Sapper's war: with ninth division engineers 1939-1945*, Sagoka Pty Ltd in association with 9th Division RAE Association NSW.

Twomey, Christina, 2018, *The Battle Within: POWs in postwar Australia*, NewSouth Publishing, Sydney.

Selected websites

Australian Red Cross Society, *Missing, wounded and prisoner of war enquiry cards* (digitised), The University of Melbourne: <https://digitised-collections.unimelb.edu.au/handle/11343/190446>

Biella/Oropa tram: <http://www.viaggiaescopri.it/davide-varesano-tramvia-biella-oropa/>

Bill Rudd: <http://www.anzacpow.com> and <http://www.campo57.com/products.html>

Cascina Veneria estate: <http://www.agricolaveneria.it/>

Cate Carrigan: <http://italytothealps.blogspot.com/2013/09/following-our-fathers-world-war-11.html>

Commonwealth War Graves Commission: <https://www.cwgc.org/>

Department of Veterans' Affairs, WW2 Nominal Roll: <http://www.ww2roll.gov.au>

Eggleston, Frederic, *Fred Eggleston's escapades Part 2*: <http://www.3squadron.org.au/subpages/Eggleston2.htm>

Evans, George, *A British POW becomes a partisan*: <http://www.bbc.co.uk/history/ww2peopleswar/stories/41/a2001141.shtml>

Kittel, Katrina, Department of Veterans' Affairs, *Our mob serving country, 100 years and beyond*: James Brennan- <http://www.dva.gov.au/i-am/aboriginal-andor-torres-strait-islander/our-mob-serving-country-100-years-and-beyond/wx7218> and Frank Page – <http://www.dva.gov.au/i-am/aboriginal-andor-torres-strait-islander/our-mob-serving-country-100-years-and-beyond/qx1639>

Museo Torino, July 1943 bombardment: <http://www.museotorino.it/view/s/acb7d7d49d6147e188377fb9e9c491ef>

Santuario di Oropa: <http://www.santuariodioropa.it/db/en/history-culture/history-of-the-sanctuary>

Theodul (Teodulo) Pass: <https://www.ultratourmonterosa.com/interesting-information/>

Yininmadyemi Memorial, City of Sydney: <https://whatson.cityofsydney.nsw.gov.au/events/yininmadyemi-thou-didst-let-fall>

The Keith Murdoch Sound Archive of Australia in the war of 1939-45

WX10009 Dodd, John (Jack), transcript of oral history recording John William 'Jack' Dodd, as a Private, 2/28th Battalion and POW in Italy, interviewed by Bill Bunbury for Keith Murdoch Sound Archive in Australia in the war of 1939–45, S00544, 1989.

WX5933 Douglas Le-Fevre, as a Private, 2/28th Battalion and POW in Italy, interviewed by Brian Wall for Keith Murdoch Sound Archive in Australia in the war of 1939-45, S00517, 10 January 1989.

WX9723 Jack Wauhop, Private, 2/32nd Battalion and a prisoner of war, interviewed by Brian Wall for Keith Murdoch Sound Archive in Australia in the war of 1939–45, S00512, 12 January 1989.

The National Archives (TNA) London

Files from the following series:

TNA, WO 208, The War Office: Directorate of Military Operations and Intelligence, and Directorate of Military Intelligence; Ministry of Defence, Defence Intelligence. Subseries Prisoner of War Reports.

TNA, WO 310/65, Shooting of Pte Batt, L.G., Clark, J.L., Smedley, J.D. at Biella, Province of Novara.

TNA, WO 311/1219, Murder of Pte. J.E. Law (NX16597) at Campo 106 Vercelli.

TNA, WO 344 series, War Office: Directorate of Military Intelligence: Liberated Prisoner of War Interrogation Questionnaires, General Questionnaire for British/American ex-prisoners of war.

TNA, WO 392, The War Office, Directorate of Prisoners of war, Prisoner of War Lists – Second World War. Sub-series WO 392/21: Imperial prisoners of war held in Italy. August 1943. Section 2: Australian Army.

Appendix 1: Nominal roll of Australian POWs at Campo 106

A note on sources:
- War Office Prisoner of War lists (TNA, WO 392, The War Office, Directorate of Prisoners of war, Prisoner of War Lists – Second World War. Sub-series WO 392/21: Imperial prisoners of war held in Italy. August 1943. Section 2: Australian Army). The file annotates 323 Australian Imperial Force POW listings as being interned at Campo 106. With reference to other sources, this number is less than half the number who were at Campo 106.
- National Archives of Australia, B883 series: Second Australian Imperial Force Personnel Dossiers, 1939-1947).
- Escaper reports held within The National Archives (TNA) - WO 208, The War Office: Directorate of Military Operations and Intelligence, and Directorate of Military Intelligence; Ministry of Defence, Defence Intelligence. Subseries Prisoner of War Reports.
- Red Cross POW cards (Missing, wounded and prisoner of war enquiry cards) accessible at The University of Melbourne's website. Dates listed on these cards include date of transfer and/or arrival to Campo 106, and indicates that transfers to Campo 106 occurred on or about 11 and 27 April 1943.
- TNA, WO 361/190 Prisoners of war, Italy: Campo 106, Vercelli file refers to a report on campo 106 following inspection on 4 June 1943. The report noted 823 (unnamed) Australians as well as 151 New Zealanders, 100 South Africans and 435 Englishmen across 23 work detachments, and that there is no base camp.

The number of POWs identified by the above sources, and as listed in the following **Nominal roll of Australian POWs at Campo 106**, fall short of the total of 823 referred to in WO 361/190. Bill Rudd believes that during transfer, a number of POWs may have been alighted near Campo 107, or that POW tallies may have doubled-up due to work across more than one Campo 106 farm.

Appendix 1: Nominal roll of Australian POWs at Campo 106

Refer to Map 1 for location of Campo 106 farms as identified through the research of Bill Rudd and Brian Sims, POW escaper reports, memoir, and interview. In addition to the mapped locations, research published by Giorgio Nascimbene (2004) includes other locations used for accommodation or labour: Cascina Vallasino (located between Olcenengo and Collobiano), Tenuta Romerana (Lignana), Cascina Impero (Salussola), Cascina Riccarda (Tronzano) and Tenuta Langosca (Villarboit). POWs may have been assigned to work locations but accommodated elsewhere. If permitted by farmers and guards, POWs could frequent taverns, *dopo lavoro*, such as Cascine Stra.

An Australian AIF POW is listed on the nominal roll if this is documented on any one of the abovementioned archival sources. To the advice of Bill Rudd, no Australian RAAF POWs were interned at Campo 106. This nominal roll is further to collaborative research with Bill Rudd, commenced on his initiation, to compile a roll of all Australian POWs held in any camp in Italy.

The military unit cited for the POWs is unit on discharge (source: Department of Veterans' Affairs online nominal roll) unless service records indicate the substantive service was within another unit.

Key:

× killed while POW
* reached Switzerland
∞ No Red Cross card evidence but mentioned in memoir or POW Report

A
WX6350 Abercrombie Ralph 2/28
NX50367 Abercrombie William 2/3PION
VX44714 Adams Arthur 3LAA
NX5488 Aiken Reginald 6 DIV CAV
NX26961 Aitken Edward 3ATANK *
QX7639 Albert Edward 2/15
WX01648 Alford Bernard 2/28
QX5457 Alford George 2/15
WX5951 Alford Leslie 2/28 *
VX29132 Allen Edgar 2/23
QX2908 Allenden Eric 2/32
WX4413 Anderson Edward 2/28
VX34767 Anderson Thomas 2/24
SX5213 Andrews Harry 2/7RAE *
QX8624 Andrews Joseph 2/2MG
NX18324 Andrews Raymond 2/13 *
WX6803 Angove Victor 2/28 *
WX14967 Archer George 2/32 *
VX37549 Armitage Leo 3LAA *

WX7579 Arnold Lawrence 2/28 *
QX8672 Arrold William 2/15 *
WX5367 Atkins Herbert 2/28
WX7292 Austin Lawson 2/28

B
NX34071 Backhouse Edward 2/3PION
VX13190 Bacon John 2/6
WX13384 Bailey Norman 2/28 *
WX5508 Bailey Stanley 2/28 *
QX1472 Baker Charles 2/32 *
WX5145 Baker Leslie 2/28 *
WX10673 Baker Sydney 2/28 *
VX52255 Baldwin Michael 2/23
WX5066 Ballard Harold 2/28
VX15782 Bannister Philip 3LAA
NX32211 Baptist Patrick 3ATANK
VX6733 Barclay Valentine 2/32
VX31735 Barker Ian 3LAA
WX15376 Barndon Albert 2/28 *
NX24504 Barry Clive 2/13 *

NX14263 Bartlett Wilfred 2/4
VX47204 Barwood William 2/24 *
VX44349 Bates Wallace 2/24
QX1929 Beach Gordon 2/15 *
WX14713 Beattie James 2/32
VX34216 Beattie Walter 2/24 *
NX60382 Beaver George 3ATANK
VX42183 Beggs Reginald 2/23 *
WX8774 Bell John 2/28
WX5930 Bell Robert 2/28 *
NX20322 Bell Ronald 3ATANK *
VX33895 Bennett Alfred 2/24 *
WX5499 Bennett Francis 2/28
QX5190 Berg Ernest 2/15 *
WX11505 Bergin Keith 2/32
WX9960 Berrey Thomas 2/28
VX20153 Berry Richard 2/23
VX54408 Bert Clive 2/3PION *
NX9333 Beston William 2/32
WX5207 Betts Albert 2/28
WX7549 Bidwell Edward 2/28 *
NX29776 Billinghurst Arthur 3ATANK *
WX9786 Birnie Frederick 2/32 *
WX7184 Black Daniel 2/28 *
VX46386 Blain Harold 2/24 ×
NX21419 Blair Wiliam 2/17 *
WX9047 Blewett Frank 2/32
WX5721 Blowfield George 2/28
NX60337 Booth Colin 3ATANK *
WX6684 Booth Stanley 2/28
PX9 Bosgard Peter 2/15
WX8857 Boskell Leonard 2/28 *
SX400 Bottroff Garth AASC *
SX737 Boulger Robert 2/3 FIELD COY *
NX69724 Boyd Eric 2/23 *
WX8927 Bowers Arthur Jack 2/28
VX47713 Bracken Edward 2/24 *
VX43313 Brear E 2/24
WX7218 Brennan James 2/28
VX47808 Bridgeman William 2/24
NX21049 Brien Gavin 2/13
VX48823 Brimacombe Harold 3LAA

WX7217 Bristow Jack 2/28
QX13418 Brockel Dawson F. 2/15 *
VX18546 Brook Douglas 2/24
QX7678 Brooks George 2/15
QX851 Brookes Lewis 2/15 *
VX45592 Brown George 2/24 *
VX42781 Brown John 2/24
QX2010 Brown Robert 2/12
VX21596 Brown Sydney 3LAA *
VX13107 Brown Wallace RAE *
WX4987 Brown William E. 2/28 *
QX6598 Brown William F. 2/15
VX25747 Browne Leo 2/23 *
VX5733 Bruce Bernard 2/7
VX34058 Bryant Ronald 2/24
WX6895 Bullock Thomas 2/28 *
QX2285 Burnett Thomas 2/32 *
WX8671 Burrows Joseph 2/28 *
NX20860 Burt James 2/1 FIELD W/S *
VX31993 Burton George 2/24 *
VX28833 Burville Bernard 2/24
VX34448 Buse George 2/24 *
QX10792 Bushnell William 2/15 *
VX11682 Busst Ian 2/3RAE
SX13742 Butler Charles 2/48
WX14981 Butterly Edward 2/32 *

C

VX32489 Caffrey Arthur 3LAA *
NX27702 Cahill Thomas 2/3PION
VX16600 Calder Kenneth 6 AASC *
VX28567 Cameron Kenneth 2/24
NX23324 Cameron Ronald 2/13 *
VX52786 Campbell Alexander 2/24
VX43960 Campbell Andrew 3LAA
NX17366 Campbell Donald 2/13 *
NX15145 Campbell Ronald 2/32
QX7889 Carey Frederick 2/15 *
NX50296 Carlile Francis 2/3PION *
VX22466 Carmichael Athol 2/24
NX51288 Carrigan Carl 3ATANK *
NX51289 Carrigan Paul 3ATANK *
NX58481 Caterson Clyde 3ATANK

Appendix 1: Nominal roll of Australian POWs at Campo 106

VX34781 Chaffey John 2/24
NX50631 Channell Burt 3ATANK
VX41005 Chapman Hillary 2/32 *
NX11450 Chard Clifford 2/1 *
WX11932 Chesson James S. 2/28 *
WX5231 Christensen Harold 2/28 *
NX11419 Clare Leslie 2/12
WX10594 Clark Edward 2/28
WX9627 Clark George H. 2/28 *
SX5055 Clark George M. 2/43 *
NX11498 Clark Henry 2/32
SX7226 Clark William 2/43
VX54170 Clarke Frederick 2/3PION
NX24360 Clarke George A. 2/13 *
WX9612 Clarkson Charles 2/28
VX47312 Clayton John 2/32
NX20404 Clifford Frank 2/3PION *
VX47792 Clifford Thomas 3LAA *
VX35181 Cody Basil 2/24
VX2053 Collins Alfred AASC *
QX8213 Collins Alfred 2/15 *
NX27858 Collins Robert 3 ATANK
VX46680 Collyer Neil 2/24 *
VX21603 Colson Norman 3LAA *
SX2560 Conner Douglas 2/1 FIELD W/S
VX23792 Connolly William 2/24 *
VX32872 Cook Walter 2/24 *
VX47973 Coombes Leslie 2/23
NX45906 Corke Neil 3LAA *
QX13679 Cotterell Alfred 2/15 *
TX146 Coulston Jack 6DiIVPOST *
QX2291 Coulthard Donald 2/32
WX8951 Cowdell Kenneth 2/28
VX3278 Cox Almond 3ATANK
QX8836 Cox Harry 2/2MG *
VX40528 Coxon Herbert 2/32
NX5531 Creasy Alton 2/4 *
VX48078 Crellin Ronald 2/24 *
NX26173 Crich Eric 2/28 *
NX201536 Croft Walter 3ATANK
VX47878 Crofts Gordon 3LAA *
VX2208 Crook Raymond AASC

NX35292 Crozier Frank 2/3PION
VX32873 Cullen Francis 2/24
WX10645 Cumpstey Harold 2/28
WX14235 Cunningham Keith 2/32 *
VX33876 Curr Frank 2/24 *
QX11367 Currington Roy 2/15
WX6544 Curtis Arthur 2/28 *
QX7686 Curtis Frederick 2/15 *

D

WX10061 Daglish Harold 2/28 *
VX33770 Dailey Albert 2/24
VX34722 Dalton Michael 2/24 *
VX38610 Dare Gordon 2/24
VX28641 Darrell Walter 2/23
QX54 Davis Eric AASC *
WX14427 Davis Harold 2/32
QX17456 Davis Leslie 2/15
VX47656 Davis Thomas 2/23 *
NX28398 Dawes James 3ATANK *
QX13454 Dawson William A. 2/15 *
NX8151 Deal William 2/1
VX28613 Dean Joseph 2/24
WX12891 Dean Ronald 2/32
NX25641 Denovan Albert 2/3PION *
VX26120 Dent John 2/23 *
QX5300 Devine Roy 2/15
NX58475 Dewberry Maxwell 3ATANK
WX15244 Dickie Reginald 2/32 *
VX28664 Dickson Harold 2/24
VX44219 Dickson Robert 2/24 *
VX28669 Dickson Stanley 2/24
WX1462 Digwood Harold 2/11 *
WX5743 Dillon Joseph 2/28 *
NX23466 Dixon John 2/13
WX10009 Dodd John 2/28 *
VX34868 Dodds William 2/24
VX1266 Doig William 2/3RAE *
VX46836 Donelly Cecil 3LAA
VX38507 Donohue Arthur 2/23
VX24151 Donovan Roy 2/23
VX34859 Doran Arthur 2/24 *
SX8381 Dornan Francis 2/48 *

QX798 Dornan Leslie 2/7RAE *
WX10529 Dorotich Jack 2/28
QX8545 Double Eric 2/15 *
SX6310 Douglas Ronald 2/10 *
VX40994 Dower Leslie 2/23 *
VX26349 Drane Henry 26ATANK *
QX6959 Drew Garvan 2/15
NX18121 Duffy Joseph 2/13
NX50270 Duggan John 3ATANK *
VX28370 Dunlop Roy 2/24 *
QX7942 Dyson Alfred 2/15

E

SX451 Eastwood Charles AASC *
VX40089 Edmondson Claude 3LAA *
QX7590 Edwards Angus 2/15
NX11212 Elliott George 2/4 *
WX10649 Elliot Henry 2/28 *
QX7333 Ellis Herbert 2/32
NX23170 Elmore Edward 2/13
NX56333 Emery Herbert 2/28 *
NX33357 Erickson Peter 3ATANK *
VX53572 Esler Robert 2/3PION *
WX13224 Ettridge Eric 2/28

F

VX48395 Fallon Charles 2/24
VX32689 Farrow Claude 3LAA *
VX28006 Farrow Cyril 3LAA *
VX48488 Farrow W.(Aka J.Williams) 2/32
WX17240 Faulkes John 2/32 *
VX41601 Fenwick Julius 2/24 *
WX1033 Ferguson Lloyd 2/28
NX16852 Ferguson Robert 2/13
NX50183 Ferrer William 2/17
VX27194 Finch Harry 2/32 *
NX51323 Fitzgerald Francis 3ATANK *
WX9147 Fitzgerald John 2/28
QX7025 Fleming Donald 2/32 *
VX46998 Fletcher John 2/23 *
WX11411 Fletcher Thomas 2/32 *
WX6905 Fogg Arthur 2/28
WX13060 Follett Charles 2/32
WX12961 Foot Henry 2/23

NX50304 Forbes Eric 2/3PION *
QX13366 Forbes William 2/15
NX2944 Ford James AASC
VX40025 Ford Ronald 2/23
VX48362 Forde Neal 2/24
VX40075 Foster Henry 2/23
NX17348 Franks Arthur 2/13 *
QX3224 Fraser Alan 2/15
VX34270 Fraser Charles 2/24 *
VX47635 Fraser James 2/23
NX23800 Freeberg Norman 2/17
WX1960 Freeman Warren 2/32
WX5388 French William 2/28
VX40342 Fullarton Jack 2/23
WX10033 Furguson Lloyd 2/28

G

QX1989 Galvin William 2/28
NX17211 Garbutt Alan 3ATANK
WX11977 Gard Bernard 2/28
WX7733 Gardiner James 2/28
NX778 Gardner Colin 9SIGS *
VX42495 Gardner John 2/23 *
QX9349 Gardner Raymond 2/7RAE
QX7028 Gardner Samuel 2/32 *
NX59278 Garretty Sidney 2/3PION
VX32518 Garrigan William 3LAA
WX3880 Gibbons Norman 2/28 *
NX29995 Gibson Claude 3ATANK *
QX8012 Giddins James 2/15
VX47985 Giles John 2/24
NX2281 Gill Alfred 2/2 *
NX53017 Gill Richard 3ATANK *
VX2210 Gillies Frank AASC *
VX35187 Gitsham Harry 2/24 *
WX2942 Goldsworthy William 2/28 *
QX8577 Gomersall Seymour 2/15
VX35212 Goodear Robert 2/24
NX5537 Goodwin Harold AASC
SX1320 Graetz Donald 2/3RAE *
WX1963 Grafton Edwin 2/28
NX56337 Graham Alexander 3ATANK
QX3989 Graham James 2/7RAE *

VX54413 Granland Ernest 2/3PION *
VX4690 Green John Brian 2/7 *
WX14707 Green Lawrence 2/32 *
WX4260 Green Peter 2/28
VX31219 Greive Henry 3LAA *
VX32516 Griffiths Alfred 2/2,3LAA *
WX14351 Griffiths Charles 2/32
WX15431 Grimsey Albert 2/28 *
VX8912 Groves Henry 2/7

H

NX17434 Hall Mervyn 2/13
VX34135 Hallowell Edgar 2/24
WX2090 Hampson Walter 2/28
SX12870 Hancock Walter 2/43
NX21076 Hancock William 2/24
TX722 Hanson Bernard 2/12 *
QX12150 Harrett Norman 2/15
QX177 Harrison Alwyn 2/32 *
VX34554 Harrison William 2/24
WX10591 Harvey William 2/32 ×
QX16551 Hassan Ray 2/15
VX34562 Hayes Ernest 2/24 *
VX50873 Hayes Francis 2/23 *
TX5749 Heald Charles 2/43
NX51056 Heath James 2/3PION
TX5618 Heazelwood Leonnard 2/43 *
VX33146 Hemphill Albert Ian 2/24 *
VX27761 Henderson Afton 2/23
VX18692 Henderson Cyril 6DiIVSIGS *
WX11469 Hendry Alexander 2/32 *
VX47078 Henman Alan 2/24
WX11416 Herbert Henry 2/32
WX8669 Hess Robert 2/28
VX28356 Hewitt Charles 2/24
WX12622 Hick Raymond 2/28
NX50707 Hoad Leonard 2/3PION *
NX17401 Hollingworth Henderson 2/13
QX11027 Holman Leonard 2/15 *
WX9065 Holmes Bramwell 2/28 *
NX11089 Holmes Ernest AASC
NX1065 Hood Raymond 2/1RAA *
QX2455 Hopes Donald 2/32

QX8542 Horder George 2/15
VX46543 Horman Colin 2/24
VX4660 Howell Frederick 2/23
WX12889 Howes Ronald 2/32
NX27773 Hoy Raleigh 2/3PION *
WX4695 Hubbard Leslie 2/28 *
NX50366 Hudson Harry 2/3PION *
VX34505 Hughes James 2/24
QX10626 Hungerford Francis 'Happy' 2/15∞
QX2993 Hunter Leonard 2/15
VX48275 Hutchinson Reginald 2/24 *
QX1232 Hutchinson Richard 2/32 *
VX34829 Hyde William 2/24
NX727 Hyland James 2/1 *
VX46380 Hynes John 2/24 *

I

QX266 Imison Donald 2/13
VX44067 Inglis Norman 3LAA *
VX34935 Irvine Victor 2/24
SX7858 Irwin Ronald 2/48 *

J

VX37065 Jackman Morris 2/32
QX17905 Jackson Leonard 2/15
VX27886 Jackson Roy 2/24 *
VX29615 Jackson Walter 2/23 *
NX15695 Jagoe Clive 2/13 *
VX25132 James Stanley 2/23 *
VX33099 James Thomas 3LAA
QX3354 Jamieson William 2/15
NX38537 Jansen Frank 3ATANK
VX31846 Jeffs Frederick 3LAA
VX34381 Jenks Roy 2/24 *
QX3237 Jobson Frank 2/7RAE *
QX21217 Jobson Ian 2/7RAE *
QX759 Jocumsen Jens 2/7RAE *
VX47125 Johns John 2/23 *
VX29238 Johnson Charles 2/23
VX41923 Johnson George 2/23
VX34438 Johnson John 2/24
QX9078 Johnson Ray 2/15 *
VX48197 Johnson Roy 26ATANK
NX21761 Johnson William 2/17 *

QX1656 Johnston RAE 2/15 *
VX37427 Jones Brinley 2/24 *
VX46863 Jones Clyde 2/24 *
NX46120 Jones Eric 3ATANK *
VX29657 Jones Keith 2/24
VX32717 Jones Lionel 2/24 *
TX597 Jones Maurice 2/12
NX51445 Jones Ray 3ATANK
SX7626 Jones Raymond 2/48
WX8349 Jones Robert 2/28 *
NX15573 Jones Ronald 2/13 *
NX59936 Jones Sydney 3ATANK
VX47799 Judd Jack 2/32? *
VX34889 Judd Maxwell 2/24 *

K

VX48290 Karnatz, Thomas 2/24
SX12776 Keats Gilbert 2/43
WX6695 Keenan John 2/28 *
VX10072 Kellett Percival 9SIGS
VX46199 Kelly Harry 2/23 *
VX36598 Kelly Thomas 2/32 *
VX24476 Kelly Thomas 2/32 *
VX32515 Kennedy Thomas 3LAA
QX22164 Kent Edgar 3ATANK *
WX2137 Kent Harold 2/32
WX9632 Kermode Thomas 2/28 *
QX5719 Kerr Leo 2/15 *
VX42959 Kimber Charles 2/23
NX12808 Kinder Arthur 2/13 *
QX5504 King David 2/32 *
VX34642 King Norman 2/24
SX8953 Kinsman Sydney 2/48 *
VX47484 Knight Colin 2/24 *
VX34773 Knight Ian 2/24
WX12167 Knight John 2/28 *
VX34393 Knight Matthew 2/24
NX35995 Knox Lloyd 2/3PION
SX6606 Kostera Louis 2/48
WX7012 Kruger Leslie 2/28

L

NX8519 Lackey John AASC
VX32578 Lamont Raymond 2/24 *

NX18898 Lane Jack 2/13 *
QX9995 Lauder Stuart 2/2MG *
NX23801 Lavallee Paul 2/17
QX7929 Lavaring Neville 2/15 *
NX25562 Lawrence Edgar 2/17
VX30924 Lawrence John 2/24 *
SX11230 Lawrie Nicol 2/43 *
NX16597 Laws John 2/17 ×
WX10052 Leach Frank 2/28 *
NX51287 Ledingham Lloyd 3ATANK *
WX4926 Lee George 2/28 *
WX5933 Le-Fevre Douglas 2/28 *
NX20543 Leonard Edward 3ATANK
NX59949 Lester Benjamin 3ATANK
WX14228 Lewis Arthur 2/32
VX1664 Liddell Clive AASC ×
QX6577 Lockie Herbert 2/15
WX6543 Loffman Philip 2/28
WX14996 Lopicic Yovan 2/32 *
WX13315 Louden Reginald 2/28
VX28382 Lucas Harold 3LAA *
NX28220 Luck Fredrick 3ATANK
SX5449 Luck William 2/43 *
VX48229 Luxford Harold 2/23
VX17367 Luxford Raymond 2/24

M

VX36944 Macgeorge Peter 3LAA
VX48130 Mackenzie Ian 2/2
VX33100 Maddern James 2/24 *
VX47708 Madin William 2/32 *
QX4351 Maher Francis AASC *
WX7942 Maher Harold 2/32
WX10252 Maher Patrick 2/32
WX1870 Mailer Frederick 2/32
WX14636 Maitland Ronald 2/32 *
WX7112 Mallins George 2/28 *
VX45165 Mandrou Alexander 2/32 *
WX2122 Marchesi Len 2/32 *
VX53646 Martin Cyril 2/24
VX10640 Martin William 2/1 *
WX7223 Martinson Stanley 2/28 *
NX35299 Mathieson Harold 2/3PION

VX32571 Matulick Edward 2/24 *
SX13037 Maynard Melvin 2/48 *
QX3733 Mazlin Norman 2/12 *
QX1500 McAlister Keith 2/32
WX9698 McCarthy George 2/32 *
VX36761 McClaren Roy 3LAA
QX2232 McClelland Robert 3ATANK∞*
VX45756 McCracken James 2/24 ×
NX21524 McDermid Duncan 2/13
QX13482 McDonald Alexander 2/15 *
QX3847 McDonald Angus 2/3RAE *
QX5895 McDonald George 2/15
VX6027 McDonald Ronald 2/8 *
VX48651 McDougal Francis 2/24
VX51782 McEwan Ronald 2/24 *
VX35662 McGavin Leslie 2/24 *
VX26797 McGillivray James 2/23 *
VX34715 McGregor Walter 2/24
NX51281 McIntosh Ronald 3ATANK
VX48203 McIntyre Ronald 2/32
VX8866 McKay Frank 2/28 *
WX15377 McKelvie George 2/32 *
VX28541 McKenzie George 2/24 *
VX48130 McKenzie Ian 26ATANK *
VX34498 McLarty Robert 2/24 *
WX7524 McLellan Alan 2/28
VX34696 McLuckie Alan 2/24 *
VX34716 McMahon Basil 2/24 *
VX32530 McMahon Jack 2/24
QX5827 McMahon Walter 2/15 *
VX31673 MacRae Robert 2/24 *
WX14477 McSwain Arthur 2/32
WX11439 Meldrum Henry 2/32 *
QX13597 Messenger John 2/15
WX14391 Miller Alan 2/32
VX33540 Miller Albert 2/24 *
NX45242 Miller Arthur 3ATANK *
VX44114 Miller David 2/24
WX11952 Miller Harry 2/28 ×
QX1975 Miller Kenneth 2/15
VX48196 Mills Charles 2/32 *
WX2973 Mills Walter 2/28

WX6564 Milroy William 2/28
QX3368 Mitchell Charles 2/15
QX8045 Mitchell Cecil 2/15 *
VX30186 Mitchell William 2/24 *
WX8815 Moir Ernest 2/28
WX8027 Molloy Maurice 2/28 *
VX35670 Molony Norman 2/23 *
SX7967 Montgomerie Alvin 2/48
VX42326 Montgomery Harry 2/24
NX23373 Moon James 2/13 *
VX29161 Mooney Kevin 2/24
WX15009 Moore Albert 2/32
QX10216 Moore James 2/15
TX383 Moore John 9SIGS *
WX7860 Moore Newton 2/28 *
NX33027 Moore, Ronald 3ATANK
WX7965 Morgan William 2/28 *
WX10462 Morley Edward 2/48
WX5575 Morris Clarence 2/28 *
WX2050 Morris Jack 2/32 *
QX1940 Morris Richard 2/15 *
QX3987 Morris William 2/15 *
WX3303 Morrissey Albert 2/28 *
NX34555 Morsillo Joseph 3ATANK *
WX13254 Mortimer John 2/28
NX40603 Moule Lloyd 3ATANK *
VX9102 Moynahan Thomas 6SIGS *
NX54257 Mudge Ross 2/3PION ×
TX1235 Mullins Harold 2/32 *
NX21061 Murray Victor 2/13
VX40095 Murtagh James 2/23

N

VX48649 Neal Ronald 2/24
WX12688 Neave Alan 2/28 *
WX12709 Neil Joseph 2/28 *
WX9950 Nelligan Frank 2/28 *
WX9903 Nelson John 2/28
WX5251 Newbey Thomas 2/28 *
QX2962 Newton Herbert 2/32 *
WX7090 Nicholls John 2/28 ×
WX10666 Nichols George 2/28 *

VX31699 Nicholson Alan 2/24 *
VX28557 Nicholson John 3LAA
NX17325 Nicol William 2/13
WX16763 Nie John 2/32 *
NX52624 Noble Robert 3ATANK *
VX32569 Norton Thomas 2/24 *
QX1994 Nott Cecil 2/15 *
WX11278 Nyal Ernest 2/32

O

WX2034 Oborne John 2/32 *
VX32499 O'Donnell Patrick 2/24
QX20453 Oldes Robert 2/32
NX35892 O'Leary Kenneth 3ATANK
WX14475 Oliver John 2/32 *
VX30023 O'Rafferty Gerald 2/24
VX34508 O'Rafferty Patrick 2/24 * ×
WX9810 Osborn William 2/32
NX6381 O'Sullivan Francis 6AASC *
NX23376 Owens John 2/13

P

NX29592 Pack Harold 2/1 PION *
QX1639 Page Frank 2/32 *
VX47735 Page Harold 2/1
WX4461 Pallot John 2/28 *
VX38325 Pannowitz William 2/32 *
WX14265 Park Havaland 2/28
VX33048 Parker James 2/24
WX14394 Parker Leslie 2/32 ×
VX33706 Parker Walter 2/24 *
SX1106 Parlett William 6AASC
NX34604 Paton Ray 3ATANK
QX3232 Payne Charles 2/7FIELD COY *
VX2556 Peachey Edward 2/2 AMB
VX9534 Peck Desmond John 2/7 *
VX31755 Peebles Stanley 2/24 *
QX3577 Peel Harland 2/12
VX35243 Percy Robert 2/24 *
NX19056 Perrott Henry 2/1 *
VX46783 Perry George 2/24
QX3365 Petersen Stanley 2/15 *
VX27577 Philpott Harold 2/23 *
QX7372 Pill Harold 2/32 *

SX6967 Plant Clyde 2/43 *
WX12186 Pleass George 2/32 *
VX40731 Pollock Horace 2/23 *
VX33372 Pope Maxwell 2/24 *
WX10094 Potter Francis 2/28
VX47124 Potter Harold 2/32
QX7984 Powell William 2/15
VX37412 Powling William 2/32
WX6079 Pratt Cyril 2/28 *
QX833 Pratt George 2/15
VX32728 Preiser Ernest 3LAA *
VX11824 Price Archibald 2/32 *
VX1476 Price Edward 2/3 FIELD COY
VX34790 Price Edwin 2/24
WX4462 Price Frederick 2/28 *
VX42421 Priest Albert 2/23
QX6908 Pritchard William 2/15 *
VX47738 Proctor Mervyn 2/23 *
VX34319 Prosser Raymond 2/24 *
WX10253 Purdy Joseph 2/32
WX7619 Putland Gordon 2/28 *

Q

QX7086 Querruell Francis 2/32
WX10321 Quick George 2/32

R

VX34693 Radnell Donald 2/24
NX13595 Ramalli Edward 2/13
VX803 Rawlinson James 2/1FLDW/S
VX54086 Ray Percy 2/3PION
WX6366 Rea George 2/32 *
NX25347 Reddan John 3ATANK *
WX10022 Reddin Frederick 2/28
NX13308 Rees Clarence D. 2/4 *
QX16528 Reese Noel 2/15 *
SX879 Reeves James SIG
WX3841 Reeves Thomas 2/28
QX1725 Reid Clarence 2/15 *
SX6604 Reid Maxwell 2/48
WX6560 Reynolds William 2/28
VX32529 Rhodes Frank 2/24
VX33373 Rhodes George 2/24 *

VX57199 Richards Harold 2/23
NX21094 Richards Jack 2/13
WX12756 Richards William 2/32
SX7532 Richardson Max 2/48 *
QX15357 Richardson Roy 2/12 *
VX47992 Richardson William 3LAA *
VX34902 Rickard Gorden 2/24 *
NX53033 Ridgway Albert 3ATANK
WX8907 Riekie Leslie 2/28
NX46456 Riordan Esca 2/4
VX31502 Robertson David 2/24 *
QX11222 Robertson Donald 2/15 *
NX50179 Robertson Harold 3ATANK
NX52814 Robinson Alfred 2/28 *
VX46816 Rodgers Ronald 2/24
VX41024 Rogers Joseph 26ATANK
NX22332 Rogers Malcolm 2/13
NX19074 Rogers Milton 2/1PION *
WX1050 Rose Clarence 2/32 *
SX8800 Rose Vivian 2/8 FIELD AMB *
WX10362 Rose William 2/32 *
WX5963 Rouse Thomas 2/28 *
WX5292 Rowe John 2/28 *
WX14424 Rowles Sydney 2/32
VX41487 Rowlings Philip 2/23
VX39694 Rudd William 2/7 RAE *
VX32857 Ruddell Henry 2/24 *
NX29871 Rundle Mervyn 2/13
VX43778 Russell Hector 2/23
VX31514 Russell John 2/24
VX32995 Russell Thomas 3LAA *
NX30501 Ryan John 2/32
QX7378 Rylands Charles 2/32

S

QX8201 Sabin Charles 2/2 MG
WX11994 Sadler Albert 2/28 *
WX6933 Salmon Allan 2/28
WX10281 Salter Robert 2/32
VX34912 Saville Francis 2/24
VX33392 Savory Frederick 2/24 *
VX32469 Scales Roy 2/24 *
VX26142 Scott Alexander 3LAA

WX15060 Scott Alfred 2/32
QX5946 Scott Ronald 2/15 *
WX5295 Scott Walter 2/28 *
NX24177 Sealy Noel 2/13 *
VX48359 Sedgman Norman 2/24
VX43003 Sedgwick Dudley 2/23
NX24949 Semple James 3ATANK
WX12267 Shaw Sydney 2/32 *
NX29579 Shaw Sydney G. 2/2 MG
WX6937 Shove Sydney 2/28 *
NX35515 Sibraa Henry 2/3PION *
VX44556 Simmonds, Henry 2/24 *
VX29525 Simmons James 2/24
VX35945 Simmons Michael 2/24
WX6900 Simmons Patrick 2/28 *
VX37657 Simpson Lewis 3LAA *
WX7977 Sinclair Colville 2/28
VX48180 Sincock Edward 2/24 *
VX48171 Sincock Herbert 2/24
VX26596 Sincock William 2/24 *
NX71206 Sing Frederick 2/13 *
WX10059 Skipworth Edward 2/28
WX3756 Sloan Mervyn 2/28 *
VX31655 Sloane John 3LAA
VX42361 Smedley Douglas 2/23 ×
VX45533 Smith Alfred 2/32
VX33912 Smith Brian 2/24 *
VX34537 Smith Claude 2/24 *
WX9093 Smith Edward 2/28
VX26109 Smith Frank 2/1FLDW/S
WX5478 Smith George 2/28
WX6614 Smith Harold 2/28
QX17734 Smith John 2/7 RAE
VX18131 Smith Leonard 2/1FLDW/S
QX5945 Smith Noel 2/15 *
WX6833 Smith William 2/28 *
QX8202 Smithwick William 2/2 MG
QX8172 Solway William 2/15 *
VX32109 Sparnon Ernest 3LAA *
VX38618 Sproule Ian 2/32
VX34730 Squires William 2/24
WX7574 Stanley Charles 2/28 *

VX28787 Steele Donald 2/24 *
TX850 Stein John 2/12 *
WX10040 Stephen Joseph 2/28
VX33491 Stephens Clifford 2/24 *
NX19374 Stephenson Harry 2/13 *
NX26130 Stevenson George 2/32
WX1839 Stokes Albert 2/32
WX12015 Stokes Arnold 2/11 AMB
WX11939 Stouse Charles 2/28 *
WX6619 Strack Albert 2/28
VX48378 Straede Oswald 2/24
WX10021 Strickland Ronald 2/28 *
WX10020 Strickland William 2/28 *
VX42137 Stuart Charles 2/23 *
WX12803 Sullivan Herbert 2/32 *

T

VX38529 Tabbiner Charles 2/32
VX46243 Tabram Frederick 2/24
NX30450 Tasker Henry 3ATANK
WX13281 Taylor Henry 2/28
NX46502 Taylor Herbert 2/17
VX34483 Taylor John 2/24
WX6013 Taylor Leonard 2/28
WX14583 Terrell Norman 2/28 *
WX5101 Thom Ronald 2/28*
VX48390 Thomas Alfred 2/24 *
WX10398 Thompson George 2/48 *
WX11914 Thompson George 2/28
WX5307 Thompson James 2/28 *
QX5870 Thompson Thomas 2/15 *
WX14193 Thompson William 2/28
VX43523 Thorne Walter 2/32
QX6922 Todd David 2/15 *
VX46073 Tomkins James 2/24
WX13405 Toovey Patrick 2/28
QX8681 Townsend Albert 2/15
QX5753 Triffett Edgar 2/15 *
VX14918 Tripovich Norman 2/32 *
VX34970 Tunks Leslie 2/24 *
NX1960 Turner Claude 2/2
WX12710 Turner Frank 2/28
TX75 Turner Joseph 2/12 *
WX10607 Turner Keith 2/28
WX12712 Turner Robert 2/28
NX13278 Turner Robert 2/13
VX33938 Twigg Charles 2/24
VX46786 Tye Thomas 2/32 *
NX23782 Tyrie Horace 2/23 *

U

VX34643 Underwood Ernest 2/24 *
VX32653 Underwood Harold 2/23 *

V

WX5229 Vardy Frederick 2/28
NX21978 Veron Francis 2/13 *
WX13239 Vigar Raymond 2/28

W

VX30736 Wade Ronald 2/24 *
WX9970 Wainewright Herbert 2/28
WX10614 Walker Bruce 2/28 *
NX53146 Walker Douglas 3ATANK
NX54410 Walker Jack 2/3PION *
VX47958 Waller William 3LAA *
QX3160 Wallis Darrell 2/11 AMB
WX6989 Walters Ernest 2/28
WX5299 Warburton Charles 2/28 *
VX52260 Ward Allen 2/24 *
WX5890 Ward Robert 2/28 *
WX5068 Warner Francis 2/28
VX44745 Waterhouse John 2/23
NX25365 Watson Edgar 2/3PION *
WX5013 Watson Harold 2/28 *
WX14400 Watson Leslie 2/32
WX5900 Watson Mervyn 2/28
WX4487 Watson Stanley 2/28 *
QX2418 Watts Harry 2/15 *
WX9723 Wauhop Jack 2/32 *
WX12725 Webb Charles 2/28
VX26590 Webb Claude 2/23
VX32483 Webb George 2/24 *
QX8236 Webb Harold 2/15
WX5438 Webber Harmon 2/28
VX23397 Webster Malcolm 3LAA
WX13002 Weedon George 2/28
NX38152 Weekes Colin 3ATANK *

NX46958 Weirs Phillip 3ATANK
WX11970 Wesley Samuel 2/28
WX5964 Westlake Bernard 2/28
VX48409 Wettenhall Roger 3LAA
NX1068 White Cedric 2/1 RAA *
NX29927 White Norman 2/13
WX13017 White Wallace 2/28
WX14338 Whitehouse Tom 2/32
VX1552 Whitham Gordon 2/32 *
VX46626 Whittingham Jack 2/23
TX360 Whyman Loyal 2/12 *
WX1863 Wiese Lawrence 2/32
WX9128 Wilbrey Arthur 2/28
WX6903 Willacott Norman 2/28
NX47829 Williams Eric 2/17
NX2979 Williams William 9DIVPROV
VX34136 Willoughby Henry 2/24 *
WX4493 Wills Maximilian 2/28 *
WX5534 Wills Victor 2/28 *
WX11748 Wilson Albert 2/28 *
NX9024 Wilson Frederick AASC *
VX35149 Wilson Jack 2/24 ×
QX5417 Wilson James 2/15 *
VX21653 Wilson John 2/24
WX15263 Wilson Keith 2/28 *

WX6100 Wilson Lloyd 2/28 *
VX34368 Wilson Richard 2/24 *
VX24892 Wilson Ronald 2/24
TX342 Wilson Stanley 2/32
VX61870 Wilson William 2/3PION
WX7185 Wilson William 2/28 *
VX14203 Winchester Arthur 2/32 *
WX11913 Winfield Edward 2/28 *
NX35880 Winter Ernest 3ATANK
WX14978 Wolfe Ernest 2/32 ×
VX47859 Wolstenholme Geoffrey 2/24
NX33270 Wood James 3ATANK
VX34421 Woodyard George 2/24
WX6058 Woosnam Norman 2/28 *
QX6608 Worsfold Michael 2/15
NX58816 Worthington Norman 2/17
WX10603 Wray Arthur 2/28
VX46959 Wrigglesworth William 3LAA
VX28988 Wycherley Rossett 2/24 *
QX5740 Wylie Robert 2/15 *

Y

VX47581 Young Allan 3LAA

Z

QX10479 Zwoerner Ronald 2/15 *

Appendix 2:
New Zealander POWs reaching Switzerland

Note on sources:
- Bill Rudd provides his compilation of New Zealander POWs as extracted from *The Final Report by the Swiss Commission for the Internment and Hospitalisation of foreign military personnel 1940-45*.
- Ken Fenton, within *Alamein to the Alps*, includes a number of New Zealander POWs (including ex-Campo 106) who reached Switzerland.
- Brian Sims's research within The National Archives (TNA) sourced a large number of WO 208 series POW Reports for New Zealander POWs reaching Switzerland. Brian's summary list of the ex-Campo 106 POW Reports is held within Bill Rudd's research collection. Brian Sims also provided a number of reports to myself, and additional reports have since been sourced for me from TNA by Neil Smith.
- The TNA, WO 392 file: The War Office, Directorate of Prisoners of war, Prisoner of War Lists – Second World War, sub-series WO 392/21: Imperial prisoners of war held in Italy August 1943, Section 4: New Zealand Army include 114 men of the 2nd New Zealand Expeditionary Force at campo 106.
- The TNA, WO 361/190 Prisoners of war, Italy: Campo 106, Vercelli file reports on Campo 106 following inspection on 4 June 1943, and reported 151 (unnamed) New Zealanders.

The 2nd New Zealand Expeditionary Force POWs listed within the WO 392 file as interned at Campo 106 as well as the POWs identified by the research of Rudd, Sims and Fenton as ex-campo 106, are marked *.

Appendix 2: New Zealander POWs reaching Switzerland

A
Arnold Allen*
Norman Allen*
William Anderson*
Leigh Andrews*
Stanley Avery*

B
Ernest Ball*
William Ballinger*
John Barker*
Stanley Barrow*
Peter Watson Bates*
Marcus Blackwood*
John Bonner*
David Boraman*
Percy Bremner*
Jack Bromley*
John Butler*
Jack Bromley*
Eric Brown*
Charles Buchan*

C
Robert Cameron*
George Cates*
Allan Chapman*
Wilbur Choat*
Wyndham Churchouse*
Ernest Clarke
Cyril Collins
William Collins*
David Conlon*
Aubrey Connolly*
Charles Coochey*
Donald Craib*
Alex Craig*
Allen Cusdin (ex-campo 120)

D
Henry Davis*
James Dawson
Paul Day
James Duncan*
Douglas Dymock*

F
Arthur Forrester*
William Frost*

G
Douglas George*
Dennis Gibbs*
Joseph Albert Giles*
William Gray
Edward Grayadler*
Alick Greygoose*
Wilfred Gyde*

H
Charly Hamilton
Sydney Hamlin*
Seton Hammond*
Ray Hand*
Henry Harrison*
Adam Heka*
David E. Higgins*
Robert Hohaia*
Leslie Holemby*
John Holland*
34900 Douglas Holley*
Reginald Hollows
Lionel Hood*
Donald Horton*
Hudson
Sylvester Hudson*

J
David Jacobs*
Lawrence Jensen*
Paul Jensen*
Leslie Jillings*
Reg Johnstone*

K
Henry Katae

L
George Loader
George London*
Frank Lowe
Roy Lunn*
William Lyons*

M
136279 C. James Maher
Edwin Martin
Rosswell Martin*
Kevin McCarthy*
13825 Gordon McLeod
James McClusky
Keith McDonald
Douglas McGee*
Clarence Meynell
Lewis Moir*
Patrick Moncur
Anglis Munro

N
Gerald Neame*

O
Robert Orr

P
Clarence Peagram*
Edward Preston*

Q
Patrick Quirk*

R
Thomas Reay*
Terence Robson
Rex Ryman

S
Edward Scanlan*
Richard Schare*
John Skilton*
George F. Smith*
Hamlet Smithson*
Ian St. George
Thomas Straker

T
Malcolm Tyson

W
Charles Williams*
Richard Willoughby*
Frederick Wilson
Frederick Wratten*
George Wright.

INDEX

Note: Chapter numbers are indexed. For end notes, the chapter number will be suffixed with 'n'.
Foreword=F, Prologue=P, Epilogue=E

> Note: *Chapter numbers* are used in this index not page numbers.

A

Abercrombie, Ralph (WX6350) 4
Absalom, Roger 5, 6, 9, 17, 21, 24
Acquadro, Eda 27
Acquadro, Elma 27
Acqui Terme 24
Adelboden 25
Afrika Corps F, 1
Agno 22
Ailoche 11
Aitken, 'Eddie' (NX26961) 25
Alagna 9, 11, 12, 13,14, 17
Alamein, *see also* Ruin Ridge 1, 2, 10, 12, 23
Albergo Compagnoni 8
Albert, Edward 'Eddie' (QX7639) 27
Albert, Tony 28
Alessandria province 23, 24
Alexander, Gen. Field-Marshal H.R. 11
Alexandria 1, 24, 25
Allen, Norman 'Norm' (NZ 23862) 10
Allied Screening Commission 9
Alpe Bill, P
Alpe Faller 13
Alpe Noveis, *see also* Hotel Alpe Noveis 11, 21
Alpini 6, 8, 11, 12, 13, 26
Amoore, Pat, British SOE 26
Andalo 8
Andenmatten, Annette 18
Anderson, 'Bloss' 2, 4, 5
Anderson, Thomas 'Tom' (VX34767) 1, 3, 4, 7, 21, 24
Andorno Micca 10, 27
Andrews, Joseph 'Joey' (QX8624) 7,21, 24
Angove, Victor 'Vic' (WX6803) 22
Ansaldi, Francesco and family 23
Antonio, Antonio Manfroi, son of Harold Sanderson E
Antrona 22
Anza River, Anzasca Valley P, 9, 13, 14, 20
Anzio 24
Aosta 9, 10, 18, 19
Apennines 19, 24
Arborio 16
'Arca', Armando Calzavara 23
Ardizzone, Armando 5
Armistice, Italian 4, 5, 6, 7, 8, 11, 12, 17
Armitage, Leo (VX37549) 7
Arolla 23
Arona 22
Arosa 25
Arro 2, 9
Avery, Stanley 'Stan' (NZ 40427) 10
AWAS, Australian Women's Army Service personnel in attendance POW reception 17/11/44, and list 25, 25n

B

Bacciagaluppi, Giuseppe 22
Badoglio, Marshal Pietro 4, 11, 17
Bailey, Norman 'Norm' (WX13384) 23

Index

Note: *Chapter numbers* are used in this index not page numbers.

Bailey, Stanley 'Stan' (WX5508) 22
Baker, 7
Balma 10
Balocco 23
Balzola 5
Bannio 17
Banzhaf, Bernhard P
Baraccone 2, 5, 9, 16
Barce 1
Bardi 24
Bardia 1
Bardonecchia 14
Barker, Ian (VX31735) 11
Barnados 2
Barndon, Albert (WX15376) 18n
Bates, Peter Watson (NZ POW) 18
Batt, Leslie 'George' (NZ POW , 61235) 27
Battalions, AIF, *see* Units
BBC reports 5, 7, 12
Bell, Jim (British SOE) 26
Beltrami, Luciano 23
Bellinzona 25
Benghazi 1, 2
Bennett, Alfred (VX33895) 8n
Berg, Ernest 'Ernie' (QX5190) 7, 14
Bern 19
Berrey, Thomas 'Tom'/'Tomaso' (WX9960)
Bersaglieri Division 8
Bianco, Rosa and family 7, 23
Bicycle, as escape vehicle 15
Biella 4, 5, 6, 9, 10, 12, 16, 18, 19, 22 27
Binns, Raymond (SX9123) 1
Bione family 24
Birch, Tony (British SOE) 26
Blain, Harold (VX46586) 24, 26
Blair, William 'Bill' (NX21419) 5, 25
Blamey, Field-Marshal Sir Thomas 25
Blewett, Frank (WX9047) 4, 21, 26
Bocchetta della Boscarola 9
Bocchetto Sessera 9
Bocchio-Monti, Maria 26
Bologna, Campo 19 8
Bolzano 3, 8
Bombay 25
Bonello, Carla 2, 3, 4, 5, 6, 28

Bonello, Giovanni 2
Bonner, John (NZ POW 65097) 8n
Booth, Colin 'Col' (NX60337) F, P, 1, 2, 5, 11, 14, 17, 18, 25, 28, E
Booth, Brian 28
Booth, Evelyn P, 28, E
Booth, Keith 28
Booth, Peter P
Booth, Ruby 3, E
Booth, Stanley (WX6684) 4
Borgomanero 23
Borgosesia 13, 15, 20, 21
Bormio 8
Bosgard, Peter (PX9) 11
Boskell, Leonard 'Len' (WX8857) 22
Bowes, Frank (NZ POW 12626) 23
Bracken, Edward 'Ted' (VX47713)
Breithorn 10
Bremner, Percy (NZ POW 44932) 8n
Brennan, James, 'Jim' (WX7218) 21, 27
Brenner Pass 8, 21, 22
Brenta Pass 8
Brescia 1
Breuil-Cervinia 10
Brianco 12
Brien, G (British POW) 14
Brig 12, 19, E
Brillaloio 11n
Brissago 22, 23
Bristow, Jack (WX7217) 4
Brown, George 'Bomber' (VX45592) 27
Bruce, Bernard (VX5733) 21
Bruno Mussolini Refuge for Alpinists 8
Brusaschetto 7, 23, 24
Bruscara family 23
Brusson 10, 19
Bryant, Ronald 'Ron' (VX34058) 5, 24, 28
'Bull', see Prando, Paolo
Bullock, Thomas 'Tom' (WX6895) 11
Buronzo 11
Burton, George 'Bluey' (VX31993) 12
Bushnell, William (QX10792) 13

C

Caffrey, Arthur (VX32489) 11
Calder, Ken 22
Calzavara, Armando 'Arca' 23

328 Shooting Through

Note: *Chapter numbers* are used in this index not page numbers.

Camandona 9
Cameron, Ronald (NX23324) 8n
Campbell, Alexander 'Alex' (VX52786) 26
Campbell, Andrew (VX43960) 11
Campello Monti 17
Campertogno 16
Campo 19, *see* Bologna
Campo 57, *see* Grupignano
Campo 78, *see* Sulmona
Campo 106, general 1, 2, 3, 6
Campo 133, *see* Grignasco
Canale Cavour 2, 11
Canisei 27
Cannobio 23
Cantua 23
Carabinieri, carabiniere 2, 5, 9, 10, 13, 17, 21, 22, 23
Carpeneto 2, 3, 4, 5, 6, 7, 22
Carpignano Sesia 11
Carrigan, Carl (NX51288) 1, 16, 28
Carrigan, Paul NX51289 1, 16, 28
Casa Nuova 11n
Casale Monferatto 5
Cascina Fantina 2
Cascina Forresto 19n
Cascina Gattesco 5
Cascina Tambarina 16
Casalrosso 22
Cassino 24
Castelletto d'Erro 24
Castelletto Merli 24
Castellone 5
Castello d'Agogno 17
Catella/Catello Angelina/Angelo Guido 26
Cedars Chalet, Lebanon 17
Cerruti, Eva 27
Cervetto 11
Cervo Valley 9, 10
Champoluc 10
Chard, Clifford (NX11450) 22n
Cheeseman, 'Fred' (British POW) 18
Cherokee Mission SOE 26
Chianti hills 24
Chiasso 23
Chiesa di San Michele 9
Chisio, Luigi 23

Chits, POW notes for helpers 7, 9, 12, 14, 15
Churchill, Winston 7
Churches, Ralph 'Crow' (SX5286) 25, E
Cigarettes 3, 7
Cittiglio 23
Cividale del Friuli 1
Clare, Leslie 'Les' (NX11419) 4
Clark, John 'Jack' (NZ POW 37158) 27
Clarke, George (NX24360) 1
Coggiola 11, 26
Col Collen 23
Col d'Olen 13
Col Ranzola 10
Colombara, Tenuta 18
Collins, Alfred (VX2053) 11, 14
Collobiano 11
Collyer, Neil 25
Colson, Norman 'Norm' (VX21603) 22
Commonwealth War Graves Commission (CWGC), Milan cemetery 22
Compagnoni, Signor 8
Como 22, 23
Conlon, David (NZ POW) 8n
Contadini, general 9, 11
Constanza, Ida 16
Contrabandieri, smugglers 8, 12, 14, 16, 22, 23
Cook, Walter 'Wally' (VX32872) 19, 25
Corke, Neil (VX45906) 11, 14
Corona, Maria E
Cossato 9
Cotterell, Afred 'Fred'/ 'Ray' (QX13679) 22
Cox, Harry (QX8836) 12
Crellin, Ronald (VX48078) 19, 25
Crevacuore 11, 21, 26
Crockatt, Norman 26
Croft, William (British POW) 18
Crook, Raymond 'Ray' (VX2208) 11, 14n
Cugnasco, Nello 5
Cunningham, Keith (WX14835) 8n
Curtis, Frederick 'Fred' (QX7686) 12

D

Dallodi/D'Allodi, Cascina Dallodi 11n
Dalton, Frank 22
Damiani, Modestino 28
Dare, Gordon (VX38610) 1, 4, 26, 28

INDEX 329

Note: *Chapter numbers* are used in this index not page numbers.

Dare, Joan 28
Davis, Harold (WX14427) 24
Davis, Thomas (VX47656) 23
Dawes, James 'Jim' (NX28398) 19
Dawson, William 'Alex'/'Peter' 11, 14
Dean, Ronald 'Jimmy' (WX12891) 4, 26
Dennis, Richard (British POW) 8
Derna 1, 12, 28
Digwood, Harold (WX1462) 25
Distelalp 18
Dodd, John 'Jack' (WX10009) 22, 25
Doig, William 'Bill' (VX1266) 22
Dolomites 8
Domodossola P, 10, 12, 22
Donato 22
Donnan, Robert 'Bob' (QX2991) 8
Dora Baltea River 1, 9
Douglas, Ronald (SX6310) 15, 20
Dower, Leslie 'Les' (VX40994) 23
Drew, Garvan 'Snowy' (QX6959) 7, 21, 24
Duggan, John 'Jack' (NX50270) 7, 23

E
Edmondson, Claude (VX40089) 10n
Eggleston, Frederic 'Eggie'/ 'Fred' (252761) 8, 25
El Regima 1
Elgg 19
Elliott, Tom (QX6017) 8, 16
Elveziro, Cabrino 16
Elvo Valley 9
Emery, Enid P
Emery, Herbert 'Nick' (NX56333) P, 1, 11, 16, 18, 28, E
English, Ian (British POW) 12, 23
Erickson, Peter (NX33357) P, 5, 11, 14, 17, 25, 28
Erto E
Esler, Robert (VX53572) 8n
Eurossola Hotel 22
Eva, friend to Col Booth P, 28, E
Evans, George (British POW) 26
Evasio family 23

F
Fai della Paganella 8
Fairbridge Society farms 2

Faulkes, John 'Ted' (WX17240) 11
Febbrario, Raimondo 21n
Fenton, Ken 7
Ferguson, Robert 11, 14n
Fitzgerald, Francis Ronald 'Fitzy'/ 'Ron' (NX51323) 16
'Five-Miler' 5, 16
Fleming, Donald (QX7025) 8n
Florence 7, 24
Fobello 13
Foglietta, Casa 4, 7
Fogg, Arthur (WX6905) 27
Fontanellato 3
Foot, MRD and Langley, JM 15, 16, 24, 25
Fountainemore 13, 18
France F, 2, 5
Francese, Benedetto 22
Fraser, Charles 'Charlie' 'Bluey'(VX34270) 10
Fraser, James 24
Freeberg, Norman 'Norm' (NX23800) 3, 11, 14
Fullarton, Jack (VX40342) 7, 24
Fuorcla Trupchun 8

G
Gaby 18, 24
Galmen 16
Gardiner, James 'Jim' (WX7733) 19
Gardner, Colin (NX778) 1, 11
Garlanda family 2
Garrigan, William 'Bill' (VX32518) 7
Gattinara 11, 23
General AE Anderson 25, E
General Pope 25
Geneva 25
Geneva Convention 2, 5, 6, 22, 26
Genoa 4, 5, 7, 24
Ghemme 11
Ghislarengo 23
Ghurka 24
Gibson, Claude 'Gus' (NX29995) 23
Giddins, James 'Tony' (QX8012) 7
Gilbert, Adrian 2, 10, 14
Giles, John (VX47985)
Gill, Richard 'Dick' (NX53017) 3, 7, 23
Gillies, Midge 3
Gillies, 'Mick' 22

Note: *Chapter numbers* are used in this index not page numbers.

Gondo 22
Gornergrat, glacier near 10
Grande Mologna 10
Grand Saint Bernard Mountain 19
Grappa 9, 13, 16
Green, John 'Brian' (VX4690) 7, 22, 25
Gressoney-Saint-Jean 10, 13, 18
Greville, Guy (British) 8
Griffiths, Alfred (VX32516) 22
Grignasco 17
Grimsey, Albert (WX15431) 22
Grupignano, Campo 57 P, 1, 2, 3, 5, 16, 28, E
Guides, child 14, 16, 19
Guides, female 20

H

Hague Convention 5
Hall, Julian (British POW) 18
Hamblin, Eric (British POW) 27
Hampson, Walter 'Wally' (WX2090) 2
Hanson, Bernard (TX722) 2n
Hanson, 'Popeye', possibly Bernard 2
Harris, Roy (WX7111) 25
Harrison, Henry (NZ POW) 8n
Harvey, William 'Stan' (WX10591) 24, 26
Hayes, Ernest 'Ernie' (WX34562) 18
Heka, Adam (NZ POW) 8n
Henderson, Darcy (NZ POW 46316) 26
HMS *Hereward* 1
HMS *Turbulent* 1
Hodgson, Thomas (NZ POW 32867) 27
Hohaia, Robert (NZ Maori POW 924) 16
Holemby, Leslie (NZ POW 26615) 8n
Holman, Leonard 'Len' (QX11027) 12, 28
Holmes, Bramwell (WX9065) 8n
Hood, Lionel (NZ POW 28201) 11
Hood, Raymond (NX1065) 22n
Horman, Colin (VX46543) 10n
Hotel Alpe Noveis 13, 14, 21
Hotel Beau Site 25
Hotel Breithorn 10
Hotel Cervin 10
Hotel Mattmark *see* Mattmark
Hotel Monte Moro 18
Hotel Portjengrat 18
Hotel Regina 25

Howe, Eddie (NX40662) 28, 28n
Hoy, Raleigh (NX27773) 27
Holman, Leonard 'Len' (QX11027) 12, 28
Hughes, James 'Jimmy' (VX34505) 7
Hungerford, Francis 'Happy' (QX10626) 26
Hyland, James 'Jim' (NX727) 22

I

Ida Donne 9
Inglis, Norman 'Ned' (VX44067) 22
Intra 14, 23
Irwin, Ronald (SX7858) 18n
Issime 18
Italy Star medal 26
Ivrea 22, 25

J

Jackman, Morris (VX37065) 12
Jackson, Roy (VX27886) 26
Jacobs, Susan 13, 23, 27, 28
James, Thomas 'Tom' (VX33099) 18
Jenks, Roy (VX34381) 10
Jewish refugees 16, 23
Jobson, Frank 'Arthur' (QX3237) 5, 16, 18, 25
Jobson, Ian 'Tim' (QX21217) 5, 16, 18
Johnson, 'Dixie' 24
Johnson, John 'Chocka' (VX34438) 5
Johnson, 'Lofty' (NZ POW) 16
Johnson, Captain 'Podge' (British POW) 8
Johnston, Mark 1, 12
Johnston, Rae (QX1656) 12
Jones, Brinley 'Brin' (VX37427) 2, 25
Jones, Keith (VX29657) 26
Jones, Sydney 'Bryce' (NX59936) 7, 14n
Jones, Robert Sydney 'Bob' (290726) 8
Jones, Ronald Houghton 'Ron' (VX4360) 16
Jones, Ronald Bonner 'Ron'/'Bones' (NX15573) 19
Judd, Jack (VX47799) 12
Judd, Maxwell 'Max' (VX34889) 12

K

Keats, Gilbert (SX12776) 12n
Keenan, John (WX6695) 10n
Kelly, Thomas (VX36598) 18n
Kelly, William (SX9027) 1n
Kent, Edgar 'Ted' (QX22164) 19, 25

Note: *Chapter numbers* are used in this index not page numbers.

Kinder, Arthur 'Jim' (NX12808) 23
King, David 'Dave' (QX5504) 12
King, Norman 'Norm' (VX34642) 2, 7, 22
Knight, Ewen (VX34777) 5
Knight, Ian (VX34773) 1, 5, 21
Knight, John 'Jack'(WX12167) 20
Knight, Matthew (VX34393) 7, 24, 25, 28
Krafft Hotel 25
Kroger, Henry 'Jack' (VX1500) 8
Kulm Hotel 25

L

Lachelle 2, 4
La Corte 2, 4, 12, 22
Lake (Lago) Como 23
Lake (Lago) della Fate (Fairies Lake) 9
Lake (Lago) Lugano 23
Lake (Lago) Maggiore 10, 14, 22, 23
Lake (Lago) Smeraldo 13
L'americani, l'americano 11
L'Aquila province 21
La Stampa magazine reporter 22
Lauder, Stuart (QX9995) 18n
Lavallee, Paul (NX23801) 1, 3, 11, 14, 28
Lavaring, Neville (QX7979) 12
Lavis 8
Law, John 'Paddles' (NX16597) 2, 28
Lawrie, Nicol 'Nick' (SX11230) 2, 7, 10, 23
Leach, Frank 'Nugget' (WX10052) 20
Ledingham, Lloyd (NX51287) 16
Le-Fevre, Douglas 'Doug' (WX5933) 1, 2, 3, 4, 5, 22, 24, 25
Liddell, Clive (VX1664) 24, 26
Lillianes 26
Livigno 8
Locarno 23
Lockie, Herbert (QX6577) 4, 7, 24
London, George (NZ POW) 25n
Lozzolo 11
Lucignana 24
Luino 22, 23
Lunn, Roy (NZ POW 32520) 11

M

MI9, MIS-X 4
Macchieraldo, or Machieraldo, Alberto, Giuseppe, Giovanni 12, 12n
Macdonald, Alastair (British, SOE) 26

Macugnaga P, 12, 13, 14, 16, 17, 19
Maddern, James (VX33100) 25
Madron Peak 8
Maher, Patrick 'Paddy' (WX10252) 25
Maitland, Ronald 'Ron' (WX14636) 1, 3, 4, 16, 18, 25
Mair, John 'Sandy' (VX38646) 8
Malga Spora 8
Manfroi, Antonio E
Marengo, Anna 26
Marseilles 25
Martin, William (NZ POW 32885) 27
Matterhorn 10, 18
Mattmark, and Hotel Mattmark P, 18, 19, 20 E
Maynard, Melvin/Allen (SX13037) 20
McCaffery, Jock (British SOE, alias 'Dr Rossi') 4n
McClelland, Robert 'Bob' (QX2232) 22
McCracken, James 'Mick' (VX45756) 23
McDonald, Donald 'Don' (NX34922) 8
McDowall, Peter (British POW) 8
McFarlane, Syd (NZ POW 480) 26
McIntosh, Ronald 'Ron' (NX51281) 16
McIntyre, Ronald 'Ron' (VX48203) 26
Mechili, Fort Mechili 1, 7, 8, 16, 23
McKelvie, George (WX15377) 22
Melbourne, POWs arrival home 17/11/1944 25
Meldrum, Henry 'Harry' (WX11439) 12
Michelone, Giuseppe and Michele 3n
Michelone, Mario 12n
Milan P, 1, 4, 5, 6, 9, 22, 23
Miller, David 19
Miller, Harry (WX11952) 23
Mills, Charles 'Charlie' (VX48196) P, 11, 16
Mitchell, William 'Bill' (VX30186) 25
Modena 8
Moir, Lewis 'Lou' (NZ POW 13359) 2, 25n
Molinetto 2
Moncalvo 24
Mondelli Pass P, 13, 16, 17, 18, E
Mondine 3, 4, 5, 20
Monscera Pass 22
Monte Barone 9, 11, 14, 17, 18, 21, 22

Note: *Chapter numbers* are used in this index not page numbers.

Monte Bianco 18
Monte Gemevola 11
Monte Greco 21
Monte Limidario 23
Monte Moro P, 9, 12, 13, 16, 17, 18, 19, 20, 22, 28, E
Monte Mucrone 26
Monte Rosa P, 9, 11, 12, 13, 16, 17, 18, 19, 20, 22, 28, E
Monte Tovo 13
Monteath, Peter F, 6, 8, 22, 28
Monti, Placida 26
Montobello National Republican Guard, GNR 27
Montonero 3, 4, 6, 15, 28
Moore, John (TX383) 10n
Moore, Newton 'Newt' (WX7860) 13, 25
Morgan, William 'Bill' (WX7965) 11
Morish, John (SX1154) 25
Moscatelli, 'Cino' 27
Mosso Santa Maria 17, 23n
Moule, Lloyd 'Mouley' (NX40603) 1, 6, 19, 22, 28
Mount Blanc 18, 26
Mount 'Pao Darla' 23
Mudge, Ross (NX54257) 22
Muff, Alois 25, E
Mussolini, Benito F, 4, 7, 14, 25, 26

N

Naples 15, 25
Nascimbene, Gianni 23
Neame, Gerald 'Gerry' (NZ POW 11278) 9, 13
Neave, Alan 'Bluey' (WX12688) 6, 9, 13, 18
Neil, Roy (VX50923) 25n
Newbey, Edward 'Ted' (WX7406) 5, 18
Newbey, Thomas 'Joe' (WX5251) 5, 16, 18
Newby, Eric (British POW) 16, 19
Nicol, William 'Bill' (NX17325) 11, 14n
Nicholls, John 'Ticker' (WX7090) 24, 26
Nicholson, Alan (VX31699) 23
Nicholson, John 'Jack' (VX28557) 18
Nie, John 'Jack' (WX16763) 23, 24, 25
Nino Bixio 1, 28
Nott, Cecil (QX1994) 22
Novara 5, 9, 12, 22, 23

O

Oborne, John (WX2034) 12
O'Flaherty, Monsignor Hugh 24
Ofental 16
Olcenengo 13
Olevano 17
Oliver, John 19
Olivero, Mariuccia 'Maria' and family 21, 26
Olivetti company 23n
Operation Avalanche 4
O'Rafferty, Gerald (VX30023) 13, 21
O'Rafferty, Patrick 'Pat' (VX34508) 13, 21, 25
Oratory of San Pellegrino 21
Organisations helping POWs 4, 6, 11, 12, 15, 20, 21, 22, 23, 24, 25, 26,
Orion 25
Orontes 25
Oropa, Santuario di Oropa and tram 9, 12, 13, 16, 17
Osborne, Kenneth, *see* Harry Miller
Oschiena, 3n
Ottenbach 25, E

P

Pack, Harold (NX29592) 20
Page, Frank 'Pagey'/ 'Brunes' (QX1639) 12
Palestro 4, 7, 23
Pannowitz, William 'Bill' (WX38325) 12, 17, 18
Pantelleria 4
Park, Havaland 'Happy' (WX14265) 5
Parker, John (NX3653) 8n
Parker, Leslie 'Les' (WX14394) 26
Parker, Walter 'Wally' (VX33706) 25
Partisans, F, 5, 6, 10, 11, 12, 13, 18, 20, 21, 23, 24, 28,
Passo Val Viola 8
Pattinson, Harold (NZ POW) 8n
Paul, Edwin 'Ted' (NX27654) 8, 25
Peachey, Edward 'Ted' (VX2556) 4, 22, 26
Pecetto 14, 16, 20
Peck, Desmond 'Johnny' (VX9534) 22, 23
Pedro, at Montonero 15
Peel, Harland 'Mickey' (QX3577) 4
Pennine Alps 7, 9, 16, 19, 23
Perazzo, Antonio 22n

Note: *Chapter numbers* are used in this index not page numbers.

Perazzo, Margherita 'Rita' 6, 28
Perrott, Henry 'Harry' (NX19056) 13
Peterson, Harold (NX12414)
Pettiva 2, 18, 23
Pianceri Alto 11, 16
Piancone 26
Piedicavallo 10, 12, 13
Piedmont, general 9
Pino brothers, and Domenico Pino 2, 5
Piode 14, 16
Pila 16
Pista Nuova 16
Pistoia 24
Ponte de Legno 8
Po River 1, 2, 5, 6, 7, 9, 13, 21, 23, 24
Pope Pius XII P
Porter, Fred (British POW) 18
Postua 11, 21
Powling, William 'Jack'/ 'China' (WX37412) 26
POWs,
    POWs, aliases 20, 23
    POWs, Allied POWs general 17
    POWs, British 5, 8, 9, 12, 13, 14n, 16, 18, 21, 24, 26
    POWs, Campo 106 cohort Appendix 1
    POWs, Canadian 3, 8
    POWs, correspondence 3, 7
    POWs, deaths 5, 18, Appendix 1
    POWs, Indigenous 12, 24, 27, 28
    POWs, Italian 10, 19, 23
    POWs, marriages 25
    POWs, New Zealanders P, 1, 2, 5, 6, 8, 9, 10, 11, 12, 14n, 16, 17, 18, 21, 23, 25, 26, 27, E
    POWs, officers 8
    POWs, organisational help to 11, 15, 22, 23
    POWs, partisan connections, see partisans
    POWs, recapture of 1, 7, 8, 12, 14, 16, 21, 22, 23, 24, 27
    POWs, reaching Allied lines 24, 25
    POWs, reaching France 26
    POWs, reaching Switzerland, general 8, 16, 17, 18, 20, 25, Appendix 1
    POWs, South African 14, 15, 17, 20, 22, 23, 24
    POWs, to German captivity 6, 8, 14
    POWs, train jumpers 8, 16, 22, 23
Prando, Paolo 6, 15, 28
Prato Isarco 1, 3
Preiser, Ernest 'Ernie' (VX32728) 18
Price, Edwin 'Ted' (VX34790) 5, 26
Price, Frederick 'Fred'(WX4462) 13
Priests, assistance to POWs P, 7, 13, 15, 17, 21, 24, 26
Prisoner of War Trust Fund 28
Pritchard, William 'Bill' (QX6908) 23
Putland, Gordon (WX7619) 19

R

Radnell, Donald 'Don' (VX34693) 2, 3, 7, 16, 22
Rayner, Vince (NX33853) 28, 28n
Rea, George (WX6366) 22
Red Cross parcels 2, 3, 5, 6, 7, 8, 9, 10, 20, 25
Reid, Clarence (QX1725) 12
Regiments, AIF, *see* Units
Reneau, Gordon (Canadian) 8
Repatriation from Switzerland 25
Repatriation, soldier settlement 28
Rhodes, George (VX33373) 18n
Richardson, Roy (QX15357) 8n
Rickard, Gorden (VX34902) 5
Rifugio Teodul 10
Rifugio Tuckett 8
Riva 16
Rivo Valdobbia 9
Robarello 2
Robertson, Donald 'Duncan' (QX11222) 19
Robinson, 'Nip', probably Alfred (NX52814) 12
Roffino, Selina 22
Rollings, Charles 1
Romagnano Sesia 23
Rome, bombing of 4
Rommel, General F, 1, 12, 22
Ronsecco 2, 21, 23, 26
Rose, William 'Bill' (WX10362) 19
Rose brothers, William 'Bill' and Clarence (WX1050) 28
Rossi, Dr 4

Note: *Chapter numbers* are used in this index not page numbers.

Rovasenda 11, 23, E
Rowe, John 'Jack' (WX5292) 26
Rudd, William 'Bill' (VX39694) P, 1, 2, 3, 5, 9, 12, 17, 24, 25, 28
Ruin Ridge, *see* Alamein
Russell, Thomas (VX32995) 18

S

Saas-Almagell 17, 18
Saas-Fee 12, 18, 19
Saas-Grund 18
Saastal, Talliboden P,16, 18 E
Sabbia 17
Sagliano Micca 17
Saint Jacques 10
Saint-Julien-en-Genevois 25
Salasco 4, 6, 22, 23
Salerno 4
Sali 12
Salussola 1, 2, 5, 9, 10, 11
Salvarini, Silvana 5
San Damiano 6, 9
San Giuseppe di Casto 27
Sanderson, Harold (NZ POW 3149) 25, E
San Germano Vercellese, Campo 106/1 2, 4, 5, 7, 12, 19
Sangro River 21
San Nazzaro Sesia, 11, 22
Santa Caterino di Valfurva 8
Santhia 12, 22
Santuario di Graglia 26
Santuario di Oropa, *see* Oropa
Saviolo, Giovanni 13
Scareno 23
Scales, Roy (VX32469) 19
Scanlan, 'Eddie' (NZ POW 40159) 9, 13
Schrieber, Vera 23
Scott, Alfred 'Scottie' (WX15060) 26
Scott, Arch (NZ POW) 16, 17
Scopello 9, 11, 14, 16
Secchia, Francesco 'Frank', Nina and Piero 11, E
Selve 16
Serfontein, Johannes 'Dan' (Sth African POW) 17
Sesia River 1, 9, 10, 11, 13, 14, 15, 16,17, 23
Sessera Valley 9
Sesto Calende 23

Sharp, Frank 'Pop' (NX60017) 8
Sharp, Keith (QX10358) 8
Shaw, John (British POW 950766) 17
Shaw, Sydney 'Syd' (WX12267) 12, 25, 28
Sheridan, Rupert 'Rupe' (VX34990) 1
Shove, 'Syd' (WX6937) 13
Sibraa, Henry 'Harry' (NX35515) 10, 25
Sidler family 25, E
Simmons 'Mick' 21
Simplon Pass 22
Sincock, Edward 'Eddie' (VX48180) 1, 13, 25
Sincock, Herbert 'Harry' (VX48171) 13, 24, 25
Sincock, William 'Bill' (VX26596) 13
Slovenia, 25, E
Smedley, Douglas 'Doug' (VX42361) 27
Smith, Brian (VX33912) 18n
Smith, Edward 'Big Bill' (WX9093) 26
Smith, John 'Jock'/'Strap' (QX17734) 5, 12, 24
Smith, Richard 'Dick' 25
Smugglers, contrabandieri 8, 12, 14, 16, 22, 23
Socraggio 23
SOE, Special Operations Executive F, 26
Soggetto, Marco E
Soldier settlement scheme 28
Sondrio province 8
Sora Valley 24
Sostegno 11
Sparnon, Ernest 'Ernie' (VX32109) 13, 18, 25
Spoletto 21
Sproule, Ian (VX38618) 26
Stanley, Charles 'Charlie' (WX7574) 19
Stanley, Peter 12
Steele, Donald 'Don' (VX28787) 11
Stefani, Bruno 24
Stelvio Pass 8
Stephenson, Harry (NX19374) 13n
Stouse, Charles 'Charlie' 5
Strickland, Ronald 'Ron' (WX10021) 16
Strickland, William 'Bill' (WX10020) 16, 20
Strona 9, 26
Stussi-Lauterburg, Jurg P, 25
Sulmona, Campo 78 1

Note: *Chapter numbers* are used in this index not page numbers.

T

Tabram, Frederick 'Fred' (VX46243) 1, 2, 4, 7, 21, 26
Tarhuna 2
Tavigliano 27
Tasker, Henry 'Jim' (NX30450)
Teodulo Pass, Theodul Pass 10, 18
Tenuta Colombara 18
Tenuta Masina 2, 9
Ternengo 9
Terrell, Norman 'Norm' (WX14583) 22
Terelle 24
Thompson, Bernard (British POW) 25
Thompson, George 'Bill' (WX10398) 12
Thompson, Leigh E
Ticino River 23
Tobruk 1, 2, 15
Toce River 9
Todd, David (QX6922) 23
Torrazzo 26
Torrente Anza 14, 17
Torrente Elvo 2
Torrente Cervo 9, 10
Torrente Lys 18
Torrente Mastallone 17
Torrente Sessera 11
Torviscosa, Campo 107 E
Trento 8, 22
Tricerro 24
Trino 7, 21, 23
Tripoli 2, 7
Trivero 26
Tripovich, Norman 'Norm' (VX14918) 12
Tronzano Vercellese 2, 3, 4, 5, 7, 10, 12, 22, 23
Turbenthal 12
Turin P, 1, 2, 4, 5, 14
Turin, bombing 4
Turlo Pass, Passo di Turlo 9, 14, 16, 17
Turner, 'Joe' (TX75) 18
Twomey, Christina Twomey 28
Tyrie, Horace (NX23782) 22

U

Udine P, 5
Units, Australian POWs' battalions and regiments (see also Appendix 1):

2/3rd Anti-Tank Regiment (3ATank) 8, 16, 23
2/3rd Light Anti-Aircraft Attack Regiment (3LAA) 1, 4, 18
2/3rd Pioneer Battalion 10, 22
2/8th Field Ambulance 1
2/13th Battalion 1
2/15th Battalion 1, 2, 4, 7, 12, 13, 23, 27
2/17th Battalion 1, 2, 23
2/23rd Battalion 24
2/24th Battalion 1, 10, 13, 23
2/28th Battalion 1, 12, 13, 20, 22, 27
2/32nd Battalion 1, 11, 12, 16, 24
Underwood, Ernest (VX34643) 10n

V

Vace E
Valais, canton of 9
Val d'ayas 10
Valdengo 9
Valtournenche 10, 23
Val Viola Pass, Passo Val Viola 8
van den Heuvel, Frederick 'Fanny' 25
Varallo 12, 13, 17
Vardy, Frederick 'Fred' (WX5229) 7, 24
Varese 23
Vatican 24
Vardy, Frederick (WX5229)
Veneria, Cascina 3, 7, 11, 16
Venetz, Augusta 18
Vercelli, city of 1, 2, 4, 5, 6, 11, 12, 13, 14, 15, 22, 23
Verdoia, Clara 19n
Vettigne 22, 23
Viancino 7
Vigar, Raymond 'Ray' (WX13239) 26
Vigliano 9, 10
Villadossola 22
Visp 10, 18
Viverone 10
Vollon 19

W

Wainewright, Herbert 'Bert' (WX9970) 26
Wald 4, 18, 25
Walker, Jack (NX54410) 8n
Walker, 'Leo' 27
Waller, William 'Bill' (VX47958) 1, 18

Note: *Chapter numbers* are used in this index not page numbers.

Warburton, Charles (WX5299) 1, 3, 4, 6, 14, 20, 25, 28
War crimes 2, 27
Ward, Robert 'Bob' (WX5890) 4, 12, 16, 17, 18
Watkins, Charles (NZ POW) 28
Watson, Len 28
Watts, Harry (QX2418) 12
Wauhop, Jack (WX9723) 1, 4, 19
Webb, Claude (VX26590) 23
Webster, Malcolm (VX2339) 26
Weedon, George (WX13002) 4
Weekes, Colin (NX38152) 1, 2, 5, 6, 9, 13, 18
West, Diana, (AWAS, VFX129059) 25, list of AWAS colleagues 17/11/1944 25n
Wil 12, 20
Wilbrey, Arthur (WX9128) 27
Willacott, Norman 'Norm (WX6903) 26
Wills, Maximilian 'Max' (WX4493) 7, 12, 16, 17, 18
Wills, Victor 'Vic' (WX5534) 16
Wilson, Albert 'Bert' (WX11748) 5, 10
Wilson, Harry (WX2743) 10
Wilson, Jack (VX35149)
Wilson, James 'Jim' (QX5417) 1, 2, 3, 7, 22
Wilson, Lloyd 'Mick' (WX6100) 11, 14
Wilson, Richard (VX34368) 23
Wilson, William 'Bill' (WX7185) 5, 10
Wolfe, Ernest (WX14978) 24, 26
Wolff, Vera 24
Women, Italian in general (*see also* mondine) 9, 11, 15, 20, 23
Wood, James 'Jim' (NX33270) 7
Woodyard, George (VX34421) 5
Woosnam, Norman 'Norm' (WX6058) 12, 17
Wrigglesworth, William 'Bill' (VX46959) 26
Wycherley, Rossett 'Ross' (VX28988) 5, 11, 17

Y

Yininmadyemi memorial to Indigenous service, Sydney 28
Young, Allan (VX47581) 18

Z

Zaninetti, Angelo 11, 21
Zaninetti, Clementina 11, 14, 21, 25
Zermatt 10, 18
Zimone 10
Zubiena 22
Zumaglia 9

Bill Rudd
Courtesy Bill Rudd

*Bill Rudd with the author at the Shrine of Remembrance August, 2018.
On 29 October 2019, Bill Rudd died. He was 101. This book is also dedicated to him.*
Courtesy of Rosa Miot

www.ingramcontent.com/pod-product-compliance
Lightning Source LLC
Chambersburg PA
CBHW031426160426
43195CB00010BB/624